Groups in Practice

Susan X Day
University of Houston
Iowa State University

ADVISERS

Rex Stockton
Indiana University

Dennis M. Kivlighan, Jr.
University of Maryland

Lahaska Press
Houghton Mifflin Company
BOSTON   NEW YORK

Publisher, Lahaska Press: Barry Fetterolf
Senior Editor, Lahaska Press: Mary Falcon
Editorial Assistant: Evangeline Bermas
Senior Project Editor: Margaret Park Bridges
Associate Manufacturing Buyer: Brian Pieragostini
Marketing Manager: Barbara LeBuhn

Cover image: © 1998 Jeannette Meyer

Credits appear on page 462, which constitutes an extension of this copyright page.

For instructors who want more information
about Lahaska Press books and teaching aids,
contact the Houghton Mifflin Faculty Services Center at:
Tel: 800-733-1717, x4034
Fax: 800-733-1810

Or visit us on the Web at:
www.lahaskapress.com

Printed in the U.S.A.

Library of Congress Control Number: 2005934058

Instructor's examination copy
  ISBN-10: 0-618-73135-0
  ISBN-13: 978-0-618-73135-0

For orders, use student text ISBNs
  ISBN-10: 0-618-38248-8
  ISBN-13: 978-0-618-38248-4

123456789—HPC—10 09 08 07 06

Contents

PART III

On Becoming a Person   173

8   *Humanist Group Theory and Practice*   175

9   *Existential Group Theory and Practice*   206

PART IV
The Unfolding of Awareness   231

10 *Psychodynamic Group Theory and Practice*   233

11 *Gestalt Group Theory and Practice*   262

PART V

A Life of Learning   291

12 *Cognitive-Behavioral Group Theory and Practice*   293

13 *Psychoeducational Group Theory and Practice*   332

Foreword

Some time back I was asked if another group counseling book would be viable. My response was that there already exist several well-done books on this topic. A new text would have to be very well written and organized in a helpful way, and needless to say, it would have to be at least as solid in coverage as the popular existing texts. In *Groups in Practice*, Susan X Day has indeed accomplished these difficult tasks.

Her text has something for everyone. The book is well organized, highly readable, and comprehensive. It seems rather trite to simply say that Day's text is very well written. So I will put it this way: Not since Irving Yalom's *The Theory and Practice of Group Psychotherapy* have I read a text written in such an engaging style. That's not to compare the two in terms of content, only that both authors' styles of communicating entice the reader to continue reading.

Day smoothly balances an extensive amount of theoretical and practical knowledge within one relatively short text. Additionally, she incorporates both classic and current research to buttress her points. There are many noteworthy chapters that I could discuss here, but space precludes their discussion in a foreword such as this. However, I must mention a well-conceptualized multicultural chapter in which Day shows how a cultural-identity perspective can foster the basic therapeutic factors of group counseling. Also, Day's readers will be treated to an especially lively introduction to Association for Specialists in Group Work (ASGW) standards and the American Counseling Association's ethical code. The reader will find personalized stories throughout the chapters as well as engaging discussion ideas.

Finally, this author has met my other criterion for a new group text; that is, she has organized it in a helpful way. Day has devised an organizational schema for her text that enables students to fit together the components of group theory and practice into a coherent and comprehensive picture of group work. The sixteen chapters are presented in a framework of six parts. Taken together, the part introductions serve as a cognitive map showing where each chapter fits into the grand scheme of things.

Certainly those who read this book will have a more complete understanding of a variety of theoretical approaches as well as useful strategies for leaders to employ in group work. In a field of many fine texts on group counseling, Susan Day's text stands out.

Rex Stockton
Indiana University

Preface

I burst into loud laughter in college social psychology class, when our lecturer commenced with the words, "What is a group?" This struck me as a hugely silly question, the answer to which was completely obvious to anyone. My only excuse is that I was a teenager, a condition that makes the rhetorical inquiries of professors seem habitually silly. Who would imagine that forty years later, I would devote much of my life to thinking about what groups are, and how and whether and why they work?

Long before this devotion, I was already convinced that groups are potent, and I've been fortunate enough to see some of the positive sides of their power. (To witness the negative side, watch the news.) The main good effect of a close human group, in broad strokes, is a hedge against the deep existential aloneness that each of us naturally faces. Counseling and psychotherapy groups specialize in mitigating the loneliness of people troubled by temporary or chronic loss of the usual pleasures in life—the most usual pleasure being the exchange of affectionate attention and good will among diverse individuals.

An Overview of Groups in Practice

Like any summary, the one above blurs the complexities of the subject. This textbook aims to expand on the complexities of group counseling in a coherent and lively fashion, and I hope to animate you with my own enthusiasm. We textbook writers always encounter the problem of what to include and what to slight, what to develop in detail and what to downplay. Let me explain the logic behind what I've included in this book and how I've elaborated upon the material.

Organization

I chose an organization that would allow me to relate psychological theories to the purposes of groups and to relevant leadership skills:

- A solid basis in interpersonal process, therapeutic factors, cultural motifs, and professional ethics is established in Part I (Group Process and Principles of Change) and Part II (Therapeutic Factors Through a Group's Stages). These are the matters that pervade all kinds of groups regardless of their theoretical approaches.

- A theoretically and empirically sound classification of groups in terms of four themes composes Parts III through VI:

  - On Becoming a Person: Becoming a whole person, with sincere social relationships and a feeling of inner harmony (Part III). This part includes humanistic and existential approaches, which emphasize group members' growth into their full human potential, in an atmosphere of caring, acceptance, and understanding.

  - The Unfolding of Awareness: Heightening awareness and bringing unconscious material to consciousness (Part IV). This part includes psychodynamic and Gestalt approaches, which expand people's insight into inner conflicts that are interfering with their well-being. These conflicts often dwell outside of awareness before counseling.

  - A Life of Learning: Learning to think, feel, and act in new ways (Part V). This part includes cognitive-behavioral and psychoeducational approaches, which depend on changing thought processes, practicing activities, and providing information that will support positive changes and healthy coping.

  - On Becoming a Citizen: Citizenship in a larger world, where we all need to live cooperatively (Part VI). This part includes Adlerian and choice-theory approaches, which orient the group members in their civic contexts. Group members are asked to choose lifestyles that lead to individual success within their society. Contributing constructively to their society is considered key to individual well-being.

Special Features

In Parts III through VI (chapters covering distinct theories), special features assist the reader.

- Each chapter begins with a selection from a primary source (Beck, Dreikurs, Rogers, and Yalom among them). The selection is followed by questions that direct your thinking to crucial features of the theory under study. In this way, you begin to engage the ideas actively rather than passively. You also get a taste of how some major figures in group therapy express themselves and may decide to read more from some of these sources.

- Plentiful samples of leader responses and brief transcripts of group episodes help you visualize interactions in progress.

- Written comments collected from members of counseling groups illustrate the participants' points of view.

- At the closing of each of these chapters, a section on Evaluation/ Assessment presents methods and instruments designed to measure whether the group is working successfully or what features of the group are working. This encourages you to become a group researcher and an evidence-based practitioner. Evaluation is an important topic in this era of accountability, and you will learn assessments that go beyond the basic client satisfaction survey.

■ Awareness of you as a person who ventures your self in the group process is a recurrent theme.

Pedagogical Features

■ **Reflections** topics encourage you to explore life experiences and personal responses to the ideas in the book, pondering the intersection of your personal and professional capacities.

■ **Small Group Exercises** allow you to discuss and practice group counseling scenes and leadership skills. You'll create your own samples of how group leaders and members interact in given situations.

■ Frequent and creative **Discussion Ideas** can be used in classroom sessions, online discussions, and private review of material. They often ask you to provide applications and examples of concepts, as well as to verbalize your understanding of material.

End-of-Chapter Learning Aids

■ The terms that are boldfaced in the chapter are defined in a **Key Terms** section at the end of each chapter.

■ **Chapter Reviews** are not mere summaries, but questions that engage you in activities such as debate, teaching, surveying, introspection, and interviewing. These enhance self-referential learning, which is proven to improve comprehension and retention of material.

■ To encourage you to read original sources, a **For Further Reading** section lists and annotates relevant articles and books.

Supplementary Videos

Transcripts can be helpful to students hungry for real-life examples of how people interact in groups. And the learning experience is richer when you can watch the actual group sessions. The brief transcripts in the text were taken from videos produced by Lahaska Press expressly to accompany this book. In these supplementary videos, you may view the episodes in the context of complete group sessions.

Acknowledgments

My publisher, Barry Fetterolf, and editor, Mary Falcon, actively assisted me in marshalling the formidable body of wisdom about groups into a streamlined, yet faithful, account. My consultants Rex Stockton and Dennis Kivlighan acted as brainstorming partners, advisers, and steady supporters throughout the writing process. Doug Carter shared hours of his wide experience in counseling groups as he painstakingly reviewed each chapter and provided apt examples and intelligent insights. The book benefited amply from detailed reviews and suggestions from professional group workers and instructors:

Francene Bellamy, Chicago State University

Alan W. Burkard, Marquette University

William J. Casile

Eric C. Chen, Fordham University

Teddi Cunningham, Valdosta State University

Rosalyn V. Green, Bowie State University

Marty Jencius, Kent State University

Michael LeBlanc, SUNY Oswego

Louis V. Paradise, University of New Orleans

Michelle Pointer, Coppin State University

Beverly A. Snyder, University of Colorado—Colorado Springs

Rick Thompson, Austin Community College

David Tobin, Gannon University

F. Robert Wilson, University of Cincinnati

Brian Carter, again, has been willing to toss his fate in with mine, and I will never cease being amazed and grateful.

Conclusion

In a 1990 address at Centenary College of Louisiana, Maya Angelou said, "We allow our ignorance to prevail upon us and make us think we can survive alone, alone in patches, alone in groups, alone in races, even alone in genders." As group workers, your vocation is to overcome that ignorance. Connections among humans may be precarious, fluid, and fragile, but they can supply what we need for a generally pleasant and civilized passage through this life.

Susan X Day
University of Houston
Iowa State University

PART I

Group Process and Principles of Change

The first three chapters of this text cover overarching topics of importance to group leaders: group dynamics, classifications of counseling groups, ethics, and group development over time. In these chapters, you will discover the major distinction between group and individual counseling—that is, the power of the group in itself. The group is a therapeutic setting in which each member learns from experience with others in relationships significantly distinct from their relationships in the everyday world.

CHAPTER 1

The Framework of Group Counseling

The Healing Power of Groups

The Panoramic Picture—Therapeutic Factors Common to Groups

The Focused Picture—A Model of Groups in Practice Today
Stray Dogs and Mermaids

ASGW Classification of Groups
Psychoeducational Groups ▪ *Counseling Groups* ▪ *Psychotherapy Groups* ▪
Task/Work Groups ▪ *The Edges Overlap*

A Theoretical and Empirical Division

Stages of Group Process

Effectiveness of Group Counseling and Therapy
Patterns Within Complexity

A famous psychiatrist recounts a personal story from 1929:

> At one time, in a very crowded schedule, three young men in therapy
> were confronted with a similar problem. In order to save time, they
> were invited for a common interview, so that this one problem could
> be discussed with them. It was rather surprising that they requested
> afterwards to have their consultations continued because they felt how
> much they had benefited from this joint session together. (Dreikurs,
> 1957/1960, p. 53)

Though Rudolf Dreikurs, a physician and educator as well as a counselor, had
used groups in public clinics since 1923 for child guidance and for alcoholics,
it had not occurred to him to see private psychotherapy clients in groups until
he was motivated by a need to save time.

The Healing Power of Groups

Saving time and money is still a driving force behind group counseling, but throughout history the group has proven itself powerful far beyond these commonplace concerns. At their best, the institutions of religion and family have flourished on the grounds of embracing their members as they are, with sins and flaws and missteps, regardless of their assets and achievements. Often groups of close friends allow each other the luxury of revealing themselves as they really are, in the knowledge that they are accepted no matter what their shortcomings and accomplishments. Many of the stories that move us deeply show a lonely person returning to a group who accepts and heals, or finding such a group. (Think of Hugh Grant in the charming 2002 film *About a Boy*, the teenaged outcasts in *The Breakfast Club* [1985], and the yuppie-turned-villager in *Local Hero* [1983].) It's no wonder that we counselors explore the restorative ingredients of an effective group.

DISCUSSION IDEA

Share with your discussion group some examples of stories in which acceptance by a group cures, heals, or improves an individual. These stories occur in mythology, fiction, and TV and movie scripts, as well as in everyday life. Why is the group curative? Does the influence work both ways—in other words, is the group changed by accepting the person?

Groups let members feel a sense of belonging, especially when they gather based on a common problem. Loneliness seems contrary to human nature, as eminent psychologists have recognized: Maslow (1968) placed **belonging** above only basic physical sustenance and safety on his hierarchy of human needs; Murray (1938) listed **affiliation** as one of the prime motivators of human behavior; and Anna Freud and Dorothy Burlingham (1947) discovered that children deprived of human handling and affection failed to thrive normally, even when their physical needs were met. Even Mary Shelley's monster, Frankenstein, merely a simulation of a human, was tragically motivated by a need for fellowship. Relief from loneliness endures as a happy ending in our songs and stories. Banishment from human companionship endures as a wretched state and a punishment.

The Panoramic Picture—Therapeutic Factors Common to Groups

"As early as 1905, Joseph Pratt began seeing his tuberculosis patients within a class format, primarily as a labor-saving device, expecting them to commit to a specified normative behavior deemed crucial to patients' sense of identification with one another, their hope of recovery, and their faith in the class, the methods, and the physician" (Fuhriman & Burlingame, 1994, p. 4).

Treating medical patients one hundred years ago—another time, another place—Pratt nonetheless zeroed in on three common therapeutic factors of group therapy: members' relationships with one another, hope, and faith in the process. The astounding accuracy of this insight has been confirmed over and over in research studies about group counseling. The most well-known refinement of these **therapeutic factors** (also called *common factors, curative factors,* and *therapeutic conditions*) comes from Yalom (1995), who organized the factors into twelve general categories:

1. Interpersonal output (talking and responding to others)
2. Interpersonal input (finding out about others' perceptions and experiences)
3. Hope (belief that the future will be better)
4. Universality (awareness of similarity with other people)
5. Cohesiveness (feeling of belonging)
6. Identification with other members and the group leader (feeling related to others and able to emulate their positive traits)
7. Self-understanding (insight into one's own motivations and behavior)
8. Family reenactment (exploring and resolving inner conflicts and patterns related to one's family of origin, through experiencing relationships similar to those)
9. Catharsis (emotional release)
10. Altruism (unselfish acts and feelings)
11. Guidance (advice and education)
12. Existential growth (exploration of basic problems of human existence)

Each of these will be analyzed in Parts I and II of this book, because they are at work in various combinations and weights no matter what the focus of the group is. "Which factors are most important?" you may reasonably ask.

DISCUSSION IDEA

The following discussion of factors will mean more to you if you first consider what factors you have experienced yourself in group settings—clubs, classes, work groups, teams, gangs, social circles, religious organizations. Share with your discussion group examples of the twelve factors above from your own life.

In 1970, Yalom (1995) and his colleagues surveyed twenty middle-class out-patients who had been in group therapy for an average of sixteen months, with goals of symptom relief and character change. These group members rated interpersonal input, catharsis, cohesiveness, and self-understanding most highly. Naturally, other researchers noted that the self-reports of middle-class clients didn't cover the territory of group counseling very well, and followed up by looking at rankings by group leaders (in contrast with rankings by group members), different kinds of clients, and different group goals. Let me give some examples:

▪ Maxmen (1973) studied 100 hospital inpatients in short-term group psychotherapy and found that instillation of hope, group cohesiveness, altruism, and universality were ranked as the top four helpful factors. Notice that only cohesiveness appears in the top four for both the Yalom outpatient group and the Maxmen inpatient group. This suggests that the setting makes a difference in what factors are therapeutic.

▪ MacNair-Semands and Lese (2000) discovered that patients' rankings of therapeutic factors depended on their own interpersonal problems (for example, dominant clients perceived a lower level of altruism than other group members did, even within the same group). So, each individual may have his or her own set of therapeutic factors according to what their needs are.

▪ Kivlighan and Mullison (1988) concurred that individuals' traits influenced what they saw as helpful, and added research on how different therapeutic factors operate at different stages of a group's life. For example, early in a group's life cohesiveness is extraordinarily important to develop.

▪ Oygard (2001) discovered a sex difference in divorce support groups: Women reported adjustment through catharsis, universality, and cohesiveness, whereas men reported adjustment through catharsis and getting a new partner. Therefore, differences such as sex, class, and ethnic background may affect what therapeutic factor stands out to what person.

▪ Pan and Lin (2004) surveyed forty-five counseling group members aged 20 to 27 in Taiwan. These college students ranked cohesiveness first and altruism last, but there was little variation among their ratings of all the factors (the range was about 1 point on a 7-point scale).

▪ Other researchers (Fuhriman, Drescher, Hanson, Henrie, & Rybicki, 1986) suggested that more valid findings would come about through boiling down the list of therapeutic factors to four inclusive concepts that would be easier for clients to understand. Kivlighan, Multon, and Brossart (1996) labeled the four broader concepts Emotional Awareness/Insight, Relationship/Climate, Other Versus Self Focus, and Problem Solving/Behavior Change.

Critical of the "contradictory and atheoretical" findings of studies ranking therapeutic factors across various types of groups and clients, Kivlighan and Holmes (2004) sought to find an empirically based classification of groups ac-

cording to what therapeutic factors were endorsed in thirty-nine previous research studies. They used cluster analysis, which categorizes objects (in this
case, studies) according to a set of variables chosen by the researcher (in this
case, therapeutic factor rankings) (Hair & Black, 2000). Thus, Kivlighan and
Holmes were able to discover four types of studies that showed high similarity
within themselves and high difference from the other types, in the way they
ranked the therapeutic factors. They examined the four types and then labeled
each group by its outstanding characteristics. They decided that the four types
could be characterized on two principles: whether they had cognitive or affective emphases (thinking or feeling), and whether they placed more value
on insight (understanding) or support (sympathy, nurturance, approval). The
four types, empirically derived, correspond to the four focuses of this textbook,
which will be explained in the next section:

- **Affective support** (the *becoming* focus): Acceptance, instillation of hope, and universality receive top rankings.
- **Affective insight** (the *awareness* focus): Acceptance, catharsis, interpersonal learning, and self-understanding receive top rankings.
- **Cognitive insight** (the *learning* focus): Vicarious learning and guidance receive top rankings.
- **Cognitive support** (the *citizenship* focus): Interpersonal learning, self-understanding, and vicarious learning receive top rankings.

The Focused Picture—A Model of Groups in Practice Today

Unless you are in private practice, you probably won't design your own groups
from the ground up. You will propose (or be assigned) groups that match the
goals of your agency or school. Veterans Administration hospitals, for example, usually offer smoking cessation and substance abuse recovery groups, and
sometimes career development groups, whereas schools hold groups for children of divorce, victims of bullying, and aggressive children. In Parts I and II
of this text, I explain many factors that operate any time people gather for a
common purpose and interact with each other. Each group can also be seen
as belonging to a type or category, with its own particularly relevant theories,
leadership skills, client bases, techniques, and dynamics. These categories are
covered in detail in Parts III, IV, V, and VI. All groups draw from common therapeutic factors, described in Parts I and II.

Along with therapeutic factors come common group leader behaviors that
activate and facilitate them. "Group therapeutic factors imply underlying leader
functions and interventions that, if performed adequately, will serve to actively
construct a group milieu where members are most likely to benefit" (Morran,
Stockton, Cline, & Teed, 1998). Therefore, in Parts I and II, I connect each factor
to one or more common leader interventions.

Stray Dogs and Mermaids

Categorization, dividing a group of similar things into distinct types, is tricky (Rosch, 1978). An ancient Chinese encyclopedia, for example, is said to categorize the animal kingdom in this way: "animals are divided into (a) those that belong to the Emperor, (b) embalmed ones, (c) those that are trained, (d) suckling pigs, (e) mermaids, (f) fabulous ones, (g) stray dogs, (h) those that are included in this classification, (i) those that tremble as if they were mad [and so on]" (Borges, 1966, p. 108). Deciding how to classify the kinds of group counseling in practice is somewhat like the efforts of the ancient Chinese encyclopedists.

ASGW Classification of Groups

The Association for Specialists in Group Work (ASGW) categorizes the field this way: psychoeducational, counseling, psychotherapy, and task/work groups (ASGW, 2000).

Psychoeducational Groups

Psychoeducational groups provide information and practice in using new knowledge. They gather for a wide variety of purposes, but each group focuses on a specific expertise. They assist mentally healthy people in dealing with life's stresses and in avoiding foreseeable problems. For example, caregivers of parents with Alzheimer's disease benefit from education about the disease given in a setting where they also gain support from others in similar situations. Children whose parents are undergoing divorces, parents of gays and lesbians, socially isolated teens, and people who have survived heart attacks are other populations served by psychoeducational groups. These are usually short-term (eight to ten one- to two-hour sessions, once or twice a week), and include ten to twelve adults, or fewer child members. If the educational component is given to large groups, discussion and exercises take place in organized subgroups, so that each person can participate.

Counseling Groups

Counseling groups serve people who need help with common problems that individuals share. Education certainly goes on in counseling groups, but the focus is on the group members themselves. Their interactions and mutual problem-solving efforts provide most of the content for group sessions, instead of educational presentations by experts. These groups are also usually short-term and have limited numbers—five to twelve for adults (Donigian & Malnati, 1977), and three to six for children. Group leaders highlight people's strengths and their ability to grapple with their problems. Examples include counseling groups for recently divorced people, support groups for Middle Eastern students on a college campus, and groups for trauma survivors. Counseling groups challenge the individual to be more self-disclosing and take more emotional risks than psychoeducation groups typically do.

Psychotherapy Groups

For people with more severe problems than psychoeducational groups and counseling groups, **psychotherapy groups** are created. Members are experiencing more prominent, more dangerous, and longer-lasting maladjustments. They may even be institutionalized. Through a process sometimes called *personality reconstruction,* groups in the psychotherapy classification aim to change people on a much deeper level than groups in any of the other ASGW classifications. This means that their established patterns of thinking, behaving, and interacting with others are examined. Leaders usually (but not always) base their work on a major psychological theory like the ones you will study in this textbook. These groups are not often time limited, though points of renewal may occur regularly. A group also may have fluctuating membership (an **open group**) in contrast to a **closed group,** which does not change membership over its course. For instance, a psychotherapy group in a hospital may always meet on Thursdays from 2 to 4 p.m., but patients come and go. Other psychotherapy groups allow a member to determine his or her own time of completion, and then replace the outgoing member with a new one. People who are survivors of child sexual abuse, addicts, and the chronically depressed or anxious are candidates for psychotherapy groups.

Task/Work Groups

While the focus of groups in the other categories is on individual growth, the focus of a **task or work group** is on getting something done. You have no doubt been a member of a task or work group yourself: a committee, a volunteer group, a drama troupe, an army unit, or a school project team. And you have no doubt noticed that the better the group dynamics, the better the task or work turns out. Group leaders trained in counseling can assist work and task groups because they understand how to manage team-building, communication, feedback, conflict resolution, power, decision making, and subgrouping among members. That is, they understand the process elements of the group, whereas the work itself provides the **content** of the group. Like a psychoeducational group, the task/work group has a definite, and sometimes abrupt, ending—when the job is done. Frequently, in order to avoid the abruptness, these groups plan a celebratory ending ritual, such as a cast party, a group meal, or a christening of the project's outcome.

The Edges Overlap

As you can see, overlap characterizes this typology: ASGW at the moment is attempting to refine the categorization (Rapin & Wilson, 2004). The first three types, especially, flow into each other easily. People seeking psychoeducation usually have needs for more than knowledge: They need human interaction, problem solving, and—well—counseling. When people join a counseling group, it often turns out that they are more seriously distressed than they appear. The group becomes psychotherapeutic. People in psychotherapeutic groups frequently need psychoeducation about their problems and symptoms (for example, post-traumatic stress disorder). And, as we have seen in many cases, being part of a work group can entail psychotherapeutic personal transformation (for example, in *Saving Private Ryan* [1998], soldiers on a dangerous mission become more noble through working together). Furthermore, labels don't always reflect what's inside. In the Veterans Administration Hospital where I worked, the patients routinely referred to their substance abusers' therapy group as their "class," which made them more willing to attend it.

The ASGW classification helps you see some general outlines. There are several other sensible classification schemes as well. You might also envision a continuum of groups, with groups that aim to prevent problems at one end and groups that aim to cure problems at the other end, and groups aiming for personal growth in the middle (Gazda, 1989).

A Theoretical and Empirical Division

I have chosen yet another approach because it allows traditional psychological theories to be intertwined with group purpose and leader techniques. Because of a research base in Kivlighan and Holmes's work (2004) and a clustering of theoretical foundations as well, I present groups in terms of four approaches to individual change:

▪ *Becoming* a whole person, with sincere social relationships and a feeling of inner harmony (Part III). This part includes humanistic and existential approaches, which emphasize group members' growth into their full human potential in an atmosphere of caring, acceptance, and understanding.

▪ Heightening *awareness* and bringing unconscious material to consciousness (Part IV). This part includes psychodynamic and Gestalt approaches, which expand people's insight into inner conflicts that are interfering with their well-being. These conflicts often dwell outside of awareness before therapy.

▪ *Learning* to think, feel, and act in new ways (Part V). This part includes psychoeducational and cognitive-behavioral approaches, which depend on changing thought processes, doing activities, and providing information that will support positive behavior changes.

▪ *Citizenship* in a larger world, where we all need to live cooperatively (Part VI). This part includes Adlerian and choice-theory approaches, which place the group members in a social context. Group members are asked to choose lifestyles that lead to individual success within their society. Contributing constructively to their society is considered key to individual success.

Stages of Group Process

A group resembles any lengthy relationship: It goes through **stages of development.** When we look at how a group is functioning at the moment (its **group process**), we can discern whether it is in its infancy, childhood, adolescence, or adulthood. Group experts are in wide agreement that a developmental path exists, but from there they look at somewhat different maps. And there's a good reason for that: Groups come in such different varieties that they naturally vary in how many stages they go through, and how long they stay in each one. A veteran group member described it this way:

> Groups often felt like a living thing. They would grow, morph, shrink, change tone, evolve. And like any personal relationship, some groups were better than others. Some would start out slow, then get really good. Some were mediocre the whole time.

Reflections

1. To help you conceptualize stages, think of two close friendships of your own. Look at the history of each, from the time you met until now. Can you divide these histories into eras? How do the processes of becoming close friends differ in each case? Can you see any underlying similarities that you could label common stages of friendship?

   For example, though my friendships are each one-of-a-kind, I seem to follow a pattern of getting to know someone in a structured setting, like on the job or working on a community project; then seeking to associate with them more within that setting; then making little trips outside the setting together; and finally, if the mutual liking persists, having the association exist in other areas of life and outlast the original setting completely.

2. Think of a small group you have belonged to—perhaps a social group, work group, or school group. Compare the early days or meetings of this group with the group today. What changes can you identify over the life of the group? Could you divide the group's life into stages? Discuss these questions with others in the same group, if you get a chance.

Many different stage models of the group have been proposed, with between three and thirteen stages labeled. Each stage involves a new task, challenge, or goal to be mastered. Generally, research has shown that groups follow a sequence that can be loosely summarized as follows:

- An initial period of caution, anxiety, and orientation, with members striving for acceptance.

■ A period in which conflicts and tension arise and the group seeks a balance between upset and tranquility. Differences that were downplayed in the initial period become points of contention.

■ A stage in which the group comes to harmony about its norms and individuals feel a sense of belonging and acceptance even during conflicts. Everyone behaves more authentically than they did in the first stage. (Of course, each person has changed since then.)

■ A stage in which goals of individuals and the group as a whole are pursued and met.

■ A final period of closure in which individuals look back over what they have experienced in the group and make separate future plans.

These stages are frequently labeled in an easy-to-remember system: *forming, storming, norming, performing,* and *adjourning* (Tuckman & Jensen, 1977) or *mourning.* The *performing* stage is also often called the *work* stage because the group's major fulfillment of purpose is concentrated in this phase. At least ten different descriptions of this development process have been proposed by group experts. They tend to divide the middle sections of the process in slightly different ways, though the overall sequence remains similar. Table 1.1 displays some of the terminology associated with the beginning, middle, and ending stages of a group. Look closely at the terms used for each stage, and you will get a sense of the interpersonal relationships and group tasks that are expected in that part of a group's life.

The descriptors in Table 1.1 illustrate a successful group as it moves through its life. Some theorists divide the middle phase into two stages, as I indicated with the dotted line. The early middle stage is transitional and involves strife, whereas in the later middle stage most of the work of the group is performed. Of course, not all groups are completely successful. Without apt leadership, the group can bog down and even dissolve when grappling with the challenges of any level. The comfort of the early stage, with its inclusiveness and dependence on the leader, can extend too long, and conflicts can be squashed rather than allowed to develop into deeper encounters. This makes for a smooth but ultimately uneventful group. Further along, the conflicts of the middle stages can become so ugly that people drop out, form rival subgroups, and fail to move beyond their differences. And the closing of the group can be soaked with disappointment and bitterness, on at least some members' parts. Termination can also be shocking if the leader has not given periodic reminders throughout the course of the group; it is common for members to be surprisingly oblivious to their group's imminent end, even when they contracted for a specified number of sessions at the beginning (Eklof, 1984).

The stage development is heavily affected by what the group's focus is, as you will see in the rest of this book. A psychoeducational group may experience little overt personal conflict (storming) and yet fulfill its goals, skipping a storming stage. For example, a group gathers because they are all people with family members who are schizophrenic. Their goal is to learn about the disorder and how they can help their loved ones, and to get some support for their sad

TABLE 1.1
Terms Describing a Group's Stages

Beginning Stage	Middle Stage	Ending Stage
Forming	Conflict	Productivity
Dependence on leader	Transition	Consolidation
Inclusion	Resistance	Control
Orientation	Questioning authority	Affection
Exploration	Tension	Adjourning
Education	Evaluation	Differentiation
Search for security and cohesion	Storming	Reinforcement
	Norming	Closing
Caution	Differentiation	Anxiety
Testing the waters	....	Separation
Exchange of information	Security within conflict	Loss
Engagement	Tolerance of conflict	Termination
	Interdependence	Reminiscence
	Emergence	Closure
	Performing	Fulfillment
	Productivity	Changing relationships
	Work	
	Power	
	Mutuality	
	Intimacy	
	Cohesion	

situation. This group may never have strong conflicts between members. In contrast, a personal growth group comprising members who suffer interpersonal problems will not fulfill its goals without struggle and confrontation between members. This type of group will be very stormy.

The duration of stages and their sequencing alters group by group, too. A short group (for example, eight sessions devoted to living with a schizophrenic family member) might complete the final stage (adjourning) in one session, while a long-term group (a year or longer) might devote four or more sessions to achieving closure. An open-membership group folds back upon its earlier processes when new members are added, and different members may experience different stages at one moment. A group member describes a combined time-limited and open system and its stages:

> After a six-month committed set of group sessions, the therapist described a break of some determined time. At that time, it was stated that the group

would continue on a certain date, and everyone was asked whether they would like to participate. Any group member not wanting to continue was asked to say goodbye to the group. Discussions were encouraged on the idea of "what it's like to say goodbye," the feelings of loss, and so on. In almost all of my groups, at least half of the members continued into the next group, and new members were added. We helped them get used to the group. In this way, the group seemed like a train, taking us all on a journey. We could get off at certain points, but always had the option of getting back on the train. I think it modeled life quite well.

Finally, it's crucial to remember that the stages of a group are not marked by fixed boundaries, but are fluid in movement (Stockton, Rohde, & Haughey, 1992). Groups also shift to earlier stages of development as they progress, just as people sometimes shift to behavior less mature than their age once in a while. Times of stress, conflict, and confusion can instigate a return to earlier stages, in both individuals and groups. Donigian and Malnati (1997) suggest that stages in sequence are clearer in time-limited groups, while longer-term groups cycle back through earlier stages more often.

DISCUSSION IDEA

Focus a discussion on Table 1.1. Relate the terms in the table to some group you have been part of or one you have observed. (Your examples do not have to be from counseling or therapy groups; they could be task or educational groups.) Talk with your classmates about successes and failures in the groups, and how these may have been related to the stages.

For example, my first resounding failure at group counseling occurred in a group of 9- to 12-year-old girls who had suffered child sexual abuse. I approached the group in the same way I would a group of teenagers or adults, neglecting to think about the alterations I needed to make for children. My major error was in not spending nearly enough time in orientation and education about the group and what was expected in it, including rules of behavior. I did not take on the authoritative role the girls could depend on. By the close of the second session, the group had dissolved into sassiness, loudness, and even pushing. I had failed in the first stage, and the group never progressed beyond it.

I had also failed to take into account developmental differences between children and adults, obviously. There are observable biological, social, intellectual, vocational, and psychological periods throughout the lifespan that must be accommodated in group work (Gazda, 1989). In the later chapters of this book, I suggest how each theoretical approach is altered for use with different client ages.

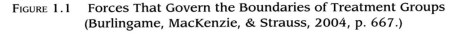

FIGURE 1.1   Forces That Govern the Boundaries of Treatment Groups (Burlingame, MacKenzie, & Strauss, 2004, p. 667.)

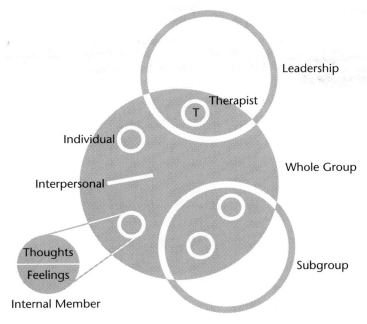

Effectiveness of Group Counseling and Therapy

Therapy in general is a difficult topic for research. Whenever we have a subject as complex as a human being, we end up asking just as many questions as we answer. However, through years of studies on the effectiveness of *individual* psychotherapy, we can say with certainty that it works: The average client who gets counseling is better off than 79 percent of similar people who do not receive counseling (Wampold, 2001). Furthermore, the gains people make in therapy are maintained over time (Nicholson & Berman, 1983). However, the interaction between the counselor and client is so intricate that exactly *why* therapy is effective remains a source of brisk controversy.

And that's just looking at two people. Invite five to twenty participants, as we do in group counseling, and the research problem becomes Byzantine. Figure 1.1 illustrates the various interacting sets, called **boundaries**, that exist in a therapy group. Any researcher would have trouble isolating elements to study within such a dynamic system. For example, just look at the leader's angle: As a counselor, there are interactions between you and an individual member, between individuals in the group, between you and the group as a whole, between you and a subgroup (like all the members on one side of a controversial topic), between individuals within a subgroup, and within yourself (the side you decide to show in sessions and the sides you keep screened). These interactions are demonstrated in Figure 1.1 by the intersections of overlapping circles. Any one of these interactions is ripe for researchers' scrutiny.

Furthermore, the terms *group therapy* and *group counseling* cover a lot of ground, from completely free-flowing conversation groups to highly structured, preplanned treatments. This variety, which on one hand makes group practice stimulating and full of possibility, on the other hand makes research on effectiveness hard to generalize to all types of group. Many people make a distinction between therapy and counseling, usually meaning that therapy concerns more deep, serious, and rare problems. However, this distinction is not consistently made nowadays, and the words *therapist* and *counselor* are used interchangeably, unless one's workplace or school traditionally prefers one or the other label. In this textbook, I use them as synonyms because my audience includes people who call themselves counselors, therapists, or both.

Reflections

1. Think of a group that you are now a part of, and consider whether you can schematize it in terms of Figure 1.1. Feel free to change the diagram or labels; for instance, the leader might be a parent, boss, elected official, teacher, or unofficial chief. Annotate your diagram with notes that explain the group in any way. Can you identify subgroups? Can you identify the interaction processes during some group encounter you remember? Can you identify which boundary or boundaries contribute to the strengths or weaknesses of your group, or both? If time permits, share your diagram with a classmate or the class as a whole.

2. The creators of Figure 1.1 use the word *boundaries* to describe the elements of the group. What do you think of using this word? How is it appropriate? Is there another way you could convey the meaning?

Patterns Within Complexity

In spite of the complexities involved, a large number of studies have examined the effectiveness of group counseling and psychotherapy. Starting in the 1990s, reviewers of group counseling research have used meta-analysis to summarize studies of group counseling effectiveness. Meta-analysis is "a general conceptual approach to problems of summarizing, integrating, and testing practical questions and theoretical issues with the results of previous research" (Mullen, Driskell, & Salas, 1998, p. 213). In meta-analysis, researchers are able to combine the results of many studies and come up with overall conclusions that are more powerful than those of any single study.

According to Kivlighan, Coleman, and Anderson (2000), the major findings of eight different meta-analyses of the group therapy effectiveness literature are very consistent. In each of the meta-analyses, the average group counseling client was found to be 75 percent better off than a comparable client who received no treatment. The relative effectiveness of group counseling was consistent across multiple measures of outcome and multiple formats of group treatment. In addition, the meta-analytic results found no outcome differences for clients treated in individual versus group therapy. These meta-analyses provide strong support for the practice of group counseling. They suggest that group counseling is at least as effective as the more traditional individual approach to treatment.

Pulling together the results of many studies that compared group therapy with individual therapy, allowing a lot of variety in both settings, Burlingame, MacKenzie, and Strauss (2004) concluded that the evidence supports the general equivalence of the two formats. That is, the client outcomes (measured in many different ways, of course) from group and individual therapy are equal.

You may think that this is surprising, because clients have to share a counselor in the group format, whereas one counselor's focus is on one client in individual formats. Sometimes clients feel the same way, that group treatment is diluted treatment. The truth is that the group *as a system* is therapeutic. The group receives much more than the attention of one counselor divided by five or eight. The common factors of group process, discussed in Part I of this book, are the active ingredients that make the experience in groups at least equivalent to individual therapy, superior for some purposes, and qualitatively different.

Some of the most structured group treatments take the theories and techniques of individual therapy and then tailor them for administration to groups. In the tailoring process, sometimes the special active ingredients of the group setting are incorporated purposely, and sometimes not. However, these ingredients tend to flavor the treatment anyway.

Burlingame et al. (2004) attempted to assess research on the effectiveness of group treatment for specific disorders (for instance, whether group treatment is especially good for depression but not as effective for panic disorders). They found their efforts hindered by two problems. First, when a group treatment was a direct application of a therapy originally designed for individual treatment, such as cognitive-behavioral therapy (CBT), it was often difficult to untangle the effects of the therapy approach from the potential contributions of being in a group. If clients in a cognitive-behavioral group improved, was it due to the CBT or due to the healing power of the group? Second, many solidly supported group treatments are always used in combinations with individual therapy, education, and medicine (dialectical behavior therapy [DBT] for borderline personality disorder is a good example). When DBT clients improve, what portion is due to group therapy, and what portion to the other treatments in the plan?

In this textbook, I take the point of view that all groups can be more effective when you make use of the common factors that fit your group's focus.

Research has compared structured, theoretically based groups with control groups, which were unstructured and without theoretical guidance. These control groups were designed to provide no treatment, so that an even comparison could be made between treatment and no treatment. They were supposed to be like the sugar pills used as placebos in drug research, appearing like the drug but not really having the main ingredient. Repeatedly, clients in the control groups, which had been considered the placebo, did just as well as those in the treatment groups! They were benefiting from the therapeutic elements of the group setting (Burlingame et al., 2004). These common therapeutic elements are the subjects of the next six chapters.

DISCUSSION IDEA

Brainstorm with your discussion group about methods you might use (or do use) to evaluate the effectiveness of group counseling. Basically, how can you tell whether a group is working or not? Discuss the pros and cons of various methods of evaluating group effectiveness.

KEY TERMS

affiliation   mutual, emotional connection among people

belonging   the feeling of membership in a group

boundaries   imaginary lines drawn around physical or psychological elements of a group, such as boundaries between the group members and the leader, or between two subgroups of members who differ, or between individuals. In a classroom, a boundary can sometimes be drawn between students who sit in the very front and students who sit in the very back

closed group   a group that does not accept new members during its life course, though some members may drop out

content   the subject matter of the group; what is said among members

counseling group   a group focused on solving or easing a life problem common to its members

group process   what happens within the group, such as team-building, communication, feedback, conflict resolution, power, decisionmaking, and subgrouping among members

open group   a group whose membership changes during its life course

personality reconstruction   a deep change in a person's basic patterns of thinking, perceiving, feeling, and behaving

psychoeducational group   a group with the purpose of imparting knowledge and assisting people in using knowledge

psychotherapy group   a group focused on a severe or chronic maladjustment common to its members

stages of group development   identifiable, sequential periods of time in a group's life. Certain challenges, interpersonal relationships, and tasks are characteristic of each period

task/work group   a group dedicated to generating something, such as a product, plan, idea, or performance

therapeutic factors   elements of group membership that contribute to members' growth and well-being; also called *curative factors, common factors,* and *therapeutic conditions*

CHAPTER REVIEW

1. List and define twelve therapeutic factors. Make up an example for each one to help you remember them.
2. What elements affect the ranking of therapeutic factors in importance? Make up your own personal ranking of therapeutic factors, reflecting what you think is important in the groups you lead or intend to lead.
3. Describe what is expected to happen in the beginning, middle, and ending stages of a group's life. You will remember this better if you visualize a group you have been in or observed.
4. In what ways do researchers study the effectiveness of group therapy? What are some difficulties in such studies? Think about what research you would like to see done in this area.
5. Pretend that a friend who is skeptical asks you what people get out of group counseling. Answer this friend as fully as you can at this point.

FOR FURTHER READING

Yalom, I. D., & Leszcz, M. (2005). *The Theory and Practice of Group Psychotherapy* (5th ed.).

This is the classic book in the field of psychotherapy groups. Chapters 1 through 4 discuss the therapeutic factors in depth. Yalom is considered the originator of therapeutic factors identification and research.

REFERENCES

Association for Specialists in Group Work. (2000). *ASGW Professional Standards for Group Counseling.* Alexandria, VA: Author.

Borges, J. L. (1966). *Other inquisitions 1937–1952.* New York: Washington Square Press.

Burlingame, G. M., MacKenzie, K. R., & Strauss, B. (2004). Small-group treatment: Evidence for effectiveness and mechanisms of change. In M. J. Lambert (Ed.), *Bergin and Garfield's handbook of psychotherapy and behavior change* (5th ed., pp. 647–696). New York: Wiley.

Donigian, J., & Malnati, R. (1997). *Systemic group therapy: A triadic model.* Pacific Grove, CA: Brooks/Cole.

Dreikurs, R. (1960). *Group psychotherapy and group approaches: Collected papers of Rudolph Dreikurs, M.D.* Chicago: Alfred Adler Institute, 1960. (Original work published 1957)

Eklof, M. (1984). The termination phase in group therapy. *Small Group Behavior, 15,* 565–571.

Freud, A., & Burlingham, D. (1947). *Infants without families.* Madison, CT: International Universities Press.

Fuhriman, A., & Burlingame, G. M. (1994). Group psychotherapy: Research and practice. In A. Fuhriman & G. M. Burlingame (Eds.). *Handbook of group psychotherapy: An empirical and clinical synthesis* (pp. 3–40). New York: Wiley.

Fuhriman, A., Drescher, S., Hanson, E., Henrie, R., & Rybicki, W. (1986). Refining the measurement of curativeness: An empirical approach. *Small Group Behavior, 17,* 186–201.

Gazda, G. M. (1989). *Group counseling: A developmental approach* (4th ed.). Boston: Allyn & Bacon.

Hair, J. F., & Black, W. C. (2000). Cluster analysis. In L. G. Grimm & P. R. Yarnold (Eds.), *Reading and understanding more multivariate statistics* (pp. 147–206). Washington, DC: American Psychological Association.

Kivlighan, D. M., & Holmes, S. E. (2004). The importance of therapeutic factors: A typology of therapeutic factors studies. In J. L. DeLucia-Waack, D. A. Gerrity, C. R. Kalodner, & M. T. Riva (Eds.), *Handbook of group counseling and psychotherapy* (pp. 23–36). Thousand Oaks, CA: Sage.

Kivlighan, D. M., & Mullison, D. (1988). Participants' perception of therapeutic factors in group counseling: The role of interpersonal style and stage of group development. *Small Group Behavior, 19,* 452–468.

Kivlighan, D. M., Jr., Multon, K. D., & Brossart, D. F. (1996). Helpful impacts in group counseling: Development of a multidimensional rating system. *Journal of Counseling Psychology, 43,* 347–355.

Kivlighan, D. M., Coleman, M. N., & Anderson, D. C. (2000). Process, outcome, and methodology in group counseling research. In S. D. Brown & R. W. Lent (Eds.), *Handbook of counseling psychology* (3rd ed., pp. 767–796). New York: Wiley.

MacNair-Semands, R. R., & Lese, K. P. (2000). Interpersonal problems and the perception of therapeutic factors in group therapy. *Small Group Research, 31,* 158–174.

Maslow, A. H. (1968). *Toward a psychology of being.* Princeton, NJ: Van Nostrand.

Maxmen, J. S. (1973). Group therapy as viewed by hospitalized patients. *Archives of General Psychiatry, 28,* 404–408.

Morran, D. K., Stockton, R., Cline, R. J., & Teed, C. (1998). Facilitating feedback exchange in groups: Leader interventions. *Journal for Specialists in Group Work, 23,* 257–268.

Mullen, B., Driskell, J. E., & Salas, E. (1998). Meta-analysis and the study of group dynamics. *Group Dynamics, 2,* 213–229.

Murray, H. A. (1938). *Explorations in personality.* New York: Oxford University Press.

Nicholson, R. A., & Berman, J. S. (1983). Is follow-up necessary in evaluating psychotherapy? *Psychological Bulletin, 93,* 261–278.

Oygard, L. (2001). Therapeutic factors in divorce support groups. *Journal of Divorce and Remarriage, 36,* 141–158.

Pan, P. J. D., & Lin, C. W. (2004). Members' perceptions of leader behaviors, group experiences, and therapeutic factors in group counseling. *Small Group Research, 35,* 174–194.

Rapin, L., & Wilson, F. R. (2004, January). Group work methods and purposes: An application matrix. Paper presented at ASGW Group Workers Conference, New York City.

Rosch, E. (1978). Principles of categorization. In E. Rosch & B. B. Lloyd (Eds.), *Cognition and categorization* (pp. 27–48). Oxford, England: Erlbaum.

Stockton, R., Rohde, R. I., & Haughey, J. (1992). The effects of structured group exercises on cohesion, engagement, avoidance, and conflict. *Small Group Research, 23,* 155–168.

Tuckman, B. W., & Jensen, M. A. C. (1977). Stages of small-group development revisited. *Group and Organizational Studies, 2,* 419–427.

Wampold, B. E. (2001). *The great psychotherapy debate: Models, methods, and findings.* Mahwah, NJ: Erlbaum.

Yalom, I. D. (1995). *The theory and practice of group psychotherapy.* New York: Basic Books.

CHAPTER 2

Small Group Dynamics and Interpersonal Theory

Group Dynamics

Interpersonal Learning Theory

> *Self-System* ▪ *Security Operations* ▪ *Interpersonal Schemas* ▪
> *Cognitive-Interpersonal Cycles*

The Group Setting: A Stage for Interpersonal Schemas

> *Honoring Feedback* ▪ *Experimentation*

Group Composition

The Group as a System

> *Totality* ▪ *Nonsummativity* ▪ *Homeostasis*

Group Dynamics and Chaos Theory

> *The Counselor's Contribution to Creative Chaos*

Think about how we define ourselves and others. When a friend introduces you to someone new, she is likely to mention your work, your relationship to other people, or both: "Shirelle is Sarah's mom; she works at the post office." "This is Jana, Tom's buddy from flight training school." Both the workplace and the social circle are commonly group settings, and these are settings that give us identity.

The relation between individual psychology and other people is at the heart of group therapy. Interpersonal activities influence a great deal of our psychological life, and the group setting can affect our habitual interpersonal activity. The group setting exposes this habitual activity for scrutiny. In counseling an individual, I get a close look at how the client approaches and responds to *me*, but I am only one person with my own set of approaches and responses. In observing an individual relating to a group, I get much richer information. For example, I learned something from the contrast in Louise's behavior in individual therapy and group counseling. Louise talked fluently in my office in individual sessions and then surprised me by holding back and remaining silent in group sessions. It emerged that she had a deeply embedded habit of nearly always trying to ensure that others' needs are met before her own.

Group Dynamics

Recall the last time when you ate dinner with another family that holds some interest for you (such as your partner's, a new friend's, or a boss's): At the table, you notice things about how family members act toward each other, who has what power over whom, what topics they discuss, the overall emotional tone that is maintained, the pace and flow of their talk, how they take turns and how long they hold the floor, and all the sorts of things that give each family its uniqueness. These are the family's **group dynamics.** For most of us, the family is our first group experience. Other groups follow as we develop, from our gang of playmates to our nursing home cronies. Kurt Lewin (1948), a social psychologist, first coined the term to describe all the things that go on in a group, both visible and invisible. *Dynamics* is a good word choice because it calls forth other images that have both palpable and unseen forces, like rushing water, the flow of electricity, breathtaking music, and the ocean tides.

Researchers in a variety of disciplines study group dynamics in many settings. Examples include how people's behavior at work is influenced by the other workers and bosses; how lynch mobs form and perform; how mixed-sex versus single-sex groups make decisions; and, of course, how happy and unhappy families operate. Even in instances as disparate as these, group dynamics have some elements in common. As we saw in Chapter 1, they have *content*, such as goals, purposes, subject matter, and exchange of information. Of most interest to counselors, they have *processes*, interactions among people in all the boundary conditions defined in Chapter 1 (Figure 1.1). In almost any group, at least a few of these processes can be identified:

problem solving

gaining and losing perspective

making alliances

tension and anxiety

elicited emotions

conflict and resolution

reality testing

negotiation

Group counseling thrives on a fascination with group dynamics and their meaning. The give-and-take among individuals in a group, after all, is what distinguishes group versus individual treatment.

SMALL GROUP EXERCISES

1. Choose one or two of the group processes listed above, and discuss examples of them from your experience in a small group. Use any kind of small group you've been in: therapy, work, classroom, family, team, and so on.

2. Discuss what someone at one of your family gatherings could tell about your group dynamics. Could an outsider see more group dynamics than an insider, or the other way around?

Interpersonal Learning Theory

Group work is based on **interpersonal learning theory,** which involves group dynamics. This theory has a large cognitive component because thinking (cognition) always accompanies feeling and experiencing when group therapy is effective (Yalom, 1995). Therefore, you will sometimes see interpersonal learning theory referred to as **cognitive-interpersonal theory.** The interweaving of feelings and thoughts is evident in the following example:

> Mark notes that his stomach tightens and he feels sad when Lauren is talking in group about her frustration that she cannot help her sister who is struggling with anorexia nervosa. A few moments later Mark realizes that he experiences quite similar stomach discomfort and frustration at moments when he feels in the middle of his divorcing parents.

Mark is identifying a physical sensation, an emotion, and a realization (a thought), and seeing how they co-exist.

Yalom would see Mark's parallel experiences of stomach discomfort inside and outside the group as an example of the group's **social microcosm.** According to the notion of the social microcosm, group members, over time, come to act and react in the group in ways similar to how they act and interact in the world. (*Microcosm* means *tiny world.*) Cognitive-interpersonal theory explains how the social microcosm comes about. Many group dynamics can be viewed in terms of cognitive-interpersonal theory.

Let me explain the theory and how it applies to the group setting. Four cognitive-interpersonal concepts are the self-system, security operations, interpersonal schema, and cognitive-interpersonal cycles. These are the topics of the next four sections.

Self-System

Harry Stack Sullivan (1953) used the term *self-system* to mean something like the personality, only with an emphasis on our concepts of who we are and how we operate in relation to other people. Sullivan is noted for taking traditional Freudian observations and explaining them through how people interact with each other instead of how internal psychological structures interact. The self-system comes about from early experience with other people, and it evolves and changes as we experience new and more complex interactions with others.

Most of us have a wide but quite recognizable repertoire of ways we relate to others. People who know us well can accurately observe when we are "not acting like ourselves." When they say this, we can almost always accept it as fact and explain it. We may not act like ourselves when we are sick, distracted, grieving, preoccupied, nervous, or self-conscious, for example. People close to us are also able to predict fairly well what our reactions to new situations will be. Think of how you can usually tell whether your best friend will like a certain movie or book.

Cognitivists call our individual repertoires *self-schemas.* In general, a schema is a pattern we impose on external reality in order to understand it and guide our responses to it. With our meeting-a-new-person schema, for example, we are able to greet, give our names, and exchange one or two superficial items of information. This schema, which everyone knows, helps us negotiate a new, unknown situation by providing a pattern to follow. Schemas operate outside of momentary awareness: When you meet someone new, you don't tell yourself, "First, greet the stranger." You follow the schema without thinking about it.

Self-schemas are patterns of emotion, thought, and behavior based on early experiences, mostly those of satisfaction, security, and anxiety. These early experiences imbue us with inclinations toward certain patterns of thought and behavior, which we then maintain. We keep them up through current attitudes, preferences, avoidances, and habits. For example, a withdrawn person chooses solitary hobbies, which maintain her self-schema because she is not brought into constant contact with others. A hostile person creates a mean world around himself. And, as you see in the following example, a condescending self-schema creates a world of inferiors:

> Rachel is a law student who sought individual counseling because "I can't trust any of those back-stabbing, gossiping, competitive law students." After being referred to group counseling, in the first session she attacked the leaders for using "psycho-babble clichés" and announced that she did not feel comfortable with the other members and was going to remain silent and "just be an observer." Her interpersonal stance of superiority to others, both in law school and initially in group, sets the stage for initial negative response to her.

Group therapy seeks to modify self-schemas that persist in harmful forms. Counselors have devised a group treatment based on interpersonal theory for borderline personality disorder, a diagnosis describing people with chronically disrupted, disappointing relationships, anger, and self-destructiveness. Interpersonal group therapy provides "a new learning experience in which, contrary to the patient's expectations, negative self-schemas are not confirmed. When this learning experience is sufficiently reinforced and consolidated, the patient is able to accommodate relational information that was previously blocked, and an altered self-schema emerges" (Marziali & Munroe-Blum, 1994, p. 64).

Reflections

1. Can you give an example of being told that you "were not acting like yourself" in some situation? In other words, think of a time when your behavior surprised people who seem to know you well. Were you able to identify what you did that was uncharacteristic, and to explain it?

2. What do you do when you want to make a good first impression on someone? What makes your efforts different from just anyone's? Relate your answers to the concept of self-system or self-schema.

Security Operations

Security operations are psychological and interpersonal strategies that serve self-esteem and preserve our self-systems. We each develop habitual behaviors that enable us to reach out to others for contact and help us avoid having others ignore or reject us. According to interpersonal theory, a sense of **security** comes from habitually predicting an experience of relatedness to others, and **anxiety** comes from habitually predicting an unraveling of personal relatedness.

In infancy, our survival depends on relatedness to other people, and attachment theorists like Bowlby (1973) believe that the roots of anxiety lie way back in infancy and childhood, in an early perception that relatedness might be disrupted or withdrawn. Our caregiver might not appear with food when we need it or could provide the food in a manner that is not reassuring. As adults, we still are attuned to possible threats to relatedness and still get anxious when we feel them in the air. Sometimes, we respond to the threat without consciously registering it (and therefore, without being able to rationally judge whether it is a real threat). On the other hand, an early perception that we can depend on our caregivers results in our being attuned to signs of relatedness to other people, and we respond to our social world from a stance of security and trust.

Examples of security operations include using self-presentation strategies such as

- looking attractive and speaking intelligently, to shore up our certainty of others' good opinion;

- diverting a conversation from anxiety-provoking subjects, like changing the subject when the topic of death encroaches; and

- screening out anxiety-provoking elements of the interaction, or automatically discounting them. This screening-out process often occurs outside of awareness, and you have witnessed one form of it in people whom you would call "insensitive."

In group Jim sometimes tells his story or reacts to another member in such exquisite detail that any group attempts to give him feedback are at least initially forestalled. Piling detail upon detail as he talks also can serve to block from his immediate awareness any difficult underlying feelings he might have.

In many counseling groups, security operations are not just a background for content, but serve as topics for discussion, unlike in ordinary interpersonal life where we may notice someone's operations but wouldn't mention them. In everyday life, we would duck into the next hallway when we see Jim approach; in a counseling group, we might point out that Jim goes on and on in tiresome detail, putting the topic right on the table.

From your study of psychology, you may recognize security operations as defense mechanisms, and they are indeed the same types of behavior. It's the "Why?" that differs. Freudians believed that defense mechanisms protected us against anxiety due to *intra*personal conflicts among id, ego, and superego, whereas Sullivan believed that security operations protect against *inter*personal anxiety.

H. S. Sullivan (1953), the first theorist to insist that interpersonal (not *intra*-personal) dynamics were primary in our personalities, called the screening-out operation **selective inattention,** and deemed it "the classic means by which we do not profit from experience which falls within the areas of our particular handicap. We don't *have* the experience from which we might profit—that is, although it occurs, we never notice what it must mean; in fact we never notice that a good deal of it has occurred at all" (p. 319).

Two other important concepts from interpersonal theory are flexibility/rigidity and lack of awareness. Kiesler (1982) thought **rigidity** and **lack of awareness** were hallmarks of interpersonal problems. Specifically, people have interpersonal problems because they interact in a rigid, nonflexible manner. Effective interpersonal actors respond to interpersonal situations in a flexible manner. They can be friendly, submissive, dominant, hostile, and all kinds of combinations, according to what the situation calls for. They aren't stuck in one style. The person with interpersonal problems responds in a rigid manner regardless of the situation. For example, Fred runs a complex division at work, and there he must be confident and aggressive. However, he acts dominant even when he's having lunch with his peers from the office, which puts them off. One major goal of group counseling is to help people become more flexible in their responses to interpersonal interactions.

The second reason that people have interpersonal problems is lack of awareness of their interpersonal style. This lack of awareness can take two forms. People can be unaware of their own interpersonal style. In other words, they have a typical way of interacting but are unable to see themselves in a reflective manner. Fred may not even realize that he *is* bullying his partners when he asserts his menu suggestions. A second form of unawareness is impact unawareness. People often are not aware of the effect that their interpersonal behavior has on others. Fred may have no idea that his peers hate it when he insists on telling them what to order for lunch. This lack of awareness occurs partly because in normal social interactions it is considered impolite to comment on how others behave or how we are affected by their behavior. One of the major ways that groups address interpersonal unawareness is through providing feedback. In a counseling group, Fred would be told that his assertiveness amounts to bullying at times.

Reflections

1. Security operations are not intrinsically harmful to us. Many of them legitimately buttress our self-esteem, for example, choosing to speak about topics you know well during job interviews or when meeting people for the first time. This choice protects you from anxiety, yet it is honest and not hurtful. Another example is starting on projects early to avoid the anxiety of a time crunch later on. Think of one of your security operations that is benign. How does it protect you from anxiety, preserve your image of yourself, or maintain your self-esteem?

2. I gave the example of Fred, who has problems of interpersonal rigidity (can't change from setting to setting) and lack of awareness (doesn't know how he appears to others). Think of an example of someone in your own life—or in fictional works—who has one or both of these problems.

Interpersonal Schemas

On one old *Star Trek* episode, the android character Data attempts a romantic relationship with a human woman, which naturally doesn't work out. When his girlfriend finally breaks up with him, Data says, "May I assume we are no longer a couple? Then I will delete the relevant programming." And he goes back to business as usual. For humans, deleting the relevant programming in interpersonal relationships is not this easy. Our programming consists of the **interpersonal schemas** we have developed over years and years. Data's "boyfriend program" was put together through a few hours of studying boyfriend behavior in books and song lyrics, and it was purely cognitive (because Data has no emotional life). It may help you to think of your interpersonal schemas as your default programs for dealing with other people. Among us humans, the interpersonal schema integrates cognitive and emotional perspectives in "a generic representation of self-other interactions" (Safran, 1990b, p. 107) with a goal of maintaining relatedness. Unfortunately, some interpersonal schemas— negative cognitive-interpersonal cycles—push this goal farther away rather than approaching it, in negative cognitive-interpersonal cycles.

Cognitive-Interpersonal Cycles

Interpersonal schemas bring about and are maintained by **cognitive-interpersonal cycles.** "Our past experiences skew our present environment and often lead us to create the very conditions that perpetuate our problems in a kind of vicious circle. For example, the people we choose and the relationships we form may confirm the dysfunctional views that we carry forward from our past and that are at the heart of many of our problems" (Arkowitz, 1992, p. 269). You probably know someone who is criticized for choosing, over and over, romantic partners who abuse them. Though they may insist that they are not consciously choosing such mates, it is no accident. Something in the nature of an abusive relationship confirms this person's interpersonal schema.

You might know people who choose to surround themselves mostly with needy people. They are most comfortable when doing something for someone else—listening to a friend's boyfriend troubles in a three-hour phone call, when they themselves have studying to do—or driving another friend to the airport when they themselves had had a movie date. Their cognitive interpersonal schema runs along the lines of "I can only feel good about myself when I am doing a favor for someone." In a group, they are going to lavish support and helpfulness on others, and feel distressed when the focus turns to them. The pattern in their life outside shows itself in their group behavior.

We may all agree that people invoke old, worn-out ways of relating to others (which may have once been functional). But, these ways now make them miserable. The psychology of learning would tell us that with enough feedback, we would change our habits of relating, just as pigeons learn to peck the right button and rats to run the right tunnels in a maze. We would all choose plans, strategies, and behaviors that would make interpersonal connection available, reliable, and satisfying.

So, how is the persistence of bad habits explained by cognitive-interpersonal theory? "The central postulate of an integrative cognitive-interpersonal perspective is that a person's maladaptive interactional patterns persist because they are based upon working models of interpersonal relationships that are consistently confirmed by the interpersonal consequences of his or her own behavior" (Safran, 1990a, p. 97). That is, the person's behavior influences the environment and shapes others' behavior back to him, in a cognitive-interpersonal cycle. Most often, the maladapted person is locked in a rigid, narrow, and extreme repertoire of engaging other people, and has the same type of expectations about how they will engage back. Here is Safran's example, which clarifies the situation well:

> As a result of important developmental experiences, a young man comes to view the maintenance of interpersonal relatedness as contingent upon his being intelligent. When he feels anxious in interpersonal situations, he attempts to reduce this anxiety by speaking in an intelligent fashion. This communication style, however, is viewed by others as unnecessarily pedantic, and distances them. In this situation the very operations that are employed to reduce the man's anxiety by increasing his sense of potential interpersonal relatedness have the impact of distancing other people from him. The more anxious he becomes, the more likely he is to engage in the very operations that are interpersonally problematic for him. (p. 98)

An important idea is that we draw certain behavior from others, which is what makes the interaction a cycle. Our own behavior influences how people respond to us. So, a woman who once got in the habit of acting helpless will continue to relate to others as a helpless person, and others are likely to react helpfully but never to take her very seriously as a competent adult. Unless they're trained counselors, they'll never react to her helplessness by acting sure that she can take care of herself, so she will never get that kind of feedback. Furthermore, repeated contact will draw impatient or avoidant reactions from others because they don't always want to help, especially since they don't ask for help in return. Why would they, when they consider this woman incompetent?

The same type of cycle can happen to someone who always appears controlled and competent. Thinking that they retain interpersonal contact by never needing support, they rarely see it offered, and they conclude that people are unhelpful and that self-sufficiency is crucial. Safran (1990a) points out that patterns like these don't show up as easy-to-see thought distortions or obvious interpersonal deficits. Only repeated instances, and lack of variation from a few interaction patterns, bring the combined cognitive and interpersonal problems to the foreground. In a group context, these patterns become obvious because opportunities abound for acting in habitual manners.

The cognitive elements that need uncovering in the three examples above are these:

■ **The intellectual one** "People will only like me if they are convinced of my high intelligence."

It can start out very subtly at first, but sometimes a group member believes that other people will respond positively to him only insofar as they perceive him to be intelligent. Thus, Brian might indirectly try to take on the group leadership role. His comments in group are restricted to psychologically astute observations about other members or the group process. It might take a while for the group to realize that self-disclosure or discussion of his own problems is never a part of Brian's interpersonal repertoire. He diverts efforts at closeness through his intellectual style.

- **The helpless one** "People will abandon me if I seem competent."

Group is a setting in which people are generally expected to share problems, so once again, it can take a while to perceive that Susan always takes on the role of asking the group for help—with her boss, with her overbearing mother, with her adolescent son. She is an active group participant but never offers constructive comments to others. Others may feel that she takes more than she gives, and resent it.

- **The competent one** "People will reject me if I show any weaknesses."

Britanny in early group sessions discussed problems in her family. She described her parents as inattentive and relatively uninvolved as she was growing up. She took considerable responsibility for herself and a younger sister. She gave helpful, accurate feedback to her fellow group members and expressed a forgiving attitude toward her parents. She was invariably cheerful—the group optimist. It took gentle, repeated work on the part of the leaders and group to tease apart some of the subtle contradictions in her presentation that finally allowed her to acknowledge some vulnerabilities. (The contradictions involved allowing herself to be manipulated by an ex-boyfriend.)

In the examples, you can see that cycles based on these cognitions have the opposite of the desired effect: The people are disliked, abandoned, and rejected. These cycles thus reinforce themselves by creating more anxiety and redoubled efforts—in the wrong direction.

The cognitive-interpersonal cycle is also referred to as a self-fulfilling prophecy (Carson, 1982) or behavioral confirmation. Self-fulfilling prophecies and behavioral confirmation emphasize the importance of **expectations** in the cognitive-interpersonal cycle. This idea will arise again when you read about the instillation of hope early in a group's life, which gives members positive expectations for themselves and their fellow group members.

Cognitive-interpersonal cycles contribute to the establishment of roles in all kinds of groups. Mudrack and Farrell (1995) emphasize that outside the formally acknowledged roles, such as leader, president, secretary, and so forth, there are always informal roles taken on habitually by members. In an author team I have worked with for many years, one member is a master of painstaking details, another one usually monitors our focus on goals during our meetings, and another can be depended on for creative solutions to problems. Without any assignment, we have fallen into these roles and are happy with them. Some group roles are emotional, such as the person who encourages others, the member who's a doomsayer, and the individual who sees the funny side of everything. Two dangers of roles are becoming stuck, as some of the examples in this section show, and disrupting the group by too much focus on individual needs to the detriment of group progress.

SMALL GROUP EXERCISES

1. In this section, you read about intellectual, helpless, and competent patterns. In your small group, come up with another example of a habitual interpersonal pattern that could elicit certain types of behavior from others. If a person never varied from this pattern, what could he or she conclude about other people? Have any of you ever seen an example of a rigid cognitive-interpersonal cycle that brings out negative reactions?

2. In group dynamics in general, a habitual interpersonal pattern is called a **role.** Some of these roles in groups are *encourager, harmonizer, opinion giver, rescuer,* and *aggressor.* From the labels, what do you think people who rigidly stick in these roles would habitually do in a counseling group? What reactions would other people have to them?

Reflections

Think about cognitive-interpersonal cycles in your own behavior. Do you draw certain types of behavior from other people? For example, my friend Sue is so exuberant and bouncy that people around her seem to come alive and become more interesting than they usually are. Do you have an effect like this? Some other consistent effect?

The Group Setting: A Stage for Interpersonal Schemas

A group of people is going to have interpersonal dynamics, under almost any circumstances. I once taught writing in a classroom where each student sat before his or her computer, and my role was mostly to provide one-on-one consultation while sitting next to each student in turn at her or his little station. Even in this individualized environment, I found that the classes I taught developed their own atmospheres, joys, and tensions, quite different from one another. One class would be hushed, serious, businesslike, with a low level of activity; another would be loud and lively, with students reading over each other's shoulders and commenting; another would be reluctant, stubborn, and negative, with complaining the main mode of communication. All were taught by the same teacher, me, in identical classrooms, with the same assignments. Something about the group explained the variations I witnessed. I found that I could often identify the key characters who were imparting their style to the group as a whole. These were people whose interpersonal schemas were displayed so vividly that they influenced the group dynamics noticeably.

Given that interpersonal schemas will inevitably operate, our job as counselors is to orient the group's dynamism to the members' psychological benefit. One way is to design a setting where individuals can get feedback on how other people see them—how their interpersonal schemas are playing out. This corrective feedback is a distinctive quality of a therapy group (Morran, Stockton, Cline, & Teed, 1998), and it involves the therapeutic factors of **interpersonal output** (talking and responding to others) and **interpersonal input** (finding out about others' perceptions and experiences). In every other setting, our social norms discourage us from making honest remarks to each other about how we're coming off interpersonally. Right now, you are holding back information that would be valuable to a friend, co-worker, or family member because in these relationships we generally choose kindness, peace, and tact over bluntness.

Honoring Feedback

In counseling groups, though, this type of feedback is often encouraged, and the givers and takers of such feedback are protected from horrible repercussions by special social norms of the group, norms that the leader helps to set and maintain. In this way, members can learn how they appear to others, an experience they may never get in ordinary polite society.

> During the middle stage of a counseling group when members revealed something emotionally painful, Megan tended immediately to redirect the group's attention to herself and tell a rather superficial story about herself. Kathy noticed this pattern and asked Megan if it were hard for her to share the difficult emotions of another person. Megan at first said, "no." The leader asked Megan what the emotional atmosphere in her family was like, especially with regard to more painful emotions. She said she usually escaped to her room when there was fighting or crying. The leader then asked John what it felt like for Megan to change the subject. He responded that at first he felt blown off. The leader helped set the stage so that Megan could less defensively hear the feedback.

Feedback also helps people recognize their own motivations, including motivations to change (Morran et al., 1998). Yalom (1995) believes that even though few people begin group therapy with the stated goal of improving interpersonal relationships, most discover that this goal underlies their stated ones. For example, it is common for people to begin a counseling group with a general stated goal of being less depressed or feeling happier. Often their "feeling less depressed" or "better about myself" goals change into more interpersonal goals—learning to trust others more, taking more risks with regard to self-disclosure, reaching out to others. Mary blurted out in a group session that it is hard for her to trust other women. She acknowledges in a later session that might be one reason why she is depressed and lonely. Joe reveals to the group that he works very hard to hide his low moods from others. People have told him that they feel they never really get to know him. A conversation from a counseling group for adults, in the example below, demonstrates some shifts in goals and new thoughts on purpose.

GROUP TRANSCRIPT: Feedback

The example here shows several instances of supportive and gently confrontational feedback from members and from the leader. Dave and Ann are the co-counselors in this group.

TALIA: I really processed a lot of the things that we talked about last week. And I enjoy groups, so I've gotten a lot just by listening to everybody. It's been a really good experience for me.

ANN: Could you talk, just a little bit, about something that you're sort of feeling like you've gotten from the group already.

TALIA: I think that I feel a little bit more grounded. When I came to the group, of course, you know I had just broken up with my boyfriend and. . . . So I was kind of all over the place and now I feel like I have a little bit more direction on what I want to do.

ANN: (Nodding in understanding) Direction . . .

DAVE: So you've gotten some advice from people who have suggested some things or . . .

TALIA: Just people talking about their own experiences has made me think about where I want to go, and where I've been. And you know some people remind me of different people in my life and different places that I've been.

DAVE: So you're feeling comfortable hearing the others, and plus you can learn some stuff.

TALIA: (Nodding in agreement) Mmhmm . . . Mmhmm . . .

ANN: I just remember a little bit that you seem to connect a lot . . .

TALIA: With Sarah.

SARA: Yeah . . .

ANN: . . . yeah with Sarah.

TALIA: We seem to have some things in common and I'm kind of feeling the same way you're feeling.

ANN: . . . relationships and stuff you talked about in the last group.

SARA: Yeah . . .

TALIA: Yeah . . .

SARAH: Do you think I should dump my boyfriend? I mean, you know? Here I am, week after week, wanting to have a baby and he doesn't want one and I don't know what to do. Is it working well for you?

TALIA: I think it's working well for me. I don't know if it would work well for you. . . . But certainly listening to you talk is making me think that I really want to be a mom. And maybe I'll adopt. I mean, I have to admit I've called a couple of places . . . yeah. But, not everybody wants to be a single mom.

SARA: (Nodding in understanding) Right. Yeah it's hard . . . . I don't even want to adopt. I just want a baby and I want a father with my baby. I just don't understand why he doesn't want one. He's old enough, he shouldn't be. . . . You know it's okay to party now and then. It's not . . .

ANN: I'm curious if the concern is about the baby, or about should I keep this relationship going.

SARA: I think this group has kind of turned my concern. When I came initially it was I want a baby, how do I make it happen? How do I make him want the baby with me. And now I'm just wondering after hearing everyone talk about relationships, is it the relationship?

Can I find someone else that would be better? You know, that can fit my life better?

ANN: I don't know.

SARA: It's really a hard thing to imagine. But, I'm not getting any younger.

TALIA: There's a light at the end of the tunnel, too, if you leave your boyfriend. It's not the end of the world.

SARA: Yeah . . .

JENNIFER: At least you have a boyfriend. I keep coming here week after week and I love coming here and giving you guys the support. But I'm still feeling just really depressed. Like, what's wrong with me? I haven't been able to find the successful relationship.

ANN: I'm curious, how you're jumping to this, what's wrong with me. And last week you were saying that your boyfriend was kind of mean to you, and he just kind of left you. And now you're saying what's wrong with me.

JENNIFER: Yeah. I mean, this isn't the first time that's happened though. It seems that my relationships that I have had progressed to a certain point and then they always leave me. There must be something wrong with me.

DAVE: What do you suppose happens.

JENNIFER: I don't know, maybe I'm too controlling. That's what he said anyhow.

ANN: That's what he told you?

JENNIFER: Yeah, that I was too bossy.

DAVE: And have other guys said that too? Or . . .

JENNIFER: No, it always seems to be a variety of reasons. I want my space, I want to go a different direction in life. This guy said I'm too bossy, but it's a variety of reasons.

ANN: So you have a lot of things that are wrong with you? Is that what you're saying.

JENNIFER: Kind of seems that way. Makes me wonder.

ANN: I hear what you're saying, is that, when you're in a relationship, maybe you guys have had similar experiences that it sort of makes you question yourself and is there something wrong with me. And on one side you sort of know, hmm, maybe not. And are sort of struggling with that.

JENNIFER: Yeah, because they know that I have some good qualities about myself. But it seems like nothing ever really pans out. Any relationship I get, they get to a certain phase and then they leave.

DAVE: It's interesting that you are willing to absorb all the blame.

JENNIFER: Mmhmm . . .

SARA: Yeah, you don't seem to be controlling to me; I know I don't know you that well.

Thinking About the Group Session

1. Review Ann's first remark to Talia. Why do you think she makes this remark at this point? What else could she have done (or added) that would help the group or Talia?

2. What has changed for Talia due to coming to group, so far? Why?

3. What has changed for Sara due to coming to group, so far? Why?

4. List the feedback comments that Jennifer receives. Do you think they are helpful? Why or why not? What other feedback could be useful?

The group leader can enhance the feedback function in a group's dynamics by paraphrasing members' feedback statements, stressing positive feedback in beginning stages of the group and encouraging the mixture of positive and corrective feedback to make it more palatable (Morran et al., 1998). Leaders can also help members phrase feedback in concrete ways: that is, "I think that Jim speaks too long, like over three minutes," rather than "Jim is self-centered." Corrective feedback is rarely given in ordinary social life, and it is a crucial feature of group counseling. In everyday interactions among equals, your bad qualities are discussed behind your back, but calm, frank, and loving direct confrontations are unusual. Group leaders and group members learn this valuable skill through practice.

In research studies, feedback has been associated with increased motivation, more awareness about the effect of one's behavior, more willingness to take risks, and more satisfaction with the group (Morran, Stockton, & Whittingham, 2004).

Experimentation

The group's dynamics can be channeled in order to let people experiment with different ways of behaving, again in a protected environment. (This protected social setting will be discussed repeatedly in later chapters.) According to cognitive interpersonal theory, people sometimes persist in ineffective behavior because they have not practiced a wide range of behaviors to see whether those work out better. The group offers a chance for this practice through **experimentation.** Group members also learn of new options through observing other people and listening to the feedback on others' behavior. Like honest feedback, these activities are performed more openly than they are in everyday life.

A participant in several different therapy groups gave these comments on typical occurrences:

> In many, many sessions, someone was completely blind to their own true feelings in a given situation. For example, a person would describe a situation where they were ignored by a loved one. When asked how that made them feel, the person would respond with some cognitive excuse or try to minimize any feelings they may have had. Only after several direct inquiries by other group members, would the person say they were actually angry or hurt, with a note of surprise themselves. To most of the other members, the feeling was obvious. But to the person describing the experience, the feeling was impossible to see without prodding.
>
> Group provided me with a safe and semi-controlled environment to attempt to break old habits of personal interaction and make real change in the way I interact with people. There is no other environment I've been in that allows me to experiment this way. Talking about it in individual therapy and then "just trying it" in real life, was just not that productive for me. Not only did group give me a playground to try out my new ideas of interacting, it taught me a lot about other people and their own life dramas. One benefit that comes to mind for me is that I've always been afraid to deal with angry people. Based on my interaction with angry people in group, I'm much more calm in real-world angry situations now.

> ## *Reflections*
>
> 1. No doubt there is someone in your life to whom you could give valuable feedback on their habitual interpersonal style. Reflect on what you could tell this person and how they might benefit from it. What would be the consequences if you gave the feedback in the course of everyday life? What conditions would you need to have in a counseling group to make you free to give this feedback to this person?
>
> 2. Have you ever purposely experimented with a new way of behaving? For instance, my friend Brian always acts as the class clown, and one semester he decided from the beginning not to clown around in any of his classes. What do you think happened? What happened when you tried it, if you did?

Group Composition

The make-up of the group will influence its interpersonal process, and different group goals and approaches suggest different tactics for selecting and rejecting potential group members. These will be discussed in later chapters under the separate approaches. In general, though, the question of similarity among members (homogeneity) and differences among members (heterogeneity) is the main issue. Group members are usually selected to be similar in some characteristics: personality features, presenting problems, sexual orientation, life events, demographics, or underlying conflicts. For example, a counseling group may include only adult male survivors of child sexual abuse, or Black adult women who are returning to college. No matter how many similarities group members share, their personal differences will be a dynamic factor in group process, and many group leaders select members who will increase the heterogeneity among the individuals. For instance, a member of an all-male personal growth group wrote, "We had quite an age span in my group. It was a mix of men from ages low 20s to mid 50s. One of the most common comments was that some older guys saw themselves in the younger guys. It really helped both parties, seeing themselves in each other's shoes." Brook (2002) stated that racial and ethnic diversity in substance abuse groups, when discussed openly, increased mutual understanding, respect, and tolerance, and made the group process increasingly effective.

Piper, McCallum, and Azim (1992) pointed out that the amount of heterogeneity that will be beneficial in a group is related to time structure, with more homogeneity desirable in shorter groups: "What proves to be stimulating in a long-term therapy group may prove to be distracting in a short-term therapy group" (p. 64). Some approaches advise group counselors to exclude clients who are suicidal, psychotic, narcissistic, or sociopathic, on the grounds that they disrupt group process too severely. Other approaches welcome these clients or target them in homogeneous groups. Regardless of composition, a group is bound to develop its own particular pattern of interpersonal processes.

The Group as a System

A new era in understanding group dynamics came from experts in family therapy, which of course is a form of group therapy. Alfred Adler in the 1920s perceived the **family system** as active in each family member's psychology, as did many therapists from a psychoanalytic background. With his child guidance clinics in Vienna and the clinics started in the United States by his student Rudolf Dreikurs, Adler was one of the first psychologists actually to treat the family as an interacting group. Adler and Dreikurs were two prominent figures in group psychoeducation: They brought together teachers and parents in their clinics to learn about and discuss family development.

Meanwhile, the social work movement at the turn of the nineteenth century integrated what we now call *family therapy* into its practice of making home visits to troubled families. Social workers observed the family group in its natural setting to identify problems that were not evident in office or individual appointments.

Clinical psychologists became more group conscious during early investigations into how schizophrenia comes about (Bateson, Jackson, Haley, & Weakland, 1956; Bowen, 1976). From these sources came a description of groups as systems in which people fulfill roles, follow rules of interaction, and habitually maintain these roles and rules even when they are harmful to the group. The family, as the first group we generally enter, gives us our first sense of who we are in the social constellation.

These insights should sound to you very much like interpersonal theory. Groups of strangers evolve into systems just as families do, and are driven by similar roles and rules.

The people in a group, like a family, are related to each other in a complex, meaningful way. The group as a system has been compared with other systems:

- A mechanical system, like a computer or machine, whose functioning is a composite of the functioning of all of its parts
- A natural system, like an ecological environment or a biological body
- A human organization, like a corporation, or a university

These comparisons apply to counseling groups as well and capture the manner in which a group is both fluid and stable. External conditions, inputs, and events create change in the system, but its way of dealing with them shows a pattern determined by the people within the group relationship.

Consider the three analogs above for human systems, in terms of groups you belong to. The part of each person (and pet) in the system, if there's a strong pattern, is a **role.** For example, in a social group you may have one person who is the brains of the operation and another who is the muscle, using the biological analogy. Someone else may act as the lubricant, smoothing the group's workings. When you and your friends prepare a meal together, one friend usually evolves as the boss, others as the manual laborers, and maybe another becomes a go-between or line supervisor (using a factory analogy). Discuss examples of groups in your lives that fit the mechanical, biological, or workplace analogs.

Three important principles applying to human interactions in groups evolved from the general systems theory of Ludwig von Bertalanffy (1968), a Hungarian biologist who theorized about organization in nature, including among humans. The principles are totality, nonsummativity, and homeostasis. When you look at a counseling group's dynamics, you can see these at work.

Totality

Totality denotes the unity of the group as a system. Changes in any part of the system affect other parts and might reverberate through the whole system (Donigian & Malnati, 1997). A dropout from a therapy group is an extreme instance. Even when the missing member was disruptive or disliked, the absence creates change for each individual and throughout the group as a whole. The longer the group has been together, the more affected it is by a dropout.

Changes in any member's external life also ripple through the system. For example, Sheri was intimidating to her groupmates Rich and Celia as their counseling group formed. She spoke frequently and forcefully. Partway through the life of the group, Sheri became preoccupied and depressed by a health problem that she didn't wish to discuss. Her new silence allowed Rich and Celia to speak out more, which changed the nature of the group by adding what in systems theory is called *new information*.

Nonsummativity

Just as a musical piece is not the sum of its notes, the group is not merely the sum of its individual members. Their combination creates a new entity with its own boundaries and tone. Thus, the principle of **nonsummativity** states that the personality of the group cannot be explained simply from the characteristics of each individual in it. The interactions of individuals and subgroups must be understood as well. This is why you receive special training in group work, so that you don't merely conduct individual-by-individual therapy in a group setting.

Homeostasis

Groups have a tendency to attempt to retain **homeostasis,** or the status quo. They deal with change in a manner characteristic of their unique totality, and this manner seeks to reestablish the state of affairs before the change, in a state of equilibrium. The tendency to control their own inner qualities is labeled *self-regulation* in both human and other biological systems. An example from family therapy occurs when a naughty child begins to behave properly; to maintain homeostasis, often a different member of the family starts causing problems. Donigian and Malnati (1997) assert that in order for a group to develop meaningfully, it must disturb its homeostasis through conflict and anxiety, which demand new behaviors in search of resolution.

Group Dynamics and Chaos Theory

The above description of groups in terms of systems theory gives added depth to models of group development that suggest a linear, one-directional series of stages. Chaos theory is an extension of systems theory that emphasizes the inadequacy of linear equations, which "cannot always describe what happens in natural systems" (Barton, 1994, p. 6). The term **chaos theory** is frightening because it makes us visualize groups in meaningless, unorganized, violent activity—that's how we use the word *chaos* in everyday life, when we say things like, "My life is in chaos," or "Heavy metal music is too chaotic for me." However, the way that chaos is understood in natural systems is not meaningless, unorganized, or violent. The term comes from physics, chemistry, and biology, where it refers to the random and unpredictable aspects of a system. It is used metaphorically to describe phenomena of human psychology. The perspective is upon the group as a dynamic, continually self-organizing system. How the group unfolds is only marginally predictable and cannot be planned in advance due to the "sheer number of variables . . . that carry a significant amount of weight, interact with each other, and contribute to idiographic [individual] development" (Meehl, 1978).

The wisdom about group dynamics that we derive from chaos theory involves the way that these human systems develop, not in a straight line but in zigzags, spirals, and overlapping repetitive revisiting of the same issues from new perspectives. Although general systems theory emphasizes homeostasis and stability, chaos theory emphasizes perturbations and disequilibrium and the rich possibilities for growth that come from spontaneous fluctuations.

Remer (1996) uses a down-to-earth example to illustrate how patterns are repeated recognizably but not at all exactly: Each time you read a certain book (especially a classic) throughout your life, you experience it differently. Let me add commentary to Remer's example: In spite of the fact that you are the same person and the book contains the same words, a multitude of influences alter the you–book system between readings. Also, it would be difficult for you to predict how you will reread the book, and even though you may be able to identify some of the influences that change your reading, most of these influences are hidden or disguised. And to make matters more complicated, the past reading of this book changed you in ways that affect what's happened to you between readings, and so it ends up affecting itself. Considering this point of view on change, chaos theory highlights the unpredictability of group dynamics and the multitude of influences (some of them tiny) that create change in the group, including the influence of the group itself.

When you think about the development of a friendship or romantic relationship of your own, you discover a nonlinear progress toward its current state. Most romantic couples reminisce about certain events or periods that systems theory would identify as *points of chaos*, or times when the relationship became more complex than mere friendship or attraction. At points of chaos, systems demand redefinition and reorganization. It's interesting that in personal relationships (like in physics), often the point of chaos is a stressful one; for example, two people working closely on a demanding project fall in love. You have no doubt seen this happen. We would rarely map out our important relationships in smooth, gradual lines but would draw lines that express sudden leaps and dips and circles.

Burlingame, Fuhriman, and Barnum (1995) intensively studied a thirty-hour, time-limited psychotherapeutic group for its entire fifteen weeks, using time series analysis of all the interactions over the course of the group's life. They found that "the group developed a stable, yet complex, nonlinear pattern of interaction" that was consistent with a chaos perspective on group process.

The Counselor's Contribution to Creative Chaos

In the chaos model, the group leader facilitates progress, not by identifying which stage the group is in but by recognizing (or creating) points of chaos and assisting in the group's multiple reorganizations. The leader does not know what is going to happen next but works by "intervening in human systems in disequilibrium without having to decide what route to follow. It is the family's [or group's] own unique properties and the random amplification of certain of its singularities that will bring it to a new stage in its development" (Elkaim, 1990, p. 31). Consequences of a particular course of action can never be completely known.

From a chaos perspective, the group grows by dealing with novel and unfamiliar challenges. The counselor structures and paces challenges to the group's existing interpersonal schemas, judging what level of crisis will evoke systemic change without undue risk (Mahoney & Moes, 1997). The variability within the members and their responses to each other, in itself, provides rich material:

> With its ever-increasing complexity, the psychotherapy group unceasingly presents the members with a novel stimulus. Because of this novelty and because of the group's inherent ambiguity (i.e., there is no obvious correct response), the process of the psychotherapy group calls into question members' old defensive solutions. . . . The demand on members to respond to new situations with new responses periodically places members at the edge of chaos. That is, because old solutions are doomed to fail, members must be poised to generate new ones continually. (Brabender, 1997, p. 229)

KEY TERMS

anxiety   in interpersonal theory, the fear of abandonment, rejection, and loneliness

chaos theory   an extension of systems theory that emphasizes the inadequacy of linear equations, instead emphasizing random and unpredictable opportunities for growth

cognitive-interpersonal cycle   a pattern of thought and action in relating to others that perpetuates itself

cognitive-interpersonal theory   a set of ideas concerning how we learn both intellectually and emotionally from others' responses to us

expectations   predictions we bring into encounters with other people

experimentation   trying out new patterns of interaction

family system   the patterns and roles established in a social group related by blood

feedback   the reactions of others to our own behavior

group dynamics   the interactions of people when they get together, both obvious and subtle

homeostasis   within an established group, the tendency to maintain the status quo

interpersonal input   what other people say and do in reference to ourselves

interpersonal learning theory   a set of ideas concerning how we learn from other people

interpersonal output   what we say and do in reference to other people

interpersonal schemas   default programs for dealing with other people

lack of awareness   inability to perceive one's impact on others

nonsummativity   the whole is more than its parts; the personality of the group cannot be explained simply from the characteristics of each individual in it

rigidity   inability to change with the situation

role   a characteristic and expected social behavior

security   in interpersonal theory, the expectation of relatedness to others

security operations   habits of behavior through which we attempt to maintain relatedness to others and escape rejection

selective inattention   failure to recognize some aspects of a situation, usually those aspects that are threatening

schemas   patterns of interaction with others, based on early experiences, mostly those of satisfaction, security, and anxiety

system   our concept of who we are and how we operate in relation to other people

social microcosm   a replica of the world in miniature

totality   the unity of a group as a system; changes in one aspect affect all other aspects

CHAPTER REVIEW

1. How is a group like a family? Consider how your own family affects the way you behave in groups.
2. Explain four cognitive-interpersonal concepts. Apply them to a group you have belonged to or observed.
3. What is the difference between feedback in groups and in everyday life? How can helpful feedback be encouraged in counseling groups?
4. What are some activities that can be described as group dynamics? Why do some of these activities remain unexamined in everyday life?
5. How does systems theory contribute to the understanding of group dynamics?

FOR FURTHER READING

Morran, D. K., Stockton, R., Cline, R. J., & Teed, C. (1998). Facilitating feedback exchange in groups: Leader interventions. *Journal for Specialists in Group Work, 23,* 257–268.

This concise article connects feedback to therapeutic factors and to successful outcome in group counseling. The authors explain eleven feedback facilitation skills for counselors. The skills are illustrated with direct quotations that help the reader visualize the group dynamics.

REFERENCES

Arkowitz, H. (1992). Integrative theories of therapy. In D. K. Freedheim (Ed.), *History of psychotherapy: A century of change* (pp. 261–303). Washington, DC: American Psychological Association.

Barton, S. (1994). Chaos, self-organization, and psychology. *American Psychologist, 49,* 5–14.

Bateson, G., Jackson, D. D., Haley, J., & Weakland, J. (1956). Toward a theory of schizophrenia. *Behavioral Science, 1,* 251–264.

Bertalanffy, L. von. (1968). *General systems theory.* New York: George Braziler.

Bowen, M. (1976). Theory in the practice of psychotherapy. In P. J. Guerin (Ed.), *Family therapy: Theory and practice* (pp. 42–90). New York: Gardner.

Bowlby, J. (1973). *Attachment and loss. Volume II: Separation: Anxiety and anger.* New York: Basic Books.

Brabender, V. (1997). Chaos and order in the psychotherapy group. In F. Masterpasqua & P. A. Perna (Eds.), *The psychological meaning of chaos* (pp. 225–252). Washington, DC: American Psychological Association.

Brook, D. W. (2002). Ethnicity and culture in the group therapy of substance abuse. In D. W. Brook & H. I. Spitz (Eds.), *The group therapy of substance abuse* (pp. 225–242). New York: Haworth Press.

Burlingame, G. M., Fuhriman, A., & Barnum, K. R. (1995). Group therapy as a nonlinear dynamical system: Analysis of therapeutic communication for chaotic patterns. In F. D. Abraham & A. R. Gilgen (Eds.), *Chaos theory in psychology* (pp. 87–106). Westport, CT: Greenwood Press.

Carson, R. C. (1982). Self-fulfilling prophecy, maladaptive behavior, and psychotherapy. In J. C. Anchon & D. J. Kiesler (Eds.), *Handbook of interpersonal psychotherapy* (pp. 64–77). New York: Pergamon Press.

Donigian, J., & Malnati, R. (1997). *Systemic group therapy: A triadic model.* Pacific Grove, CA: Brooks/Cole.

Elkaim, M. (1990). *If you love me, don't love me: Constructions of reality and change in family therapy* (H. Chubb, Trans.). New York: Basic Books. (Original work published 1989)

Kiesler, D. J. (1982). Interpersonal theory for personality and psychotherapy. In J. C. Anchon & D. J. Kiesler (Eds.), *Handbook of interpersonal psychotherapy* (pp. 3–24). New York: Pergamon Press.

Lewin, K. (1948). *Resolving social conflicts: Selected papers on group dynamics.* New York: Harper.

Mahoney, M. J., & Moes, A. J. (1997). Complexity and psychotherapy: Promising dialogues and practical issues. In F. Masterpasqua & P. A. Perna (Eds.), *The psychological meaning of chaos* (pp. 177–198). Washington, DC: American Psychological Association.

Marziali, E., & Munroe-Blum, H. (1994). *Interpersonal group psychotherapy for borderline personality disorder.* New York: Basic Books.

Meehl, P. E. (1978). Theoretical risks and tabular asterisks: Sir Karl, Sir Ronald, and the slow progress of soft psychology. *Journal of Consulting and Clinical Psychology, 46,* 806–834.

Morran, D. K., Stockton, R., Cline, R. J., & Teed, C. (1998). Facilitating feedback exchange in groups: Leader interventions. *Journal for Specialists in Group Work, 23,* 257–268.

Morran, D. K., Stockton, R., & Whittingham, M. H. (2004). Effective leader interventions for counseling and psychotherapy groups. In J. L. DeLucia-Waack, D. A. Gerrity, C. R. Kalodner, & M. T. Riva (Eds.), *Handbook of group counseling and psychotherapy* (pp. 91–101). Thousand Oaks, CA: Sage.

Mudrack, P., & Farrell, G. (1995). An examination of functional role behavior and its consequences for individuals in group settings. *Small Group Research, 26,* 542–571.

Piper, W. E., McCallum, M., & Azim, H. F. A. (1992). *Adaptation to loss through short-term group psychotherapy.* New York: Guilford Press.

Remer, R. (1996). Chaos theory: The canon of creativity. *Journal of Group Psychotherapy, Psychodrama, and Sociometry, 48,* 145–155.

Safran, J. D. (1990a). Towards a refinement of cognitive therapy in light of interpersonal theory: I. Theory. *Clinical Psychology Review, 10,* 87–105.

Safran, J. D. (1990b). Towards a refinement of cognitive therapy in light of interpersonal theory: II. Practice. *Clinical Psychology Review, 10,* 107–121.

Sullivan, H. S. (1953). *The interpersonal theory of psychiatry.* New York: W. W. Norton.

Yalom, I. D. (1995). *The theory and practice of group psychotherapy.* New York: Basic Books.

CHAPTER **3**

Professional Standards (ASGW) and Ethics in Group Practice

Codes of Ethics and Best Practice Guidelines

Examination of Self

Informed Consent

> *Screening Process* ▪ *Freedom to Choose to Participate* ▪ *Psychological Risks* ▪ *Signed Consent*

Confidentiality

Relationships Outside Group

Multicultural Sensitivity

Leader Competence and Responsibility

Legal Practice

Use an Ethical Decision-Making Model

Ethics Related to Theoretical Approaches

> *Ethical Concerns in Existential and Humanistic Groups* ▪ *Ethical Concerns in Psychodynamic and Gestalt Groups* ▪ *Ethical Concerns in Psychoeducational and Cognitive-Behavioral Groups* ▪ *Ethical Concerns in Adlerian and Choice-Theory Approaches*

Personality and Ethics

During your training as a group leader, probably in connection with the course you are taking now, you will be practicing as a group leader and member. You may already be in a practice group of trainees, or observing or co-leading a counseling group. Therefore, ethical considerations need to

46

be highlighted in this early chapter so that you will be able to note situations where consulting about ethics is necessary. This chapter gives an overview of topics in ethics to prepare you for more detailed discussion in your training.

Codes of Ethics and Best Practice Guidelines

Occupational groups establish ethical codes to identify the standards to which practitioners are expected to adhere. Most ethical codes, no matter what profession they guide, include principles concerning confidentiality, avoiding harm, competence, and accountability, so you will see these topics covered in code documents for physicians, attorneys, and accountants, as well as for mental health professionals. Your certification process will involve studying your code and knowing it well. The websites for major professional counselors' codes follow.

American Counseling Association	*www.counseling.org/resources/ethics.htm#ce*
American Psychological Association	*www.apa.org/ethics/code2002.html*
American Association for Marriage and Family Therapy	*www.aamft.org/resources/lrmplan/ ethics/index_nm.asp*
American Mental Health Counselors Association	*www.amhca.org/code/*
National Association of Social Workers	*www.naswdc.org/practice*
Association for Specialists in Group Work	*www.asgw.org/best.htm*
American Group Therapy Association	*www.groupsinc.org/group/ethicalguide.html*

Group workers follow the ethical code of the American Counseling Association (ACA, 1995). The Association for Specialists in Group Work (ASGW, 1989, 1998, 2000) has followed up the code of ACA, its parent organization, with documents clarifying how the ethics code applies specifically to group work. These codes provide general principles from which to extrapolate in specific situations. One of these follow-up documents, ASGW's Best Practice Guidelines, appears below. Read through these guidelines now so that you are aware of the matters they cover. Though you won't memorize most of them, it's good to know where you can find the principles when you need them and the general thrust of the rules.

Association for Specialists in Group Work Best Practice Guidelines

Approved by the ASGW Executive Board, March 29, 1998

Prepared by: Lynn Rapin and Linda Keel,
ASGW Ethics Committee Co-Chairs

The Association for Specialists in Group Work (ASGW) is a division of the American Counseling Association whose members are interested in and specialize in group work. We value the creation of community; service to our members, clients, and the profession; and value leadership as a process to facilitate the growth and development of individuals and groups.

The Association for Specialists in Group Work recognizes the commitment of its members to the Code of Ethics and Standards of Practice (as revised in 1995) of its parent organization, the American Counseling Association, and nothing in this document shall be construed to supplant that code. These Best Practice Guidelines are intended to clarify the application of the ACA Code of Ethics and Standards of Practice to the field of group work by defining Group Workers' responsibility and scope of practice involving those activities, strategies and interventions that are consistent and current with effective and appropriate professional ethical and community standards. ASGW views ethical process as being integral to group work and views Group Workers as ethical agents. Group Workers, by their very nature in being responsible and responsive to their group members, necessarily embrace a certain potential for ethical vulnerability. It is incumbent upon Group Workers to give considerable attention to the intent and context of their actions because the attempts of Group Workers to influence human behavior through group work always have ethical implications. These Best Practice Guidelines address Group Workers' responsibilities in planning, performing and processing groups.

Section A: Best Practice in Planning

A.1. Professional Context and Regulatory Requirements
  Group Workers actively know, understand and apply the ACA Code of Ethics and Standards of Best Practice, the ASGW Professional Standards for the Training of Group Workers, these ASGW Best Practice Guidelines, the ASGW diversity competencies, the ACA Multicultural Guidelines, relevant state laws, accreditation requirements, relevant National Board for Certified Counselors Codes and Standards, their organization's standards, and insurance requirements impacting the practice of group work.

A.2. Scope of Practice and Conceptual Framework
  Group Workers define the scope of practice related to the core and specialization competencies defined in the ASGW Training Standards. Group Workers are aware of personal strengths and weaknesses in leading groups. Group Workers develop and are able to articulate a general conceptual framework to guide practice and

a rationale for use of techniques that are to be used. Group Workers limit their practice to those areas for which they meet the training criteria established by the ASGW Training Standards.

A.3. Assessment

a. *Assessment of self.* Group Workers actively assess their knowledge and skills related to the specific group(s) offered. Group Workers assess their values, beliefs and theoretical orientation and how these impact upon the group, particularly when working with a diverse and multicultural population.

b. *Ecological assessment.* Group Workers assess community needs, agency or organization resources, sponsoring organization mission, staff competency, attitudes regarding group work, professional training levels of potential group leaders regarding group work, client attitudes regarding group work, and multicultural and diversity considerations. Group Workers use this information as the basis for making decisions related to their group practice, or to the implementation of groups for which they have supervisory, evaluation, or oversight responsibilities.

A.4. Program Development and Evaluation

a. Group Workers identify the type(s) of group(s) to be offered and how they relate to community needs.

b. Group Workers concisely state in writing the purpose and goals of the group. Group Workers also identify the role of the group members in influencing or determining the group goals.

c. Group Workers set fees consistent with the organization's fee schedule, taking into consideration the financial status and locality of prospective group members.

d. Group Workers choose techniques and a leadership style appropriate to the type(s) of group(s) being offered.

e. Group Workers have an evaluation plan consistent with regulatory, organization and insurance requirements, where appropriate.

f. Group Workers take into consideration current professional guidelines when using technology, including but not limited to Internet communication.

A.5. Resources

Group Workers coordinate resources related to the kind of group(s) and group activities to be provided, such as: adequate funding; the appropriateness and availability of a trained co-leader; space and privacy requirements for the type(s) of group(s) being offered; marketing and recruiting; and appropriate collaboration with other community agencies and organizations.

A.6. Professional Disclosure Statement

Group Workers have a professional disclosure statement which includes information on confidentiality and exceptions to confidentiality, theoretical orientation, information on the nature, purpose(s) and goals of the group, the group services that can be provided, the role and responsibility of group members and leaders, Group Workers' qualifications to conduct the specific group(s), specific licenses, certifications and professional affiliations, and address of licensing/credentialing body.

A.7. Group and Member Preparation

   a. Group Workers screen prospective group members if appropriate to the type of group being offered. When selection of group members is appropriate, Group Workers identify group members whose needs and goals are compatible with the goals of the group.

   b. Group Workers facilitate informed consent. Group Workers provide in oral and written form to prospective members (when appropriate to group type): the professional disclosure statement; group purpose and goals; group participation expectations including voluntary and involuntary membership; role expectations of members and leader(s); policies related to entering and exiting the group; policies governing substance use; policies and procedures governing mandated groups (where relevant); documentation requirements; disclosure of information to others; implications of out-of-group contact or involvement among members; procedures for consultation between group leader(s) and group member(s); fees and time parameters; and potential impacts of group participation.

   c. Group Workers obtain the appropriate consent forms for work with minors and other dependent group members.

   d. Group Workers define confidentiality and its limits (for example, legal and ethical exceptions and expectations; waivers implicit with treatment plans, documentation and insurance usage). Group Workers have the responsibility to inform all group participants of the need for confidentiality, potential consequences of breaching confidentiality and that legal privilege does not apply to group discussions (unless provided by state statute).

A.8. Professional Development

Group Workers recognize that professional growth is a continuous, ongoing, developmental process throughout their career.

   a. Group Workers remain current and increase knowledge and skill competencies through activities such as continuing education, professional supervision, and participation in personal and professional development activities.

   b. Group Workers seek consultation and/or supervision regarding ethical concerns that interfere with effective functioning as a group leader. Supervisors have the responsibility to keep abreast of consultation, group theory, process, and adhere to related ethical guidelines.

   c. Group Workers seek appropriate professional assistance for their own personal problems or conflicts that are likely to impair their professional judgment or work performance.

   d. Group Workers seek consultation and supervision to ensure appropriate practice whenever working with a group for which all knowledge and skill competencies have not been achieved.

   e. Group Workers keep abreast of group research and development.

A.9. Trends and Technological Changes

Group Workers are aware of and responsive to technological changes as they affect society and the profession. These include but are not limited to changes in mental health delivery systems; legislative and insurance industry reforms; shifting population demographics and client needs; and technological advances in Internet and other communication and delivery systems. Group Workers adhere to ethical guidelines related to the use of developing technologies.

Section B: Best Practice in Performing

B.1. Self Knowledge

Group Workers are aware of and monitor their strengths and weaknesses and the effects these have on group members.

B.2. Group Competencies

Group Workers have a basic knowledge of groups and the principles of group dynamics, and are able to perform the core group competencies, as described in the ASGW Professional Standards for the Training of Group Workers. Additionally, Group Workers have adequate understanding and skill in any group specialty area chosen for practice (psychotherapy, counseling, task, psychoeducation, as described in the ASGW Training Standards).

B.3. Group Plan Adaptation

a. Group Workers apply and modify knowledge, skills and techniques appropriate to group type and stage, and to the unique needs of various cultural and ethnic groups.
b. Group Workers monitor the group's progress toward the group goals and plan.
c. Group Workers clearly define and maintain ethical, professional, and social relationship boundaries with group members as appropriate to their role in the organization and the type of group being offered.

B.4. Therapeutic Conditions and Dynamics

Group Workers understand and are able to implement appropriate models of group development, process observation and therapeutic conditions.

B.5. Meaning

Group Workers assist members in generating meaning from the group experience.

B.6. Collaboration

Group Workers assist members in developing individual goals and respect group members as co-equal partners in the group experience.

B.7. Evaluation

Group Workers include evaluation (both formal and informal) between sessions and at the conclusion of the group.

B.8. Diversity

Group Workers practice with broad sensitivity to client differences including but not limited to ethnic, gender, religious, sexual, psychological maturity, economic class, family history, physical characteristics or limitations, and geographic location. Group Workers continuously seek information regarding the cultural issues of the diverse population with whom they are working both by interaction with participants and from using outside resources.

B.9. Ethical Surveillance

Group Workers employ an appropriate ethical decision making model in responding to ethical challenges and issues and in determining courses of action and behavior for self and group members. In addition, Group Workers employ applicable standards as promulgated by ACA, ASGW, or other appropriate professional organizations.

Section C: Best Practice in Group Processing

C.1. Processing Schedule
Group Workers process the workings of the group with themselves, group members, supervisors or other colleagues, as appropriate. This may include assessing progress on group and member goals, leader behaviors and techniques, group dynamics and interventions; developing understanding and acceptance of meaning. Processing may occur both within sessions and before and after each session, at time of termination, and later follow up, as appropriate.

C.2. Reflective Practice
Group Workers attend to opportunities to synthesize theory and practice and to incorporate learning outcomes into ongoing groups. Group Workers attend to session dynamics of members and their interactions and also attend to the relationship between session dynamics and leader values, cognition and affect.

C.3. Evaluation and Follow-Up
   a. Group Workers evaluate process and outcomes. Results are used for ongoing program planning, improvement and revisions of current group and/or to contribute to professional research literature. Group Workers follow all applicable policies and standards in using group material for research and reports.
   b. Group Workers conduct follow-up contact with group members, as appropriate, to assess outcomes or when requested by a group member(s).

C.4. Consultation and Training with Other Organizations
Group Workers provide consultation and training to organizations in and out of their setting, when appropriate. Group Workers seek out consultation as needed with competent professional persons knowledgeable about group work.

■ ■ ■

DISCUSSION IDEAS

1. Before addressing these discussion ideas, look up ASGW's Training Standards at *www.asgw.org*. Discuss the situations in which these standards might be useful. Why do you think the professional organization created this document?

2. In section A.4.f., group workers are required to follow professional guidelines in Internet communications. Section A.9. urges awareness of ethical guidelines for using developing technologies. Why would the ASGW ethics committee specifically mention new technologies in this document? Brainstorm about the difficulties these sections might be meant to preclude.

3. Section B.6. explains "Collaboration." Explain why this section is important to group workers. For example, what would an *unequal* group situation look like? What ethical harm could ensue?

4. As you read the Best Practice Guidelines, what sections were unexpected or surprising to you? Can you surmise why these were included?

_____

The following sections will expand on several key topics in ethical behavior for group counselors.

Examination of Self

Sections A.8., Professional Development, and B.1., Self-Knowledge, request that group counselors seek self-knowledge. Think for a moment about why you want to be a group counselor. Think also about what type of group you would refuse to lead, if you had the option. What kind of people do you have the most respect for? These kinds of questions help you assess your own motivations, values, and biases. You are exhorted to understand yourself thoroughly. In many situations, you will have to decide whether you are making judgments based on clinical evidence or based on your own needs and wishes.

Many counselor educators exhort trainees to join a personal growth group (or other relevant group) themselves (e.g., Corey, Corey, & Callanan, 2002). Such groups can help you understand your own world view, your own prejudices, and your own habitual patterns, as well as how these affect your counseling of other people. Furthermore, the experience of being a group member is extremely valuable in furthering your grasp of how the people in your group feel. Even as a mature counselor, I found myself nervous and worried about how to behave when I joined a therapy group as a member. Going through this myself gave me more insight than classroom learning ever did.

Informed Consent

Good ethics demand that you let people know what they're getting into when they join your group. This means that each member gives you **informed consent** to be treated in the group, and this consent includes several elements.

Screening Process

In the best situations, you will be able to see each potential group member privately in advance and explain the nature of the group and what to expect (see Section A.7., Group and Member Preparation). At this point, you can also make a judgment about whether the person will be able to benefit from your group and whether they will contribute to the group's growth. Some individuals can be harmed by, or do damage to, the group. If you judge the person as unsuitable for your group, ethically you must have some alternative to offer.

How do you determine suitability? Trotzer (1999) lists three basic criteria. He looks for evidence that each member possesses qualities that

1. enable a process of give and take to occur,
2. demonstrate a degree of interpersonal initiative, and
3. indicate awareness of the interpersonal influence of others. (p. 202)

Trotzer believes that if these positive qualities exist, disruptive personality traits can be worked out within the group.

Yalom (1995) points out that suitability depends on the nature of the group's purpose. For heterogeneous (mixed problems), outpatient, therapy-oriented groups, he lists poor candidates: "brain-damaged, paranoid, hypochondriacal, addicted to drugs or alcohol, acutely psychotic, or sociopathic" (p. 219). Notice that these are all people who would have difficulty meeting one or more of Trotzer's (1999) three criteria. However, if the group is dedicated to working on one of these particular problems, they are expressly included. Group counseling has been designed for people with all of these disorders, in homogeneous collections (for example, see the range of applications in DeLucia-Waack, Gerrity, Kalodner, & Riva, 2004).

In many situations, you are unable to screen out members in individual sessions ahead of time. This demands that you make informed consent and discussion of group process a focus of the initial session. Emphasize that each member is privately deciding whether the group is right for her or him and that they are free to interview you about the group during this session. Point out that there is no indignity in dropping out after this session (if you are running a voluntary group). If you sense that a member is poorly suited to the group, make a point of drawing him or her aside for discussion of the matter after the session.

In the **screening** process, find out what, if any, other mental health professionals the client is seeing currently. Arrange with the client for permission to talk to these other people so that you can coordinate your efforts effectively.

Freedom to Choose to Participate

In most groups you lead, you will offer each member freedom to withdraw at any time. This may seem obvious, but actually people in distress often don't realize their rights or tend to be passive about them. Most group leaders ask for members to discuss their leave-taking in a group session. This way, if their withdrawal is due to a misunderstanding or perceived threat, it can perhaps be prevented.

Members also have the freedom not to participate in a group activity, yet stay in the group. This means that they don't even have to speak. In some instances, group members are mandated; that is, they don't have a choice about joining the group. They could be court-ordered, or the group could be part of their institutional treatment. Mandated members need to be informed that they can passively withdraw while still attending. (You will learn methods of encouraging all members to participate fully, but the truth is that they don't have to.)

Psychological Risks

As with any psychological intervention, risks arise with group counseling. Group members may feel abused by other group members, for example, due to emotional exchanges that are bound to happen. Intense emotional experiences sometimes carry members off in impulsive directions outside of group sessions. For example, one member called her sister and gave her what-for after a highly emotional group session and then the next day was sorry she'd done it. Sometimes, the group experience engenders lifestyle changes that affect other people in a member's life. Though many times the changes are positive in the long run, they may be upsetting. This is a risk worth discussing ahead of time.

Though you don't want to frighten people off, it is ethical to let members know that they are taking some risks and that you will minimize these as much as possible. You also want to remind them to take the other group members' risks into account in choosing how to behave.

Signed Consent

It's not enough to discuss these matters orally. Your client should sign a document that explains their rights and your expectations for group membership, and both you and the member should keep a signed copy. This ethical responsibility is covered in Sections A.6., Professional Disclosure Statement, and A.7., Group and Member Preparation, of the Best Practices. If you work within a service or institution, the organization will have a standard form, and you may want to add one of your own that reflects your individuality. Be sure to okay your phraseology with your supervisor.

An informed consent document for an existing men's therapy group is reprinted in Figure 3.1. (Names and places have been changed.) Read it carefully as a model for your own informed consent form.

FIGURE **3.1 Sample Informed Consent Form**

Information for Our Clients

Welcome to Group Therapy! We appreciate your trust and the opportunity to be of help to you. This information is designed to answer some of your questions about group therapy and the expectations we will have for each other. Please read this thoroughly before you sign the consent form on the last page.

In general, group psychotherapy, like individual psychotherapy, is intended to help people who are interested in personal growth and who would like to improve their ability to manage difficulties and problems in their lives. This group is specifically designed for men wanting to develop their capacity for effective interpersonal relating. We live in a culture in which men struggle to define themselves. Issues such as fear, competitiveness, intimacy, communication, sexuality, anger, depression, failure, guilt, and inadequacy dominate the private thoughts of men. Discovering that other men share these contemplations can lead to greater understanding and freedom from how they negatively control our lives. Men who participate in this group can expect to gain greater levels of personal insight, deepen their potential for genuine empathy, and achieve greater levels of self-confidence.

How Does it Work?

This group is designed to be a "process" or "therapy" group rather than a "support" group. This does not mean it will not be supportive, but that the emphasis will be on helping each group member work on his individual needs in the context of the interpersonal relationships existing in the group. For this reason, not everyone in the group will be dealing with the same problems or issues. We want to provide you with an opportunity to be exposed to a variety of perspectives on your problems and to offer your thoughts to others, as well. While each group member will be different in many respects, it is likely you will also find many similarities among yourselves. Frequently, the people you meet in the group will remind you of others in your past or current life with whom you have difficulty. The group will provide you a safe place to effectively work through these situations.

As group co-leaders, our job will be to help facilitate this process. We will not have an agenda each week to impose on you, or a series of questions for you to answer. For the most part, issues will arise spontaneously from the group as you will be free to bring to group your thoughts, feelings, reactions, options, and attitudes to share with the other group members. The other group members, in turn, will respond with their own thoughts and feelings, as well as feedback, encouragement, support, or sometimes even criticism. Our purpose as leaders will be to keep the group on track while providing a safe environment for you to share and be heard.

Risks exist in most every worthwhile endeavor and this group therapy is no exception. It is important to understand that some risks exist. For instance, there can be no complete guarantee of confidentiality. Other group members may annoy or irritate you. Sometimes people feel anxious or hurt after a group session because they have

FIGURE **3.1** *(continued)*

been misunderstood or criticized by other group members. If you have concerns about any potential risks, please feel free to speak privately with either Dr. Brady or Dr. Horton.

What is Expected from You?

This group is designed to run for nine months. Each group member is making a commitment to stay for that length of time so that the benefits of the group experience can be fully realized. At the end of nine months each participant will be given an opportunity to continue with the group for another ten months or to withdraw. Although therapy is always voluntary and one can withdraw at any time for any reason, this commitment to the group is essential to achieve its fullest success. You are expected to be present each week and come on time. Of course, illness or out of town travel may occasionally prevent your participation. However, for the group to be a benefit to you, regular and reliable participation is a must. If you know you will be gone for a week, it will be important to let the other group members know the week prior to your absence.

The benefits of this group are closely tied to the sense of safety you have with each other. Therefore you are required to keep confidential all information discussed in the group, including the names and identities of the other group members. This confidentiality needs to be absolute, even in regard to your closest friends or family members. You will never be required to talk or reveal any intimate issue you do not wish to reveal. However, it is clear that the benefits of group therapy are tied to participation. The more open you are, and the more willing you are to talk about yourself, the more you will gain from this experience. There are no subjects that are off limits.

Technical Details

This group is designed for eight to ten men and two therapists. Once we have begun to work together we will not add additional members until the nine-month period of commitment is complete. This will allow trust and safety to develop between group members over time, while minimizing the disruption of adding new members.

Each group session will last for one hour and twenty minutes. For the sake of continuity and to avoid interruption, please arrive on time and do not plan to leave early.

Fees for the group are $50 per session. These are to be paid to Dr. Brady, one month in advance. There will be no refunds for missed sessions. If you have insurance which will cover you in group psychotherapy Dr. Brady will submit a bill to your insurance company for you if you would like. (Remember, your insurance also will not pay for missed sessions). Please be sure to provide him with your current insurance information.

Your Therapists

Both Dr. Horton and Dr. Brady are in individual private practice as licensed psychologists in the State of Illinois. However, we are collaborating together in regard to this group. We each are experienced in group, individual, family, and couple psychotherapy. If either Dr. Horton or Dr. Brady is unavailable for a session, the group will continue with just one

Figure 3.1 *(continued)*

therapist for that week. If for some reason both are unavailable, you will be contacted as soon as possible regarding cancellation and/or rescheduling.

We are licensed by the State of Illinois, Division of Professional Regulation, 320 W. Washington, Springfield, IL, 62786 (www.idfpr.com).

Agreement

I, Beau W. Brady, Psy.D., and I, Tom Horton, Psy.D., having no reason to believe that this client is not fully competent to give full consent to treatment and believing this client fully understands the issues raised above because either I or my professional colleague have personally informed the client of the above stated issues and points, discussed them, and responded to all questions raised, agree to enter into group psychotherapy with this client as is indicated by my signature below:

_____(signature)
Beau W. Brady, Psy.D.

Today's date is: _____

_____(signature)
Tom Horton, Psy.D.

Today's date is: _____

I, _____(print your name), have read (or had read to me) the issues and points stated above, discussed them where I was not clear about them, had my questions fully answered, and understood and agree to comply with them, and agree to enter into psychotherapy with this therapist as indicated by my signature below:

_____(signature)

Today's date is: _____

Please return your signed copy of this agreement to Dr. Horton or Dr. Brady and we will return to you a photocopy for your records. We truly appreciate the opportunity you have given us to be of professional service to you and are eager to receive your questions, comments, suggestions or concerns at any time. We look forward to a successful and beneficial relationship with you. If, as we proceed, you are fully satisfied with our work, we would appreciate your referring other people to us who might benefit from our services.

DISCUSSION IDEAS

1. Reread the Information for Our Clients statement next to ASGW's Best Practice Guidelines. Find at least six of the principles reflected in the document.
2. Considering the Best Practice Guidelines, can you think of any additions that should be made to Information for Our Clients?
3. This model is from a men's interpersonal growth group. What revisions would be needed for a different type of membership? Think about a teenaged men's group, a mixed-sex depression group, a middle-aged women's group, or whatever type of group you lead or intend to lead in the future.

Confidentiality

Everyone in the group must agree that revelations and events in the sessions will be kept private from outsiders. This **confidentiality** is extremely important. Members rely on it when they disclose personal information, and without it, trust breaks down. The confidentiality agreement needs to be stressed during screening and also referred to once in a while during the course of the group. If confidentiality is broken, discussion in the group on what to do about it ensues. The group needs to decide how each member can talk with significant others about what they did in sessions or what they have learned, without treading on other members' rights to privacy.

Confidentiality has limits. The counselor might go to outsiders (like state agencies) if a person is a clear danger to him- or herself, or sometimes specific others; if a court commands a disclosure; if child abuse is revealed; or if the member gives permission for the counselor to disclose. Each state has legal mandates on such matters that you will learn for your credentials.

If you will be presenting your work to a supervisor or to a training team (like your classmates), inform your group of this and promise not to reveal their names on printed material. On video or audiotapes that you share with colleagues, names might crop up. Let members know that revelations to these other professionals are bound by confidentiality rules, too. That is, your supervisors and colleagues can't discuss what you present about your group with outsiders.

You need to emphasize in screening that group members themselves are responsible for confidentiality; you can only guarantee your own part. In individual counseling, you can promise that a client's disclosures will be properly protected, but in group counseling you can't make that promise. The group members must rely on each other to protect each other's confidentiality. How to achieve this is discussed further in the next chapter.

DISCUSSION IDEA

Share examples of breaches of confidentiality that people in your small group have witnessed. Has anyone in your discussion group accidentally breached confidentiality? What situations most tempt you to discuss counseling experiences outside of professional settings?

Relationships Outside Group

Usually, **dual relationships**—two potentially conflicting roles in each other's lives, such as buddy *and* counselor, or husband *and* group co-member—are discouraged. This advisory applies to client-counselor, member-member, counselor-supervisor, and educator-trainee associations. A dual relationship can lead to special treatment and power motifs that erode the group's unity.

Romantic and sexual relationships between the group leader and a member are wholly prohibited. The question of socializing and romance among group members has invited more varied points of view in the profession. Some experts see the development of personal relationships as natural and healthy as long as the associations are known to the group as a whole, whereas other experts require members to make contracts not to socialize outside of the group as long as it runs.

DISCUSSION IDEA

Explore the question of dual relationships further. How does the type of group influence your decision about whether members ought to socialize outside of sessions? What relationships between counselor and group member outside sessions would you find acceptable (that is, nonconflicting)?

Multicultural Sensitivity

In several ways, an ethical group counselor monitors herself or himself to avoid prejudice toward or against members due to client differences: "ethnic, gender, religious, sexual, psychological maturity, economic class, family history, physical characteristics or limitations, and geographical location" (ASGW, 1998, Section B.8). The counselor also seeks accurate education about how people are influenced by culture, color, physical ability, and other categorizing features. Through making these efforts, we aspire to **multicultural sensitivity.** The Association for Specialists in Group Work has developed a document to help you, *Principles for Diversity-Competent Group Workers*, available at *www.asgw.org*.

Leader Competence and Responsibility

The Association for Specialists in Group Work (ASGW, 2000) provides standards for the training of group leaders, including course work and experience in practicing group skills. Your certification process will require documentation of certain educational accomplishments. Education is never complete, of course. Ethical counselors continue to learn through reading, professional organizations, conferences, and continued supervision.

You are encouraged to learn new techniques and theories but are limited ethically to practice only the ones you have competence within unless you are closely supervised by someone who has the proper credentials. For example, if you have not run a group based on choice theory (Chapter 15), you need to line up a supervisor who is expert in this approach.

Furthermore, you are responsible for understanding the effects and aims of the techniques you use. When you encourage the unleashing of strong emotions, you are ready to deal with the upshot. This includes planning time to wind down in the session after intensely stimulating techniques. You only use techniques with an understanding of the theoretical basis for them; this is essential for establishing faith in the treatment (Frank & Frank, 1991). Your responsibility includes referring members who do not benefit from the group to some other treatment where they may fare better.

Finally, you have charge of terminating the group in a way that leaves members feeling closure rather than cut off. Openly discussing feelings about the group's end should be an activity planned for the final stage of the group's lifetime, not only in the last session.

Legal Practice

Knowledge of your state's laws that affect you, such as parental consent for treatment of minors and mandated reporting of child abuse, will keep you from accidentally breaking the law. Like a physician, you can be civilly sued for malpractice, and most counseling malpractice suits come from client complaints of sexual misconduct and breaking of confidentiality. You are also open to suits for negligence and for departing from the **standard of care** for your community; that is, what people can reasonably expect when they receive counseling—for example, you should refrain from procedures that are perceived as bizarre and exotic in your community, even if you trust in them. Be sure to carry professional liability insurance, usually available through your professional organization. The American Counseling Association offers a plan.

Failure to protect a group member from physical harm can result in legal liability (Paradise & Kirby, 1990). The nature of some groups leads to emotion-laden, angry interactions that can lead to physical attack, especially if members have poor impulse control. The leader is charged with taking reasonable precautions against these occurrences, for instance, having a ban on physical aggression in the written consent statement. Careful screening can help, though some groups must admit violent members as part of their mission. You need to decide on how you will intervene when you perceive physical danger brewing and be vigilant in monitoring for it during group sessions.

Another source of legal action is failure to follow appropriate billing practices. Paradise and Kirby (1990) mention the particular fraud of billing members for individual therapy when they are actually in a group, which costs less. Another fraud is signing third-party (insurance) forms for supervisees without obtaining the supervisee's co-signature (that is, pretending that you led the group when your supervisee really led the group). Many counselors don't realize that it's also fraudulent to waive a member's co-payment without informing the insurer.

Use an Ethical Decision-Making Model

Section B.9. of the Guidelines requires the group worker to maintain "ethical surveillance." Many ethical decisions come naturally when you consider the principles of the ethical codes of ACA (1995) and ASGW (1989, 1998). However, many times your situation is a true dilemma, in which the correct course of action is unclear. In a dilemma, each of your choices of action involves some ethical gray areas. By their nature, the ethical codes and principles are too general to deal with thorny problems specifically. You need a good system for deciding what actions to take (or not to take) when you're in such a dilemma.

An example of such a system is provided by Sileo and Kopala (1993). These authors acknowledge that "situations that involve breaching confidentiality, reporting an individual to authorities, protecting a potential victim, or confronting a colleague, can lead to feelings of anxiety, doubt, hesitation, anger, and confusion" (p. 89). Sileo and Kopala produced an A-B-C-D-E Worksheet to help you weigh situations and choose the best approach, knowing that maybe no approach is perfect. I summarize their guidelines here:

■ **A is for Assessment**   Examine each factor in the situation, such as the client's strengths, resources, and weaknesses; your own values, fears, and biases; and other information such as test results and medical consultations.

■ **B is for Benefit**   Remember that we are compelled to promote human welfare *and* to avoid doing harm. The balance is not always clear. Consider which decision will benefit the most individuals.

■ **C is for Consequences and Consultation**   Think of what therapeutic, legal, and ethical outcomes are likely given different choices of action. At this point, it's crucial to talk with other professionals about the implications of your choices because you may not be able to think of them alone.

■ **D is for Duty**   Most of the time, your duty lies with your client first and foremost. However, with minor children, your duty probably includes parents or guardians. When working in institutions, be clear with yourself and others on whether your duty is to the employer (the school or prison, for example) or to the individual client.

- **E is for Education**   Know and reread ethical guidelines of your professional organization. Stay informed about the laws in your state, when state laws conflict with professional ethics, and what to do in the case of such conflict.

Keeping a written record of your decision-making process cannot be over-emphasized. Writing helps you think straight and brainstorm about possibilities. The document you write as you go along shows that you have tried your best to serve your clients well and will assist you if you need to justify your actions legally or professionally.

DISCUSSION IDEAS

1. Give a specific (maybe real, maybe invented) example of a situation in which A, B, C, D, or E would be applicable. Think of an example for each letter of the guidelines.
2. Practice applying the A-B-C-D-E Worksheet to a situation: A classmate or your instructor will provide a description of an ethical dilemma not readily solved by reading ethical codes. Brainstorm through the A-B-C-D-E list together. After you're done, discuss any ideas that you might have ignored without a systematic approach.

Ethics Related to Theoretical Approaches

Parts III, IV, V, and VI of this textbook each deal with categories of theoretical approaches.

- Part III, On Becoming a Person, focuses on humanistic and existential approaches, which emphasize group members' growth into their full human potential, in an atmosphere of caring, acceptance, and understanding.
- Part IV, The Unfolding of Awareness, focuses on psychodynamic and Gestalt approaches, which expand people's insight into inner conflicts that are interfering with their well-being, conflicts that previously existed outside of awareness.
- Part V, A Life of Learning, focuses on psychoeducational and cognitive-behavioral approaches, which depend on changing thought processes and providing information that will support positive behavior changes.
- Part VI, On Becoming a Citizen, focuses on Adlerian and choice-theory approaches, which place the group members in a social context and ask them to choose lifestyles leading to success within a society and constructive contributions to that society.

Each category invites further exploration of certain ethical concerns, due to the nature of its theoretical basis. Though all the ethical principles above apply to all counseling groups, in the following sections I expand upon concerns specifically salient to each category. No doubt you will be able to identify the issues relevant to the groups you lead or intend to lead.

Ethical Concerns in Existential and Humanistic Groups

Trust and openness are keystones of existential-humanist group therapy. Thus, members must feel assured of confidentiality. Among adult groups, levels of confidentiality may be negotiated: Members may discuss, for example, whether they will talk about other members outside of sessions anonymously, or not at all. In younger groups, including teenagers and children whose judgment and impulse control are not fully developed, a written statement of a promise to protect each other's privacy helps to cement the idea of confidentiality, though of course it cannot be perfectly enforced (Jacobs & Schimmel, 2005). In schools, it is preferable to get parental permission for a student to attend a counseling group. Always consult your school's and your state's policy on parental permission because these rules vary considerably from site to site.

According to many of our ethics codes, we are bound to inform clients about what will happen to them in counseling. This presents a special problem for person-centered humanistic and existential groups because there is no easily set forth plan for the group. Carl Rogers's person-centered groups are the most common instantiation of humanistic theory. In these groups, the group's activities are not preplanned by the counselor. It's hard to say that we can fully inform people at the outset what will happen, when we don't know. The group's unpredictability is part of its philosophy of being. To be ethical, your informed consent document needs to describe the types of conversations or (in child groups) activities that are likely to occur, to explain confidentiality and its limits, to ask for assent to audio or videotaping (if you plan to tape), and to explain how data from the group will be used in research reports (if it will).

One common criticism of person-centered humanistic small-group work is that it produces long-term psychological distress in some members, who are often labeled *casualties* (Hall, Hall, Harris, Hay, Biddulph, & Duffy, 1999). This criticism was especially targeted at the brief, intense forms of encounter groups and marathon groups that thrived in the late 1960s and the 1970s (e.g., Rogers, 1967). The group experience does involve serious emotional challenges. However, in general, group therapy has a lower incidence of negative effects than individual psychotherapy, perhaps because group counselors do not operate in the privacy that individual counselors do (MacKenzie, 2002).

A survey of ninety-two members of Rogerian small groups between 1976 and 1996 found that though about 12 percent suffered short-term distress, only two people claimed long-term damage (Hall et al., 1999). Interestingly, many more of these former members believed that *other* members of their groups were casualties. These identified casualties included people who failed to contribute to the group process, those who were too emotionally vulnerable to cope with short-term distress, and those who were victimized by scapegoating or incompetence on the facilitator's part. Obviously, however, these people rarely saw themselves the same way or did not report it on the survey.

The democratic nature of person-centered theory demands that its practice is not restricted to licensed professionals, and this has created some problems. Some people who take up the banner of encounter and personal-growth groups are not well trained and have personal agendas for fulfilling their own needs through group leadership. There has been outright exploitation of clients in such cases. On a less flagrant level, group leaders who are encouraged to be genuine can take self-disclosure too far and become objects of a group's focus rather than facilitators of their growth. The best way for you to avoid this problem is to examine your own behavior, asking yourself whose needs are foremost in your group work. Listening to tapes of your group sessions will help you see whether you are speaking more than any other individual in the group, always a danger sign. If this is true, seek consultation with another group counselor who will help you get out of the limelight.

Ethical Concerns in Psychodynamic and Gestalt Groups

A major ethical concern for many practitioners of psychodynamic therapies is **scope of practice.** Specialists are disturbed that counselors describe their practices as Gestalt or psychodynamic when they are not thoroughly educated about the approaches, thus harming the public image of the approach and perhaps misleading clients. Section C.2. of the ACA Code of Ethics (available at *www. counseling.org*) describes Professional Competence:

> **Boundaries of Competence**   Counselors practice only within the boundaries of their competence, based on their education, training, supervised experience, state and national professional credentials, and appropriate professional experience. . . .
>
> **New Specialty Areas of Practice**   Counselors practice in specialty areas new to them only after appropriate education, training, and supervised experience. While developing skills in new specialty areas, counselors take steps to ensure the competence of their work and to protect others from possible harm.
>
> **Qualified for Employment**   Counselors accept employment only for positions for which they are qualified by education, training, supervised experience, state and national professional credentials, and appropriate professional experience.

Almost any working counselor includes some psychodynamic elements in his or her conceptualizations of clients (see Prochaska & Norcross, 1999, for a survey), and many counselors integrate techniques from psychodynamic and Gestalt analysis into their group practice. However, to label yourself publicly with one of these orientations—"I am a Gestalt psychologist"—implies, ethically, that you have had advanced training and even certification in the theory and technique. This training is usually pursued in postgraduate study. Many of the training programs can be pursued while you are a working counselor.

If you are attracted to a specific approach discussed in Part III, look at these websites with information on advanced training:

www.Gestaltassociates.com   Describes postgraduate training in Gestalt therapy, with one-, two-, and four-year programs leading to different levels of expertise.

www.psychologia.sk/linky/index-178.htm   Describes more than twenty training sites for psychoanalytic and psychodynamic academic work.

www.itaa-net.org   Is the website for the International Transactional Analysis Association. Here you can find descriptions of one- to five-year training as a practitioner and five- to seven-year training as a supervisor or instructor of transactional analysis.

www.asgpp.org   The website for the American Society of Group Psychotherapy and Psychodrama, an organization established in 1942 by J. L. Moreno. The site lists, by state and country, institutes and training programs leading to certification in psychodrama.

Ethical Concerns in Psychoeducational and Cognitive-Behavioral Groups

The sticky issue of confidentiality in group counseling was introduced in this chapter. Basically, confidentiality is impossible to guarantee in groups because group members are not held to professional and legal codes as counselors are (Rapin, 2004). However, group members are exhorted to protect each other's privacy, and discussions of confidentiality are followed up throughout the group's life to reinforce the notion.

In psychoeducational and cognitive-behavioral groups, another confidentiality issue arises. Because there is psychoeducation involved, these groups include printed materials, tapes, and even videotapes of their own sessions for individual review. Meanwhile, the record-keeping involved means that each group member owns pages of a revealing nature, such as descriptions of anxiety-producing incidents, ratings of distress intensity, episodes of relapse, charts of daily activities, thought records, and so forth. Each member might feel differently about the openness of all this material: One person might leave it lying around her house for anyone to see and discuss, whereas another keeps it under lock and key. Again, no group member is bound legally to protect his or her own materials, but an early discussion of the matter will help everyone see how the others feel about it and, one hopes, lead to a consensus about how the materials will be handled. This is especially important when group members also share other settings, such as school classes and workplaces: One member's cavalier attitude toward the group materials may affect another member. For example, a high school student who shows her thought records to a friend innocently lets the friend know what other group members are doing, too.

Behavior modification, an earlier label for behavior therapy, gained a negative image from imaginative portrayals like George Orwell's *1984* (1949) and Anthony Burgess's *A Clockwork Orange* (1962; made into a film by Stanley Kubrick in 1971). These works portrayed massive social control of individual behavior. At the expense of spirituality, moral choice, and human dignity, citizens were behaviorally conditioned into passivity and conformity. Some critics still view behaviorist techniques as ethically dangerous. Who, they ask, chooses the goals—the individual or a social system that benefits from conformity? These are serious questions in an age when managed care and public institutions channel troubled people into the most cost-effective treatment—which is often group counseling.

Certainly, behavioral control of prison inmates, mental patients, and students is frequently done for the benefit of the institution rather than the individuals. **Involuntary assignment** of members to group work is a real dilemma for the counselor (Wessler, 1983). This involves, at times, including members into the group that you would otherwise refer to individual therapy. Remember that each member has a right to determine her or his level of participation; however, the counselor must make sure that each member understands the consequences of both participation and nonparticipation (Morgan, 2004).

Similar to concerns about social control for behaviorist techniques, a worry exists about how cognitive techniques seem to indoctrinate people into certain ways of thinking. Patterson (1980) notes that the techniques of brainwashing—persuasion, suggestions, and repetition—are the same as Albert Ellis's Rational Emotive Behavior Therapy and may have their effect in the same way, especially when the "indoctrinator genuinely and sincerely believes in what he or she is indoctrinating and is concerned about the subject's accepting it" (p. 93). Group pressure can certainly be coercive, and people have later regretted what they did or said in a group session.

Other critics, too, have alerted us that the vocabulary of cognitive models can be learned superficially, like the jargon of any specialized pursuit, and can be manipulated to avoid or justify all kinds of behavior. On the other hand, I see the collaborative style of most cognitive-behavioral counselors as protective against brainwashing, because the group members are encouraged to set clear goals and evaluate their own progress toward them. In many ways, clients of this type of therapy have a much better idea of what will be done in counseling than clients in other types of groups. The sound ethical principles of the counselor are the foundation of whether the group work is sincerely focused on the welfare of the members.

Cognitive-behavioral treatments are structured, have measurable results, and are designed for time-limited interventions (in most cases). These qualities have suited them for manualization, in which a series of printed procedures and materials are standardized so that counselors everywhere can follow the same treatment plan. Critics wonder whether this amount of prescriptiveness is optimal, suspecting that it belittles the complexity of each individual client (Strupp & Anderson, 1997). Many critics also envision a lowering of training standards, allowing for paraprofessionals to deliver manualized treatments at lower costs than fully credentialed counselors and psychologists would. This is a controversy that has been debated in legal and political settings.

Ethical Concerns in Adlerian and Choice-Theory Approaches

Both Adlerian and reality therapy (the outgrowth of choice theory) have been criticized for valuing society's interests over individual interests. This has happened because both emphasize that a person exists within a social context and that individual happiness must be found within this context. Adlerians believe that well-being always involves contributing to society, and choice theorists believe that an individual must accept the constraints of social institutions when formulating goals. ASGW's Best Practice Guidelines emphasize the development of individual goals (Section B.6.). Thus, group counselors with a citizenship focus must guard against being agents of institutions or governments more than advocates of individual clients. This is especially true of reality therapists, whose clients are often delinquents, failing students, prisoners, addicts, and people on the edges of society.

Reality therapists have been accused of endorsing submission to authority and environmental limitations, of paying more attention to conformity than creative living. Their confrontations with clients have been tinged with judgmentalism, and their insistence on individual responsibility has ignored the no-win situations that marginal groups and individuals find themselves in. They also make use of peer pressure, sometimes in ways that many counselors would find unacceptable. However, these questionable ethics are not inherent in choice theory; they are matters that require vigilance among all counselors. Nevertheless, reality therapy may attract professionals who wish to exert authority and provide strong guidance. This issue leads to the topic of how personality relates to ethical behavior.

Personality and Ethics

In the above sections, I have related ethics to theory. You will find, however, that the ethical issues you focus upon as a practitioner will also be related to your own personality. You may fall prey to some ethical violations more than others. For example, counselors who are highly nurturant and supportive need to beware of fostering ongoing dependency in their group members because nurturant people enjoy allowing others to lean on them. Although a period of dependency is expected in early stages of group counseling, the ethical goal for each client is independence from the therapist. Another counselor who has led a sheltered life may need to work especially hard on sensitivity to diverse worldviews and lifestyles among group members. This counselor may feel legitimate shock when confronted with clients who consider wife-beating a necessity, or who have never cleaned their own houses, or who have had five abortions so far. However, the group leader must model equanimity about such messages so that they can be processed effectively by the group.

R e f l e c t i o n

Consider your foremost personality characteristics in relation to which ethical issues will be most meaningful in your development as a group worker. This will be an enlightening topic to discuss with your friends and classmates.

KEY TERMS

confidentiality protecting the privacy of group members by not revealing information and discussions within the group to nonmembers

decision-making model a systematic step-by-step plan for analyzing ethical dilemmas

dual relationships for members and counselor, holding two or more potentially conflicting roles in each other's lives

informed consent the group member's agreement to participate in group activities, usually outlined in a written document and signed

involuntary assignment attendance in a counseling group required by parties other than the member, such as courts and school authorities

multicultural sensitivity actions based on awareness and accurate education about individual differences related to membership in identifiable categories: race, ethnicity, handedness, sex, religion, and so on

scope of practice the range of procedures and techniques that a counselor may ethically apply, usually defined by training and supervision

screening making decisions about each potential member's suitability for the group

standard of care the procedures of mental health treatment that a person could reasonably expect in a certain community

CHAPTER REVIEW

1. Memorize the elements necessary to an informed consent document. Write an informed consent document for one type of group you lead or intend to lead.

2. What is an ethical dilemma? Describe an example of an ethical dilemma and follow it through a decision-making model.

3. Explain how different ethical issues may be more or less problematic depending on the type of group you are leading.

4. Describe some activities that would help prepare you to deal with the ethical questions that come up in group work.

5. "For the group worker, nearly every intervention has potential ethical ramifications" (Paradise & Siegelwaks, 1982, p. 164). Explain this statement, providing several examples and references to the Best Practice Guidelines.

FOR FURTHER READING

Welfel, E. R. (2002). Ethics in counseling and psychotherapy: Standards, research, and emerging issues (2nd ed.). Pacific Grove, CA: Brooks/Cole.

This book aims to help you grapple with true ethical dilemmas—that is, cases in which the best course of action is unclear or the ideal is impossible. Welfel offers a nine-step decision-making model. She also spans history by introducing classic writings in the field of ethics as well as discussing the latest debates. Examples of difficult cases are analyzed.

Gumaer, J., & Martin, D. (1990). Group ethics: A multimodal model for training knowledge and skill competencies. *Journal for Specialists in Group Work, 15,* 94–103.

This nine-page article provides an excellent review of training knowledge and competencies for ethical group counseling. The authors have created an acronym, GROUPETHICS, and provide a table summarizing essential points. Post a copy of this table at your desk!

www.groupsinc.org/pubs/GS-0499.html

This website displays an article by renowned group specialist K. Roy MacKenzie, "Professional Ethics and the Group Psychotherapist." The article takes up two topics: (1) How are the well-established ethical guidelines for individual clinical work adapted to the group environment? and (2) What are the ethical implications that arise when doing group work in a managed care environment?

kspope.com/ethcodes/index.php

This website provides links to over one hundred therapy, counseling, forensic, and related ethical and practice codes developed by professional organizations. All the codes listed are online. Here is the place to find ethics codes for specialized groups such as the Employee Assistance Program Professionals Association, the Clinical Social Work Federation, and the Feminist Therapy Institute.

REFERENCES

American Counseling Association. (1995). *Code of ethics and standards of practice.* Alexandria, VA: Author. (Available at *www.counseling.org*.)

Association for Specialists in Group Work. (1989). *Ethical guidelines for group counselors.* Alexandria, VA: Author.

Association for Specialists in Group Work. (1998). Best practice guidelines. *Journal for Specialists in Group Work, 23,* 237–244.

Association for Specialists in Group Work. (2000). *ASGW Professional Standards for Group Counseling.* Alexandria, VA: Author.

Corey, G., Corey, M. S., & Callanan, P. (2002). *Issues and ethics in the helping professions* (6th ed.). Monterey, CA: Wadsworth.

DeLucia-Waack, J. L., Gerrity, D. A., Kalodner, C. R., & Riva, M. T. (Eds.). (2004). *Handbook of group counseling and psychotherapy.* Thousand Oaks, CA: Sage.

Frank, J. D., & Frank, J. B. (1991). *Persuasion and healing: A comparative study of psychotherapy* (3rd ed.). Baltimore: Johns Hopkins University Press.

Hall, E., Hall, C., Harris, B., Hay, D., Biddulph, M., & Duffy, T. (1999). An evaluation of the long-term outcomes of small-group work for counsellor development. *British Journal of Guidance & Counseling, 27,* 99–112.

Jacobs, E., & Schimmel, C. (2005). Small group counseling. In C. A. Sink (Ed.), *Contemporary school counseling* (pp. 82–115). Boston: Lahaska/Houghton Mifflin.

MacKenzie, K. R. (2002). Effective group psychotherapies. In F. W. Kaslow & J. Lebow (Eds.), *Comprehensive handbook of psychotherapy: Volume 4: Integrative/eclectic* (pp. 521–542). New York: Wiley.

Morgan, R. D. (2004). Groups with offenders and mandated clients. In J. L. DeLucia-Waack, D. A. Gerrity, C. R. Kalodner, & M. T. Riva (Eds.), *Handbook of group counseling and psychotherapy* (pp. 388–400). Thousand Oaks, CA: Sage.

Paradise, L. V., & Kirby, P. C. (1990). Some perspectives on the legal liability of group counseling in private practice. *Journal for Specialists in Group Work, 15,* 114–118.

Patterson, C. H. (1980). *Theories of counseling and psychotherapy* (3rd ed.). New York: Harper & Row.

Prochaska, J. O., & Norcross, J. C. (1999). *Systems of psychotherapy: A transtheoretical analysis* (4th ed.). Pacific Grove, CA: Brooks/Cole.

Rapin, L. S. (2004). Guidelines for ethical and legal practice in counseling and psychotherapy groups. In J. L. DeLucia-Waack, D. A. Gerrity, C. R. Kalodner, & M. T. Riva (Eds.), *Handbook of group counseling and psychotherapy* (pp. 151–165). Thousand Oaks, CA: Sage.

Rogers, C. R. (1967). *The process of the basic encounter group.* In J. F. T. Bugental (Ed.), *Challenges of humanistic psychology* (pp. 261–276). New York: McGraw-Hill.

Sileo, F.J., & Kopala, M. (1993). An A-B-C-D-E worksheet for promoting beneficence when considering ethical issues. *Counseling & Values, 37* 89–96.

Strupp, H. H., & Anderson, T. (1997). On the limitations of therapy manuals. *Clinical Psychology: Science and Practice, 4,* 76–82.

Trotzer, J. P. (1999). *The counselor and the group* (3rd ed.). Philadelphia, PA: Accelerated Development.

Wessler, R. L. (1983). Rational-emotive therapy in groups. In A. Freeman (Ed.), *Cognitive therapy with couples and groups* (pp. 43–65). New York: Plenum Press.

Yalom, I. D. (1995). *The theory and practice of group psychotherapy* (4th ed.). New York: Basic Books.

PART II

Therapeutic Factors Through a Group's Stages

I n the next four chapters, the therapeutic factors and some of the leadership skills that foster these factors are examined in detail. I have chosen to begin with factors that are especially prominent in early stages of the group and follow with factors that usually develop later. The multicultural point of view is interpreted as a foundation for many of the curative factors.

Most group experts believe that therapeutic factors underlie success, no matter what theoretical basis the treatment follows. All the factors work together, so it's somewhat artificial to divide them. However, for ease of explication the division is necessary. Similarly, any factor operates at any time during the group, so the order of presentation is somewhat arbitrary.

CHAPTER **4**

Hope, Universality, Cohesiveness, and Identification

The early stages of a counseling group are "characterized by indirect attempts to discover the nature and boundaries of the task" (Tuckman, 1965, p. 388) and often involve some suspicion and fear about the new situation. What role the counselor will take is one question that members explore, and so is the question of what relationships are expected among members. In this chapter, I have chosen four therapeutic factors that are logically related to group development in these early stages. When well established, these factors inform the entire course of the group.

Instillation of Hope

Hope plays a pivotal role in improvement, in any counseling setting (Snyder, Michael, & Cheavens, 1999). Summarizing research on contributions to successful change, Lambert (1992) estimated that hope, in the form of expectancy of positive change, accounted for 15 percent of a client's improvement (with the therapeutic alliance, client circumstances, and specific counseling techniques accounting for the rest). This may sound like a small percentage, but in looking at something as complex as human behavior, *anything* that can be identified this strongly is impressive.

The dreadful weight of hopelessness is probably familiar to you. It robs you of energy, zest for life, and even curiosity. For Adler (1929), the battle against terrible problems could not defeat a person emotionally: hopelessness about them could. Adler wrote that psychopathology equals a feeling of discouragement, a feeling that oneself and the world are not going to change, and the resulting feeling that it's worthless to try. The therapist's first goal, as he saw it, is to encourage the client, making her or him feel that change is possible and worth the effort.

People come to therapy when they are demoralized, "unable to envision a pathway or make movement toward a desired goal" (Snyder et al., 1999, p. 181). When you look at the process this way, generating new pathways or revising goals, or both, constitute improvement. For instance, many clients are discouraged in their love lives; they need to rewrite the script, especially if they feel they are acting out the same old story again and again.

Because institutionalization often vividly marks the exhaustion of alternatives, inpatient groups indicate that they place greater importance on instillation of hope than outpatient groups do (Kivlighan & Mullison, 1988). One enheartening aspect of all this is that frequently hope doesn't need much spark to be rekindled. Many clients, just by seeking or accepting help, have already made an important decision on the side of hope. The group mode has some built-in advantages here because members surely are at different points in their ability to cope with problems and enjoy life. It's inspirational to see others who are pulling through a bit better than one's self. In fact, it may be more inspirational to see someone just slightly ahead than someone already in a state of joy and fulfillment. In their experience with bereavement groups for schoolchildren, Samide and Stockton (2002) noted that some of the children "experience hope

Reflection

Why might you be more hopeful about your own problem when you witness someone who is still struggling with a similar problem, with some success? Have you ever experienced this phenomenon or seen it in someone else?

as they see students who are further along in the process and can attest to the fact that life does go on" (p. 199).

Therapists' Contributions to Hope

As a group counselor, your own belief and confidence in group therapy is a powerful influence. Share your convictions about the mode's effectiveness with your clients and show optimism. Present yourself as determined to help and as someone who has seen success in your groups. If you hold individual sessions to prepare group members, these are prime settings in which to exude hopefulness. When you are leading an open group that continually incorporates new members as old ones leave, point out improvements other members have made when a new person joins. Your hopefulness can be infectious. Hope translates into increased energy to try.

Lack of belief in the effectiveness of mental health treatment is a significant predictor of dropout (Edlund, Wang, Berglund, Katz, Lin, & Kessler, 2002; MacNair-Semands, 2002). In group therapy, repeated dropouts are demoralizing for everyone. Put effort into preventing early dropouts by reiterating that sticking with the group, even when doubtful, will be rewarding. Here's how one group leader says this:

> I have a lot of confidence in this group, maybe more than you have at this point. There are times when you feel like it's just too much trouble for too little gain. At those times, I want you to remember what I am saying today: Ride out the bumpy parts because the journey will be worth it. That's what I do, and it always works out that way.

In the early stages, presenting yourself as an authority is advantageous to building hope. The client should see the counselor as having an explanation for problems and an approach that the client can accept (Frank & Frank, 1991). This is why it's a good idea to share your theoretical framework (in brief form) from the start. What I mean by this is to construct a summary of your beliefs about the sources of clients' problems and the mechanisms of change. You may not have a clear idea yourself yet, but by the end of this course, you will. I will encourage you in later chapters to practice conveying your theory to nonprofessionals.

SMALL GROUP EXERCISE

Write a script for what you might say in a first group session to inspire hope. Collaborate to come up with just two or three sentences that capture the message. Write versions for young children, adolescents, and adults. If possible, target a specific type of group that you lead or intend to lead. Take turns reading the scripts out loud and critiquing them.

Building Hope Through Dispelling Discouraging Myths

Like any new situation, group counseling brings up several concerns among potential participants (Stockton & Toth, 2000), and these may cause lack of hope. Among adults, and perhaps some teens, there are ideas about group therapy that run counter to hope. It's best to discuss these misleading ideas early, partly to dispel them and partly to demonstrate that you are willing to deal openly and calmly with disputable topics. People may come into group therapy believing one or more of these myths (MacKenzie, 2001):

▪ **Group therapy is a second-rate treatment.** Clients may have been assigned to group therapy because it is cheaper than individual, or they may feel that they are not interesting or promising enough cases for anyone to help individually. You need to emphasize that there are advantages to group therapy and that it has special features unavailable in individual therapy.

▪ **I will be forced to make confessions of my darkest secrets.** Clients think that somehow the group or the counselor has magical powers to compel uncovering of dreadful information. Be sure to point out that they always have the choice of what to say and how much detail to reveal. They may have good reasons to keep some secrets. Remind them that openness about their feelings is encouraged but that usually the focus is on present feelings, not digging into past sins.

▪ **I can't learn anything from other losers.** Clients don't want to belong to this club of misfits. To answer this sentiment, you can appeal to altruism (which I will discuss in Chapter 6): Group members find that helping others is therapeutic in itself. Furthermore, you can appeal to a sense of fairness that most people possess: You need to look beyond the surface to judge others. People in distress are naturally not at their best, but who knows what lies beneath? One group member said, "'I can't learn from losers' was my immediate first thought, right before my first session of my first group. Ten minutes into that first session, after the introductions, I realized that there were nine other people *similar* to myself. It was as if we all showed up with our bags packed, ready for a trip. We all had that in common. What we brought in our bags was all different."

▪ **No one will like me.** Though it's somewhat at odds with the last myth, people are able to hold both of these ideas at once. Reassure clients that most group members eventually feel mutually close and supportive, even though there are rocky times. Remind them that they have a fresh start in this group and are not burdened by the others' already set ideas about them (except in cases where members do already have set ideas about each other).

▪ **Emotional storms will break loose, and no one will know what to do about it.** Many clients fear the unleashing of strong emotions, and they know that this tumult may happen in the group therapy setting. They need reassurance that powerful feelings will not lead to pandemonium and that you are competent to contain any crisis that comes up.

■ **I can't talk about my problems in front of a group.** If the group is composed of strangers, a client may feel uncomfortable with the idea of discussing personal matters. You can maintain that they can ease their way into the process by listening and responding to others until they are ready to talk about themselves. If the group is composed of people they know or see regularly, like many school-based groups, you should mention that everyone in the group will be bound by a serious agreement of confidentiality. What goes on in the group stays in the group.

Many group counselors prefer to see each potential member individually before they join the group. In this pre-orientation, the counselor is able to convey hope, dispel myths, and inform the client what to expect. However, in many situations you won't have the luxury of an hour with each person individually, and you will need to deal with orientation inside group sessions.

With young children and many adolescents, parents or guardians need much the same early information about the group experience because they may have the fears listed above. It's desirable to instill hope in the significant others of group members and energize their support. In schools and other institutions, administrators and staff need to be persuaded that the group is worth the efforts and inconvenience it may entail for them (Dansby, 1996); therefore, they need hope, too. Emphasize to everyone that what is learned in group will last long after the group experience is over.

DISCUSSION IDEA

Brainstorm with your discussion group to list the advantages of group over individual counseling. Which of these advantages would you like to stress for potential group members? Which ones would work to instill hope in you if you were a group member? Which ones are important to motivate the cooperation of teachers and staff in a school where you lead a student group?

SMALL GROUP EXERCISES

1. Write a leaflet inviting high school students to a Changing Families group. (This group is for people whose family unit is changing membership through divorce, remarriage, or integration of other members.) Select two members of the discussion group to role-play a high school student and a parent and respond to the leaflet from their perspectives. If time permits, exchange leaflets with other discussion groups and discuss similarities and differences.

2. Role-play a situation in which a school counselor must persuade a parent that a withdrawn middle school child would benefit from coming to group counseling after school once a week. Assume that this arrangement would cause some practical problems (picking the child up at a different time, coordinating other family activities).

Universality

Malik is a single father of three, ages 2 through 4, with only a twenty-eight-month span between their birthdays. He joined a support group for single parents on the urging of his physician, whom Malik had asked for anxiety medication. The doctor encouraged Malik to look into the support group first because he knew that beyond his children Malik had no social group.

In the second session of group, Malik buried his head in his hands and said wretchedly, "I have to admit it—sometimes I think my children are little monsters put on this earth to make my life miserable!" To his utter surprise, the other members burst into laughter, saying that they felt exactly the same way on a regular basis. Several of the mothers reassured him that *everyone* felt that way sometimes. Malik later reported this incident as a breakthrough: "I realized that *I* wasn't a monster for having these thoughts!" He felt his anxiety loosen its hold in the embrace of his peers' laughter.

The experience of commonality, or **universality,** is a potent pain reliever. Many people coming to counseling feel alone; social isolation is a reality for them. Some have developed interpersonal habits that push other people away, as I explained in Chapter 2. Others, like Malik, have become isolated by the demands of their daily lives as well. Without the chance to learn about other people's inner experiences, people stigmatize themselves for impulses they consider uniquely ugly. Discovering that they are ugly in quite a common way is a huge relief.

A sense of universality can open up discussion of problems that previously have been suffered alone. This was demonstrated in responses to the television program *Without a Trace,* which deals with FBI efforts to find people who've disappeared. After one episode about a 12-year-old who tried to kill himself, the show displayed a phone number for a suicide prevention hotline. The hotline got 400 calls in three minutes, when the average is 800 calls a day (Keveney, 2004). Simply making the topic of suicide an open one on prime-time TV brought on a surge of people ready to talk about it.

Knowing that you are not alone in the world destigmatizes your behavior, even when it is shocking or illegal. Seeing others struggling with the same problems is especially important in the early stages of a group (Kivlighan & Mullison, 1988). A realization of universality may be an early form of self-understanding, another therapeutic factor in group counseling (Fuhriman, Drescher, Hanson,

Henrie, & Rybicki, 1986). Self-understanding denotes an intellectual and emotional insight about one's own behavior; simply realizing that one's behavior is not unique is an insight.

Reflections

Universality often explains the appeal of artistic works and cultural products. For example, in reaching for descriptions of themselves, my clients often bring up their similarity to specific fictional characters. Think of an instance in which you found your own feelings, thoughts, or behavior mirrored in a story, film, or television show. Did this reflection of your self lead to any insights? What emotions were associated with seeing this reflection?

Universality can be detected even in our most private thoughts. We all have secrets. Little do we know that our secrets are likely to be very similar to those of the person sitting next to us. Yalom (1995) found that when people are asked to think of three personal secrets, they follow the same themes. One secret is a feeling of basic inadequacy, sometimes called the *imposter syndrome.* We feel that we are not really as good as we present ourselves to others. The second secret is a fear that we are alienated interpersonally, for example, unable to love fully and unselfishly. The third is usually some sexual secret. When a professor tried this experiment in a class I took, we found that these were indeed the themes of our secrets. Knowing that even one's deepest secrets are like those of the person sitting next to you is a realization of universality.

Therapists' Tasks in Establishing Universality

You as the counselor can help by reflecting the commonalities among your group members early in the process in an intervention called **linking** (Morran, Stockton, & Whittingham, 2004). Connecting the remarks of various people by pointing out underlying similarities is one helpful technique:

- "As you introduced yourselves, I noticed that all of you talked about your jobs. It sounded like your work is important to all of you, and you all are concerned about doing well at work. How did you end up in the jobs you have?"

- "Susan, Mark, and Sonia have all mentioned that being alone is difficult for them. How many of you feel that way? Could the rest of you each talk about this? Are there certain times of day or days of the week that stand out? Let's hear from each of you, starting with Al." (This technique, a very common one, is called a *go-around.*)

■ "Gosh, everyone here is from someplace else—you're all transplants geographically. What's that like?"

■ "I notice that all of you are here due to the influence of someone else, not on your own incentive. What were some of your thoughts about that as you got ready for our meeting tonight?"

These examples show the relatively nonthreatening topics that can be elicited early, providing a common base. Yet, you can see that each one could develop emotional depth. Because in early stages clients expect you to guide the conversation, you can steer the discussion's direction toward universal topics. Later in the group's development, divergent experiences and points of view are fruitful, but for now you can emphasize the "We're all in the same boat" theme.

The following example shows the counselor, Ann, helping members of a women's group connect their experiences through linking, highlighting the universality in their themes while acknowledging diversity.

GROUP TRANSCRIPT: Linking

Valerie: Well, part of the reason why I came to this group, too, is because I was feeling so alone and I didn't have any friends. Everything was for, in my family. And I wanted connection with other women and to learn how to form friendships that had some . . . some meaning . . . um . . . outside of just my family life. So just being able to hear what you're going through, um, makes me feel, although I'm struggling, that my problems, you know, a luxury problem, to use Judy's term, just to be here and be part of this is helpful to me.

Ann: And just as, sort of being here and being part of this, what is it that you would like to offer to Alice?

Valerie: Just comfort, an ear, a connection, um . . .

Alice: I don't think that it's possible to be comforted. I mean, I knew there were problems in the marriage, I mean, I know what you are saying about what you're feeling. I was, there was something missing, you know, an intimacy with my husband, but I thought that was just sort of normal . . . you know . . . as time goes on and I'm involved with the children and they require,

you know, my attention so much. And I thought, well maybe it will come back. And now, I don't know if I want it to come back. Because I don't feel that I can ever forgive him and have that, you know, intimacy again.

Valerie: And perhaps that's how we got to help each other to get through what we're struggling with. It's, we all have choices to make. And we can listen to each other and perhaps offer suggestions.

Judy: Are you going to follow through and find a counselor, for couples, for you know, to work with him and yourself?

Alice: I'm just so angered at him I don't know if I want to, you know, to stay.

Valerie: But you don't know if you want him to leave either?

Alice: I think it's mainly because of the children, to tell you the truth. I think if the children weren't there I would, you know, break off from him. So perhaps that's what I should do but (sighs).

Ann: It's so hard to know what to do right now.

Judy: Is there a time constraint? I mean, I'm sure it feels that way, but you could look at it as open ended at this point and just calm yourself that way.

ALICE: I can't, I just can't bear to have him around. I wish he would just move out and give me some space. But that will all just hurt the children if he moves out.

ANN: (Looking at Tammie and Betsy) Let me just check in with the two of you and just see where you're at because you're listening a lot and . . .

TAMMIE: Well I'm, I'm kind of feeling like Valerie, but my issues are, are really not anywhere near as dramatic as yours (looking at Alice). And I'm just thinking maybe I'm just being selfish because, you know, my husband is gone all the time and he's a good provider. And now that my kids are older my life is just centered around them. And I'm wondering what am I going to do now that I don't have to go to their sports games and take them to music festivals. And you know, I've just been centered on being somebody's mother. And I'm thinking, you know, that doesn't sound very important to me, listening to what Alice is going through right now.

ANN: Although it does sound like, you know, you in some ways and Alice are sort of grappling with same kind of thing of now, there's a stage in my life and how am I going to accommodate that. What am I going to do in this case with my husband and my kids? In your case, how do I want to live my life?

TAMMIE: I feel like I have to redefine myself and I . . . I dunno . . .

ANN: What about you Betsy, where are you at with all of this?

BETSY: I guess, you know, at the risk of sounding self-centered, I can understand in one way some of the dilemma. But, as you know I'm not married, I don't have kids, and I am really feeling like I'm having a little difficulty relating to what you're saying. Um . . . Maybe I should be in a different group um . . . Because as I kind of mentioned in the last couple groups that, you know, I'm constantly looking for that kind of relationship and have, you know, had relationships with men over a lot of years but, you know, I think we're on, my thoughts are going, is really looking back to the best times I've had, and actually, I think it'd be college and you know my best friend Alison. And, you know that's a big one.

ANN: So are you sort of . . . Let's just check in and see. You're sort of wondering like, am I even interested in men and maybe I'm thinking about whether I'm interested in women and who I feel comfortable with in terms of . . .

BETSY: And if that's the case, I'm again for my own salvation judging what you're saying whatever your issues are, there's a whole lot of support out there for whatever moves you make, as lonely as you might feel. I'm sitting here thinking if this is true, if I am attracted to and would ever consider having a relationship with another woman, it's a pretty scary world out there . . .

ALICE: At least you don't, that's all you have to think about is what you're feeling, I mean in some ways I wish I didn't have children, I would never not want my children, you know, my children, but in some ways I just wish I were free of that burden, you know, to go back and make a different choice . . .

BETSY: But still . . .

ANN: And one of the things I am hearing, Alison, I'm hearing Betsy say, is that she is feeling so alone and so sort of isolated by having this feeling, by having this attraction that she's wondering about, that it sort of puts her on the outside, that she sort of feeling so alone, in this group, as well as out there is that . . .

JUDY: That's what I heard, too. I mean, that's a biggie. . . . And to uh . . . you know after living your life with one sexual orientation and a sanctioned one and a supported one and then yeah, it's like a frontier.

ANN: Sounds like you are really connecting with Betsy. What's that doing for you to hear Betsy talk about what she's talking about right now.

JUDY: Maybe I'm relating just because of, because I'm scared at this point in my life and you know I'm picking up on what I'd imagine is fear, unknown.

ANN: Which is what I'm hearing Betsy talk about, too? Tammie, a lot of you guys, it's that fear of entering new territory here, I don't know what to do, I feel unknown, in this group and certainly out there. (Looking at Tammie) What's going on for you?

TAMMIE: I was just thinking about what you just said, and I was thinking if it were me, I would be thinking what are other people going to think, and how is your family going to feel if you explored this.

ANN: Did you want to ask Betsy if she wanted to talk about those things?

TAMMIE: Well I'm curious, I'm curious about, you know how, what that would bring on if you decided to explore that more.

BETSY: An avalanche in any direction you look in. You know, I work in a school. You know, I'm the advisor to the gay/straight alliance there. So one would think, oh, great liberal school. Right? Can you imagine how that would play out? I think about my family, that's adopted kids, my brother and you know, this is stretching the envelope to older parents. You know I even sit here and a piece of me says you know how will you keep this confidential, how will you judge me, look at me, you know it's an amazing insecurity; that is why I'm still on the fence . . . but . . . having trouble relating and it's not pinning one person's problem that is better or worse than another's but I

feel like I'm alone, I'm separate somehow in trying to wade through this.

ALICE: Both you and Judy though have this, you know, at least you have the issue attracted to someone. I mean, that's something that is so foreign to me now. I haven't felt that sort of attraction to anyone. I have just been so involved in my children that I can't even imagine a relationship, not just with my husband or for anyone.

ANN: That sort of reminds me of what you've been talking about, Tammie, you are so involved with your kids, and (looks at Valerie) you to some extent, too. So involved with your kids, that um . . . Sometimes with those relationships you don't even think about them, and they sort of form a life of their own and all of a sudden you are forced to look at it.

Thinking About the Session

1. In this transcript, there seems to be a struggle about whose problems are worse or more important. Is this struggle resolved? What efforts do people make to resolve it? What might you do as the leader when such a struggle comes up?

2. How does the group respond to Betsy's inclination toward lesbianism? At one point Betsy wonders whether she should be in a different group. Should she? Do you find Ann's and others' efforts to emphasize shared aspects, or universality, convincing? What might you say if you were in Ann's position? What would you do if you were Betsy?

3. List instances of Ann's linking interventions. What other remarks of Ann's are intended to enhance group process, in your opinion? Explain why.

Socially isolated people could easily have missed out on messages that most of us take for granted. I remember one time when I casually mentioned to a client, "Well, everyone feels two opposite ways at once about something, sometimes." The client later told me that this was a tremendously reassuring statement. He had felt that he was weird for liking and disliking some of his girlfriend's qualities at the same time. Then, he thought of several different situations in which he felt opposing ways. Seeing this as a common human dilemma eased his mind. My pointing out the universality of his feeling was effective.

The counselor skills coming into play at this point are clarifying, summarizing, and reflecting feelings in such a way that commonality is underlined. These skills, and several others, are labeled **active listening skills** to distinguish them from passive listening. Passive listening gives no clear response to the speakers.

Clarifying "Several of you have talked about your unhappiness when you're alone. Listening closely, I felt that you weren't *always* unhappy when alone, but mainly at times when you imagine that most other people are socializing, having a good time. Is that right?"

Summarizing "If I'm hearing correctly, you all get much more from your work than just an income. You feel personally committed to the job and proud of it."

Reflecting feelings "So, this worry that you talk about concerning money, it seems like something that nags at you all the time, like a background stress."

SMALL GROUP EXERCISE

Choose one member of your group to play the counselor. Everyone else, take a turn introducing yourself as though you didn't already know the others in the group. The counselor's task is to pull together the introductions and emphasize commonalities, both during the introductions and after everyone is through. Then, other group members can point out commonalities that they noticed. Using one commonality you underlined, design an open-ended question based upon it that would invite a deeper level of discussion if your group members are willing. Do this with the other commonalities as time permits.

Emphasizing Commonality in Physical Space

Your arrangement of the group's room can also lead to feelings of equality, an element of commonality. In most cases, you will not be choosing the furniture. However, work with what you have to ensure that every member can make eye contact with every other member so that no one is visually left out. Ideally, all the seating should be on the same level with no member (including you) sitting higher than others; a higher level seems naturally to imply more power and authority, as we see in schoolrooms and churches. A circle is the best form to keep in mind. It would be nice if all the seats were comfortable and noiseless, as well. (This is rarely true even in our own homes, but it's something to aspire to.) Think your furnishings through carefully. One group leader told me that her clinic had invested in beautiful, adjustable, office-type chairs for the group room and it had been a mistake because some group members could hardly resist rolling around and continually fiddling with the adjustments.

Elements ranging from the way you speak and listen to how the seating is arranged will affect the development of universality. Feelings of commonality allow the group to achieve cohesiveness, the next common factor discussed.

Cohesiveness

As shown in Figure 4.1, Maslow's (1970) famous hierarchy of human needs is arranged in levels. These levels are in order, with the most basic needs at the bottom of the pyramid and the highest level needs at the top. The needs motivate our thoughts and actions in this order. The basic, lower level needs like food (physiological) and protection (safety) must be relatively taken care of before we are motivated by higher level needs. Notice that after the needs that are physical, belongingness takes the next place. This means that we are highly motivated by a need for belongingness, unless we are in terrible circumstances like starvation or bombing raids. We can also look at the hierarchy from a developmental point of view: infants and children require physiological care and safety, while by the time they are adolescents, the need for belongingness appears to drive their behavior. This is one reason group counseling is a great mode for teenagers. A key difference between group and individual therapy is that group gives members an opportunity to experience *belonging*. Esteem, the feeling of being valuable, and self-actualization, the feeling that one has reached one's full potential, depend on having the need for belonging fulfilled because belonging comes earlier in the hierarchy. In terms of group therapy, we can make use of this basic human drive by assisting the group to experience cohesiveness (also called *cohesion*).

Defining Cohesiveness

Cohesiveness is an analog of the therapeutic alliance in individual therapy (Budman et al., 1989; Yalom, 1995). The therapeutic alliance is the relationship between client and counselor that allows them to work successfully together, and both thoughts and emotions are involved. It is the strongest predictor of outcome in individual therapy.

In a parallel manner, a cohesive relationship among the group members (including the leader) is necessary for other therapeutic factors to operate (Fuhriman et al., 1986). Several therapeutic factors can operate both as conditions for change and as mechanisms for change (Fuhriman, Drescher, & Burlingame, 1984), and cohesiveness is a good example. Cohesiveness alone acts in a

FIGURE 4.1   Maslow's (1970) Hierarchy of Human Needs

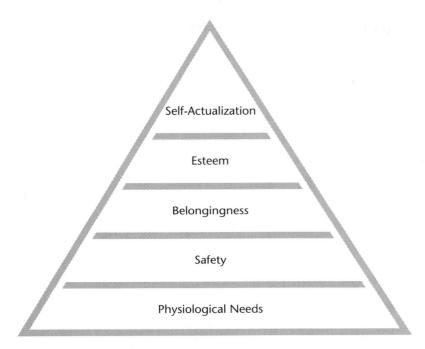

positive way through the feeling of belonging (a condition for change), and cohesiveness also acts as a soil in which other good things can grow (a mechanism for change).

The group's feeling of togetherness as a whole, and the individual member's feeling of being accepted by the group, are components of cohesiveness. Some of the synonyms you may hear used are *solidarity, in-group identity, we-ness,* and *esprit de corps.* Cohesion is more than the compatibility of the group members because diverse personalities can still achieve it, and personalities that are alike can still fail to achieve it. Cohesion can be accomplished in many ways—support, caring, listening, sharing experiences, identifying with the leader, feeling strongly about a common task or goal. Members may feel different individual levels of belonging, and group cohesiveness can ebb and flow over the life of a group (Yalom, 1995).

A research team at Harvard Community Mental Health Plan developed a scale to measure group cohesion. After extensive investigation of existing studies and literature, they chose this definition:

> Cohesion is what keeps members coming to the group; but, it is also what keeps members giving to one another under circumstances where for periods of time there may not be many clear or direct rewards for the givers except vicarious learning and

the knowledge that they are helping others. Cohesion may also allow the members to sustain an involvement with the group, even in the face of strong or frightening emotionality, such as confrontation and hostility. (Budman et al., 1987, p. 80)

The Harvard group realized that several elements compose cohesion, so they named five dimensions and one overall (global) dimension. A group could be located on a continuum between the two extremes named in each of these dimensions:

1. Withdrawal and self-absorption versus interest and involvement.
2. Mistrust versus trust.
3. Disruption versus cooperation.
4. Abusiveness versus expressed caring.
5. Unfocused versus focused themes.
6. Global fragmentation versus cohesion (in the sense of unity). (pp. 80–81)

R e f l e c t i o n

Think of at least one group in which you have felt cohesiveness. This may be a committee, a social group like a club or gang, a religious group, a work team, classmates, a military squad, or a group based on similar strengths or problems. I have a friend who felt unexpectedly strong cohesion develop in her physical therapy group, which was composed of strangers who'd happened to have heart attacks around the same time. Jot down your thoughts on what created the cohesion you experienced in one specific group.

How Cohesiveness Works

Cohesiveness works in ways explainable by interpersonal learning theory (see Chapter 2). Being accepted counters the feeling that you are unacceptable, a feeling many troubled people have. An unusual security can be found in a cohesive group, a comforting contrast from the everyday background tension of feeling that you don't belong and that you tread uncertain ground among other people.

Remember that feedback from the group is a major form of interpersonal learning. *The more the group is cohesive, the more persuasive group judgment can be.* Although feedback from authorities and rivals may usually be rejected as mean-spirited or faulty, feedback from within your own in-group is more compelling. For example, an adolescent who is nagged by parents for being sullen and by teachers for being silent may pay much more attention to a cohesive group who gives the same type of feedback.

The Harvard study group emphasized that cohesion gives members strength to stay involved in the group even when strong emotions, confrontation, and hostility arise. The cohesive group is less threatening than the rest of the world. This opens up lines of communication, even between hostile members. People are willing to go through the discomfort of dealing with a conflict if the group has solidarity—if they don't fear that the group will fly apart in a storm of emotion. For example, in one group I co-led, a woman disclosed that she frequently hated another group member, a man, for being so attractive and speaking so well. She saw him as a smooth-talking cad. He retorted that he was sick and tired of being criticized, especially by rich brats like her. The two were able to talk about their points of view and engage the opinions of the others. It turned out that the woman was reacting to her own awful experiences with slick, smooth-talking men and the man was defensive about taking flak for his two strong points (which he felt were about the only ones he had). Not being wealthy was one of his sore spots, so naturally he brought up her social class when defending himself. In this encounter, what would have been the parting shots in everyday life were just the beginning of a dialog that ended in deeper understanding and a feeling of commonality about being hit in one's sore spots. The topic of how stereotypes (slick deceiver, rich brat) distort perceptions of each other brought up examples from minority members in the group.

"As members are able to go beyond the mere statement of position, as they begin to understand the other's experiential world, past and present, and view the other's position from their own frame of reference, they may begin to understand that the other's point of view may be as appropriate for that person as their own is for themselves" (Yalom, 1995, p. 65).

Recent research reflects well on group cohesion as a moderator of the social comparison effect. The social comparison effect says that you gain self-esteem when you outperform others and lose self-esteem when you are outperformed. This would predict a constant competitiveness among group members. However, Gardner, Gabriel, and Hochschild (2002) discovered that when the self expands and thinks in "we" rather than "I" terms, "self-evaluation shifts from emphasizing individualistic social comparison to more interdependent social reflection" (p. 250). Thus in a cohesive group, each member's self-esteem is enhanced by each other member's successes.

A member of a young adult personal growth group put it powerfully:

> B started crying today. She has never really been ready. I was so excited about that. I felt a sorrow for her. I'm just so mad that everyone's life has to be so depressing. I commented on how I feel; like I need to be the one to change the vicious cycle of generations past. B has the best personality. I just felt like taking all of her pain away. T really gave all of herself today too. I was crying so hard for her. I felt so horrible. The cohesion of the group is so intense that it is amazing. I finally felt the weight of T's burden.

DISCUSSION IDEAS

1. Do you belong to any categories of people that are often stereotyped? (For instance, computer nerds, blondes, fraternity men, intellectuals, soccer moms.) If you can, share an example of being misperceived because of another's reactions to something about you that stereotyped you in her or his perception. Can you think of an example in which you and another person were able to get beyond the stereotype? How did that happen? Did the process fit into the explanation of cohesiveness? Interpersonal learning?

2. What stereotypes might group members apply to you, the counselor, at a first session? How do you (or would you) deal with the situation?

Practical Effects of Cohesion

People who feel part of the group have good attendance and low dropout rates. Others are influenced to do the same. In counseling groups, poor attendance and dropouts discourage the other members, making them wonder: "Is this group worthless to all these other people? Maybe it's worthless to me." As you already know, hope is basic to group success, and seeing others give up subverts hope. Cohesion keeps people attending even though some sessions are unhelpful personally or distressing. In brief forms of group therapy, attendance is obviously especially important.

In many studies, cohesion has been a good predictor of outcome; that is, the more cohesive the group is, the more improvement is made by members (Kivlighan & Tarrant, 2001). Budman and his colleagues (1989) at Harvard found that member improvement was most strongly associated with cohesiveness early in the group's development. Clients consistently rate cohesiveness as an important part of their improvement in surveys (Yalom, 1995). Groups scoring high on cohesion (rated by members) generated a higher number of improved clients than low-cohesion groups.

Leaders' Contributions to Cohesiveness

Your job as group leader is to increase cohesiveness early in the group's life, to make people feel "We're in this together." One technique is to develop a history together. Having an experience with this and only this bunch of people has a bonding effect, as army buddies and graduate-school cohorts can attest. You can design a history-building experience. In an intensive group seminar I attended with groups specialist David Hutchinson, he arranged for all of us to do a nighttime maze walk together. This strange, eerie, candle-lit event, quite outside the realm of everyday life, was something that we shared together and that brought us together emotionally. The maze walk was a good choice because it was pleasant, easy, and not frightening, as well as inspirational to some. Sometimes working groups do outdoor activities like rope courses for similar purposes.

Another way for group leaders to foster cohesiveness is to encourage continuity from session to session. This can be done by asking members whether they have had any new or unshared reactions as they thought back about the group over the week. Cohesion is also fostered by encouraging group members to think about the group and its members between sessions.

Researchers in one study (Marmarosh & Corazzini, 1997) taught group members to think about their group membership during their day-to-day activities. Participants in the control condition received general information about counseling, whereas those in the experimental condition were guided through an examination of the value of their counseling group and carried a card with them that symbolized their group membership. After one week, group members who received the experimental intervention had greater collective self-esteem than those who received general information. This study indicates that conscious reminders of the group increased cohesion, in terms of members' positive evaluations of the collective.

Sharing food and food preparation, celebrations, field trips, or performances, even films, can provide a group with its own history. A sense of in-groupness can be enhanced with rituals and traditions, like always opening the session the same way or always sitting in the same arrangement. Predictability is desirable when building group identity.

SMALL GROUP EXERCISE

Come up with other ideas for creating a group history. Think in particular of groups that have legal, physical, or institutional restrictions. What could be done in a school setting? An inpatient setting? What might be done with specific age groups, like 8-year-olds or elderly clients?

"In group treatment leaders should probably de-emphasize their relationships with the individual group members and focus on creating a therapeutic group climate" (Kivlighan & Tarrant, 2001, p. 231). Thus, you will need to monitor carefully the amount of attention given to individuals at first, speaking often to the group as a whole and using the word *we* often to refer to the group.

If you can, establish the optimal group size for cohesion. This is five to eight members (Posthuma, 1999) to maximize opportunities for interaction and closeness. "Cohesion tends to be weaker and morale tends to be lower in larger groups than in comparable smaller ones" (Luft, 1984, p. 23). Larger groups, of course, lend themselves more to the development of subgroups and factions (Thomas & Fink, 1963). Two- or three-person groups have different characteristics than larger ones, with less expression of dissatisfaction and disagreement (Thomas & Fink, 1963), though in long-running groups occasional sessions with only two or three members attending have been successful. Like many situations in the real world, your group size may not be under your control. Policies of your institution or agency and the room available at your site may be determining factors.

Many of the skills that operate at the early stage involve your modeling of desirable behaviors that promote cohesion. I will discuss modeling more in the next section, but some points are relevant here. Modeling means demonstrating by example: for instance, a parent serves as a powerful model for a child. Sometimes it's frightening to see your child behaving just as you do, in ways you never intended! A notoriously well-dressed friend of mine was shocked to see her six-year-old stepdaughter becoming fussy and perfectionist about what she wore to school, within three weeks of their moving in together.

The message is, naturally, that you want to model behaviors that you want the group to adopt. A tone of caring and a habit of self-expressiveness on your part encourages the same in others and develops an atmosphere of closeness. Redirecting members' talk toward the group rather than straight toward you is a major feat at early stages. If you can do this, you encourage group interdependence.

SMALL GROUP EXERCISE

Look at the group member statements below. They were directed at you, the counselor, during a second session. Brainstorm some ways that you could redirect the talk to the group. Then, practice redirection by having a classmate make the statement, with another student speaking directly to the client.

▪ "I'm not sure I belong in this group at all."
▪ "Do you think there's any hope for my marriage, even though my husband won't go to counseling?"
▪ "I have a lot of good ideas about how to help people. I'm just a people person."

Maintaining Cohesiveness During Hostility

At some point, you may encounter members' expressing hostility toward you for being too bossy or too nondirective, too unhelpful, too cool, or some such deficit. This is normal, especially after the very first sessions in which everyone usually concentrates on being nice. You can provide a great model by tolerating negative feelings without getting angry or defensive and by showing that there's no permanent harm done by the conflict. You can

- accept the criticism and delve into more explanation,
- ask the group what they would like to see you do and the pros and cons of their suggestions,
- say that you will consider their point of view before next time,
- refuse to let the situation stay intense for too long, and
- generally come up with the types of responses that you want them eventually to give each other under fire.

You may also see the group turning hostility upon one of its members (before, after, or instead of you). This event is a **scapegoating** process, in which the loose dissatisfaction and anxiety of the group get assigned to one person's fault. At early stages of the group, it's important for you to protect the scapegoat. This means giving some support and backing to the individual, perhaps explaining to the group the phenomenon of scapegoating and showing your acceptance that it's natural but not beneficial. Even members who don't like this intervention at the time get the message that you will protect members from getting trashed, *including them*. Again, reassurance that conflict and hostility won't have the last word here contributes to group cohesiveness. "Protecting interventions may be valuable at any point in the group, but should be particularly useful in promoting a feeling of safety during the initial stage when members are uncertain about their roles" (Morran et al., 2004, p. 93).

In Budman and colleagues' (1989) research, observers of videotapes rated cohesiveness. The outcome of each counseling group was measured by members' self-reports on a self-esteem questionnaire and a symptom checklist. The researchers explored how cohesion was related to outcome. The higher the level of group cohesion in the first thirty minutes of each session, the more positive the outcome was: "Apparently, it is the rapidity of pulling together and working on a therapeutic task that is most indicative of the future outcome of the group" (Budman et al., 1989, p. 349). This interesting finding suggests that as a group leader, you need to use tactics that enhance cohesiveness at the beginning of each session.

The more cohesiveness is developed, the more members will want to be adequate citizens of this little community. They will be motivated to identify with one another and with the group leader.

Identification, Norming, and Modeling

Yalom (1995) notes that group members rate **identification** low when ranking the importance of curative factors. However, he also notes that they may be thinking of identification as mimicry, or imitation of the leader or other members. Most people have little respect for mere imitation. Yalom points out that there are many other ways in which we agree to become alike when we form a cohesive group. Two of these more subtle identification processes are

norming and **modeling.** Both are processes of becoming alike, but are more complex than imitation.

Without thinking about punishment or legality, most of us behave according to a set of rules most of the time. Some of these rules are expressed, but many are not expressed unless there's a reason, like someone's breaking one of them. The rules of a group, big or small, are its **norms,** based on *normative*, or usual, behavior. Even a loosely organized social group has its norms, often unstated. For example, study groups in law school often become so close that they sleep on each other's couches and raid each other's refrigerators, even at ages when unrelated people wouldn't usually do these things. They have established special norms that fit their situation.

Norms also govern whom we talk to about what, how formal we are expected to be among others, how much influence we wield, and how much humor or messing around is allowable. *The strongest norms serve to maintain the group's existence over time and to make the group's goals attainable.* The law students help each other learn difficult material, and suspending the usual rules of guesthood gives them the time flexibility they need: They can sleep and eat at each other's houses. Furthermore, norms equalize power: "Established groups also impose their norms on individuals, even strong dominant individuals" (Luft, 1984, p. 19). Thus, in a way the group has a mind of its own bent on self-survival.

Group norms include both prescriptive ones, indicating what behaviors and attitudes should occur, and proscriptive ones, indicating behaviors and attitudes that should be avoided in group sessions.

R e f l e c t i o n s

As a newcomer to some established social group, what norms do you notice? Think about a specific case in your life, such as having dinner at another child's home, staying overnight, joining a different group of friends, being on a new job, and moving to a new school. Were some norms expressed directly, such as, "We pray before dinner in this house"? What norms were expressed indirectly (you noticed that everyone defers to Dad in conversation)? Discuss your examples in class if time permits.

A counseling group has norms, some clearly expressed from the beginning and some coming about gradually in both organized and accidental ways. Because of the socially alienated lives group members may lead, this may be the only place where they are motivated to be sensitive to group norms and adhere to them—the only place they have a chance to fit in or haven't already set themselves up in a pattern that is hard for others to let go of. The new group is an opportunity to start from scratch. Yalom (1995) pointed out that increased acceptance in the group will lead to increased interpersonal effectiveness in life outside of sessions—"by augmenting self-esteem and by reinforcing adaptive social skills" (p. 61). Many people see this effect as one of the big advantages of group over individual therapy: the group is a little world that mirrors the outside world. In contrast, the relationship with a counselor in individual therapy is remarkably different from situations in the real world (Trotzer, 1999). The group becomes its own culture. "The group is often seen as a more neutral zone in which to establish a working threshold without the intensity that accompanies individual relationships. The process of accommodating to the group norms is a prosocial experience that has important value in social adaptation outside the group itself" (MacKenzie, 2001, p. 503). Thus, becoming more alike, or identification with each other, is more than an act of imitation.

Negotiating Common Norms

MacKenzie (2001) suggests that common, constructive group norms be articulated early, with norms unique to a particular group developing over time. He suggests the following general list:

1. On-time and regular attendance is expected.
2. Communication goes in all directions, not predominantly through the leader.
3. Interaction is fluid, generally not lengthy on one person at a time, a "take turns" model.
4. Active participation is expected.
5. There is a nonjudgmental acceptance of others.
6. The members see the group as basically supportive and safe.
7. Self-disclosure is anticipated.
8. An interest in understanding one's self is expected.
9. There is an eagerness for change.
10. Risk taking with new behaviors is rewarded.
11. Identifying problematic aspects of others does not involve uncharitable criticism. (p. 503)

Members often indicate that discussing norms in early group sessions was very helpful to them. Some people are so socially alienated that in outside life, it seems to them that norms arrive out of the blue—that there is a secret set of rules they've never seen. They appreciate the clarity of developing them in the group.

DISCUSSION IDEAS

1. MacKenzie developed the list above with personality disorders in mind. Consider the general list in terms of a different type of group. For example, how would you phrase the norms for a group of adolescents in a school setting? What extra points might you include? What will you include in a list of norms for the type of group you lead or intend to lead?

2. Do you think you need items about coming to the group high, admitting to criminal behavior in group, or touching other members? What might you omit from MacKenzie's list? After discussing these questions, choose a type of group and make up a revised list.

David Hutchinson, groups specialist, suggests that a basic list be discussed at a group's first meeting and posted on the wall in positive terms (for example, "We will start at 7 p.m. sharp" rather than "No lateness allowed"). One critical topic to discuss is **confidentiality,** a much more complex matter in group than in individual counseling. In both cases, the counselor is bound by strict professional ethics regarding confidentiality, but in groups, the counselor cannot guarantee that members will maintain confidentiality. Group members must be bound by **consensual norms** instead. Most people will agree that they don't want to be talked about outside the group, but they also realize that they will want to discuss the group with outsiders, especially significant others (Dies, 1994). Many groups decide that they will limit members to speaking only about their own group experiences outside of group and that they will not use the names of other group members when doing so. It's important to bring up the question of what to do when there *is* a slip-up. Open disclosure to the group about what happened and what it means is usually encouraged. With children, discussing past instances when someone told their secret and how they felt about it can lead into talk about keeping secret what happens in the group.

The confidentiality discussion allows the counselor to underline commonality and to set an atmosphere of equal involvement and acceptance. It is indeed a subject important to each member, and all have a stake in hammering out a policy that protects the group. When group members see each other regularly outside and share outside acquaintances, such as in a school or workplace, reassurance about confidentiality is especially crucial. It is a norm that exerts great power in its adherence and its breach.

DISCUSSION IDEA

Group leaders differ heatedly on norms of lateness and attendance. Some do not allow late members into the session at all, and some drop a member after a certain number of absences. Discuss the various forms that a lateness and attendance norm could take. How are the norms related to the type of group you are leading or intend to lead? What effects on group cohesion are created by different policies?

Some norms, such as levels of self-disclosure and intensity of emotional expression, are set more subtly by each group. Some groups are stormy and confessional, whereas others are more subdued. This variation is natural and reflects the personalities of the members. David Hutchinson points out that contrary to popular opinion, not every group unleashes dramatic affect. A group can meet its goals and have intense meaning for members without tempests. However, the leader needs to have a sense of whether a group's norm of smooth surfaces is holding back progress by limiting acceptable topics. Tactics for taking discussions to deeper levels, with or without passionate expression, will be discussed many times in this textbook.

Norming Through Modeling

By serving as an example, the counselor has a huge influence on the group's norms. Clients model their counselors' patterns of thinking and behaving (Snyder et al., 1999). Some of your early modeling tasks as a therapist include

- modeling acceptance of your own self and frailties.
- modeling a level of self-disclosure appropriate to the group at this stage.
- exemplifying an "explore rather than dismiss" approach to conflict. That is, rather than passing over a potential conflict, focus in on it—unlike polite conversation habits.
- demonstrating nondefensive responding. For instance, don't jump to deny personal accusations, but think aloud how the accuser must be feeling and thinking.
- modeling a level of humor that relieves tension without dodging the topic.
- openly reflecting on process (commenting on what is going on in the here-and-now of the group). Calmly mentioning conflicts that you suspect between members, rather than ignoring them, is an example.
- modeling inclusiveness. Ask silent members to express their thoughts. Make efforts to avoid even the appearance of favoritism.
- modeling support. Express positive responses and sympathy actively.
- showing how to disagree without insult. Start by summarizing what the person you disagree with has said so that you are sure you have understood it correctly.

▪ paying attention to the positive. Try to find the strengths and adaptive behaviors in a member's story.

▪ normalizing the types of activities you will want the group to do—round robin, role play, discussion, checking in—by incorporating light versions into early sessions.

DISCUSSION IDEA

In your discussion group or as a class, come up with one example of each modeling task of the eleven listed above. Use examples from a group you have witnessed or from an imagined group situation. Each example should include a direct quotation, or script, for what the leader says and does.

Here's an illustration to get you started: A member of the group says she feels ashamed that she's been divorced. Counselor models limited self-disclosure: "I've been divorced myself, and you'll probably learn more details about that when we all get to know each other better."

Making the Most of Intragroup Modeling

Group members model not only after the leader but also after each other. They derive norms of behavior based on other members. This phenomenon speeds progress when new members join an ongoing group and imitate the seasoned members. As I mentioned before, the example of members who are more advanced in dealing with their problems is therapeutic in itself. Many leaders openly ask experienced group members to help new ones learn the ropes, which can uncover group norms that have been unspoken. For instance, an old member might say to a new one, "We don't talk about the close-up details of sex. Too much information!" and the others might agree laughingly, although this norm has never been articulated before.

Early on, you may notice members who are clearly more able to model openness and responsiveness to others. You can use this to the group's advantage by letting them lead off on topics or by asking them to take the first turn at risks like role-playing. Seeing others take risks (and live through embarrassment, in some cases) is inspirational to shy or fearful members. The message: Vulnerability is safe here. A member of a Gestalt-oriented group said this about modeling:

> One common situation is anger expression. There have always been one or two group members who have no problem expressing anger. I remember one guy who

was doing everything he could to deny and ignore some angry feelings about his mother. He eventually said that he wanted to express his anger in a "constructive" way, which puzzled us all. He went on to say that he admired the other members that could get angry. After a while, he finally let loose.

Using **rounds,** with each member in turn responding to some prompt, is a good way to get examples of behavior out on the table. In the first stages, you may want to use an imagined narrative and ask each member to give a response. One professor used this narrative in a counseling skills group:

> You arrange to meet a friend at 9 p.m. at a party. This party is made up of his acquaintances, whom you don't know yourself but would like to know. You arrive on time and the party is in swing, but your friend isn't there yet. Your friend still hasn't got there at 9:10. Let's say he doesn't have a phone. How do you feel? What do you think? What do you do?

I liked this narrative because it gave each person freedom to respond at a comfortable level, yet reveal something personal. Some people were very self-disclosing and thoughtful, and set the tone for others. The situation also invites some humor. Furthermore, the professor used opportunities to admire the richness of diversity in the ways people dealt with the problem, modeling an inclusiveness and acceptance that came to characterize these counseling trainees in general.

In this chapter, you have seen how the therapeutic factors meld. Through identification with the leader and other group members, evolving through the processes of norming and modeling, an individual joins a cohesive group and experiences the precious sense of belonging and hope.

DISCUSSION IDEAS

1. With your discussion group, brainstorm a narrative that could be used to initiate a *round* in a group. The narrative above, about the party, appeals to college-aged students. Choose a different group, such as 9-year-olds, high school students, or parents of toddlers, and write a narrative that might serve the same purposes. Remember that you want a situation that is not too threatening, encourages self-disclosure, highlights diversity, and invites humor. Make paper or electronic copies of your narrative for everyone in the class.

2. Design another activity for a group that would enhance any of the curative factors in this chapter: hope, universality, cohesiveness, and identification through norming and modeling. Make copies of your activity for your class. If time permits, critique the activities in class

KEY TERMS

active listening skills   methods of responding perceptibly and purposefully to what others are saying

clarifying   taking general statements by group members and making them more specific, pointing out specific elements in common

cohesiveness (cohesion)   a sense of togetherness with the group as a whole

confidentiality   the promise that members and leaders will not reveal what is said in the group to outsiders, except in certain clearly stated circumstances (e.g., the counselor must report child abuse to authorities)

consensual norms   rules and standards of behavior that come about through agreement among members of the group, in contrast with rules and standards that are legal or institutional

hope   a feeling and belief that the future will be an improvement over the present

identification   a perception of being like someone else; associating oneself with another's qualities, characteristics, and views

linking   drawing together several comments by group members to show their commonalities

modeling   using someone else's behavior as a pattern for your own; or purposely behaving in a way you want others to imitate

norming   setting rules and standards within the group

norms   rules and standards within the group; these include both *dos* and *don'ts* and may be stated or unstated

reflecting feelings   repeating, in different words, the emotions expressed by group members; the purpose may be to enhance commonality or to check for accuracy

rounds   a group process in which each member in turn gets an opportunity to respond to a prompt, such as a topic, question, or scenario

scapegoating   blaming one person for several problems in the group; choosing one person as the focus of group frustration or anxiety

summarizing   making a statement that consolidates what group members are saying

universality   commonality; a feeling that one is not alone or unique, especially in negative experiences

CHAPTER REVIEW

1. What are some effects of social isolation on the individual? How does group therapy ameliorate these effects?

2. Defend either cohesiveness or hope as the fundamental therapeutic factor in group counseling.

3. What are the effects of group size on cohesion? What do you think is the ideal number for the type of group you lead or intend to lead in the future, and why?

4. Explain several ways a counselor could usefully respond to criticism or hostility from group members. Discuss why these ways are beneficial.

5. Discuss the relationship between identification, modeling, and norming.
6. How is norming involved in systems theory (Chapter 2)? Relate norming to how the different elements of a system interact.

FOR FURTHER READING

Luft, J. (1984). *Group processes: An introduction to group dynamics* (3rd ed.). Mountain View, CA: Mayfield.

> *This classic book brings together, in a highly readable form, basic theory and research on processes underlying all kinds of groups. Principles of group dynamics are illustrated in the applied areas of organizational behavior, teaching, training, and psychology.*

REFERENCES

Adler, A. (1929). *Problems of neurosis.* London: Kegan Paul.

Budman, S. H., Demby, A., Feldstein, M., Redondo, J., Scherz, B., Bennett, M. J., Koppenaal, G., Daley, B. S., Hunter, M., & Ellis, J. (1987). Preliminary findings on a new instrument to measure cohesion in group psychotherapy. *International Journal of Group Psychotherapy, 37,* 75–94.

Budman, S. H., Soldz, S., Demby, A., Feldstein, M., Springer, T., & Davis, S. (1989). Cohesion, alliance and outcome in group psychotherapy. *Psychiatry, 52,* 339–350.

Dansby, V. S. (1996). Group work within the school system: Survey of implementation and leadership role issues. *Journal for Specialists in Group Work, 21,* 232–242.

Dies, R. R. (1994). The therapists' role in group treatments. In H. S. Bernard & K. Roy MacKenzie (Eds.), *Basics of group psychotherapy* (pp. 60–99). New York: Guilford Press.

Edlund, M. J., Wang, P. S., Berglund, P. A., Katz, S. J., Lin, E., & Kessler, R. C. (2002). Dropping out of mental health treatment: Patterns and predictors among epidemiological survey respondents in the United States and Ontario. *American Journal of Psychiatry, 159,* 845–848.

Frank, J. D., & Frank, J. B. (1991). *Persuasion and healing: A comparative study of psychotherapy* (3rd ed.). Baltimore: Johns Hopkins University Press.

Fuhriman, A., Drescher, S., & Burlingame, G. (1984). Conceptualizing small group process. *Small Group Behavior, 15,* 427–440.

Fuhriman, A., Drescher, S., Hanson, E., Henrie, R., & Rybicki, W. (1986). Refining the measurement of curativeness: An empirical approach. *Small Group Behavior, 17,* 186–201.

Gardner, W. L., Gabriel, S., & Hochschild, L. (2002). When you and I are "we," you are not threatening: The role of self-expansion in social comparison. *Journal of Personality and Social Psychology, 82,* 239–251.

Keveney, B. (2004, Feb. 19). "Without a Trace" right on track. *Wall Street Journal,* 1D.

Kivlighan, D. M., & Mullison, D. (1988). Participants' perception of therapeutic factors in group counseling. *Small Group Behavior, 19,* 452–468.

Kivlighan, D. M., & Tarrant, J. M. (2001). Does group climate mediate the group leadership-group member outcome relationship? A test of Yalom's hypotheses about leadership priorities. *Group Dynamics: Theory, Research, and Practice, 5,* 230–234.

Lambert, M. J. (1992). Implications of outcome research for psychotherapy integration. In J. C. Norcross & M. R. Goldstein (Eds.), *Handbook of psychotherapy integration* (pp. 94–129). New York: Basic Books.

Luft, J. (1984). *Group processes: An introduction to group dynamics* (3rd ed.). Mountain View, CA: Mayfield.

MacKenzie, K. R. (1987). Therapeutic factors in group psychotherapy: A contemporary view. *Group, 11,* 26–34.

MacKenzie, K. R. (2001). Group psychotherapy. In W. J. Livesley (Ed.), *Handbook of personality: Theory, research, and treatment* (pp. 497–526). New York: Guilford Press.

MacNair-Semands, R. R. (2002). Predicting attendance and expectations for group therapy. *Group Dynamics, 6,* 219–228.

Marmarosh, C. L., & Corazzini, J. G. (1997). Putting the group in your pocket: Using collective identity to enhance personal and collective self-esteem. *Group Dynamics, 1,* 65–74.

Maslow, A. H. (1970). *Motivation and personality* (2nd ed.). New York: Harper & Row.

Morran, D. K., Stockton, R., & Whittingham, M. H. (2004). Effective leader interventions for counseling and psychotherapy groups. In J. L. DeLucia-Waack, D. A. Gerrity, C. R. Kalodner, & M. T. Riva (Eds.), *Handbook of group counseling and psychotherapy* (pp. 91–103). Thousand Oaks, CA: Sage.

Posthuma, B. W. (1999). *Small groups in counseling and therapy: Process and leadership* (3rd ed.). Boston: Allyn & Bacon.

Samide, L. L., & Stockton, R. (2002). Letting go of grief: Bereavement groups for children in the school setting. *Journal for Specialists in Group Work, 27,* 192–204.

Snyder, C. R., Michael, S. T., & Cheavens, J. S. (1999). Hope as a psychotherapeutic foundation of common factors, placebos, and expectancies. In M. A. Hubble, B. L. Duncan, & S. D. Miller (Eds.), *The heart and soul of change: What works in therapy* (pp. 179–200). Washington, DC: American Psychological Association.

Stockton, R., & Toth, P. (2000). Small group counseling in school settings. In J. Wittmer (Ed.). *Managing your school counseling programs: K-12 Developmental Strategies* (2nd ed., pp. 111–119). Minneapolis: Educational Media Corporation.

Thomas, E. J., & Fink, C. F. (1963). Effects of group size. *Psychological Bulletin, 60,* 371–384.

Trotzer, J. P. (1999). *The counselor and the group* (3rd ed.). Philadelphia: Accelerated Development.

Tuckman, B. W. (1965). Developmental sequence in small groups. *Psychological Bulletin, 63*, 384–399.

Yalom, I. D. (1995). *The theory and practice of group psychotherapy.* New York: Basic Books.

CHAPTER **5**

Self-Understanding, Family Reenactment, and Catharsis

Self-Understanding and Insight
Artful Questioning Toward Insight ▪ *Interpretation as Insight* ▪ *Confrontation Leading to Insight*

Family Reenactment

The Counselor's Role in Family Reenactment

Catharsis

The Counselor's Stewardship of Catharsis

Processing Group Events

While early stages of group process dwell upon the similarities among members and develop norms based on agreement, the group does not rest in this harmonious state (Donigian & Malnati, 1997). Conflicts and differences must arise and find resolution, or at least acceptance. As members get used to open communication and feedback, they become more productive in achieving separate and group goals. Confrontation is done constructively, not given or taken as personal attack (Trotzer, 1999). Although hope, universality, cohesion, and norming underlie many of the group's interactions, another set of therapeutic factors grows and persists throughout the course of a successful group. In this chapter, I discuss three of these factors—self-understanding, family reenactment, and catharsis—and how the group leader can cultivate them.

Self-Understanding and Insight

It's a rare person who doesn't want to understand herself or himself better. Go to the magazine section of your bookstore, and you will see dozens of self-quizzes offering the readers a chance to find out something about their personal qualities. Furthermore, we like to see our lives as coherent narratives (White & Epston, 1990) with story lines that make sense, for better or worse. **Self-understanding** is critical in any personal problem-solving effort. When I run groups for people with writer's block, I find that they often make plans that totally lack self-knowledge or try to ignore it. For example, a person who has never been a morning person decides to force herself to get up and write between 5 and 7 a.m. An easily distracted person insists on working at home. These efforts are bound for failure because they include the seeds of their own destruction. Soon, the first person will sleep, and the second will do the dishes and water the plants. Thus, not only do we all need to understand ourselves, we also need to apply our understanding to life's challenges.

Understanding something about oneself that was previously hidden represents **insight**. Yalom (1995) outlines four levels of insight and elucidates how self-understanding by group members corresponds with insight:

- **Interpersonal insight** A member realizes how he or she is perceived by other people. A teenager in a mixed-age group was surprised to hear all the other members agree that she was unusually poised for her age when her inner experience was one of awkwardness.

- **Interactional insight** A member understands a pattern of his or her own behavior, such as ignoring certain types of people, currying favor with powerful people, competing all the time.

- **Motivational insight** A member learns the emotional reason behind her or his patterns of behavior. For example, a reserved person realizes that she fears an uncontrollable eruption of feeling if she lets a little bit out.

- **Genetic insight** A member understands how his or her personal history influenced current behavior, thoughts, and feelings. A self-conscious person may be able to trace her feelings to childhood years when she had to wear an eye patch to correct an eye disorder; her difference from others made her try not to call attention to herself.

Reflection

Once in a while, we have insight into our little oddities or quirks. I hate to share my food in restaurants, quite unreasonably and also quite out of synch with the conventions of my social group. I remembered recently that I was such a slow eater as a child that my brother and father would both help themselves to my plate to hurry me along. In a moment of insight, I realized that this might be the history of my not wanting to share off my plate as an adult. This was what Yalom calls *a genetic insight*. Think of a case in which you have had one of the four types of insight described above.

Artful Questioning Toward Insight

In the group setting, insights often come about through questioning. One of the most important modeling functions of the group leader is the role of questioner. Group members usually have no problem asking questions of each other, but the questions may not be the best ones for furthering goals. For instance, they may ask about concrete details of a situation or about motivations of someone outside the group. The group can learn to ask better questions by imitating the therapist's questioning style. For instance, the counselor demonstrates taking the discussion to a deeper level.

> **SALLY:** I can't believe the horrible traffic now that the 247 spur is closed off. I was just steaming trying to get my errands run on Saturday. It ruined my day off.
>
> **JUDD:** Yeah, I was late coming here tonight because of some idiot that cut halfway across the road and just sat there. Everybody was backed up. I felt like getting out and socking him.
>
> **JEFF:** Drivers like that make me furious.
>
> **LEADER:** Let me bring something up. You all look really pissed off when you're talking about this traffic thing. You talk about being angry. What's happening here? You know that with the new construction, you've got to start out earlier for everything. But you're way more angry than just that. Let's talk about the experience of getting so mad in traffic. Like, how does it start out? Where do you feel it first?

In this example, the counselor deepens the topic from complaining about traffic to thinking about the experience of anger. The discussion has many more meaningful directions to move from there than from its original level.

The counselor also models focusing on process rather than content in cases where content is outweighing process. Often, the focus needs to be steered toward the members rather than outside characters. Content involves facts, details, and descriptions of people and events outside of the group, whereas process involves modes of action and interaction within the group session. The following example shows the counselor intervening in an unfruitful discussion. After three members speak, the counselor makes a process comment followed by a shift of focus.

> **JEANNIE:** My mom doesn't let me do anything. She thinks I'll get kidnapped or something if I just go to the mall to be with my friends.
>
> **JULIO:** Yeah, my grandma is that way. She is so uptight. Like she wants a list of who I'm with and where we're going and every little thing.
>
> **SARAH:** And then you just end up lying because they are asking, asking, asking. They are so clueless.

COUNSELOR: I bet you could all just keep giving examples of your parents or grandparents acting this way. What about y'all? What have you tried so far to deal with this problem, other than lying? Has anybody had any success in changing the situation?

In this dialog, the counselor points out the group process (they are taking turns giving examples of the same thing) and moves the group to a focus on their own behavior rather than their parents' or grandparents'. Without this gentle intervention, the group members might continue in a content-matching vein.

Thinking fast, the counselor uses questions to clarify members' remarks and lead to insight. Often, members grope for words to explain their experience, and a counselor, through practice and theory, has a more ready phraseology. If a member's contributions remain confused and jumbled, others may lose interest and let their minds wander (Jacobs, Masson, & Harvill, 2002). They may also slap their own template of concerns onto the discourse and begin talking about themselves. Jacobs, Masson, and Harvill emphasize the leader's responsibility to clarify what matters are being dealt with. Here's an example:

SOFIA: I can't even go out and scrape my windshield without hearing my father's voice. I know I don't have the right kind of scraper for ice. He always has the right tool. The garbage bags are the same way. I end up overstuffing them and stuff falls out. He'd just be disgusted with me. The other day I burst into tears when I was taking out the trash.

LEADER: Sofia just gave us two examples of how she gets nagged by her father even though he's not there. In her mind, she can hear him criticizing her, even the way she does little household things. He might as well be right there pestering her. He was never happy with anything you did. Is that about right, Sofia?

In this example, you can see how the group leader brings the topic—the critical inner parent—into focus. Without this clarification, other group members might take up the topic of irritating household tasks and their own problems with them. Notice that the therapist does not clarify remarks by finishing clients' sentences or jumping in right away; she finds a way to summarize meaningfully after the client is through (or gives up).

The counselor uses questions to invite group members to get involved. Instead of responding to an individual's statements, she can wait through the silence until someone else responds, making eye contact with the rest of the group. She can also ask out loud for group input:

LEADER: I know what Sofia's talking about—I can sometimes imagine the look on my mother's face if she saw what I was serving for dinner! How about the rest of you? Do you ever feel that you have an inner voice criticizing what you do?

The dialogue below shows a group experiencing conflict among its members. Dave, the counselor, uses strategic questions and comments to help them develop insight rather than remain mired in repetition of the same arguments.

GROUP TRANSCRIPT: Leader Questions and Comments

DAVE: This is really interesting, that basic thing in this group is people wanting connection, and a proved connection. And yet, what you have going on here is contentiousness for the second week in a row. How is it that we can, you know? I'm not, uhh, I don't have any big problem with conflict. You know, I think that oftentimes conflict can be the underpinning of something better on the other side. But I'm kind of wondering how we can work this through in a way that helps you get some of the connections you want. A couple of things occur to me, one is talking personally and not telling other people how to behave, and another one is talking about how I feel, instead of what I think you should do. I guess they're variations of the same thing, but, uh, I don't know, I'm open to any ideas, too.

SARA: I think that that would work well. I feel like it's turned into us telling each other what's wrong, and us sharing with each other what's wrong.

JENNIFER: I agree and I think that people have to be respectful that we all come from different places. Have different values and beliefs and grew up completely different.

DAVE: Well I'll just say too, in terms of my own relationships, my own intimate relationships, the times when I get in trouble are the times when I am essentially telling other people what to do and not taking responsibility for myself. That's just personal, I don't have any idea if that is at all true for you.

MICHAEL: I'm far less comfortable speaking about myself. And I am actually listening to you guys for whatever it's worth. You know

chiming in saying how I feel. That's just, you know, it's just easier.

DAVE: What's that all about talking about yourself?

MICHAEL: Well, I mean, it's just, you know, I don't find it absolutely necessary to divulge everything from my personal life. It's just more comfortable when it's . . .

ANDREW: I totally, I hear you.

SARA: Aren't we here to divulge about ourselves though? I don't really want any one of you to tell me what I am supposed to do. I want you to listen and then share about yourselves, too. Even if it's hard.

ANDREW: I think we're on the same page on that one. I agree.

DAVE: This is one of those times where, as a group leader, I am trying to figure out, well, is there something that I should do to make it easier for people to talk about themselves. Especially when they don't have a comfort level with that, or enjoy it much. And a part of me thinks, well, I should just wait it out and just see what happens.

TALIA: We've made it uncomfortable, I think, to share about ourselves in some respects, too, and I guess I'll take a responsibility with that. Like last week when Mike tried to share about himself and I jumped on him, and I feel like that's what happened with Andrew today, when he tried to share about himself that Dana jumped on him. So I can see why people wouldn't want to share. That it doesn't feel like a real safe place right now.

SARA: Last week when I was talking about Brad and Mike was kind of defending Brad, I felt like why am I even here, like to just have this conversation again with somebody else defending themselves against my viewpoint. And it's, you know, definitely when I went home I felt kind of bummed about all that. It seems like it would be a lot helpful if we were each other's friends and listened and didn't fight with each other about it.

DAVE: Any reactions to that?

ANDREW: I'm just having a hard time trying to figure out what, you know, what's the appropriate, umm, you know, you mentioned a few different, I can't even remember. You said, you know friend or also like group mates, you know different, umm, you know, relationships even just interacting in the circle. So it's also difficult, I never . . . done this before so I'm not sure like what the, how you're supposed to go through that, or what the normal process is. You know, I'm probably partly to blame for, you know, just not really knowing how to act in this group. You know, what's the normal you know, what does a normal guy in a group counseling chair, what does he do, or you know, like how to respond or . . .

DAVE: Yep . . .

TALIA: But isn't that why we're here? Just to figure out how to interact with other people and . . .

DAVE: We've done a bit of finding out how it doesn't work. Well, one piece of information you got was, at least one person in the group would really love to hear what you had to say as long as you could be at least a little more concise and as long as you listened more to what she had to say. So there's one, you know, piece of feedback.

ANDREW: I would listen all day. You know? But it's just silent.

DAVE: Well, is that, I mean, you could do that, you could just retreat. That doesn't sound like what was going on either.

ANDREW: No, you know, I'm just kind of trying to find that balance point. I took that one to heart.

DAVE: It's interesting, there's a new, I mean I sense a new, almost a new softness in the group. And kind of a choice point around, there could be something interesting things that happen now if somebody wants to kind of get out there.

ANDREW: I feel like I really have been getting to know everybody fairly well except for Jenn. Right? Yeah? Is . . . Uhh, I don't know. Where do you sit on these topics, I guess?

JENN: Mmhmm . . .

DAVE: You're saying you would like to listen to her a little bit.

ANDREW: Yeah.

JENNIFER: Well, I guess up until this point, I've just been feeling so bummed about what's been transpiring in my life that I really haven't felt like sharing or had the energy to. But after last week and . . . when Ann said to me, do you think it was all your fault or something along those lines. I went home, and I was doing a lot of thinking this week and realize that, no, it's not all my fault. But I do realize there are things about my personality that I put out there that also place me in those types of situations with men. That I can change and do differently. I think I like to be with men I feel like I can kind of take care of them. Well, and, umm, that's not my job, and I know I need to look at that more. But after last week I started to realize that about myself, which is very different. And I'm not in any hurry to rush out into a relationship, and I need to figure out things about myself and really look at it more deeply.

DANA: I think that's all I'm trying to tell you, if I could just bring it back to Andrew, is that, you know, maybe attacking you isn't the

continues

right way to go about it. But what I'm trying is, maybe you need to figure out a little bit of more about yourself, and like you know, I mean like, what you like to do yourself, by yourself. It might make it easier on your mission.

DAVE: At least that's something that's working for you.

DANA: Yeah. Well yeah . . . and Jenn seems to be on . . . I just think that it would work for everybody.

DAVE: And I would like to point out that, uh, you kind of invited Jenn to talk. Listened, seemed to really take it in. I really appreciated it. You know? If I were in Jenn's seat anyway, I would have really appreciated it being heard out like that.

ANDREW: I just had a feeling that, I don't know, that Jenn her, much from her situation seems even a little bit like mine, except different, you know, different points on the spectrum there, but, I don't know, I'm just trying to figure out what's going on with everybody.

DAVE: So we only got about a minute or so. Umm, want to check in with people see how you're doing. Any observations about the group that you'd like to make?

SARA: I feel like we're grieving somebody's death or something right now.

DAVE: Hmm . . . Mmhmm, that there's a sadness.

SARA: Yeah. Last week we when we left we were all fired up and angry. And this week I feel like, sad.

TALIA: But maybe we're mourning the loss of that anger. And now we've come to a new place where, you know it was, it was great to hear from Jenn because we haven't heard from her. So I feel, it does feel a little bit sad but it feels like maybe next week we can really dive in and really make some progress.

DAVE: Well, this has all been, this has all been really interesting for me anyway and part of the, part of the progress. Hard . . . Anybody else?

DANA: I don't feel like I have to, should apologize every week to Andrew but again I'm just feeling really sorry.

ANDREW: Yeah, I mean, you shouldn't feel sorry like, I'm not a sorry sad individual, and have to feel bad . . .

DANA: . . . but still I'm sorry.

ANDREW: I know. But, you know, you, you just, just give me a break, I guess, at some points. Just realize that, you know, if I wasn't conscious of these types of things going on I wouldn't be here. And so like, you know, I don't know really, I'm confused about what your prerogative is. I'm kind of feeling, you know, tension or even pressure. So you know, I'm just going to have to think about that and just try to figure out where you're trying to go with that, what you're trying to say.

DAVE: What he's saying his purpose is, is trying to do is make contact and get to know him. Is that, is that right?

DANA: I need to separate the issues between my family and his issues.

Thinking About the Group Session

1. Reread Dave's speech at the beginning of the group. Imagine yourself in the group. What are the good points of Dave's talk? What are the bad points, if any? If you got a chance to rephrase his speech, how might you change it?

2. What is the conflict in the group, as far as you can tell? When is it brought up directly? How are Michael and Andrew unified in opposition to the women in the group? How are Michael and Andrew differentiated in

the group? Is the struggle between men and women, or what?

3. Read through all of Dave's comments in a row, skipping group members' remarks. He is very active in this session. What do you think of that? Is he too active? Why or why not? How will you decide how active to be when your group is in conflict?

4. There is a change in tone within this group transcript. Where is this change, and why do you think it comes about? Do you think things will be different in the next session? How? Who will change, and why do you think so?

SMALL GROUP EXERCISE

In this exercise, take on the roles of group members, and identify a volunteer to act as a group leader. Begin a discussion among group members that might be considered small talk about your daily lives, annoyances, and memories. While this discussion occurs, the group leader tries to identify opportunities to use questions to deepen the level of the discussion, to lead to potential insights. After ten or fifteen minutes, process the experience. See how members felt about the guidance of the leader. What were their reactions to the questioning? Did any members see other opportunities to use questioning toward insight? Your instructor may convene the whole class to talk about the exercise.

Interpretation as Insight

When a group member makes a statement that fits into a pattern or framework, the therapist tends to be aware of the pattern before other members of the group are. After all, the therapist has a background of theoretical connections assisting in the **interpretation** of statements and behavior. Therefore, the counselor offers tentative insights for the group to consider. Remember that all four kinds of insight involve recognition of patterns. For instance, in one situation a group member mentions several times that she is older than the rest of the group. The counselor might encourage insight by making one of the following remarks:

■ "You just said that you have several years on the other people here. I get the impression that your age has given you some wisdom that the group can benefit from. What is that all about?"

■ "It seems as though you are afraid that no one here can really understand your situation because we're younger. Why do you think that younger people would have a hard time understanding you? I'm not saying it's not true; I just want to hear your line of thinking."

▪ "Since your age keeps coming up, I'm wondering if you feel that you missed out on something in your younger years. What do you think you missed?"

Any of these questions need follow-up to see whether the individual and the group can discern the same pattern the counselor perceives. Notice that none of them are phrased as undebatable truths. They are open-ended. The member might well say, "My birthday is next week, so my age is on my mind tonight. I usually don't even think about it in here."

Dies (1994) offers general guidelines for interpretations, based on research into group process. I summarize these guidelines here and give some examples:

▪ Interpretations that invite generalizations from interactions in group sessions to interactions outside the group are frequently considered highly beneficial. A therapist might ask, "You said that you hate it when your father and uncle argue. Do you also hate it when people in this group have arguments?" Or, in the other direction, "You are often ready to discuss who is to blame in situations that other group members describe. You help to untangle who is at fault. Is this true of you at work, or in your family, too?"

▪ Especially in short-term groups, clients appreciate interpretations that focus on their impact on other people and point out their patterns of behavior more than abstract interpretations of their motives and personal history.

▪ Counselors need to be careful about making interpretations using psychological jargon and speculative stretching. Clients want to see the concrete evidence that leads directly to an interpretive inference. For example, a leader might say, "Four times today you steered the discussion to deciding who is to blame. Help us understand why this is important."

▪ Interpretations should be phrased tentatively, not as judgments or final wisdom. The counselor above might ask, "It seems to me like you are more comfortable when you have decided where to place blame. Is this accurate, do you think?"

▪ Interpretations are more likely to have influence when emotional arousal is also present.

Researchers have studied what kinds of interpretations are given by counselors of various stripes and what kinds of interpretations are associated with good client outcomes. Flowers and colleagues (Flowers & Booraem, 1990a) compared cognitive-behavioral groups with psychodynamic groups and found that both clients and therapists in cognitive-behavioral groups made more interpretations of people's prevalent impact on others (interactional insights), whereas those in psychodynamic groups made more historical cause interpretations (genetic insights). This makes sense because psychodynamic theory places importance on childhood roots of psychological problems and cognitive-behavioral theory stresses current habits, no matter how they arose. The interactional insights, according to a second study by Flowers and colleagues (Flowers & Booraem, 1990b), were most effective in producing positive outcomes. Second most effective were impact-on-others interpretations (interpersonal insight), and third were historical interpretations (genetic insight).

Take note that in this research, the clients followed the types of interpretations modeled by the counselors in both kinds of therapy: The members of cognitive-behavioral groups spoke like cognitive-behaviorists, and the members of psychodynamic groups spoke like psychodynamic therapists. The powers of modeling and norming were at work in determining how clients looked at things.

DISCUSSION IDEA

Imagine yourselves as counselors in the following situations. For each one, brainstorm several interpretations that could be offered and what kinds of insight might result. Be as creative as you wish. Think of open-ended ways to offer an interpretation to the group.

1. A man consistently ignores the statements of women members in the group.

2. A group member always jokes around about her shortcomings as a parent.

3. One person always arrives five or ten minutes late, immediately apologizes, and gives a new reason for lateness every time.

Confrontation Leading to Insight

Some of the questions and interpretations in the examples above could also be considered **confrontations**, conscious attempts to help members explore their own experiences in new ways. A confrontation is "an invitation to engage in self-examination" (Johnson & Johnson, 2003, p. 535). This self-examination is not usually expected to be pleasant, which is what distinguishes confrontation from support. Being asked to recognize your flower arranging skills is supportive; being asked what you are avoiding by spending so many hours at flower arrangement is a confrontation. Many group counselors like the puzzled-and-confused confrontation approach: "I'm puzzled when I see someone as bright as you spend so much time at flower arranging . . . Can you help me understand that?" Confrontations often concern incongruities or seeming contradictions in what a person does or says.

In everyday use, we speak of confrontations as being somewhat aggressive or hostile, but in counseling groups they are not. Confronting someone kindly but powerfully is a skill that comes with practice. When I first started as a counselor, my confrontations were so mild that neither my clients nor my supervisor noticed them at all! I had to learn to highlight confrontations by making eye contact, speaking more slowly, isolating them from other responses, and repeating them in different words if the first try didn't seem to get through. In contrast, other trainees need to tone down their confrontations so clients do not feel attacked and react defensively.

R e f l e c t i o n s

How do you feel about confrontations? Have you ever had to confront someone about their behavior or motivations? Think about situations with roommates, romantic partners, siblings, and teammates, as well as clients. Do you avoid confrontations? Do you think that you are a person who has to learn to confront more forcefully or a person who needs to tone down confrontations?

In Parts III through IV of this book, you will read about the various levels and kinds of confrontation that fit with specific types of group work. In general, though, you need to confront yourself about confrontation. It's an action that can come from your own need for power, your dislike for a group member, your own memories of someone outside the group, your hostility, and other inner sources that are not fair to inflict on group targets. In training, I was surprised by classmates who sparkled with relish when they reported angry confrontations with their clients, and I thought that their own personal needs were coming to the fore. Ask yourself, "Am I confronting this client to express myself or to help him?"

Both interpretation and confrontation are subjects of controversy in our field. Various theoretical stances endorse differing levels of interpretation and confrontation, with a range from preferring none at all to recommending vigorous forms.

Family Reenactment

According to traditional psychodynamic thought, we are all mightily influenced by our primary families of origin. In fact, almost all practicing clinicians agree with this principle. Experts disagree on how much to make of this principle in individual therapy, and the same disagreement exists among group counseling experts. With this in mind, let me explain briefly the workings of the past in the present group setting, especially **family reenactment,** the repetition of the roles and patterns experienced in the family of origin.

Most people turn a small group into a sample family, whether they are aware of it or not. In the rare cases in which the family background has been relatively smooth and satisfactory, so are the small groups in current life. For example, take Otto, a person who has accepted his father's wisdom and authority so far and has found this authority to be legitimate and trustworthy so far. When Otto joins a group with an older male leader, he feels protected and cooperative. On the other hand, take Louie, whose father was a ruthless and unpredictable bully. The same male leader whom Otto accepts happily may continually make Louie angry and rebellious, with an underlying fear. These cases show how we *recapitulate the primary family group* (Yalom, 1995). Our ways of becoming attached to and relating to others are at least partly motivated outside of our awareness, by traces of what happened in childhood (Westen, 1998).

The therapy group is the ideal setting for projecting family roles and relationships. The counselor is a parental figure, and frequently a man and woman co-therapy team deliberately mirror parental pairs (Donigian & Malnati, 1997; Yalom, 1995). Among group members, styles of relating to parents blossom—competing for their attention, attempting to unseat their power, rebelling against their rule, appeasing them like gods, forming coalitions to influence them, testing their affection, seeking favor. Sibling rivalries also spring up, as group members struggle for status among themselves. In a children's group I once led, one child was developmentally much younger than her chronological age, and the other children fell into big-brother and big-sister roles, alternating between teasing her and protecting her, but never seeing her as an equal. She willingly complied with her little-sister status because that is what she was used to at home.

Ideally, the group would explore the meaning of such roles and offer opportunities to practice new ones, as members play parts that are more in line with satisfying age-appropriate relationships. Yalom (1995) stressed that early family conflicts should be relived correctively, "working through unfinished business from long ago" (p. 15) so that members are no longer stuck in ineffective patterns. For instance, the rebellious Louie could be helped by several group phenomena:

- experience with an authority figure who is dependable, trustworthy, and benevolent
- seeing other members who relate without hostility to the leader, and observing that they are not harmed
- getting feedback from other group members who point out that he acts angry toward the leader without basis; and
- practicing a more open response to leadership.

We shouldn't forget that the family gets reenacted in a positive way as well as a conflicted one in the group setting. A close brotherly and sisterly feeling grows as members work together in an emotionally intimate setting. For some members, this is a new pleasure. They may experience the group as the family they never had.

The Counselor's Role in Family Reenactment

Therapists must highlight and attend to the relationships among members because these offer a large range of opportunities for corrective family experience. If I had been a more seasoned therapist in the children's group I mentioned earlier, I would have designed exercises in which the little-sister child, Ana, took leadership, with the other children following in subordinate roles. I also might have helped the children verbally process what was happening, maybe asking, "What do you think Ana is thinking right now? Guess what she is feeling, and she can tell you whether you guessed right." In other words, I would use the group to subvert or explore the roles that they were stuck in.

Counselors help group members see the ways they are reenacting family roles by giving **feedback on patterns** of relating. They also encourage member-to-member feedback; members may accept feedback from each other better than from the leader (Morran, Stockton, & Whittingham, 2004). Feedback means expressing one's own observations or reactions to another person's contribution. Careful balancing of positive and confrontational feedback allows the leader to keep a running gauge of the group's capacity for introspection.

CELESTE: I'd talk more about my date with Will but I can see Brianna's disapproval all over her. She thinks I shouldn't be seeing an ex-convict.

BRIANNA: I didn't say a thing! I just worry about your safety.

CELESTE: Well, don't! Who I date is my own business. I don't need you to protect me.

PHILIP: You two are acting just like my wife and teenaged daughter!

LEADER: Maybe Philip's on to something. Celeste, I've noticed a few times that when someone shows concern for you, you really bristle. It's like you're rejecting motherly stuff. Is there anything to that, do you think?

CELESTE: Yeah, my mother was incredibly over-protective. I hate that.

PHILIP: You're probably still rebelling when you don't even need to. No one's going to ground you!

CELESTE: It's hard for me to hear people worrying about me. I guess I do feel like they're going to forbid me to do this or that, or restrict me somehow.

BRIANNA: I'm about the age to be Celeste's mother. I do feel motherly to all of you sometimes.

There are obviously plenty of directions to go with this lively discussion. The depth of processing would depend on the goals of the group as well as the stage of readiness to discuss touchy emotional matters in this group. At an early stage, the leader might leave the conversation here with a summary like, "We'll probably all be acting out family dynamics as this group goes along. We can learn from the family patterns we see repeated here, and even change the ones we don't like."

The changes in pattern often flow from **corrective emotional experiences,** which "lead to modifications of maladaptive thoughts, emotions, and patterns of behavior" (Wessler & Hankin, 1988, p. 214). The small group, with its similarity to the outside world and family, provides occasions in which to experiment with new interactions in safety. People have a chance to broaden their scope of relating to others who remind them of their family members (Andronico & Horne, 2004). For instance, Celeste may eventually learn that her group members worry about her without strings attached; their affection is not packaged with control. A corrective experience occurs when she finds solace or help in their concern without feeling engulfed or bullied.

This corrective experience may be possible because even though the group member is casting others in roles from her own past, the feeling she has toward them is diluted. For instance, Clory resists any questions by the female co-therapist because her own mother was extremely intrusive. She automatically feels interrogated when a parental authority figure asks her anything. However, because the co-counselor is really not her mother and is not as anxiety-provoking, Clory finds it easier to see her pattern and to experiment with responding to questions from the counselor. In this way, she opens the door to a new kind of experience.

An advantage of group over individual counseling in this regard is that the counselor can observe multiple targets of family reenactment. In individual therapy, the therapist usually has access to the client's relationship with one (or one type of) figure—mother, father, sister, grandmother—because the therapist is cast in one role. In group, the counselor can see several enactments with various members of the group. A group member also may have automatic responses to the group as a whole in the role of family—for instance, a person who always felt himself to be an outsider in his family will probably recapitulate this feeling in group, feeling like an outcast and being treated as one. In this case, the growth of cohesion and universality will be a corrective emotional experience.

DISCUSSION IDEA

Think of groups you belong to or observe in terms of family. Many groups actually call themselves *a family* on occasion, appreciating this type of relationship. Discuss whether you can see family-type interactions going on in the groups you are thinking about—are there members who take on parental roles and child-type roles? Is there sibling rivalry? What are the power relationships like compared to families' power structures? Your classmates' examples will help you develop your ideas on this subject.

Catharsis

Experiencing and expressing strong emotions is associated with healing in many areas of life. For instance, most funeral rituals allow socially approved release of sorrow and regret. Aristotle elevated **catharsis,** purgation of strong emotion, as a noble goal of tragedy on the stage: Through identifying with the tragic hero, the audience discharges an excess of emotional elements and returns to health, which is seen as a balanced state of affect. Plato thought of catharsis as the harmonious merging of the soul, collected from all parts of the body. Catharsis has also been defined as a spiritual and moral cleansing process, with intense passion leading to relief and calm. The process is associated with insight and wisdom. In everyday life, a good cry, a hearty laugh, or a vicious game of racquetball can leave us with a feeling of being cleansed, which is catharsis.

Since Freud, release of strong feelings has been part of psychotherapy, and repression of affect has been considered harmful. However, the idea that untrammeled exhibition of emotion is salubrious in itself enjoyed only brief popularity in the late 1960s and early 1970s and was soon abandoned, with research showing that angry actions do not dissipate anger but breed more (e.g., Bushman, Baumeister, & Stack, 1999). The uncontrolled discharge of feelings can be hazardous if the high state of arousal is not resolved (Crouch, Bloch, & Wanlass, 1994).

"The open expression of affect is, without question, vital to the group therapeutic process; in its absence, a group would degenerate into a sterile academic exercise. Yet it is only part of the process and must be complemented by other factors" (Yalom, 1995, p. 81). As I said in Chapter 1, there must be a cognitive aspect connected with catharsis: The group members must connect the emotional ventilation with some insight. A timid group member once flew into a rage when another group member questioned the accuracy of her statement about a typing rule, even knowing that she was a lifelong typist. She surprised herself and all of us with the intensity of her anger, as she leaped from her chair and kicked it backwards, yelling and crying. The insight that grew from the shocking event, with its innocuous occasion, was that the typist simmered with resentment that she was never given respect. When she was doubted by an amateur on a subject in which she was obviously expert, it was the last straw. The safety of a cohesive group allowed her to express feelings that murmured within her all the time without conscious explanation. Outside, this anger had expressed itself in many small ways, such as petty theft from the workplace and obstructionism in processing paperwork. She needed to make direct demands for acknowledgment instead of these covert acts of aggression, and during the course of the group she was able to make some progress in this regard. At the same time, each of the other group members realized that there was someone in their life outside group whose skills they habitually slighted. They had to wonder whether this person nursed a rage like the typist's.

Powerful catharsis cements the bonds among group members when the group is past its early, exploratory stage. (In early sessions, a member's emotional outburst can frighten everyone.) However, some cathartic events are not notably explosive. For some people, really letting go takes a mild form of expression that, to them, is just as intense as an outburst.

An experienced group client wrote, "There was an intangible lesson learned with any catharsis, even without analyzing it. It brought the group together in a way that nothing else could. It seemed almost ritualistic, like initiation into a club." This client connected catharsis with cohesiveness.

A member of a child therapy group explained catharsis in a postsession report this way: "It was important to me because I feel like I released a little bit of hurt off my chest, and people listened to what I had to say."

From a young adult in group: "When T. and O. started to tell the group about their experience as children, they told us that they never truly experienced childhood. This was a subject that really related to me. I understood everything they said and could really relate to the feelings of anger. It was a chance for me to let out many of my hidden angers directed toward my mother for not letting me be a child. My expression of anger and hurt, in turn, ignited the same responses in both T. and O. as well as N. It really felt good to let out some of my anger to other people besides myself. It felt like I was lifting a huge weight off my shoulders." This group member associated the experiences of universality with catharsis.

The Counselor's Stewardship of Catharsis

The group leader holds a delicate responsibility in regard to catharsis. By picking up on the feeling portion of group members' remarks and reflecting feelings back, a counselor can intensify attention to emotional expression: "We do control our clients' behavior even in nondirective therapy, by reinforcing certain types of talk. It's unavoidable, since randomly responding to the client would be quite unhelpful" (Day, 2004, p. 168). An illustration of various responses will help:

> ANTONIO: Last night was bad, my birthday dinner. I thought that Rudy should remember that I really dislike raisins, and he put them in my carrot cake. Then he just said that he thought carrot cake needed raisins and that they were in all the recipes. But it was *my* birthday cake.

LEADER, VERSION 1: Rudy paid attention to the traditions of carrot cake instead of your preferences. [restating, addressing the situation]

or

LEADER, VERSION 2: You were disappointed on a special day. [keeping the feeling on a mild level]

or

LEADER, VERSION 3: You said it was "bad." How was it bad? How would you describe your feelings? [going deeper into feelings but keeping them in the past]

or

LEADER, VERSION 4: Pretend I'm Rudy. What would you say to me, if there were no consequences at all? [inviting a cathartic reaction if Antonio has one, putting feelings in the here and now, giving Rudy a chance to show how much anger he feels]

Notice that at each **level of response,** the counselor is increasing the possibility of the unexpected or extreme reaction. Don't conclude that the most intense level is always the best. Sometimes your group is not ready for heavy emotional expression; and sometimes you feel that they need to see how they can modulate emotions by labeling them distinctly. For example, you will find clients who jump directly to anger without recognizing gradations like irritation and disappointment. They need help in recalibrating their emotional thermometers, and a response like "You were disappointed on a special day" is fully appropriate.

When you increase emotional expression and intensity, you foster group disarray. People have strong feelings in response to strong feelings, and suddenly you have five to eight people with idiosyncratic irrational reactions all at once. Your group needs to trust that you can handle the disorder and protect them from lasting harm.

DISCUSSION IDEAS

1. Brainstorm about ways in which you can respond when your group becomes highly emotional. How will you decide whether to intervene or let things take their own course? How long will you allow a storm to last? What kinds of intervention could help resolve an episode?

2. Now, discuss how you can prepare yourself for such situations. Where can you get practice in the essential art of managing groups caught up in emotions? Where can you observe good group management?

Not all emotional release is cathartic. You will sometimes find members who have an extremely expressive style, and this style is an interpersonal pattern that fends off self-exploration and acceptance of feedback. Uncontrollable tears or vicious anger, for example, puts a quick stop to incisive questioning and confrontation. When a group member repeatedly uses emotions in this way, it's time to temporarily stop it with a time-out style tactic called *blocking,* or cutting off:

> LEADER: Jamie, I'd like to give you a few minutes to collect yourself and take a few deep breaths. [Addressing another member] Sienna, the look on your face during the last few minutes said to me that you're having some intense reactions yourself. Do you want to tell us what's going on?

While emotional arousal usually facilitates learning, too much arousal makes it impossible to process information. You see this occurring in bad cases of test anxiety, when a person's brain won't work normally due to emotional static. In the example above, the leader moves attention to another member, realizing that Jamie won't benefit from a group focus on her at the moment. In case Jamie's emotional storms are a bid for attention, this tactic also avoids rewarding and abetting the behavior.

Extreme cathartic displays can be frightening, especially in the early stage of a group. Members observing such a display can be clueless about how they should respond and whether such displays are going to be expected from everyone. The cathartic individual needs to be reassured that the group is a safe place to vent; at the same time, the rest of the group needs assurance that people express themselves meaningfully at many different levels of intensity, not all of them fervent. Your task in early sessions is to present yourself as a trustworthy lightning rod if things get too stormy. It's important not to lose members to emotional overload at the outset.

Think through catharsis in terms of your group's goals when you are planning the group. In some groups, intense expression of feeling will not advance the group's purpose at all and should always be calmed. These matters will be considered in Parts III through VI of this text, where specific types of groups are discussed.

SMALL GROUP EXERCISE

Divide the class into three small groups. Each group receives an assignment of two of the following terms for counselor interventions:

Questioning

Clarifying

Interpretation

Confrontation

Giving feedback

Blocking (or cutting off)

Brainstorm in your small group for examples of your terms from groups you have been in or observed (not necessarily counseling groups but also classrooms, workplaces, interest groups, and task groups). Together, write a brief definition of each term along with a good example. Have two group members role-play one of your examples before the whole class, and see whether the class can identify the counselor's intervention.

Processing Group Events

I have described in this chapter many ways that the leader can help the group gain self-understanding (insight), incur corrective emotional experiences related to family reenactment, and foster beneficial catharsis. All of these activities can be subsumed under the skill of **processing.** Stockton, Morran, and Nitza (2000) offer an eloquent definition of processing:

> Processing can be defined as capitalizing on significant happenings in the here-and-now interactions of the group to help members reflect on the meaning of their experience; better understand their own thoughts, feelings, and actions; and generalize what is learned to their life outside the group. (p. 345)

Without processing, group activities and discussions may remain unrelated to insight, to life outside the group setting, and to meeting individuals' goals (Glass & Benshoff, 1999). The emotional surges of catharsis can calm down without any learning coming from them. Thus, processing is an important part of the counselor's role in promoting therapeutic factors.

Stockton, Morran, and Nitza (2000) outline four interrelated steps in processing:

1. **Identify critical incidents.** As group leaders gain experience, they become good at identifying events that have potential for promoting change. These are indicated by intense reactions to the event by group members, repeated patterns or themes in the group, references to group goals, notable successes and failures, and body language that suggests strong feelings. Not all critical incidents should be processed; important ones will repeat themselves in various ways. The group leader begins by focusing the group's attention on the event.

2. **Examine the incident and member reactions.** Each member is offered an opportunity to think and speak about his or her thoughts and emotions concerning the incident. Sometimes this is done through rounds. Artful

questioning, discussed earlier in this chapter, maintains a **here-and-now focus**, in which immediate reactions are elicited. Remember that the counselor models a here-and-now focus by maintaining attention to what is happening in this group, today, rather than to individual members, in the past or outside the group.

3. **Derive meaning and insight from the event.** In this step, feedback is crucial. Critical incidents bring up themes and patterns for each group member, which are the content of interpersonal feedback from other members and the leader. Members are encouraged to compare their immediate reactions with past reactions and to see commonalities. They develop hypotheses, insights based on general statements about what they have learned about themselves.

4. **Apply what's learned toward personal change.** Members finally consider how they could apply what they have derived from the critical incident processing to their lives outside the group. This consideration can follow from connecting insights to individual and group goals. What changes are implied through the processing of the incident? The group can brainstorm about strategies for change. (Adapted from pp. 347–352)

The authors point out that this four-step map must be applied flexibly. At times, some members may complete all four steps, while others complete the first two. You as the leader benefit from having the map in your mind, even when the destination is not quite achieved.

KEY TERMS

blocking protecting one or more group members through stopping some damaging behavior in the group

catharsis experiencing and expressing strong emotions, usually associated with healing; the healing usually involves both emotional and cognitive elements

confrontation a challenge to another person to examine what she or he does or says; often, a confrontation points out an apparent incongruity or contradiction; therapeutic confrontations are intended to lead to insight

corrective emotional experience a reliving, in group, of a situation parallel to an old situation, only with a more positive resolution than the old one

had; usually, old negative emotions are resolved through this process

family reenactment in groups, the repetition of roles and patterns from one's family of origin, with other members treated like family members

feedback on patterns giving another person one's perceptions of her or his repeated actions and themes, with an aim of enhancing insight; sometimes feedback is given to check on the accuracy of the giver's perceptions

genetic insight an understanding about how one's personal history influenced one's current behavior, thoughts, and feelings

here-and-now focus   dwelling on the present occurrences within the group, rather than past occurrences outside or within the group

insight   a new understanding about one's patterns of thought, feeling, behavior, and problems

interactional insight   a realization about a pattern in how one behaves toward other people

interpersonal insight   a realization about how one is perceived by other people

interpretation   a statement, often tentatively phrased, focused on helping a group member or members gain insight into current or past reactions and behavior

level of response   degree of intensity invited by a leader's questions or comments; leaders can adjust the depth of reaction elicited according to group members' readiness

motivational insight   a realization about the emotional reason underlying one's patterns of behavior

processing   focusing on a significant happening in the here-and-now interactions of the group to help members understand their reactions, find meaning in the experiences, and generalize what they learn

self-understanding   cognitive comprehension of one's own thoughts, feelings, and behavior

CHAPTER REVIEW

1. In group counseling, what interpretations are most useful? What kinds of interpretations are usually not well received? Can you speculate on why?

2. Give an example of a confrontation. Review your own feelings about confrontations.

3. Why does group counseling tend to generate more family reenactment and feedback on personal patterns than individual counseling does?

4. Describe an example of a corrective emotional experience from your own life, your observations, or fictional portrayals.

5. Imagine or remember a critical incident in group counseling. In a format like a play, depict a group going through the four steps of processing this incident.

FOR FURTHER READING

Jacobs, E. E., Masson, R. L., & Harvill, R. L. (2002). *Group counseling: Strategies and skills* (4th ed.). Pacific Grove, CA: Brooks/Cole.

This is a practical, hands-on book that goes into detail on many techniques for group counseling. Beginning and closing a group, maintaining focus, cutting off and drawing out, using rounds and dyads, structuring exercises, and dealing with problem situations are specifically described. The text is a reassuring tool for beginning group leaders.

REFERENCES

Andronico, M. P., & Horne, A. M. (2004). Counseling men in groups: The role of myths, therapeutic factors, leadership, and rituals. In J. L. DeLucia-Waack, D. A. Gerrity, C. R. Kalodner, & M. T. Riva (Eds.), *Handbook of group counseling and Psychotherapy* (pp. 456–468). Thousand Oaks, CA: Sage.

Bushman, B. J., Baumeister, R. F., & Stack, A. D. (1999). Catharsis, aggression, and persuasive influence: Self-fulfilling or self-defeating prophecies? *Journal of Personality and Social Psychology, 76,* 367–376.

Crouch, E. C., Bloch, S., & Wanlass, J. (1994). Therapeutic factors: Interpersonal and intrapersonal mechanisms. In A. Fuhriman & G. M. Burlingame (Eds.), *Handbook of group psychotherapy: An empirical and clinical synthesis* (pp. 269–315). New York: Wiley.

Day, S. X. (2004). *Theory and design in counseling and psychotherapy.* Boston: Lahaska Press/Houghton Mifflin.

Dies, R. R. (1994). The therapists' role in group treatments. In H. S. Bernard & K. Roy MacKenzie (Eds.), *Basics of group psychotherapy* (pp. 60–99). New York: Guilford Press.

Donigian, J., & Malnati, R. (1997). *Systemic group therapy: A triadic model.* Pacific Grove, CA: Brooks/Cole.

Flowers, J. V., & Booraem, C. D. (1990a). The effects of different types of interpretation on outcome in group psychotherapy. *Group, 14,* 81–88.

Flowers, J. V., & Booraem, C. D. (1990b). The frequency and effect on outcome of different types of interpretation in psychodynamic and cognitive-behavioral group psychotherapy. *International Journal of Group Psychotherapy, 40,* 203–214.

Glass, J. S., & Benshoff, J. M. (1999). PARS: A processing model for beginning group leaders. *Journal for Specialists in Group Work, 24,* 15–26.

Jacobs, E. E., Masson, R. L., & Harvill, R. L. (2002). *Group counseling: Strategies and skills* (4th ed.). Pacific Grove, CA: Brooks/Cole.

Johnson, D. W., & Johnson, F. P. (2003). *Joining together: Group theory and group skills* (8th ed.). Boston: Allyn & Bacon.

Morran, D. K., Stockton, R., & Whittingham, M. H. (2004). Effective leader interventions for counseling and psychotherapy groups. In J. L. DeLucia-Waack, D. A. Gerrity, C. R. Kalodner, & M. T. Riva (Eds.), *Handbook of group counseling and psychotherapy* (pp. 91–103). Thousand Oaks, CA: Sage.

Stockton, R., Morran, D. K., & Nitza, A. G. (2000). Processing group events: A conceptual map for leaders. *Journal for Specialists in Group Work, 25,* 343–355.

Trotzer, J. P. (1999). *The counselor and the group.* Philadelphia, PA: Accelerated Development.

Wessler, R. L., & Hankin, S. (1988). Rational-emotive therapy and related cognitively oriented psychotherapies. In S. Long (Ed.), *Six group therapies* (pp. 159–215). New York: Plenum Press.

Westen, D. (1998). The scientific legacy of Sigmund Freud: Toward a psychodynami-cally informed psychological science. *Psychological Bulletin, 124,* 333–371.

White, M., & Epston, D. (1990). *Narrative means to therapeutic ends.* New York: Norton.

Yalom, I. D. (1995). *The theory and practice of group psychotherapy.* New York: Basic Books.

CHAPTER **6**

Altruism, Guidance, and Existential Growth

T his chapter completes a survey of the twelve therapeutic factors and the therapist's contributions to their cultivation.

Altruism

Altruism redeems the sullied character: this is a lesson that delights us through the ages. In the 1988 film *Rain Man*, self-centered Charlie Babbit takes on the care of his autistic brother purely for greed—he hopes to claim a huge inheritance. Over the course of the movie, Charlie's motivations change. He learns to love selflessly, and thereby he finds peace and wholeness. The film received five Academy Awards. We adore such tales, and for good reason.

Altruism is unselfish behavior—an act that rewards a person other than the one performing the act, at some cost to the person acting (Brown, 1986). The act is motivated by concern for another's welfare. In a group, for instance, altruism is at work when we devote most of a session to helping one member with a pressing problem, even though all members have their own problems. Several features of group therapy facilitate altruism.

▪ A cohesive group experiences a feeling of closeness, and social theorists agree that "in close relationships psychological altruism, self-sacrifice for the welfare of others, is common" (p. 106).

▪ Many counseling groups include members who have few or no close relationships outside, and therefore experience scant altruism on either the giving or getting side. They are thirsty for an encounter with this pleasant virtue.

▪ Furthermore, a strong group norm of helpfulness exists from the beginning. When social psychologists have studied whether or not people will help a stranger in an emergency, the major principle determining helpfulness has been shown to be "the clarity with which the *responsibility* to help fell to a particular person or persons" (p. 105). In the therapy-group setting, this responsibility is very clear and often expressed verbally.

You may wonder whether the second part of the definition of altruism—that the altruistic act is done at some cost to the person acting—holds true in groups; that is, what do group members sacrifice in helping another member? Basically, they sacrifice the attention of the leader and the other members, which could be devoted to their own concerns. In public settings, people operate more on the expectation that one good act will be rewarded with a return benefit **(exchange theory),** but most people in close relationships do not keep strict account of who is ahead and who is behind. They are motivated by thoughts of the other person's welfare rather than eventual payoffs. The associations among group members definitely qualify as close relationships.

Reflections

Think about altruism versus exchange theory in your own social interactions. List five important relationships, and then rank them according to their altruism level. Include both balanced relationships—in which altruism goes both ways—and relationships in which one person contributes most of the altruism. What are some differences between your number one and number five relationships on this ranked list?

People who seek therapy have often lost their sense of their own worth. This worth is rebuilt when they see that they have helped someone else in group therapy. Through accepting, supporting, and being truthful with others, they find that they are indeed valuable citizens of this little community. Unlike their counselors in one-to-one situations, they are not paid for these services; the help is given in a spirit of altruism. For the unfortunate souls who swear "Everyone's always looking out for themselves," altruistic relationships are a happy surprise, and having these within group opens the possibility that they can exist outside as well.

Some people in counseling know that they are worthwhile members of society, but wonder whether they merely act out expected duties by bringing home the paycheck, watching the children, cleaning the house, driving the carpool, calling relatives. They go through the motions. Their sense of spontaneous, fresh responsiveness is absent. But altruism in group revives this sense. Altruistic reactions to others in a therapy group cannot be discounted as pro forma or inauthentic. They are outside the normal demands of life, and people gain self-respect through their own helping impulses. Alfred Adler (1927/1957) often suggested that his patients perform selfless activities in their communities as part of their cure, knowing that **social interest** gave meaning to life. He believed that humans have an innate orientation toward promoting each other's welfare—that altruism is a built-in need. Furthermore, Adler emphasized that many emotionally troubled people suffer from too much dwelling on their own problems and that distraction and social comparison with the less fortunate would naturally be salutary.

A young adult in a personal growth group wrote:

The event that was most important for me related to L. One of my goals for the session was to sit back and listen deeply to those talking instead of trying to insert myself at all times. I was doing this for the most part 'cause nothing was really being directed at me. I noticed L. getting into slight confrontations with W. but just assumed that these were just things working themselves out. Then I noticed L. kind of jump on T. It was as if something triggered inside of me. It had nothing to do with my ego, though, but was rather, as if there were an observer inside me unrelated to my ego. I asked L. if there was something wrong. She asked me why I would ask that. I answered that it seemed that some chords were getting struck in her more than usual. She began to tear up, said that she had a rough day, a friend was in the hospital. I hugged her and was able to tell her I cared for her. It was a unique experience for me to be totally concerned for her, not myself. I was pleased with my ability to pick up on others' feelings if I was sitting back and listening.

The Therapist's Promotion of Altruism

By its very nature, altruism cannot be forced; the counselor plays a facilitating role by creating a fertile atmosphere. Recall that a clear sense of responsibility for the welfare of others is the main principle that determined helpful behavior in experimental studies. This sense can grow from the group's development of norms ("We are committed to helping each other") and from the counselor's positive reinforcement.

> **LEADER:** Today we spent about half an hour focused on Jan's feelings about losing her boyfriend. I want to point out that everyone in the group got involved in giving Jan support and helping her sort out her reactions, and some of you shared some parallel experiences that were painful to talk about but valuable. You were all unselfish in devoting this time to another person's problem, and as Jan said, it really helped her. Five or six weeks ago, I'm not sure we would have been this way. I think some of you might have been impatient, or shy, or too miserable in yourself to reach out like you did today. What do you think?

In such a way, the leader highlights the altruistic nature of the group and compliments it as a sign of progress.

As group leaders, we need to take some heed: not everything that looks like altruism is positive. For example, a person who gives help and never takes it may be deflecting attention from his own situation (in a typical interpersonal strategy). Furthermore, some people are already altruistic in the extreme, deriving their self-worth almost entirely from service to others. In either case, strangely enough, helpfulness doesn't help. The group needs to confront the pattern.

Altruism, Guidance, and Advice

Many times, altruistic helping involves providing guidance and **advice.** I often tell my friends that I am happy to give them advice because I'm reluctant to give any to my counseling clients. My friends can have the overflow. My training program, like most others, frowned upon advice-giving to clients (e.g., Gladding, 2005). The reasoning behind this is that clients don't benefit from solutions that come from outside; they benefit from change that originates within themselves. As professionals, we try to refrain from imposing our judgments on what clients should do. Most troubled people have had plenty of advice (some of it good advice) that has not helped them a bit. In group counseling, you will observe advice and guidance coming both from members and from leaders, usually with altruistic motives.

Retrospectively, neither therapists nor clients rate advice very highly in contributing to a good outcome (Yalom, 1995). However, in my own experience, clients have often mentioned a piece of advice given by me or another group member when asked at termination what was most valuable from therapy. In training, I once had an embarrassing experience when a client went on and on about the great piece of advice I had once given him, during a termination session that was being audiotaped for my supervisor to hear. I knew my supervisor would disapprove, and though I tried to lead my client off this topic, he was unswerving. (Luckily, my supervisor saw the humor in the situation.)

Flowers (1979) perceived that *advice* needed a multidimensional definition to refine research evaluating its effectiveness. He identified four types of advice for his research project at a state hospital:

1. **Simple Advice**   simple statements about what the client should do without clearly operationalizing how to do it, such as, "You should not set fires when you get mad."

2. **Alternatives**   statements of two or more possible ways of dealing with the problem in which the client has the choice of which to try, such as, "You should get more active with your fellow ward members. You could play cards or you could get involved in some of the sporting events."

3. **Instruction**   statements of a single advisement clearly broken down into the steps necessary for client success, such as, "You should get more involved in the activities on the ward. I think you should start with volleyball since you have already said you like it. The volleyball game usually starts at 10. At 9:45 you should come to the office and see me and have tennis shoes on and be ready to play. We will walk out and then you will be at the court a little early and be ready to be chosen for a team when the players are chosen."

4. **Process Advice**   statements or advisements that only have to do with the process of the group as it is being conducted, such as, "I think you should speak to more people in the group and not always direct your comments to me." (pp. 307–308)

From these definitions, it's clear that merely referring to "advice" is not adequate for our purposes as group counselors. In Flowers's research, advice receivers (simulated clients) rated as "good therapeutic responses" about 40 percent of simple advice statements, 100 percent of alternatives statements, 75 percent of instruction statements, and 67 percent of process advice statements. Clients were told only to identify "good therapeutic responses"; they didn't know that types of advice were under study. Supporting Flowers's findings in real settings among mental-hospital clients, simple advice was the least effective in producing a good outcome, with instructions and alternatives predicting significantly more client improvement.

Advice senders (real therapists) who rated their own "good therapeutic responses" did not concur with the advice receivers. The senders considered 74 percent of their simple advice, 11 percent of their alternatives, 50 percent of their instructions, and 47 percent of their process advice as "good therapeutic responses." In other words, they rated simple advice as more valuable and all the others as less valuable than the clients did. Notice the huge contrast in ratings of alternatives-type advice: 100 percent of it valued by clients versus 11 percent valued by counselors. Therapists seem to overrate their own simple advice (74 percent helpful). Perhaps this is why training programs stress avoidance of advice-giving in general: We tend to overestimate our own pearls of wisdom.

Instructions and alternatives types of advice might better be called **guidance**, an elaborated form of advice. In contrast with simple advice, guidance is certainly involved in problem solving, a process that almost any group engages in. Guidance is offered by other members of the group as well as the leader. For instance, one group I co-led brainstormed about how a member could ameliorate her isolation as the only woman in her advanced chemistry courses. The suggestions ranged from building her inner tolerance of isolation, to identifying approachable classmates for assistance, to making friendship overtures. She was able to accept two of the alternatives and put them into practice, reporting in the next weeks on her efforts. Other useful advice I've seen given and taken in group therapy included practical tips on getting ready to come out to parents (as homosexual), confronting racism at work, and adjustment to crowding in dorm life.

Homework assignments given by a counselor can be seen as instructive advice. For example, a client reported the following experience:

> In one case, when I was talking about the lack of personal relationships, he [the therapist] asked me what I do to help facilitate them. I had to admit that I didn't make much of an effort. He challenged me on this, and gave me a "homework" assignment to seek out opportunities for personal connections. Based on that comment, I sought out a deeper relationship with a friend at work, and pursued a weekly lunch with him, where we could discuss meaningful things in our lives. It was the best thing I could have done to extend what I learned in group, to put it into practice in the real world.

Counselors' Stance on Guidance and Advice

Direct advice given by members occurs in every therapy group. It is a basic form of communication, and some members may believe that it is what they are supposed to give and receive in group counseling. Often advice giving is the major way that new group members have of interacting with each other or acting altruistically. Your job is to ensure that advice-giving is not the main event of the group and that the type of advice given is elaborated enough to be useful. Remember to turn simple advice into alternatives, instructions, or process commentary if you can.

The process of advice-giving is more engaging than the content in many cases. In a session, you may want to make "advice" the topic of group discussion.

■ What types of advice do members get on the outside? Who gives it?

- When is it helpful?
- What feelings come out in you when you get advice?
- Why does the "Yes, but . . ." pattern of response happen?

Such a discussion will bring forward critiques of simple advice, awareness that will serve the group well in the future. It will also reveal the positive motivations behind many statements of simple advice. For example, "Tell him to get lost!" is not offered as a serious course of action but instead is intended to express support and mutual outrage. In contrast, sometimes advice is a form of one-upsmanship, setting up the adviser as wiser than the advisee. A frequent adviser may be masking his or her own problems, or minimizing a problem that is too close for comfort by giving oversimplified solutions ("Just say no"). Ormont (2004) explains advice givers who maintain their stance as "isolates," outsiders in the group:

> Some peripheral members distance themselves from the rest of the members by giving advice. . . . These advice givers are isolates in the profoundest sense, but they disguise their isolation in what seems like heartfelt concern. Every comment they dole out on "how to do it better" separates them further from their listeners. They can always be identified because their advice is unsolicited. Isolates do not bother with understanding; if they were truly generous, they would listen as well as instruct, and they would counsel only when it was requested (and even then they would limit their guidance). But such consideration would bring them closer to others than they want to be. (pp. 71–72)

Sometimes, group leaders themselves offer advice too quickly, in order to avoid a deeper discussion that unnerves them for some reason. We always need to consider our own motivations for giving advice, especially when the topic is one that makes us uncomfortable.

You might engage the group members in the subject of the strengths and weaknesses of advice giving by asking them to reflect on some advice-giving that has just occurred in the group. In reference to an advice interaction, the group leader can ask the advice receiver to reflect on what was helpful or not helpful in the interaction. The group leader can also ask the advice giver or other group members to generate non-advice alternatives for the interaction that just happened. In general, it is better for the group members to come to a mutual understanding of the benefits and detriments of advice-giving and formulate their own rules for advice-giving than for the leader to lay down certain prescriptions.

Sometimes specific members' advice must be directly handled. For instance, people may give advice that is wrong or off-base. A man advising another man to smack his sassy wife once in a while can't be countenanced, nor can a teen telling another teen how to hide drugs better. Advice that blurs the focus by long narration of the adviser's own experiences needs to be curtailed. Counselors need to develop blocking or cutting-off techniques in such cases. This is often difficult because we are well socialized not to interrupt. However, our job requires us to intervene sometimes. Sometimes it's enough to make a hand signal, such as an open-palm Stop gesture, and then continue by asking the adviser or the group to talk more about the advice. Tone of voice is important in cutting off; appearing angry or shocked might make people back off from strong statements in group. A tone of quiet reason is better, and some clarification of why you are cutting off, if someone else in the group doesn't pick up the cue. "Let me stop you here . . ." and "I need to jump in here . . ." and "Before you get too far into this, let's see what other people think. . . ." are good openings to keep at hand.

SMALL GROUP EXERCISE

Role play as members of a counseling group, having one person volunteer to describe a recurrent problem or irritant in her everyday life. Another volunteer should provide some bad or over-lengthy advice. Each other person in your group should practice cutting off or blocking the adviser and using a question to take the discussion to a more meaningful level. Discuss your feelings as complainer, advisee, or leader during this practice session.

Existential Growth

The last category of therapeutic factors Yalom (1995) included are those that allow people in group therapy to grapple with the most basic problems of human existence; appropriately, these are called **existential factors.** Some philosophers and psychologists identify themselves as *existentialists,* meaning that they focus mostly on these factors. Yalom constructed an inventory to assess the operation of his twelve therapeutic factors, which he used in studying their importance to group members (as discussed in Chapter 1). The five items of this inventory that represent the therapeutic factor of **existential growth** are these:

1. Recognizing that life is at times unfair and unjust
2. Recognizing that ultimately there is no escape from some of life's pain or from death
3. Recognizing that no matter how close I get to other people, I must still face life alone

4. Facing the basic issues of my life and death, and thus living my life more honestly and being less caught up in trivialities

5. Learning that I must take ultimate responsibility for the way I live my life no matter how much guidance and support I get from others (p. 88)

Reading over these items, you can see that they hang together by a common thread: They are realizations about the hard facts of life. How deeply have you acknowledged these five statements? Existential psychologists believe that beneath specific problems and personality defects are always problems inherent to all human existence. Clemmont Vontress, considered by many to be one of the founders of cross-cultural counseling theory, believes that these universals make the existential model suitable for clients of any cultural background: "Since I began reading African, Asian, and Arab writers, I have learned that people all over the world try to make sense of life" (1996, p. 161). Yalom (1980) outlined the four basic problems we all confront in one way or another: meaninglessness, freedom, isolation, and death. They are all part of the package deal we get with being born. In the following sections, I will explain each basic problem more fully.

Meaninglessness

At some point, we all wonder why we were ever born or what our purpose on earth might be. We ponder the meaning of life. According to existential thought, the universe is not designed, purposeful, or coherent. There is no pre-set and stable meaning in life. But people need a sense of meaning, or they fall prey to hopelessness, discouragement, and emptiness—the essence of depression. We must create meaning for ourselves. Subjective well-being demands that we are able to balance the immediate situation against something bigger than ourselves. We want to see a pattern in what happens to us and our loved ones, but existentialists say that we must weave that pattern ourselves. In group therapy, clients are exposed to each other's constructions of meaningfulness and meaninglessness, which serve as comparison points to investigate their own stance. An exploration of their own **values** is usually involved: "Values provide us with a blueprint for life conduct: values tell us not only *why* we live but *how* to live" (May & Yalom, 2000, p. 286).

People in nursing homes compose one population for whom meaning may be especially precarious. The move from familiar surroundings, followed by a new environment that threatens privacy and individuality, undermines the residents' sense of meaningful continuity to life and its closing. A nursing-home therapy group based on writing and sharing writings (Schuster, 1998) provided "a unique opportunity for establishing a discourse community which encourages expression and the search for larger meaning in a world which is often bereft of purpose" (p. 148). Such groups are a topic of Chapter 9.

DISCUSSION IDEA

Below is a list of values—activities and qualities that people consider meaningful. Check off all the values that are important to you. Then, put a second checkmark next to the three that are most important.

____ Achievement

____ Beauty

____ Career success

____ Child rearing

____ Creativity

____ Fame

____ Friendship

____ Health and fitness

____ Helping others

____ Independence

____ Learning and knowledge

____ Love and romance

____ Nature/outdoors activities

____ Order

____ Possessions

____ Power

____ Prestige and admiration

____ Security

____ Variety

____ Wealth

Discuss your decision-making process with your group. (This exercise is adapted from Seligman, 2001.) When you enter a group therapy setting, can you see how your values might come into play?

Freedom

It may seem odd to view freedom as a problem. In the existential sense, we have some extent of freedom even in the most restrictive circumstances, and that means that we have the burden of choice at all times. Viktor Frankl's (1946/1984) account of his four years in Nazi concentration camps serves as a touchstone text for learning about mental and spiritual freedom within terrible physical enslavement. He observed that prisoners who found something to live for survived longer than those who gave up. Frankl applied his revelations to human psychology in general, saying that though we may not choose what happens to us, we choose our attitudes toward it and what we make of it. The idea of choice is a major theme in counseling groups, as members discover that their typical behavior is not set in stone (Holt, 1990).

Existentialists see freedom as a great responsibility because having freedom of choice means taking personal responsibility for choices. People blame parents, spouses, bosses, or society's injustices, but in existential terms responsibility includes not blaming others for one's own inner state. Thus, people who explain their bad behavior, failures, or interpersonal problems by pointing to abuse in childhood (or other past trauma) are dodging the freedom to change, choosing to make something positive out of the negative. This positive transformation often involves caring for other people and striving for their happiness or their relief from pain. The group counseling setting, through providing an outlet for altruism and empathy, expedites this transformation.

Isolation

We are ultimately alone. This fact strikes us most forcefully in times of crisis or profound change. Because we have a sense of self and individuality, we also have a sense of aloneness: I am the only I there is. When people are dying, they are keenly aware of their isolation, and many terminally ill patients turn away from others in the last part of their lives. We are alone in the final decision about how we should live as well. As the Christian hymn goes, "You have to walk this lonesome valley by yourself—nobody else can walk it for you."

Loving relationships relieve our isolation, and for most of us the pursuit and maintenance of such relationships is a primary value. Seeing your friend or loved one as a whole being, not as an object to relieve your isolation or serve your other needs, is the ideal. This type of relationship was described in Martin Buber's (1970) book *I and Thou,* and it is referred to as an **I/Thou relationship.** In an I/Thou relationship, "one must truly listen to the other: relinquish stereotypes and anticipations of the other, and allow oneself to be shaped by the other's response. . . . one must lose or transcend oneself" (Yalom, 1980, p. 365). However, existential isolation persists in the face of intimacy, and we live the human paradox of being related to yet separate from other people. This paradox permeates the group therapy setting.

May and Yalom (2000) see an important part of existential psychotherapy as learning what you *cannot* get from others—what you must create from within. This is a hard lesson, as you probably know. Our romantic films and songs would lead us to believe that the perfect love partner meets every need. Notice that the films and songs are almost all about the *beginning* of love, not the middle or the end, where existential aloneness reigns. Remember that after years of experience leading groups, Yalom (1995) concluded that interpersonal alienation was a major reason people seek therapy.

Reflections

Choose one or more of the three topics below to consider privately or to write about.

1. How comfortable are you with isolation? Think of the last time you were alone for more than a few minutes without a structured task to do. What did you do, how did you feel, and why?

2. What do you do while alone? How many of these activities are distractions from loneliness and how many are expressions of your wishes and will?

3. Do you ever seek companionship just because you are lonely? Have you ever been lonely even when you are among other people?

Death

Every therapy group is made up of people who are dying. Our lives are finite; we and our loved ones will die. Psychologically, we struggle with this reality by defending ourselves against it, starting early in childhood. As children, we defend against the threat by a belief in specialness (for various reasons, death will not happen to *us*) and belief in the ultimate rescuer, a wondrous parental figure who will save us from harm. As adults, we defend against death in the same irrational ways, perhaps in bigger words.

We also lessen our anxieties about death by leading meaningful lives (by our own definitions, of course). "A sense of fulfillment, a feeling that life has been well lived, mitigates against the terror of death" (Yalom, 1980, p. 208). I come from a family of teachers, and our belief that we have altered many students' lives for the better has given us a sense that we leave a legacy behind when we die. Creative artists, counselors, architects, medical workers, builders, ecologists, and sometimes parents feel similar comfort in how their contributions to humanity and nature will survive beyond their life spans.

Too great a fear of death leads to "a life dedicated more to safety, survival, and relief from pain than to growth and fulfillment" (Yalom, 1980, p. 208). Because pursuit of a meaningful goal usually involves taking risks, both great and small, a person motivated by death anxiety will avoid the pursuit and choose the course of security. In contrast, acceptance of the limits of a lifetime motivates us to use the time we have to create a meaningful existence: to live *authentically*, on our own terms. In a paradoxical way, an awareness of death impels us to live with zest and creativity.

In many subcultures in the United States, discussing death is discouraged, especially discussing our own deaths. A group therapy setting provides a place to ponder deep concerns with mortality without worrying or offending significant others outside the group (Donigian & Malnati, 1997). Greenstein (2000) developed a Meaning-Centered Group Psychotherapy in which people with advanced cancer can grapple with their impending death: "Perhaps, the ultimate usefulness of Meaning-Centered Group Psychotherapy is in helping foster a feeling of connectedness both between people and within each individual, as illness forces him or her to explore those issues that are truly meaningful and important at this critical point in his or her life" (p. 510).

The Counselor and Existential Inquiry

I believe that a group therapist does well to keep the four existential problems (meaninglessness, freedom, isolation, and death) in mind when analyzing a group session's content and emotional tone. One of these problems could be the strand that holds an otherwise scattered discussion together. For example, a counselor was disappointed in a group session that, on the surface, consisted of a series of unrelated and individualistic gripes about the foibles of members' romantic partners. It seemed to him that he was hosting a whining party. Then he realized that everyone was indirectly talking about their problems with isolation and the fact that their loved ones failed to keep isolation at bay. When he was able to suggest this theme to the group, the discussion turned to a more vibrant and more fruitful level.

Many times, identifying the existential content is a technique for "taking groups deeper," a basic leadership skill emphasized by group specialist Ed Jacobs (2004). Jacobs exhorts counselors to process boring, superficial, repetitive, or irrelevant material by deepening the focus through questions. Consideration of the four existential problems can help us formulate these questions, as you saw in the example above.

SMALL GROUP EXERCISES

1. Existential themes are pervasive. To prove this to yourself, brainstorm in your small discussion group to list current songs, films, plays, or novels that have at their heart one of the four existential problems: meaninglessness, freedom, isolation, and death.

2. Convene your group and begin with a period of small talk on whatever topic comes up, for instance, whatever you might discuss at a party or when running into each other at the bookstore. After five or ten minutes of small talk, attempt to come up with some questions that would lead the discussion to a deeper level. Think about the four existential themes to help you formulate questions. Your instructor may ask you to discuss the experience with the class as a whole if time permits.

The Shadow Side: Destructive Factors in Groups

The therapeutic factors of groups operate strongly and dependably, but of course there are other forces of negativity that threaten a group's healthy functioning. McClure (1994) asserts that all groups contain the seeds of their own undoing or stagnation. He discusses four **destructive factors,** characteristics that inhibit a group's growth:

1. **Psychic Numbing**   When members continually conform to principles, opinions, and norms that contradict their own privately held values, they deaden themselves to the tension of the disparity between their inner and outer existence. They become able to participate in discussions and behaviors they morally abhor with little discomfort. This numbing, McClure (1994) believes, creates physical, emotional, and spiritual damage and stops group development in its tracks.

2. **Dependence on the Leader for Direction**   When members are unable to challenge the leader during the early stages of the group's life and choose the role of follower rather than leader, they do not take responsibility for the direction of the group. Thus, they never have to plan, decide, or take risks. This situation can be exacerbated by a leader who enjoys the group's obedience and loyalty and suppresses criticism. If members do not act independently, they remain stuck in regressive, childlike roles.

3. **Group Narcissism**   An unhealthy sense of cohesiveness can develop through hatred of another group or even creation of an out-group to dislike. The group focuses on the deficiencies of the out-group and overlooks its own. McClure (1994) reminds us that often the flaws members loathe in the out-group are the very attributes they themselves disown within themselves. For example, a middle-school clique whose parents are working class may label another clique as snobby and pretentious when the rival clique comes from the upper class and dresses better. The working class girls probably wish they too had money for clothes, but they disown this desire.

4. **Avoidance of Conflict and Dissent**   The three characteristics above all develop partly from a group's punishment of discord. When the group has not negotiated norms for dealing with conflict, dissenters are silenced, and minority views are seen as corrupt or disloyal. The group's range of acceptable opinions is narrowed as it refines its dogma and restricts its exploration of options. Many of the therapeutic factors simply can't operate in an atmosphere that stifles conflict.

The group leader needs sensitivity to dissension and how dissenters are treated within sessions. The leader should model open-mindedness and attention to minority points of view. A sample from a parenting group shows the counselor modeling sensitivity to dissension: "Did we all decide that giving out candy for children's especially good behavior is reasonable? Julius, you look to me like you don't agree. And you didn't have much to say in the discussion. Is there something else we should think about before we decide?"

Reflections

Consider whether you have ever seen any of the four destructive factors at work in a group. What were the outcomes in the group you are thinking of?

Assessment of Therapeutic Factors in Groups

Now that you have read about the therapeutic factors and how you as a counselor will be contributing to them, you probably want to know how to judge how they are operating in groups you lead or belong to.

Group counseling and therapy specialists have developed several ways of concretely assessing what happens during group counseling. I will be introducing these to you throughout this book. Let me begin with a simple system for getting an idea of what is important to members of your group, called the **Critical Incident Report** (Hurd, 1996). At the end of each session, have each member answer three questions on paper:

1. From today's session, describe a situation in which you think you experienced a change in how you usually think, feel, or act. Please describe what happened and why it was important to you.

2. Please rate how important this was to you:

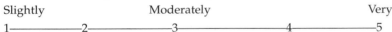

Slightly		Moderately		Very
1	2	3	4	5

3. Was there a time during the group when you think that another group member experienced a change in how they usually think, feel, or act? If so, please describe what happened and how it affected you. (It may or may not be the same event that was important to you.) (p. 44)

Reading these responses will give you an impression of how your clients are experiencing the group, which may be quite different from your own judgment.

Kivlighan, Multon, and Brossart (1996) have developed a way of sorting the clients' responses into categories (including Yalom's therapeutic factors) so that you are able to group their critical incidents into a form easier to handle conceptually. Kivlighan and colleagues boil the incidents down to four overall factors: Emotional Awareness/Insight, Relationship/Climate, Other Versus Self Focus, and Problem Solving/Behavior Change. If you chart the factors session by session over time, you can see whether the group's impact changes over time, and how. The categorization scheme, the **Group Counseling Helpful Impacts Scale,** appears in Table 6.1.

TABLE 6.1
Group Counseling Helpful Impacts Scale*

0=Not at all   1=Slightly   2=Somewhat   3=Pretty Much   4=Very Much

1.	Realized something new about myself	0 1 2 3 4
2.	Realized something new about someone else	0 1 2 3 4
3.	More aware of or clearer about feelings, experiences	0 1 2 3 4
4.	Definition of problems for me to work on	0 1 2 3 4
5	Progress toward knowing what to do about problems	0 1 2 3 4
6.	Feeling my therapist or other group members understand me	0 1 2 3 4
7.	Feel supported or encouraged	0 1 2 3 4
8.	Feel relieved, more comfortable	0 1 2 3 4
9.	Feel more involved in therapy or inclined to work harder	0 1 2 3 4
10.	Feel closer to my therapist or other group members	0 1 2 3 4
11.	Provision of significant material about self and/or interpersonal relationships	0 1 2 3 4
12.	Description-exploration of the personal nature and meaning of feelings	0 1 2 3 4
13.	Emergence of previously warded-off material	0 1 2 3 4
14.	Expression of insight/understanding	0 1 2 3 4
15.	Expressive communication	0 1 2 3 4
16.	Expression of good working relationship with therapist or other group members	0 1 2 3 4
17.	Expression of strong feelings towards therapist or other group members	0 1 2 3 4
18.	Expression of strong feelings in personal life situations	0 1 2 3 4
19.	Manifest presence of substantially new personality state	0 1 2 3 4
20.	Undertaking new ways of being and behaving in the imminent extra-therapy life situation	0 1 2 3 4
21.	Expression or report of changes in target behaviors	0 1 2 3 4
22.	Expression of a welcomed general state of well-being	0 1 2 3 4
23.	Catharsis	0 1 2 3 4
24.	Self-disclosure	0 1 2 3 4
25.	Learning from Interpersonal Actions	0 1 2 3 4
26.	Universality	0 1 2 3 4
27.	Acceptance	0 1 2 3 4
28.	Altruism	0 1 2 3 4
29.	Guidance	0 1 2 3 4
30.	Self-understanding	0 1 2 3 4
31.	Vicarious Learning	0 1 2 3 4
32.	Instillation of Hope	0 1 2 3 4

Emotional Awareness-Insight (average of items 1, 3, 11, 12, 13, 14, 15, 17, 23); Relationship-Climate (average of items 6, 7, 8, 9, 10, 16, 22, 27); Other Versus Self Focus (average of items 2, 24(R), 26, 28, 31); Problem Solving-Behavior Change (average of items 4, 5, 20, 21, 30).

*GCHIS; Kivlighan, Multon, & Brossart, 1996.

Conclusion

In these opening chapters, you have read about abstract principles like cathar-sis and altruism. I have also provided examples of how these principles are made concrete in counselors' and group members' behavior. The abstract and concrete elements are tightly intertwined and work together to produce an in-terpersonal experience that removes barriers, allowing clients to discover new paths to satisfaction and meaning in life.

KEY TERMS

advice   statements meant to influence how someone else behaves or thinks; often given for altruistic reasons

alternatives   advice given in statements of two or more possible ways of dealing with something

altruism   helping others, with unselfish motives and often with self-sacrifice

Critical Incident Report   a standard method for as-sessing what group members consider important in a session or set of sessions

destructive factors   psychic numbing, dependence on the leader, avoidance of conflict, and group narcissism; dangerous qualities that may develop in groups, undermining therapeutic factors

exchange theory   a social psychology explanation of interpersonal behavior, including how we balance what we put into a relationship with what we ex-pect to get out of it

existential factors   universal dilemmas of life, such as grappling with meaninglessness, death, isola-tion, and freedom

existential growth   development of strategies and philosophy to grapple with existential factors

Group Counseling Helpful Impacts Scale   a stan-dard system of analyzing members' reports about positive group events, this scale boils the thera-peutic factors down to four concepts: Emotional Awareness/Insight, Relationship/Climate, Other Versus Self Focus, and Problem Solving/Behavior Change

guidance   an elaborated form of advice, used in problem solving

I/Thou relationship   an association in which one sees a friend or loved one as a whole being, not as an object to relieve isolation or serve other needs

instruction   statements of advice broken down into the steps necessary for success

process advice   statements of advice about the proc-ess of the group as it is being conducted

simple advice   statements about what someone else should do, without elaboration

social interest   concern with the welfare of other people

values   principles, standards, and qualities a person considers desirable

CHAPTER REVIEW

1. Look up definitions and discussions of altruism in dictionaries, on the Web, and in reference books concerning philosophy in order to deepen your un-derstanding of the term.

2. What is the relationship of advice and guidance to the therapeutic factor of altruism in group counseling?

3. For three days, jot down every instance of advice you encounter, given to you or others. Classify each instance according to the four types of advice

outlined in this chapter. Consider whether each instance was probably helpful or not, and why.

4. Choose a friend from outside your class to help you explore existentialism. Summarize the four existential problems from this chapter, and discuss with your friend how these problems manifest themselves in your lives.

5. Why would a group counselor be interested in using the Critical Incident Report and the Group Counseling Helpful Impacts Scale?

FOR FURTHER READING

Frankl, V. (1984). *Man's search for meaning*. Boston: Washington Square Press. (Original work published 1946)

The first-person account of Frankl's years in Nazi death camps, this book explores topics of altruism, values, and existential growth in a gripping narrative. Frankl developed his psychology of human motivation from this concentration camp experience. Many readers have found this a life-changing book, with complex ideas explained in everyday language.

REFERENCES

Adler, A. (1957). *Understanding human nature* (W. Beran Wolfe, Trans.). New York: Fawcett. (Original work published 1927)

Brown, R. (1986). *Social psychology* (2nd. ed.). New York: Free Press.

Buber, M. (1970). *I and thou* (W. Kaufman, Trans.). New York: Scribner's.

Donigian, J., & Malnati, R. (1997). *Systemic group therapy: A triadic model.* Pacific Grove, CA: Brooks/Cole.

Flowers, J. V. (1979). The differential outcome effects of simple advice, alternatives and instructions in group psychotherapy. *International Journal of Group Psychotherapy, 29,* 305–315.

Frankl, V. (1984). *Man's search for meaning*. Boston: Washington Square Press. (Original work published 1946)

Gladding, S. T. (2005). The right to struggle. *Counseling Today, 47,* 5.

Greenstein, M. (2000). The house that's on fire: Meaning-centered psychotherapy pilot group for cancer patients. *American Journal of Psychotherapy, 54,* 501–511.

Holt, H. Existential group analysis. (1990). In I. L. Kutash & A. Wolf (Eds.), *The group psychotherapist's handbook* (pp. 175–190). New York: Columbia University Press.

Hurd, L. J. (1996). A task analysis of change episodes in group psychotherapy. (Doctoral dissertation, University of Utah, 1996). *Dissertation Abstracts International, 57,* 21–53.

Jacobs, E. E. (2004, January). *Taking groups to a deeper level using theories and creative techniques.* Paper presented at the meeting of the Association for Specialists in Group Work, New York, New York.

Kivlighan, D. M., Multon, K. D., & Brossart, D. F. (1996). Helpful impacts in group counseling: Development of a multidimensional rating system. *Journal of Counseling Psychology, 43,* 347–355.

May, R., & Yalom, I. (2000). Existential psychotherapy. In R. J. Corsini & D. Wedding (Eds.), *Current psychotherapies* (6th ed., pp. 273–302). Itasca, IL: Peacock.

McClure, B. A. (1994). The shadow side of regressive groups. *Counseling & Values, 38,* 77–90.

Ormont, L. R. (2004). Drawing the isolate into the group flow. *Group Analysis, 37,* 65–76.

Schuster, E. (1998). A community bound by words: Reflections on a nursing home writing group. *Journal of Aging Studies, 12,* 137–148.

Seligman, L. (2001). *Systems, strategies, and skills of counseling and psychotherapy.* Upper Saddle River, NJ: Prentice-Hall.

Vontress, C. E. (1996). A personal retrospective on cross-cultural counseling. *Journal of Multicultural Counseling and Development, 24,* 156–167.

Yalom, I. D. (1980). *Existential psychotherapy.* New York: Basic Books.

Yalom, I. D. (1995). *The theory and practice of group psychotherapy.* New York: Basic Books.

CHAPTER **7**

Cultural Identity in Groups

I often hear counselors say they're frustrated by the feeling that they are struggling to repair the world one person at a time. As group therapists, we can envision the larger effects of our efforts. We are fortunate to participate in "one of the central adaptive challenges in contemporary society—negotiating intergroup interactions" (DeSteno, Dasgupta, Bartlett, & Cajdric, 2004, p. 323). Categorical membership—what race, gender, class, culture, and subculture a person belongs to—has been newly emphasized in modern counseling theory in the last fifty years or so. The freedoms and constraints of our life situations determine so much of our psychological make-up that mental health professionals consider these conditions in helping others understand themselves, their strengths, and their dilemmas. The differences among us act as teachers. These differences, in my opinion, can even be considered an additional therapeutic factor in group counseling.

Why Do Differences Matter?

"It's a small world," we say, and "People are the same all over." The Golden Rule prescribes that we treat others as we would like to be treated. Sayings like these reflect the commonality among human beings, a commonality that is huge. Our most basic needs, like sustenance, safety, belonging, communication, meaning, and power, are probably shared (Wubbolding, 2000). Personality across the globe is mixed from the same fundamental ingredients: extraversion, openness to experience, agreeableness, conscientiousness, and neuroticism, and their opposites (McCrae & Costa, 1997; Paunonen, Jackson, Trzebinski, & Forsterling, 1992). People universally wish to acquire and keep positive self-regard (Sedikides, Gaertner, & Toguchi, 2003). We all look at the world of human activity as divided up into the same categories: social, enterprising, artistic, systematic, realistic (hands-on), and intellectual (Day & Rounds, 1998). And we all face a common fate, death.

On the other hand, our societal context determines important differences, such as

- how and when we express these common needs, personality traits, and perceptions (e.g., Sedikides et al., 2003);
- how we put them in order of priority in our lives; and
- how free we are to follow whatever inner compass our genes provide us.

The context involves our culture and our personality (which partly derives from culture). Each person exists in a web of demands, some of which are common human demands, some of which are dictated by the mainstream culture where they live, some of which are determined by the subcultures to which they belong, and some of which may spring from unique personal attributes.

We usually describe ourselves in terms of categories we belong to; prominently, we identify our sex. Then, we might list our age, job, geographical location and background, social class, ethnic background, and race. Often, we would describe ourselves by some other categories we belong to that are important to our identity: for example, by homo- or bi-sexuality, disability, school name, religion, fame, political faction, parentage, hobby, ancestry, or other distinctive status. Each member of a counseling group comes in with a blend of categorical memberships and an inner sense of which memberships are meaningful in understanding him or her.

Each of us combines a personal, individual identity with a social, collective identity. **Collective identity** includes membership in family, teams, cliques, schools, communities, countries, gender, ethnicity, and race. A positive collective identity can enhance one's personal identity. One reason for a counseling group's effectiveness may be that the group becomes a new, positive collective identity for its members. Marmarosh and Corazzini (1997) found that an intervention designed to focus group members on their group identity enhanced their personal self-esteem.

Reflection

Think about your favorite fantasies as a child. How were they related to your situation at birth—your race, gender, class, culture, generation, and subculture? Can you think of a friend who had childhood fantasies different from your own, with differences you can trace back to situations at birth?

Do Differences Imply Different Pictures of Psychological Health and Illness?

Existentialists like Yalom (1980) view all of us as struggling with matters of meaninglessness, mortality, responsibility, and freedom. I agree with this conceptualization, so the question is, are categorical distinctions merely colorful overlays on these basic human struggles, or do they really make a difference in psychological terms?

I think that they do make a difference to us as mental health professionals. A core collection of mental health disorders are diagnosed worldwide (Comas-Diaz, 1996): schizophrenia, bipolar disorder (that is, depression with at least one manic episode), major depression, and the anxiety disorders involving phobias, panic, and obsessive compulsive disorder. Exactly how these disorders are acted out, how they develop over time, how they are treated, and whether they improve are matters heavily influenced by culture (including the cultures determined by gender and class). For example:

- Among depressed children, boys are more likely to openly misbehave (externalize), whereas girls are more likely to withdraw (internalize) (Keiley, Lofthouse, Bates, Dodge, & Pettit, 2003).

- In Asian cultures, anxiety is often expressed in terms of bodily aches and pains (Hsu & Folstein, 1997; Tanaka-Matsumi & Higginbotham, 1996), whereas an anxious European might express constant worry instead.

- Low-income clients are more likely to receive brief, drug-centered therapy than their middle- or upper-class counterparts (Lott, 2002) who are more likely to receive longer, insight-oriented therapy from higher-status professionals.

- For both White and Black students who are high achievers, academically advantageous behaviors and attitudes are the same. But these behaviors and attitudes were associated with introjective depression in Black but not in White adolescents (Arroyo & Zigler, 1995).

- Many studies show consistently low use of mental health services by African Americans, Asian Americans, and Latinos, although these groups report similar levels of psychological distress as others in this country (Lee & Ramirez, 2000).

- Empirical studies found that adolescents with physical disabilities have lower self-esteem than able-bodied teens (Specht, King, & Frances, 1998).

- The experience of racism usually results in psychological and physiological stress responses (Clark, Anderson, Clark, & Williams, 1999).

- Newly Americanized children experience role conflict between their immigrant parents' expectations and their own desires (Ponce, 2001).

- A U.S. Surgeon General report concluded that racial and ethnic minorities receive strikingly less mental health care, resulting in a greater disability burden (Smedley & Smedley, 2005).

- In general, people are likely to attribute credit for positive events to themselves and attribute negative events to causes outside themselves. This is called the *self-serving attributional bias*. However, Asian samples displayed significantly smaller self-serving attributional biases than United States or other Western samples (Mezulis, Abramson, Hyde, & Hankin, 2004). Children and older adults displayed the largest biases.

These are convincing bits of evidence that category differences have real effects in the way people experience our world, are treated by others, think about themselves, and behave. These varying experiences will be manifest among the members of the groups you lead. Using them as opportunities for new interpersonal patterns is one of the joys of group leadership.

DISCUSSION IDEA

Brainstorm for additional examples of how categorical differences may affect psychological states. For instance, do fat people and thin people have differing ways of experiencing the world? What special world do strikingly attractive people experience? Do these experiences affect psychological phenomena?

What Is Culture, Anyway?

The term *culture* includes cities and symphonies and weird tattoos, but much more. Culture includes habits of thought, feeling, and behavior that were invented by humans (or other animals) and taught to contemporaries and descendants, but not practiced among all groups of the same species (Begley, 2004). This means that knowledge, belief, art, morals, law, and customs vary among human cultures. So, for instance, happiness is experienced among all humans; but glad, laughing, buoyant greetings on the street are usual only among certain groups of humans, such as the Yoruba of Nigeria. These greetings, then, are part of a tribal culture. The same enthusiastic greeting pattern also may be part of an ethnic culture (the Irish) and a professional culture (counselors). Naturally, not all Yoruba, Irish, and counselors are peppy greeters; the behavior is the norm and cannot predict how an individual will behave when you meet her on the street on any given day.

Culture is sometimes directly connected to racial identity, ethnic identity, and geographical background. Today, we recognize that culture is also a property of sexual orientation, disability groups, religion, economic class, generation, and occupation. This broader definition of culture is synonymous with **diversity,** when we speak of a robust, colorful mixture of cultures as desirable.

Categorizing Cultures for Counseling Purposes

The family is the first teacher of culture. McGoldrick and Giordano (1996) state that "Ethnicity remains a major form of group identification and a major determinant of our family patterns and belief systems." Do you agree? In the following passage, McGoldrick and Giordano describe ethnic traits in a way that was popularized in the late twentieth century:

> Certain common ethnic traits have been described as typical for families of one or another group. For example, Jewish families are often seen as valuing education, success, family connections, encouragement of children, democratic principles, verbal expression, shared suffering, and having a propensity to guilt and a love for eating. Anglos have been characterized as generally emphasizing control, personal responsibility, independence, individuality, stoicism, keeping up appearances, and

moderation in everything. By contrast, Italian American families are generally described as valuing the family more than the individual; considering food a major source of emotional as well as physical nourishment; and having strong traditional male-female roles, with loyalty flowing through personal relationships. African Americans are often described as favoring an informal kinship network and spiritual values. Their strength to survive is a powerful resource, and they tend to have more flexibility in family roles than many other groups. In Hispanic cultures, family togetherness and respect, especially for elders, are valued concepts. People are appreciated more for their character than for merely their vocational success. They may also hold on to traditional notions of a woman's role as the virgin and the sacrificial sainted mother, who tolerates her husband's adventures and absence with forbearance. Chinese families stress harmony and interdependence in relationships, respect for one's place in the line of generations, ancestor worship, saving face, and food as an emotional and spiritual expression. For Asian Indians, purity, sacrifice, passivity, and a spiritual orientation are core values, and death is seen as just one more phase in the life cycle that includes many rebirths. (p. 10)

_____

SMALL GROUP EXERCISE

Do you know families who fit any of the ethnic trait descriptions in the passage above? Do you know families who do not fit the description of their ethnic traits? In your own family, how does your ethnic background affect values and beliefs, if it does?

_____

Many group therapy handbooks discuss multiculturalism in terms of these conventional divisions, as McGoldrick and Giordano did. However, minute by minute such an approach becomes more and more simplistic in our country today. Clear characterizations of people by ethnic or racial category depended in the past on stable, separate, and intact cultures, which we rarely see now. How many generations will experience such clear-cut splits along the lines of cultural traditions? It could be that within the next two generations, people will be thinking of themselves as world citizens due to television and computers, which "penetrate local experience and allow access to information and persons in many other places" (Arnett, 2002, p. 778). This globalization process can be seen in youth cultures in places like India, Japan, and Africa, which share more with each other (and with U.S. youth culture) than with the old local cultures of their own countries. Furthermore, the traditional hierarchy of placing men over women is being toppled worldwide, at least in its most pernicious forms. "The values of the global culture are based on individualism, free market economics, and democracy and include freedom of choice, individual rights, openness to change, and tolerance of differences" (p. 779). The world's youth, except where governments prevent citizens from communicating with the rest of the globe, will probably develop a **complex hybrid identity** that won't be geographically determined.

The notion of biologically distinct racial groups, though still used in some circles, has been discredited among biologists, anthropologists, and experts in other disciplines. "Racial distinctions fail on all three counts [of definition]: that is, they are not genetically discrete, are not reliably measured, and are not scientifically meaningful" (Smedley & Smedley, 2005). When everyday people make generalizations about race, they usually refer to a visible characteristic like skin color, and they are usually confounding it with ethnicity. Ethnicity refers to shared cultural features among a group, which distinguish these people from others—such as language, geography, ancestry, beliefs, religion, values, food habits, and dress. Ethnic groups are not fixed and stable. They change, like other cultural characteristics. Individuals accept new ethnic influences and reject old ones, and their ethnicity is self-defined.

DISCUSSION IDEA

To what extent do people in your classroom possess "complex hybrid identities"? For example, do you switch codes of politeness or conversation according to the cultural setting you are in, without feeling that switching is inauthentic? What problems do you predict that globalization of identity might entail?

Generalizations and Prejudice

In his farsighted text *The Nature of Prejudice* (1954), Gordon Allport provided the **contact hypothesis,** which states that personal interactions between groups can eliminate their prejudices. Allport defined prejudice as "an antipathy based upon a faulty and inflexible generalization" (p. 9). Making generalizations about people is a natural part of human cognitive processes. We depend on generalizations to determine our behavior toward others, especially when we don't know them; for example, we are solicitous about the comfort of elderly people because they belong to a group whom we consider frail. Allport didn't extend the word *prejudice* to these benign biases, though benign biases can also be based on flawed generalizations. *Antipathy* based on generalizations makes for negative behavior ranging from snobbery to war.

Generalizations can go bad in a few major ways, which are often summarized as tenets of social psychology (e.g., Brown, 1986; Stuart, 2004).

■ One is the **fundamental attribution error,** of which we are all guilty. We look at another person's behavior and attribute it to an enduring characteristic of the person—for example, their moral character or basic personality. We look at our own behavior and attribute it to the situation. So, if you overcharge me, you are a cheat; if I overcharge you, I made an addition error on your check because I was distracted at the moment.

▦ A second generalization problem is the **ecological fallacy,** which is assuming that one individual possesses some trait on the average level for the larger population he or she belongs to. My gay friend Nick laughs because people are always surprised to find that he doesn't care at all what he wears; they apply the ecological fallacy and believe that each gay man will have most gay men's sartorial interests.

▦ A third error is the **atomistic fallacy,** in which the qualities of one member are generalized to belong to the whole group they represent. Especially when we are exposed to one or only a few members of a category, we tend to use them as representatives of their whole category. For instance, an adult man who knows very few women well tends to reason by atomistic fallacy that all women share the characteristics of his mother, sister, and wife.

A report of applying Gestalt dreamwork with students and professors at two Taiwan universities was refreshingly honest about faulty generalizations (Coven, 2004). Coven wished to share his enthusiasm for Gestalt theory and dreamwork in groups, which usually involves intense emotions, vivid self-expression, and profuse self-disclosure. He had learned "that Asians are hesitant to share problems and display emotions" (p. 177) and naturally had doubts about whether they would participate fully. He was surprised to find that they were enthusiastic, energetic, and self-revealing in the dreamwork demonstrations: "My expectations that the Taiwanese students and professors would be cognitive and reserved were not validated" (p. 181). If Coven had originally decided that the dreamwork exercises were culturally inappropriate for the Taiwanese, everyone would have been deprived of a meaningful experience.

DISCUSSION IDEAS

1. Give your own examples of the fundamental attribution error, the ecological fallacy, and the atomistic fallacy.

2. As a class, create a group counseling activity that will alert group members to these mistakes in thinking about others. First, create the activity targeted at young adults, as though you were holding it at a college counseling center. Then, discuss how you would hold the group for a high school group and a junior high school group. What problems do you need to predict and plan for, for each age level? Do any of you think that your own visible cultural markers (like age, skin color, or sex) will affect your group counselees' reactions to the exercise you create?

3. Do you believe that this kind of exercise is relevant in all types of group counseling? Why or why not?

Conditions for Making Contact Work Against Prejudice

Allport (1954) defined four conditions under which personal contact reduces prejudice:

- equal status in the situation
- common goals
- no intergroup competition (for scarce or limited resources like food, money, or safety)
- authority sanction (that is, the contact is supported by law, custom, or social atmosphere)

Teams at work, school, neighborhoods, and wars have certainly experienced a lowering of prejudice when they meet these conditions. Looking back at the first six chapters of this book, you can see how a well-run counseling group meets these conditions beautifully. This is why I say that we have an opportunity to improve the world on a significant scale.

As I see it, the common goals and authority sanction are elements established early in a group or maybe even before it meets when the goal is formally announced: "Join a Women's Self-Esteem Group" or "Parents Without Partners." The very fact that members are coming to group means that law, custom, or social atmosphere have given the go-ahead.

The problematic conditions for group leaders are making sure that all members maintain equal status and managing intergroup competition. Early in a group's development, intergroup competition often takes the form of vying for the leader's attention and approval. Later, it may take the form of vying for the center of attention. Inequality and competition are process features for which you must develop antennas because members may be far too immersed in content or their own emotions to notice.

Allport's contact hypothesis has been proven out over the last fifty years in many different research studies using children, adults, various prejudice types, and diverse experimental designs. Of particular application to our pursuits is the idea that an individual will follow a group's norms, so if a prejudice-free environment becomes valued by the group, individuals will not only conform outwardly but also internalize the unprejudiced attitude (Crandall, Eshleman, & O'Brien, 2002). Furthermore, the more highly valued the group is, the more each individual will internalize its norms: "The more desirable the group, the more people will wish to follow its lead" (p. 376). This is one reason why development of cohesion (discussed in Chapter 4) is such an important group task.

Contact with other cultures creates change in surprisingly subtle ways, even outside of our awareness. On a standard perceptual task (judging the length of a line in a frame), Japanese in Japan usually make a certain type of error, whereas Americans in America make a different type of error. In their own countries, they do not usually make the other nation's type of error. However, people who had lived in the other culture (Japanese in America and Americans in Japan) for as little as four months came to make mistakes in the pattern of their host culture, not in that of their own culture (Kitayama, Duffy, Kawamura, & Larsen, 2003). The fact that cultural variations in a nonsocial aspect of behavior like perception can be transmitted through contact is an intriguing prospect in terms of how keenly we affect each other.

Evidence of malleability within individuals also supports the idea that we are not inevitably driven by our original cultural programming. According to a frequently verified generalization, people from the Western world have an individualistic orientation, whereas those from the Eastern world have a collectivist orientation. For example, people from the United States see themselves as unique and autonomous individuals, whereas people from Hong Kong see themselves as embedded in a larger social network such as extended family and ancestry. Although the generality holds true, researchers found that individuals from the United States and Hong Kong endorsed values counter to their cultural description after reading stories that emphasize these values (Gardner, Gabriel, & Lee, 1999). For example, Hong Kong natives endorsed individualism after reading stories that brought up the theme of individualism, and United States natives endorsed collectivism after reading stories that brought up a collectivist theme. Therefore, the situation affected individuals more than their cultural background did— more good news for those of us who strive for change through group work.

Aspirations in Multiculturalism

Given that generalizations such as "The Hispanic family is extremely close" are receding in relevance, what is a counselor of heterogeneous groups with complex hybrid identities to do? The American Counseling Association, the Association for Specialists in Group Work, and the American Psychological Association all require us to seek wisdom about the cultural diversity among our clients. In a recent *Professional Psychology: Research and Practice* article, R. B. Stuart (2004) provides us with twelve forward-looking guidelines that facilitate multicultural competence:

1. Develop skill in discovering each person's unique cultural outlook.
2. Acknowledge and control personal biases by articulating your worldview and evaluating its sources and validity.
3. Develop sensitivity to cultural differences without overemphasizing them.
4. Uncouple theory from culture.
5. Develop a sufficiently complex set of cultural categories.
6. Critically evaluate the methods used to collect culturally relevant data before applying the findings in psychological services.
7. Develop a means of determining a person's acceptance of relevant cultural themes.

8. Develop a means of determining the salience of ethnic identity for each client.

9. Match any psychological tests to client characteristics.

10. Contextualize all assessments.

11. Consider clients' ethnic and worldviews in selecting therapists, intervention goals, and methods.

12. Respect clients' beliefs, but attempt to change them when necessary. (p. 6)

I will expand on several of his points in the following discussion, adding commentary on how they apply to the group counseling endeavor.

Each Person's Unique Cultural Outlook

Prejudgments about individuals from any group can fall far from the mark, partly because each of us is a member of several different groups. "Human beings love to divide the world and its inhabitants into pairs of opposites," wrote Carol Tavris (1992, p. 90). We often hold **mirror-image stereotypes:** opposite notions of two groups simultaneously (if men are warlike, women must be peaceful). Ideas of men and women as opposites are present in ancient Eastern and Western philosophy, in psychodynamic and Jungian theory, in theories that label men *instrumental* and women *expressive,* and in feminist versions of men's *rationality* as opposed to women's *relationality*. Where there is a visible difference, this tendency toward thinking in opposites appears; Westerners' treasuring of individualism must find its mirror in Easterners' value of collectivism. Even parents in discussing their two children tend to describe them in mirror-image terms (Sam is outgoing, but Rashika is shy). However, thinking like this makes differences seem permanent and stable, which limits the amount of potential improvement there can be in relationships and social policies. The mirror-image stereotype also suggests that there is a nice symmetry going on, obscuring real-life inequalities between the opposites.

Reflections

Have you noticed any other examples of mirror-image stereotyping? For example, is a group that you belong to often described in contrast to some other group? Think about the way people talk about Republicans and Democrats, Greeks and independents, rich and poor. Do the mirror-image stereotypes distort reality in harmless or dangerous ways?

You need to encourage members of your group to develop more textured portraits of themselves and each other. In fact, an open discussion of mirror images and their flaws can lead to productive, nonthreatening exploration of the topic. Start the discussion with some less affectively loaded opposites that might be perceived within your current group: for example, working class versus professional class, urban versus rural, morning people versus night owls, spender versus saver, extrovert versus introvert. See where talking about mirror images takes you.

The dialogue below concerns a struggle in a mixed-sex group about the mirror-image generalizations that people of each gender make about each other. The counselors, Dave and Ann, encourage members to examine general statements and personal reactions beyond the level of stereotyping each other.

GROUP TRANSCRIPT: Stereotypes

ANDREW: I mean, men struggle with that commitment [starting a family]. You know what I mean? That's a tough one.

ANN: That's sort of a part of being male. Is that what you're saying?

ANDREW: Yeah, you know it's also a part of being female. It's that that's such a, you know, you only have, you know, a few, certain amount of, a couple, three, one kids in your whole lifetime. And that's just, it's such a, you know, within nine months or within, you know, the second that the, you know, the baby is born, you can, no matter how you look at it, that's just a total life changing moment. You know, an instant where, you know, you take one breath and, and then as soon as you let that breath out everything is different.

ANN: What do you think that does for men? Like, what is that for them. Is there a feeling there that they might have or . . .

ANDREW: Yeah, definitely nervousness, umm, you know, scared, pride, you know, it's reward for, umm, you know for, being alive and for, you know, trying to give life to the, you know to the world and, give back,

you know, there's, there's a lot of different feelings in there. And there's, you know, a whole different range you can get with all of them. So you know . . .

ANN: So do you think those enter into real . . . Like when you go out to meet women, do you think all of those feelings of fear, and pride, and sort of nervousness go into the bar with you. You know what I'm meaning?

ANDREW: Yeah. Absolutely. . . absolutely. I mean it's part . . . For me I don't, you know I'm not . . . that's a long . . . You know, the thing about a baby is a long ways off for me but those, those same feelings about trying to present myself and trying to enter into a relationship, a new relationship that, you know . . .

ANN: They're there.

ANDREW: They're there . . . they're there. Oh yeah.

ANN: So how like. . . what happens with those? So how do you manage those?

ANDREW: I just . . . I don't know. Try to umm. . . try to use them for a positive I guess. Try to umm, you know, use them to my advantage somehow, or just try to recognize that umm, I'm feeling nervous because of, umm, you know I'm worried that I'm going to get, you know, a rejection that night. Or that, you know, I'm going to speak with somebody for a while, think things are is going great and then, you know, ask somebody for their number and then I'm going to get laughed at. Those . . .

ANN: Sort of like what Jennifer's been talking about?

ANDREW: Yeah.

JENNIFER: (Nodding) Mmhmm . . .

ANN: Right? Isn't that what you've kind of heard here?

ANDREW: Yeah. Definitely. You know, we are umm, we are kind of in the same, same boat from the uh, you know, from on both sides of the genders. So you know . . . I just wanted to get back from that same point though . . . It's such a . . . You know, guys worry about that commitment but, on any given day you can find yourself in the opposite, where the man wants to have umm, a child or you know really wants to have a baby and start a family and that he can't find someone to, you know, to uh um, to join him with that, you know, or even if his partner can't join him with that . . .

DAVE: And you have some big time yearnings . . . to find a partner?

ANDREW: Yes . . . yeah. That's uh, that's probably the goal right now. As far, you know, just . . . for living yeah. That's uh . . .

DAVE: And so there's all those guys out there, and then there's you.

ANDREW: Exactly, yeah. And so it's hard for me in particular to hear a lot of the sentiment where, you know, the noncommittal, nonrelationship, you know, not trying to be umm, a father for Brad's point of view, or just not trying to do all of that stuff because

I see that as a set of responsibilities that I'm able to even tap into. You know, good responsibilities.

DAVE: Well there's at least one suggestion that perhaps you're looking for love in the wrong places.

ANDREW: Same, yeah, old song but, it's uh, you know, where to look, I guess, if it were easy, then you know I'm sure a few of us wouldn't be here today. So it's, you know, maybe the wrong places but umm . . .

DAVE: So it's the commitment issue, I mean, I hear that one. But I also hear some resistance, at least part, some of the women in the group, to the whole notion of righteousness and, you know, being right all the time, that there's something about that is of some concern as well.

TALIA: I think it infringes on our space as women to have somebody who is always right.

ANN: Has that happened in here for you?

TALIA: Yes.

ANN: Could you talk a little bit about what had happened.

TALIA: I feel like it didn't happen today, but I guess it was last week.

ANN: What happened?

TALIA: That when I was speaking about my boyfriend and how he always felt like he was right. I felt like Mike jumped on me a little bit.

ANN: Do you remember what Mike said last week?

TALIA: Umm . . . I think it was something like, "Why don't you just give him [the boyfriend] a break?"

ANN: Could you tell Mike what that did, just talk to him for a second about how that was for you when he said that.

TALIA: It made me feel like he didn't respect who I was as a female and as a member of this group.

Thinking About the Example

1. What stereotype of men is Andrew fighting against in the first part of the session? Is this stereotype of men present in your own culture? Do you think that Andrew convinces the group of his point of view? Why or why not? How does Ann help him make his arguments?

2. For a long period, only Andrew and Ann, and later Dave, interact, while others are silent.

What do you think of this? If you were one of the silent members, what might you be thinking? If you were one of the counselors, would you try to include others? How might you do this?

3. Go back to where other group members come into the discussion. Why do they enter the discussion? What changes when they do?

4. You witnessed some interaction from this group in Chapter 5. Has the conflict between men and women in the group changed? If you were the leader, what would you say at the beginning of the next session?

Each Person's Acceptance of Cultural Themes

In child-raising, one of the most potent cultural transmission routes, some people imitate exactly the way they were raised themselves. Some do this on purpose because they believe they were brought up right, whereas some are shocked and chagrined when they find themselves acting like their own parents, and try to stop. Other people make a concerted effort to raise their children in opposite ways from their own upbringing. You probably know both kinds. These are examples of how people respond differently to their cultural backgrounds: accepting, rejecting, and modifying them. The process of accepting cultural givens is called *acculturation,* and people are acculturated at different levels to each of the cultural environments they experience.

Social class provides an illustration. Some people are very proud to be working class and incorporate it into their identity and personal style. Others who belong to the working class rarely think about their class status at all. Their identity and personal style may be tied to some other category they belong to, such as Black, lesbian, or Christian.

DISCUSSION IDEAS

1. Social science experiments have definitively discovered that certain ingredients ensure group hostility:

   - **Ethnocentrism,** setting a higher value on the assets and traits of your group than other groups

▪ **Stereotyping,** believing that groups have quite distinct character profiles

▪ **Unfair distribution of scarce resources** (R. Brown, 1986)

Discuss examples of intergroup hostility that you have seen yourself, and see whether the three ingredients existed. Can these ingredients explain hostility between boys and girls and men and women? Neighborhood gangs? Neighborhood ethnic groups? High school cliques? (Remember that scarce resources can take many forms, not just money—grades, trophies, prizes, attention, praise, opportunity, advancement, and status are resources, too.)

2. As a counselor, how might you see such hostility affecting your therapy groups? Mention both overt and subtle ways that hostility can show itself.

Evaluate the Evidence

Three of Stuart's (2004) guidelines revolve around critical thinking about multicultural differences. This is a time to evaluate what you hear and read thoughtfully and dispassionately. Generalizations made from research results need to be tempered by considering how many people were in the study's sample and how those people were gathered. For instance, a 1980 study stating that it explored "the differences in thinking and social action that exist between members of 40 different modern nations" (Hofstede, 1980, p. 11) was based on a very large number of survey respondents; however, all of them worked for one large multinational business corporation. This study is still referenced in summaries of cultural differences, in spite of the specialized nature of the people sampled. Similar critiques apply to the human samples used in making assertions about intelligence differences among racial groups (for example, Lane, 1994).

The same thoughtfulness should be used when you look at a person's scores on psychological tests. Though we don't usually do standardized testing on counseling group members, we sometimes receive testing results from referral sources. Often, instruments developed in one culture have been used to evaluate clients from another. This may be no problem at all, but it deserves some consideration.

Stuart's (2004) precept to "Uncouple theory from culture" is another matter of critical thinking. The theory of individualistic versus collectivist thought processes, which I discussed earlier in this chapter, serves as an example of what Stuart means. The theory itself is handy in analyzing how any individual looks at the world—no matter whether they are Westerners or Easterners. Does this group member consider herself a unique and independent individual, or an integral thread in the tapestry of her family? How does this individualism or collectivism show itself in her relations to other group members? In "uncoupling" the theory from its connection with geographical groupings, it becomes a psychological variable worth looking at in all people. Another instance of **uncoupling,** then, is that we can think of *machismo* as a value that can exist in non-Latinos and in women. You could probably rate yourself on a scale of machismo (or individualism/collectivism) no matter whether you belong to the groups conventionally associated with these qualities. A similar situation prevails in terms of preferring directive or nondirective counseling. It's an important continuum, but we cannot predict by group membership what any individual will prefer or whether what they seem to prefer will be the most helpful to them.

Stanley Sue (1998), in defining cultural competence among counselors, proposed three desirable characteristics:

- **Being scientifically-minded**   Forming hypotheses rather than working from conclusions about culturally different clients.
- **Dynamic sizing**   Knowing when to generalize and when to individualize in thinking about clients.
- **Culture-specific expertise**   Having specialized knowledge about the cultural groups we usually encounter, including acquaintance with the sociopolitical influences that affect them, and the ability to find this information about unfamiliar cultural groups.

Improve Yourself

In training as a counselor, you have consistently been encouraged to reflect upon the stereotypes, biases, and prejudices that you once considered natural. Research supports the common-sense idea that forming firm intentions and plans not to judge people in stereotypical manners really does inhibit the automatic habits of stereotypical beliefs and prejudicial feelings (Gollwitzer, 1999). In Gollwitzer's study, experimental participants were able to suppress automatic gender stereotypes, negative evaluations of the homeless, and judgments of the elderly by consciously planning to eliminate these biased thoughts when the occasion came up. This is excellent news for counselors who wish to derail their automatic thoughts about diverse groups.

You can broaden your view of human variability by being open to the ample resources available in our society. *The Handbook of Group Counseling and Psychotherapy* (DeLucia-Waack, Gerrity, Kalodner, & Riva, 2004) includes ten chapters about groups that include or comprise multicultural members, and other books in our field provide similar chapters. The Center for Research on Education, Diversity, and Excellence (*www.crede.ucsc.edu*) provides rich material that is frequently updated. Reading essays and fiction by minority and immigrant authors is always enlightening. If the groups you lead frequently include speakers of another particular language, it is respectful and illuminating to learn some of that language—at least the proper pronunciation of names, holidays, and places.

Examine Your Implicit Attitudes

Psychologists have developed measures of prejudice and stereotypes that operate outside conscious awareness or control (e.g., Nosek, Banaji, & Greenwald, 2002). The Implicit Association Test (IAT; a demonstration is found at *https://implicit.harvard.edu/implicit/*) provides a concrete experience of the greater ease of some associations (e.g., old with bad) over others (e.g., young with bad) and the relatively automatic nature of such associations. As a result, it clarifies potential dissociations between your conscious and unconscious attitudes and beliefs.

SMALL GROUP EXERCISE

Movies are an easy and enjoyable way to find out how other people live and think. I will list several that I consider rewarding. In your small group, brainstorm to add more titles (and their multicultural topics if the title doesn't suffice). Make copies of your list for the class as a whole.

A Thousand Acres (1997)
The Banger Sisters (2002)
Beloved (1998)
Born on the Fourth of July (1989)
The Breakfast Club (1985)
Breaking Away (1979)
City Slickers (1991)
Cocoon (1985)
In the Heat of the Night (1967)
The Joy Luck Club (1993)
Kissing Jessica Stein (2002)
Love! Valor! Compassion! (1996)
Mask (1988)
Monsoon Wedding (2001)
Monsters Ball (2002)
Real Women Have Curves (2002)
Saturday Night Fever (1977)
Shall We Dance? (1996)

Beliefs and Change

Those of us who endorse a multicultural perspective and attempt a nonjudgmental point of view on value systems unlike our own eventually experience moral conflicts because our own value systems come into play and we believe that they are right. If we didn't value human equality, freedom and dignity of all, and relief from human misery, we wouldn't be interested in multicultural-ism in the first place (Fowers & Richardson,1996). But what do we do when asked to accept cultural practices that don't share those values, which seem so natural to us? For example, racism, sexism, heterosexism, and ethnocentricity are ingrained in more cultures than not and are expressed in practices such as ethnic cleansing, prisoner abuse, female circumcision, female infanticide, perse-cution of gays and lesbians, and tossing troublesome wives into the fire. Negy (2000) fears that multicultural educational materials too often present "defen-sive and romanticized cultural characterizations" (p. 442). How can therapists challenge practices they see as crippling and oppressive without being "psy-chological colonialists" (Kliman, 1994)? Luckily, such cultures include their own dissidents with whom we can fairly side. Moreover, with globalization will come shared values of "freedom of choice, individual rights, openness to change, and tolerance of differences" (Arnett, 2002, p. 779), partly because these are the expressed values of the countries that energize television and computer proliferation and partly because these values are needed to unify people across cultural and national boundaries.

Fortunately, in group therapy the leader is not the only voice that can argue against practices that disrespect human freedom and dignity. This is one reason that your group needs to develop ways to tolerate conflict openly, without cut-ting it off or ignoring it as we do in polite society. The handling of confrontation is critical. "Controlling the intensity of conflict in a group is a key determinant of its eventual success because excessive curbing of conflict can result in superfi-ciality, whereas excessive conflict can result in alienation" (Merta, 1995, p. 579).

Moving Beyond Victimhood

In this country and most others, women and minorities of various kinds are victimized. Feeling safe from unequal treatment, prejudice, and violence is re-served for a specific slice of the American apple pie. However, the awareness of being a victim or potential victim isn't a life sentence of doormat status, nor is it a license to float on a raft of self-pity and expect special favors. When individu-als wish to excuse their bad behavior through their own victimization (past and present), they irritate and exasperate the rest of us (and the members of their counseling group). Often, their identity as victims blocks the development of a more positive identity for themselves.

Remember that it is extremely healing when a client realizes that his or her suffering is not self-made, that there is an explanation for it outside the individual, in society and culture. Victims of childhood sexual abuse provide moving examples of the huge relief stemming from externalizing the causes of the abuse. Gender- and culture-based therapies make use of these explana-tions as elements in self-understanding and action, not as a stopping place. The word *empowerment* comes up again and again, obviously the opposite of vic-timhood. Empowerment entails developing and discovering competence and self-direction in as many spheres of life as possible, not giving up helplessly or exploiting one's victimized status. In a counseling group that is working effectively, members confront each other when they act too much like victims.

How Cultural Perspective Kindles Insight

One way that we understand ourselves is by contrast with others. We frequently say that we gain perspective by being around people different from ourselves; for example, parents and teachers are often delighted by seeing things through a child's eyes. One of the charms of travel is brushing against ways of life quite at odds with one's own taken-for-granted patterns. I remember an Austrian friend telling me that in her country, women of all classes received government support to stay home with their infants and toddlers, "because mothers' work is important to our country's well-being." This was such a different way of thinking about the matter that I could practically feel my brain ticking.

Even when members look outwardly similar, a group encounter is bound to be multicultural. "The behavior of group members is greatly influenced by their cultural backgrounds in the areas of communication style, relational patterns, and interaction with the therapist" (Tseng, 2003, p. 316). Remember that cultural background includes sets of beliefs and values transmitted through families and social settings. In the United States today, most of us partake of more than one cultural background. Simone, a medical student, came from a background strong in the Puritan work ethic and also strong in Jamaican musical and culinary heritage. As Simone goes through training, she will become enculturated in the customs, manners, and ways of perceiving that are unique to the medical profession. She will blend these cultures into her own unique, complex hybrid identity.

Though sometimes multiculturalism is considered a problem for groups to navigate (e.g., Tseng, 2003), I think that members offer each other new perspectives due to their different backgrounds. For example, a parent who constantly tries to please her demanding eight-year-old daughter can learn from a parent whose culture endorses stricter obedience from children and sees parental dominance as natural. A person whose family avoided competition can observe the inspiriting zest that competition provides for a different family. As we come to understand various ways of living and looking at things, we allow new cultures to enter our own identities and enrich them.

A group's diverse makeup can also help free members from previous prejudices. When social barriers exist between people represented in a counseling group, welcome transformations are likely to occur if the disparate members can be kept in the group. A powerful enemy of prejudice is group effort toward superordinate goals—shared purposes that override differences and require cooperation (Myers, 2001). This has been proven in many research studies. Because cooperative effort is the cornerstone of a therapy group, culture clashes are likely to be negotiated in the service of larger objectives.

The Therapist's Contributions to Cultural Perspective

Today, all counselors, including specialists in group counseling, are trained in multicultural sensitivity. The American Psychological Association (1993), the American Counseling Association, and the Association for Specialists in Group Work all express commitment to diversity in official documents (respectively, *www.apa.org/pi/oema,*   *www.counseling.org/site/PageServer?pagename=resources_ diversity,* and *www.asgw.org/diversity.htm*). We strive to be conscious of the variety of values, styles, and assumptions (including our own) represented in any group we lead (Yau, 2004). This variety is a great source of learning material for everyone in the group. Our interventions make a difference in whether the material is used to the group's advantage.

The counselor models openness to discussion of cultural differences. Pretending to be culture-blind in the service of equality closes the door on opportunities to learn from each other. On the other hand, group leaders must be able to see underlying similarities among disparate people in order to enhance cohesion and universality. Pulling together similar content from various members' remarks is called *linking*, a skill discussed in Chapter 4. Frequently, members from one background believe that they have cornered the market on a certain human commodity.

CHO: My parents are completely behind me in support, as long as it's about academics. Anything else, oh no, they're suspicious . . .

TING: Oh, yeah, that's the Chinese thing. My dad is so narrow, also. School is the important thing, not my artwork or social life.

JACK: Hey, my parents aren't Chinese and they're the same way. They grew up without education and had to work such hard manual jobs that they are trying to make up for it through my schooling.

COUNSELOR: So, parents can emphasize academics for all kinds of reasons. What is your reaction to it? It sounds like Cho, Ting, and Jack all resent it. Anyone else want to chime in on the topic?

The counselor points out commonalities across the cultures of national origin and social class but also invites other perspectives from group members. In a diverse group, it could easily be that someone takes the parents' side in this conflict, and productive discussion can ensue.

Sometimes the counselor's sensitivity to multicultural issues must take the form of *cutting off* or *blocking*, that is, intervening to stop a member from talking. Extreme positions are examples: Members may be unaware that they are hurting the group's progress when they complain about their Puerto Rican neighbors in language full of generalizations, go on about the overall stupidity of Republicans, or speak as though accepting Christ is the answer to all problems. When a member talks at length in terms that are hurtful and inaccurate, the therapist must stop the talk. Usually there is a kernel of feeling that the counselor can redirect to the whole group.

> **BOB:** (continuing after a few similar sentences) It's a battle of the sexes. The feminists just want us to deny our basic nature as men. Yeah, we like to look at naked women, and the feminists are jealous because they're dogs and want to censor everything . . .

> **LEADER:** Bob, let me jump in here. Some people here don't agree with you about what feminism is, and we aren't here to judge different groups. But let's follow up on your idea of feeling like there's a war between the sexes. Everyone stand up. This north wall stands for thinking there's a huge split between the sexes, and this south wall stands for thinking that men and women are more alike than different. Everybody go stand about where your belief on this would be located between the north and south wall. Choose anywhere you like between the two extremes so we can see how we're distributed on this.

The counselor has cut Bob off without cutting him out—that is, his concern is still represented. The intervention also marks a clear break from Bob's tirade by changing to a physical activity, and it will help people in the group envision that there is a range of opinions on this topic, without each person having to speak about it. (Thanks to Ed Jacobs [2004] for the movement exercise.)

SMALL GROUP EXERCISE

Each member should describe elements of his or her cultural background. Discuss what elements are relevant to group counseling, and how. Which elements are visible or easily discernible? Which elements would need to be purposely revealed? Which elements would you think important to discuss with a group you are leading, and why? Were any of you surprised at something you discovered about your classmates?

Commonalities to Keep in Mind

Keep in mind our overall goals. Many of the group counselor's tasks involve concepts of "what is normal, socially acceptable, and valued, and of what facilitates the individual's integration into roles considered personally and socially meaningful" (Dumas, Rollock, Prinz, Hops, & Blechman, 1999). Our own and our clients' gender and cultural backgrounds affect these concepts intimately. However, there are common features that define a core of healthy functioning, regardless of one's background or current setting:

▪ accurate understanding of social expectations;

- reasonable assessments of our own interests, capabilities, and limitations;
- good control over our own behavior;
- cognitive and behavioral flexibility;
- energy; and
- hope for the future (Day & Rottinghaus, 2003).

A common feature of all good counseling is "an appreciation of the context in which problems and solutions occur and a sensitivity to the context" (Coleman, 1988, p. 154). Categorical memberships are certainly contexts. Multicultural competence, from this viewpoint, is unified with general counseling competence.

DISCUSSION IDEA

Elaborate on the six common features listed above. Give explanations of how each one contributes to psychological well-being (or how its lack contributes to distress). From Chapters 1 through 6, choose concepts of group counseling that apply to each of the six features. For example, building and following group norms contributes to a member's *accurate understanding of social expectations.*

KEY TERMS

acculturation the process of accepting cultural norms, standards, values, and identity

atomistic fallacy assuming that the qualities of one member belong to the whole group they represent

collective identity a sense of membership in an identifiable category; family, teams, cliques, schools, cities, countries, gender, ethnicity, profession, and race are examples

complex hybrid identity a sense of self that is based on several different collective identities, not necessarily including geographical, racial, or ethnic categorization

contact hypothesis the idea that personal interactions between groups can eliminate their prejudices against each other

culture habits of thought, feeling, and behavior that were invented by humans (or other animals) and taught to contemporaries and descendants, but not practiced among all groups of the same species

diversity the mixture of several cultures within a setting such as a country, school, or profession

ecological fallacy assuming that one individual possesses some trait on the level that is average for the larger population they belong to

empowerment developing and discovering competence and self-direction in as many spheres of life as possible

fundamental attribution error explaining other people's behavior by their enduring characteristics, while explaining our own behavior by situational demands

linking focusing on commonalities among several statements or sentiments

mirror-image stereotyping a tendency to perceive two differing people or groups as opposites

norm a typical model

prejudice a prejudgment, usually negative, based on a generalization

uncoupling removing categorical labels from meaningful theoretical constructs

CHAPTER REVIEW QUESTIONS

1. Explain how diversity within a counseling group is a therapeutic factor or how it helps develop other therapeutic factors.

2. Write a description of your own and one friend's complex hybrid identities. Show your descriptions to this friend and invite his or her comments.

3. Why are conventional divisions by ethnicity and race becoming illogical in today's world? Give examples.

4. Explain conditions under which the contact hypothesis works. How does group counseling fulfill these conditions?

5. Why is the concept of acculturation important in thinking about diversity in the groups you lead?

6. If you joined a practice that served a population with some collective identities unfamiliar to you, how would you go about educating yourself?

7. What are six common features of healthy personalities worldwide? Can you think of additions to the list of six?

FOR FURTHER READING

Stuart, R. B. (2004). Twelve practical suggestions for achieving multicultural competence. *Professional Psychology: Research and Practice, 35,* 3–9.

This article served as an organizational guide for Chapter 7. In just six pages, the piece summarizes up-to-date thinking about multicultural competence. It also refers to relevant research findings concerning this topic and explains several myths about it. The reference list guides you to many ovular articles on specific ethnic and racial groups.

Fuertes, J. N., & Gretchen, D. (2001). Emerging theories of multicultural counseling. In J. Ponterotto, J. M. Cases, L. A. Suzuki, & C. M. Alexander (Eds.), *Handbook of multicultural counseling* (2nd ed., pp. 509–541). Thousand Oaks, CA: Sage.

These authors review nine contemporary theories of multicultural counseling. A table summarizes the major points of each theory, very useful for background in the area for your certification examinations. The discussion has a decidedly positive slant on all the theories.

Weinrach, S. G., & Thomas, K. R. (2002). A critical analysis of the multicultural counseling competencies: Implications for the practice of mental health counseling. *Journal of Mental Health Counseling, 1,* 20–35.

The authors discuss the Multicultural Counseling Competencies created for the American Counseling Association in 1996. Their critical analysis provides a view that balances the genial stance of the Fuertes and Gretchen chapter (above).

REFERENCES

Allport, G. W. (1954). *The nature of prejudice.* Cambridge, MA: Addison-Wesley.

American Psychological Association. (1993). Guidelines for providers of psychological services to ethnic, linguistic, and culturally diverse populations. *American Psychologist, 48,* 45–48.

Arnett, J. J. (2002). The psychology of globalization. *American Psychologist, 57,* 774–783.

Arroyo, C. G., & Zigler, E. (1995). Racial identity, academic achievement, and the psychological well-being of economically disadvantaged adolescents. *Journal of Personality and Social Psychology, 69,* 903–914.

Begley, S. (2004, May 7). Cultures of animals may provide insights into human behavior. *Wall Street Journal,* p. B1.

Brown, R. (1986). *Social psychology* (2nd ed.). New York: Free Press.

Clark, R., Anderson, N. B., Clark, V. R., & Williams, D. R. (1999). Racism as a stressor for African Americans. *American Psychologist, 54,* 805–816.

Coleman, H. L. K. (1998). General and multicultural counseling competency: Apples and oranges? *Journal of Multicultural Counseling and Development, 26,* 147–156.

Comas-Diaz, L. (1996). Cultural considerations in diagnosis. In F. W. Kaslow (Ed.), *Handbook of relational diagnosis and dysfunctional family patterns* (pp. 152–170). New York: Wiley.

Coven, A. B. (2004). Gestalt group dreamwork demonstrations in Taiwan. *Journal for Specialists in Group Work, 29,* 175–184.

Crandall, C. S., Eshleman, A., & O'Brien, L. (2002). Social norms and the expression and suppression of prejudice: The struggle for internalization. *Journal of Personality and Social Psychology, 82,* 359–378.

Day, S. X, & Rottinghaus, P. (2003). The healthy personality. In B. Walsh (Ed.), *Counseling psychology and optimal human functioning* (pp. 1–25). Mahwah, NJ: Erlbaum.

Day, S. X, & Rounds, J. (1998). Universality of vocational interest structure among racial and ethnic minorities. *American Psychologist, 53,* 728–736.

DeLucia-Waack, J. L., Gerrity, D. A., Kalodner, C. R., & Riva, M. T. (2004). *Handbook of group counseling and psychotherapy.* Thousand Oaks, CA: Sage.

DeSteno, D., Dasgupta, N., Bartlett, M. Y., & Cajdric, A. (2004). Prejudice from thin air: The effect of emotion on automatic intergroup attitudes. *Psychological Science, 15,* 319–324.

Dumas, J. E., Rollock, D., Prinz, R. J., Hops, H., & Blechman, E. A. (1999). Cultural sensitivity: Problems and solutions in applied and preventive intervention. *Applied and Preventive Psychology, 8,* 175–196.

Fowers, B. J., & Richardson, F. C. (1996). Why is multiculturalism good? *American Psychologist, 51,* 609–621.

Gardner, W. L., Gabriel, S., & Lee, A. Y. (1999). "I" value freedom, but "we" value relationships: Self-construal priming mirrors cultural differences in judgment. *Psychological Science, 10,* 321–326.

Gollwitzer, P. M. (1999). Implementation intentions: Strong effects of simple plans. *American Psychologist, 54,* 493–503.

Hofstede, G. (1980). *Culture's consequences: International differences in work-related values.* Beverly Hills, CA: Sage.

Hsu, G., & Folstein, M. F. (1997). Somatoform disorders in Caucasian and Chinese Americans. *Journal of Nervous and Mental Disease, 185,* 382–387.

Jacobs, E. (2004, January). Talking groups to a deeper level using theories and creative techniques. Workshop presented at the meeting of the Association for Specialists in Group Work, New York, New York.

Keiley, M. K., Lofthouse, N., Bates, J. E., Dodge, K. A., & Pettit, G. S. (2003). Differential risks of covarying and pure components in mother and teacher reports of externalizing and internalizing behavior across ages 5 to 14. *Journal of Abnormal Child Psychology, 31,* 267–283.

Kitayama, S., Duffy, S., Kawamura, T., & Larsen, J. T. (2003). Perceiving an object and its context in different cultures: A cultural look at New Look. *Psychological Science, 14,* 201–206.

Kliman, J. (1994). The interweaving of gender, class, and race in family therapy. In M. P. Mirkin, (Ed.), *Women in context* (pp. 25–47). New York: Guilford Press.

Lane, C. (1994, Dec. 1). The tainted sources of *The Bell Curve. New York Review of Books, 41,* 1–2.

Lee, R. M., & Ramirez, M. (2000). The history, current status, and future of multicultural psychotherapy. In I. Cuaellar & A. Paniagua (Eds.), *Handbook of multicultural mental health* (pp. 279–309). San Diego, CA: Academic Press.

Lott, B. (2002). Cognitive and behavioral distancing from the poor. *American Psychologist, 57,* 100–110.

Marmarosh, C. L., & Corazzini, J. G. (1997). Putting the group in your pocket: Using collective identity to enhance personal and collective self-esteem. *Group Dynamics, 1,* 65–74.

McCrae, R. R., & Costa, P. T. (1997). Personality trait structure as a human universal. *American Psychologist, 52,* 509–516.

McGoldrick, M., & Giordano, J. (1996). Overview: Ethnicity and family therapy. In M. McGoldrick, J. K. Pearce, & J. Giordano (Eds.), *Ethnicity and family therapy* (pp. 1–27). New York: Guilford Press.

Merta, R. J. (1995). Group work: Multicultural perspectives. In J. G. Ponterotto, J. M. Casas, L. A. Suzuki, & C. M. Alexander (Eds.), *Handbook of multicultural counseling* (pp. 567–580). Thousand Oaks, CA: Sage.

Mezulis, A. H., Abramson, L. Y., Hyde, J. S., & Hankin, B. L. (2004). Is there a universal positivity bias in attributions? A meta-analytic review of individual, developmental, and cultural differences in the self-serving attributional bias. *Psychological Bulletin, 130,* 711–747.

Myers, D. G. (2001). *Psychology* (6th ed.). New York: Worth.

Negy, C. (2000). Limitations of the multicultural approach to psychotherapy with diverse clients. In I. Cuaellar & A. Paniagua (Eds.), *Handbook of multicultural mental health* (pp. 439–453). San Diego, CA: Academic Press.

Nosek, B. A., Banaji, M., & Greenwald, A. G. (2002). Harvesting implicit group attitudes and beliefs from a demonstration web site. *Group Dynamics, 6,* 101–115.

Paunonen, S. V., Jackson, D. N., Trzebinski, J., & Forsterling, F. (1992). Personality structure across cultures: A multimethod evaluation. *Journal of Personality and Social Psychology, 62,* 447–456.

Ponce, D. E. (2001). The adolescent. In W. S. Tseng & J. Streltzer (Eds.), *Culture and psychotherapy: A guide to clinical practice* (pp. 193–208). Washington, DC: American Psychiatric Press.

Sedikides, C., Gaertner, L, & Toguchi, Y. (2003). Pancultural self-enhancement. *Journal of Personality and Social Psychology, 84*, 60–79.

Smedley, A., & Smedley, B. D. (2005). Race as biology is fiction, racism as a social problem is real. *American Psychologist, 16*, 16–26.

Specht, J. A., King, G. A., & Frances, P. V. (1998). A preliminary study of strategies for maintaining self-esteem in adolescents with physical disabilities. *Canadian Journal of Rehabilitation, 11*, 109–116.

Stuart, R. B. (2004). Twelve practical suggestions for achieving multicultural competence. *Profession Psychology: Research and Practice, 35*, 3–9.

Sue, S. (1998). In search of cultural competence in psychotherapy and counseling. *American Psychologist, 53*, 440–448.

Tavris, C. (1992). *The mismeasure of woman.* New York: Simon & Schuster.

Tanaka-Matsumi, J., & Higginbotham, H. N. (1996). Behavioral approaches to counseling across cultures. In P. B. Pederson, J. G. Draguns, W. J. Lonner, & J. E. Trimble, (Eds.), *Counseling across cultures* (4th ed., pp. 266–292). Thousand Oaks, CA: Sage.

Tseng, W-S. (2003). Clinician's guide to cultural psychiatry. San Diego, CA: Academic Press.

Wubbolding, R. E. (2000). *Reality therapy for the 21st century.* Philadelphia, PA: Brunner-Routledge.

Yau, T. Y. (2004). Guidelines for facilitating groups with international college students. In J. L. DeLucia-Waack, D. A. Gerrity, C. R. Kalodner, & M. T. Riva (Eds.), *Handbook of group counseling and psychotherapy* (pp. 253–264). Thousand Oaks, CA: Sage.

Yalom, I. D. (1980). *Existential psychotherapy.* New York: Basic Books.

PART III

On Becoming a Person

The first category of groups I explain in detail, in Chapters 8 and 9, flows most directly from the common therapeutic factors surveyed so far: humanist and existential groups. These groups are structured more by the people within them than by an outside curriculum, and they draw on the interpersonal powers of the group itself to do their work. They emphasize affect (emotion) and support. For the title of Part III, I have borrowed from Carl Rogers the phrase "on becoming a person," which describes the category succinctly.

CHAPTER 8

Humanist Group Theory and Practice

A Selection from *Carl Rogers on Encounter Groups*

Essential Concepts in Humanist Theory
> *The Phenomenological Stance* ▪ *Innate Striving for Self-Actualization* ▪ *Person-Centered Counseling*

Group Dynamics

Leadership Skills
> *Necessary and Sufficient Conditions of Therapy* ▪ *Therapist Congruence* ▪ *Unconditional Positive Regard* ▪ *Empathy* ▪ *Differences from Friends and Loved Ones*

Techniques in Humanist Group Counseling
> *Listening* ▪ *Nondirective Responding* ▪ *Socratic Dialogue* ▪ *Self-Disclosure*

Problems Addressed by Humanist Groups
> *Saving the World*

Adaptations to Clients' Ages
> *Play Therapy* ▪ *Transitions of Adolescence* ▪ *Groups for Parents and Teachers*

Evaluating Humanist Groups

The positive and constructive side of human life is the benchmark of humanist counseling, rather than the troubled, psychopathological side. An inborn **actualizing tendency** impels each of us toward our highest potential, and an **organismic valuing process** naturally operates, leading us to choices that are healthy for ourselves and humanity in general. We are essentially good, and if we are able to act as trustworthy and genuine beings, we act with **authenticity.** In the following passages, Carl Rogers writes about person-centered group therapy, the major existential humanist approach in practice today. Rogers is the major figure associated with this approach.

A Selection from

Carl Rogers on Encounter Groups

by Carl Rogers (1970)

Because of the unstructured nature of the group, the major problem faced by the participants is how they are going to use their time together. . . . Often there is consternation, anxiety, and irritation at first—particularly because of the lack of structure. Only gradually does it become evident that the major aim of nearly every member is to find ways of relating to other members of the group and to himself. Then as they gradually, tentatively, and fearfully explore their feelings and attitudes toward one another and toward themselves, it becomes increasingly evident that what they have first presented are facades, masks. Only cautiously do the real feelings and real persons emerge. The contrast between the outer shell and the inner person becomes more and more apparent as the hours go by. Little by little, a sense of genuine communication builds up, and the person who has been thoroughly walled off from others comes out with some small segment of his actual feelings. Usually his attitude has been that his real feelings will be quite unacceptable to other members of the group. To his astonishment, he finds that he is more accepted the more real that he becomes. Negative feelings are often especially feared, since it seems certain to each individual that his angry or jealous feelings cannot possibly be accepted by another. Thus one of the most common developments is that a sense of trust slowly begins to build, and also a sense of warmth and liking for other members of the group. . . . Participants feel a closeness and intimacy which they have not felt even with their spouses or members of their own family, because they have revealed themselves here more deeply and more fully than to those in their own family circle.

Thus, in such a group the individual comes to know himself and each of the others more completely than is possible in the usual social or working relationships. He becomes deeply acquainted with the other members and with his own inner self, the self that otherwise tends to be hidden behind his facade. . . . Hence he relates better to others, both in the group and later in the everyday life situation. (pp. 8–9)

OPERATING IN TERMS OF MY FEELINGS

I have learned to be more and more free in making use of my own feelings as they exist in the moment, whether in relation to the group as a whole, or to one individual, or to myself. I nearly always feel a genuine and present concern for each member and for the group as a whole. It is hard to give any reason for this. It is just a fact. I value each person; but this valuing carries no guarantee of a permanent relationship. It is a concern and feeling which exists now. I think I feel it more clearly because I am not saying it is or will be permanent.

I believe I am quite sensitive to moments when an individual is feeling a readiness to speak or is close to pain or tears or anger. Thus one might say, "Let's give Carlene a chance," or "You look as though you are really troubled about something. Do you want to let us in on it?"

It is probably particularly to hurt that I respond with empathic understanding. This desire to understand, and to stand psychologically with the person in pain, probably grows in part out of my therapeutic experience.

I endeavor to voice any *persisting* feelings which I am experiencing toward an individual or toward the group, in any significant or continuing relationship. Obviously such expressions will not come at the very beginning, since feelings are not yet persistent ones. I might, for example, take a dislike to someone's behavior during the first ten minutes the group is together, but would be unlikely to voice it at that time. If the feeling persists, however, I would express it . . . .

I *trust* the feelings, words, impulses, fantasies, that emerge in me. In this way I am using more than my conscious self, drawing on some of the capacities of my whole organism. For example, "I suddenly had the fantasy that you are a princess, and that you would love it if we were all your subjects." Or, "I sense that you are the judge as well as the accused, and that you are saying sternly to yourself, 'You are guilty on every count.'"

Or the intuition may be a bit more complex. While a responsible business executive is speaking, I may suddenly have the fantasy of the small boy he is carrying around within himself—the small boy that he was, shy, inadequate, fearful—a child he endeavors to deny, of whom he is ashamed. And I am wishing that he would love and cherish this youngster. So I may voice this fantasy—not as something true, but as a fantasy in me. Often this brings a surprising depth of reaction and profound insights. (pp. 52–53)

Exploring Carl Rogers on Encounter Groups

1. In his writing, Rogers repeatedly emphasized that person-centered groups are unstructured. In the passage above, he mentions that people find this anxiety-provoking and irritating at first. Why is this true? Have you ever been in a group so unstructured that you were anxious or irritated? What happened to that group?

2. What is "the contrast between the outer shell and the inner person" (paragraph 1)? Do you think this describes everyone? What are some of the facades that middle school, high school, and college students usually feel compelled to wear? What about children: Do you think they are genuine, without facades? What masks do other roles in life seem to require—of mothers, fathers, nurses, teachers, counselors, social workers, managers, secretaries, psychology students?

3. What do you think of the idea that people are more accepted by the group the more real they become (paragraph 1)? Give an example of a time when you have seen this principle in action or when you have seen it fail to hold up.

4. From reading paragraph 2, can you summarize the important changes Rogers believes happen to people due to group therapy? Review the concepts of existential awareness in Chapter 6. Which concepts apply to Rogers's ideas?
5. When you read the specific examples of Rogers's using his own feelings and fantasies, in the last two paragraphs of the passage reprinted above, what was your immediate reaction? Would you like to be in a group where this happened? Why or why not? When counselors have fantasies like this, what do you think they are picking up on?
6. What impression of Carl Rogers as a person do you get from reading his words? List three adjectives that you think describe him.
7. Does Rogers's use of male pronouns seem old-fashioned to you today? When did it become standard to use the plural or both genders in writing about counseling and psychology? What does the *Publication Manual of the American Psychological Association* (2001) say about the matter?

■ ■ ■

A first step in understanding the humanists is to contrast them with what they stood against. Freud thought that humans are born with ruinous drives that have to be suppressed or redirected in civilized society; humanists believe that constructive inborn drives should be expressed and celebrated. Maslow (1968) augmented Freud's conceptions: We have not only the internalized conscience coming from our parents (the superego) but also an "intrinsic conscience . . . based upon the unconscious and preconscious perception of our own nature, of our own destiny, or our own capacities, of our own 'call' in life" (p. 7). Rogers made an analogy between the actualizing tendency and infants' learning to walk; in spite of painful episodes of falling down, the child naturally persists in moving forward toward behavior that signifies maturity and freedom. Obviously, humanism entails an optimistic view of human nature.

Essential Concepts in Humanist Theory

As you can gather from the excerpt reprinted at the opening of this chapter, Carl Rogers believed that the best counseling relationship resembled not a meeting between the expert and the needy but an **existential encounter,** in which both parties behave authentically, without pretense or power plays (Bachelor & Horvath, 1999).

The Phenomenological Stance

The **phenomenological stance** unifies existential, humanistic, multicultural, and most modern psychological theories. This stance contrasts with a strict structural stance like classical psychoanalysis. A structural approach embraces the idea that our psyches can be divided into parts and that different parts need fixing depending upon the type of psychological distress. The structuralist believes that a person's problem can be corralled off and separated from him or her as a person.

In contrast, in the phenomenological point of view, reality is determined by how each individual perceives and understands it, and therefore, reality is different for each person. The counselor strives to enter the client's phenomenological world, seeing both problems and strengths as part of this world. A person's whole being is considered a system, in which each feature influences other features, and a change in one feature changes the entire picture. As you may remember from Chapter 2, a system is much more than the sum of its parts.

The humanist counselor does not purposefully acquire a life history from each client, as therapists of many other stripes do. Early on, Rogers (1940) realized that "Our most profound emotional patterns are as evident in our daily experience as in our past history, as plain in the immediate counseling relationship as in our childhood reactions" (p. 162). A client's whole system of responses is what each one brings into counseling, and this system will make itself clear in the group setting. Just as a fingerprint you leave at an unfamiliar setting will still identify you, your behavior in a group setting is uniquely yours.

Innate Striving for Self-Actualization

The term *self-actualization* is associated with Abraham Maslow and is the pinnacle of his pyramid-shaped hierarchy of human needs: physiological needs, safety, belongingness and love, respect, self-esteem, and self-actualization (see Figure 4.1). Maslow (1968) wrote that self-actualization can be defined in four ways:

> as ongoing actualization of potentials, capacities and talents, as fulfillment of mission (or call, fate, destiny, or vocation), as a fuller knowledge of, and acceptance of, the person's own intrinsic nature, as an unceasing trend toward unity, integration or synergy within the person. (p. 25)

Like Maslow, Rogers viewed self-actualization as an innate impulse. The humanist approach is based on an active, affirmative, growth-oriented idea of human nature. Our distinctive potentials struggle for expression:

> The muscular person likes to use his muscles, indeed, *has* to use them in order to self-actualize, and to achieve the subjective feeling of harmonious, uninhibited, satisfying functioning which is so important an aspect of psychological health. People with intelligence must use their intelligence, people with eyes must use their eyes, people with the capacity to love have the *impulse* to love and the *need* to love in order to feel healthy. Capacities clamor to be used, and cease their clamor only when they *are* used sufficiently. (Maslow, 1968, p. 152)

We naturally move toward self-actualization, though for most people, the movement is a continuous process, an act of becoming that is never utterly completed. Self-actualization is not the same thing as selfishness; it may come in many forms, including self-sacrifice for the betterment of a group or for a spiritual goal, as well as the heights of individual achievement. The humanistic group is an arena for allowing self-actualizing impulses to be discovered and for self-restricting habits to be confronted. This group works against the ways that we limit ourselves in order to feel safe, to avoid taking risks. Trust in self-actualizing tendencies is the bedrock of humanist group therapy, in which all members are treated as naturally capable of helping each other.

Humanists broke away from conventional psychology by examining highly functioning, happy people. Study of the healthy personality, which has long been the province of counseling psychology, is today more widespread in the field, with a strong, well-funded *positive psychology* movement (Seligman & Csikszentmihalyi, 2000). This movement investigates subjective well-being, optimism, the spiritual experience, and similar subjects. These are keystones of humanistic group counseling. Remember to think of these subjects in contrast with therapies that focus on people being sick or broken.

A thwarted need for self-actualization is the source of psychological distress: "If this essential core of the person is denied or suppressed, he gets sick sometimes in obvious ways, sometimes in subtle ways, sometimes immediately, sometimes later" (Maslow, 1968, p. 4).

DISCUSSION IDEAS

1. Do you personally trust in people's self-actualizing tendencies? What are some arguments *against* the existence of self-actualizing tendencies?

2. Do you share the humanist tenet that a human is born good, rather than born as a blank slate or born with good and evil struggling for power? Take a class show of hands to see which point of view is most popular in the room. If time permits, debate the issue.

Person-Centered Counseling

The therapy closely identified with Carl Rogers is called **person-centered.** This may sound odd, because you assume that all counseling is centered on the person. But the term gives us a handle on the unique qualities of this counseling approach. Other approaches you will study are much more technique-centered, theory-centered, and even therapist-centered, and that's the difference Rogers was emphasizing with his choice of person-centered. Person-centered approaches are also called **nondirective** because the group convener doesn't direct the action. The phenomenological basis is clear in the holistic approach of person-centered groups. They emphasize growth and discovery rather than fixing specific problems. Frequently, the clients are healthy in that they have relationships and support themselves (if adults) or manage at some basic level the tasks expected at their age (if children and teens). In each client's case, there is something missing to life. This could be said of all of us.

When we encounter other people at an honest, open level, in a safe environment, positive personal growth is bound to occur, according to humanists. **Encounter groups,** in fact, were popular in the 1970s, a rich historical period for group therapy. These were time-limited, emotionally intense, person-centered experiences; people would go for a weekend encounter in which they would meet in a group all day (and sometimes all night, in marathon groups). The ordinary counselor is not likely to lead groups like these, though they are still available here and there.

It takes a deeply positive belief in the goodness of human nature to organize a counseling group and then enter it as an equal member, with no agenda, trusting that the right things will happen—that is, that curative factors will kick in. The roles, style, and sequence (stages) of each group will be harmonious with the needs of that unique group. Rogers over and over insists that this is the case. "The most fundamental and pervasive concept in person-centered therapy is trust" (Raskin & Rogers, 2000, p. 133). Once an atmosphere of genuineness, expressiveness, caring, and understanding is established among a group, goals and methods will evolve from within it, rather than being brought in from outside by the leader. This is one reason that person-centered counseling in groups is usually taught by example rather than book instruction. The person of the therapist is a critical ingredient.

Group Dynamics

Groups based on humanistic theory are unstructured, allowing the members to grope toward their own potential rather than providing them with a framework (which could potentially be limiting). Though the therapist does not direct or control group development, Rogers (1967) perceived a natural course of events that he could predict after leading many, many groups. This **fifteen-stage process** shows his faith in the self-actualizing tendency of the group if left to its own devices. The word *stages* does not quite capture the overlapping, concurrent nature of the process, but it is useful for description.

1. **Milling around** Members stay on a superficial level of talk. They try to figure out how to proceed with the group, since the leader does not take charge. There is silence, discontinuity, and frustration.

2. **Resistance to personal expression or exploration** Members are ambivalent about whether they want to hear revelations from others or to express their own hidden selves. Whether or not to trust the group is a big question.

3. **Description of past feelings** People are willing to describe feelings existing "then and there," such as how certain situations have made them angry or sad.

4. **Expression of negative feelings** The first "here-and-now" feelings expressed are frequently negative ones toward other members or toward the group facilitator for not leading enough. Rogers speculated that negative expressions test the trustworthiness of the group and leader—whether negativity will be punished. He also thought that being rejected for negative statements is less painful than being rejected for positive ones, and therefore members make the less risky disclosures first.

5. **Expression and exploration of personally meaningful material** Once negative feelings have been expressed without horrible results, an individual takes the chance of disclosing a deeper facet of self. Members show different levels of acceptance and nonacceptance of such disclosures.

6. **Expression of immediate interpersonal feelings in the group** In an increased climate of trust, expressions of present feelings toward each other arise. Rogers gives several examples: "I feel threatened by your silence"; "You remind me of my mother, with whom I had a tough time"; "To me you're like a breath of fresh air in the group" (p. 266).

7. **Development of a healing capacity in the group** A number of members show ability to deal with others' pain and suffering in a naturally therapeutic way. Members with this intuitive capacity act as models for others. Rogers believed the ability was much more common than we usually assume.

8. **Self-acceptance and the beginning of change** Individuals become closer to their own feelings and accepting of their needs. According to Rogers, this authenticity is the basis for openness to experience and change.

9. **Cracking of facades** Concurrently with the other processes described here, the group demands that each individual drop his or her social masks.

10. **Individual receives feedback** Because of increasing genuineness, each member gets important information about how they really appear to others.

11. **Confrontation** In Rogers's terms, confrontation is an intense form of interpersonal feedback, in which one member levels with another one about his or her perceptions and judgments. This can be positive or negative, more often negative.

12. **Helping relationship outside group sessions** The groups Rogers was holding when he developed the fifteen stages allowed for members to spend time listening and talking outside of group sessions. Rogers saw this as a healthy occurrence. Many kinds of groups today discourage members from socializing outside of the group, for several reasons.

13. **Basic encounter** Throughout the processes just described, people get closer to each other and experience a directness of contact that is unusual in everyday life. Rogers wrote: "This appears to be one of the most central, intense, and change-producing aspects of such a group experience" (p. 270).

14. **Expression of positive feelings and closeness** Warmth, group spirit, and trust grow as members feel affirmation of the positive sides of themselves, even from people who know their worst sides.

15. **Behavior changes** Changes in behavior within the group grow throughout the trust-building process. The final test of the group's transformative experience is how the members translate it into their behavior in the rest of their lives. People report subtle as well as drastic improvements interpersonally.

Leadership Skills

The skills of the leader in humanistic group work seem to me almost personality characteristics rather than skills. The leader must be a certain type of person, more than anything else, to assist such a group in their self-determination. You have probably been thinking, while reading this chapter, about whether you would be a good humanist group counselor. From my reading and observation, I have made up a list of questions to ask yourself and discuss with your friends and classmates. The answers will guide you in whether you would enjoy practicing and prosper as a humanist group therapist.

- Do you talk with strangers, like your seatmates on an airplane or bus? That is, do you enjoy conversation that has no defined point, no personal advantage, no ulterior motive?
- Do you remember the details of people's stories even without reason to do so? Do you think about such stories later?
- Do you stay in touch with friends from the past?
- Do you become absorbed in movies and novels?
- When about to enter a strange social situation, do you look forward to it or feel nervous or dreadful? Do you like the unpredictable nature of social situations?
- Do you have a generally positive view of human nature?
- What types of people do you have a hard time being tolerant of? What do you do about this?
- Do you have a reputation for staying calm in turmoil? For taking criticism calmly?
- In your inner life, is there an easy translation between feelings and ideas? Or do you prefer to keep them separate?

Think about your discussions and thoughts on these matters as you read the next section on Carl Rogers's descriptions of the conditions you must engender for this type of counseling group to fulfill its mission. Keep in mind that not everyone is cut out for this type of work; a different theory and approach may suit your personality better.

Necessary and Sufficient Conditions of Therapy

Rogers's most famous and controversial assertion concerned what he called the **necessary and sufficient conditions** of therapy. By *necessary*, he meant that constructive change cannot happen unless these conditions are present. By *sufficient*, Rogers meant that no other theoretical backing or technical skills need to be applied to a case. Improvement will come about naturally if his six conditions are met. The *sufficiency* assertion is much more controversial than the *necessary* one. Rogers derived his list not only from his memory, notes, and observations but also from analysis of audiotaped sessions. It was not until the 1940s that this technology was used as a research tool, and Rogers was a pioneer. The ability to review taped sessions allowed researchers to analyze much more accurate data than their memories, notes, and impressions could provide.

I will quote directly from Rogers's (1957) article in which he listed the six conditions. For constructive personality change to occur, it is necessary that these conditions exist and continue over a period of time:

1. Two persons are in psychological contact.
2. The first, whom we shall term the client, is in a state of incongruence, being vulnerable or anxious.
3. The second person, whom we shall term the therapist, is congruent or integrated in the relationship.
4. The therapist experiences unconditional positive regard for the client.
5. The therapist experiences an empathic understanding of the client's internal frame of reference and endeavors to communicate this experience to the client.
6. The communication to the client of the therapists' empathic understanding and unconditional positive regard is to a minimal degree achieved.

No other conditions are necessary. If these six conditions exist, and continue over a period of time, this is *sufficient*. The process of constructive personality change will follow. (p. 96, italics mine)

Items 3, 4, and 5 describe qualities of the therapist. You will often see references to Rogers's *three* **facilitative conditions,** and these are **congruence** (also called *genuineness* or *authenticity*), **unconditional positive regard** (*nonpossessive warmth*), and **accurate empathy** (*understanding*). The facilitative conditions are sometimes labeled with shorthand terms, "the core conditions" or "the conditions." (Items 1, 2 and 6 are contextual variables and are less often debated.) Later in Rogers's life, he became mostly involved in group rather than one-on-one counseling and extended the conditions to that setting as well. In group therapy, the group leader takes advantage of the infectious nature of modeling: He or she demonstrates the three facilitative conditions, and group members consciously or unconsciously imitate them in the way they relate to each other.

Therapist Congruence

The therapist must present him or herself as a person (in contrast with playing a role as teacher or confessor). Congruence is "the opposite of presenting a facade, either knowingly or unknowingly" (Rogers, 1957, p. 97). The counselor's feelings, thoughts, and actions are not at odds, though all his or her thoughts and feelings are not expressed. For example, when a group member declares that she's finally found Mr. Right, you as a group leader might inwardly groan, but you would probably decide not to voice your reaction. Your decision is not a breach in congruence because the thought is not *at odds with* your behavior; it is just not appropriate at the time. The incongruent response would be, "That's wonderful! You deserve the right guy after all your turmoil." This response is incongruent, inauthentic, and ungenuine. In this situation, it would be desirable to let another group member express her doubts about Mr. Right Number Twelve. A process of selection constantly operates during your sessions. Therapist incongruence would be exemplified by your saying, "I am so happy for you," when you really doubt that the new Mr. Right is any better than his predecessors. A Rogerian would maintain genuineness by saying something like, "Tell me, how would you define 'Mr. Right'?" Another Rogerian might choose an honest personal response (a self-disclosure), like, "It seems to me that this label 'Mr. Right' puts a lot of responsibility on his back. Is this new relationship carrying more weight than it can hold?"

In child therapy, children act impulsively and call forth some kind of reaction; the counselor's congruence is often tested (Ellinwood & Raskin, 1993). Landreth (2002) explores the dilemma of a child-centered therapist who nonetheless must set limits on dangerous behavior:

> If the therapist's attitude really is one of trust and a belief that the child will respond responsibly, then the therapist will respond accordingly with calmness. The fact of the matter is that if a child is standing 10 feet away from the therapist threatening to shoot the therapist with a dart gun, the therapist cannot move fast enough to get across the room and stop the child before the trigger is pulled. Therefore, the therapist may as well sit there with calmness and trust that if she responds appropriately, the child will respond responsibly. If the therapist were to jump out of her chair and attempt to grab the gun, her behavior would communicate a message of, "I don't trust you." The child is then left to carry out the original intent because, "She really expects me to." Such moments of intense interaction can be anxiety-provoking for the therapist and quickly reveal deeper attitudes, beliefs, and motivation. Inexperienced play therapists should not be discouraged, however, if they experience some anxiety or perhaps even a bit of rejection of the child who persists in pushing the limit, threatening or verging on actually breaking the limit. There is only one way the therapist can learn that children really can be trusted in such situations and that is to "weather the storm" and in the process discover children really can and will control their behavior if responded to appropriately. (p. 247)

To many clients, therapist congruence and genuineness are not only judged within a session. Singh and Tudor (1997) offer a multicultural point of view on therapist congruence, emphasizing that many clients look at the genuineness of a leader not only within a session but also in how the therapist behaves as a member of the community, in everyday transactions and social action. "This perspective is not unusual in . . . societies in which the therapist/healer/sha-man/wise woman/man is both a part of and separate from their society: an accepted and respected outsider" (p. 40). Such a consideration is critical when you play several roles in a culture, such as being a college entrance counselor, a teacher, a speech team coach, and a group counselor, all in one school—or a nurse on a ward as well as a group counselor in a hospital. Your honesty and straightforwardness at the local convenience store or insurance office are part of your professional congruence. The consistency of your behavior in your various roles will affect how group members judge your congruence.

Unconditional Positive Regard

Unconditional positive regard is what you feel when your infant in your arms stares into your eyes or when your dog sees you picking up the leash for a walk in the snow. We seek this delicious acceptance from other people and rarely get it. It entails "a warm acceptance of each aspect of the client's experience as being a part of that client . . . no *conditions* of acceptance, no feeling of 'I like you only *if* you are thus and so'" (Rogers, 1957, p. 97). Such an acceptance is especially curative when clients are used to *conditional acceptance*—"You are a good son if you take over farming our land"; "I will love you if you move up in your corporation"; "Daughters of mine don't drink"; "I will leave you if you continue to be anxious."

The counselor will stick with the clients when they flounder at their job, decide not to farm, keep drinking too much, or continue to be anxious.

> The client-centered therapist respects the client's self-directing abilities and consistently evidences respect for these abilities in practice. This philosophy holds, in unabated and perhaps more dramatic forms, when children are the clients, because children are commonly regarded and treated as immature, not responsible, not knowing enough, requiring guidance and supervision, and needing to be molded. (Ellinwood & Raskin, 1993, p. 259).

The same could be said for adolescents and even college students, and for adult clients who have been *infantilized*—that is, treated as though they were children. The trust that counselors and other group members show them may be the first suggestion that they are, indeed, trustworthy (Seligman, 2001).

Within a session, positive regard is often shown by a sympathetic rewording of what the client has said and by background verbalizations of "uh-huh" and "mmm-hmm." Through analyzing tape recordings of a long-term treatment, Truax (1966) found that Rogers selectively applied these positive reinforcements, giving them when the client spoke in a style similar to Rogers's, about

R e f l e c t i o n s

Who is the person for whom you feel the   What are the limits of your unconditional
most unconditional positive regard? Why?   regard for this person?

the same types of content. True to learning theory, the client over time did more of these things, having learned what Rogers liked to hear. Truax's study tells us that we do control group members' behavior even in nondirective therapy, by reinforcing certain types of talk.

Listen to your own tapes and be aware of how your patterns reinforce your group members. For example, if you take a great deal of comfort from the spiritual side of life, you may be subtly reinforcing these values when your clients speak of spiritual matters. You may *not* respond at all when your clients speak in a self-oriented way about their worldly ambitions and secular ethics. This would be a subtle imposition of your own values on your clients, outside of your awareness. Remember that the whole group is likely to follow your lead.

Empathy

In the jargon of today's youth, a sentence that catches my ear is, "She *gets* me" or "He *gets* me." This charming turn of phrase means that "She" or "He" has empathy for the speaker. To have empathy is "to sense the client's anger, fear, or confusion as if it were your own, yet without your own anger, fear, or confusions getting bound up in it" (Rogers, 1957, p. 99). The same goes for the client's happiness, success, and hope. The empathetic counselor tries to see the world from the point of view of people in the group, entering their phenomenological world. When a client feels this understanding, she feels "really free to explore all the hidden nooks and frightening crannies" of her experience (Rogers, 1961, p. 34). Freedom is an outgrowth of receiving accurate empathy. Ardent, responsive attention to group members' thoughts and feelings means that we *get* them.

The redemptive view of human worth exemplified by qualities like empathy and warmth might seem questionable in the light of real-world problems, but Rogerian conditions have research support for application to tough problems. In one experiment (Truax, Wargo, & Silber, 1966), lower-class teenaged girls who had misbehaved severely enough to end up in a correctional facility were divided into a group that received therapy from a counselor high in accurate empathy and nonpossessive warmth and a control group who received the minimal treatments the institution offered. The girls offered accurate empathy and nonpossessive warmth spent significantly more time out of the institution in the year after treatment, had significantly reduced scores on delinquency-related personality tests, and showed increased congruence between self-concept and ideal self.

SMALL GROUP EXERCISE

Sometime in the coming week, encourage a friend to talk to you about a tough decision, a dilemma, or a disappointment they encounter. Attempt to listen with full attention and empathy, without turning the conversation to your own similar problems. After the experience, jot down honestly what it felt like for you and what kind of things ran through your head. Bring your jottings to your small group and discuss what you have learned.

Differences from Friends and Loved Ones

Genuineness, unconditional positive regard, and accurate empathy are found in many affectionate relationships. Your best friends, your spouses, and your chosen social group come through with these qualities. So you may wonder, "Why would I need group counseling? Why can't I just talk with my friends about my problems?" Rogers (1957) provided an answer to such questions:

> For brief moments, at least, many good friendships fulfill the six conditions. Usually this is only momentarily, however, and then empathy falters, the positive regard becomes conditional, or the congruence of the 'therapist' friend becomes overlaid by some degree of facade or defensiveness. Thus the therapeutic relationship is seen as a heightening of the constructive qualities which often exist in part in other relationships, and an extension through time of qualities which in other relationships tend at best to be momentary. (p. 101)

From this viewpoint, the best friends, families, and gangs of your clients usually have some stake or personal advantage or disadvantage in what the clients think, feel, and do, whereas counseling group members are usually people less affected by each other's behavior outside of group, at least in the long term. They can afford to be more honest and direct. Consider, for example, a man's choice not to take over the family farm: His family, his friends, his fiancée, and his workmates far away from the farm all have their own wishes about his decision. His counseling group can more clearly focus on the situation he's facing.

Techniques in Humanist Group Counseling

Rogers (1970) was emphatically anti-technique: he eschewed structured exercises, guided drama, homework, interpretive remarks, analyses, plans, and gimmicks. These go against the natural processes that he trusted to operate in a group. However, this did not prevent the proliferation of books, videotapes, and cassettes on Rogerian and person-centered techniques. It's true that there are techniques that go along with focusing on the organismic tendencies of the group. In humanistic therapy, as we know, group members do learn to behave in certain ways consistent with self-discovery and altruistic bonding, and they learn from the therapist's model first. The group leader stays alert for appropriate moments to model the therapeutic conditions of empathy, warmth, acceptance, and genuineness discussed above, for example. As the person in the group least tied up in his or her own problems, the leader is usually most able to decide when to seize which moment as a learning opportunity.

Listening

With around fifty years of contribution to person-centered development, Godfrey Barrett-Lennard (1988) puts primary emphasis on sensitive or empathic listening as a healing technique:

> Sensitive listening refers broadly to listening in which individuals feel that their communication—and thus potentially their inner self—is heard and understood. Such listening is not only directed to the other's intended verbal messages but also, as Rogers illustrates, to messages that come in other ways, perhaps without clear awareness on the sender's part. In sensitive listening, one is receptive to the full spectrum of the other's experience. The other person feels that you have tuned in, that you have indeed heard him or her, perhaps that you may almost know at this moment how the other's world is. Generally this is also accompanied by a feeling of being prized or accepted and trusted. This is so because this particular kind of listening, in its full expression, is rare and implies that the listener is not standing apart but is close to the point of touching the other's understanding. (pp. 416–417)

From Barrett-Lennard's description, you can see how empathic listening relates to the development of a humanistic group. He outlines four effects of sensitive listening, which I will summarize and exemplify:

1. **Personal healing and growth** By being properly heard, we hear ourselves less fearfully and more clearly. In one group, a woman spoke of her boyfriend's Internet habit with such a strong hostile tone that two other women mentioned the emotional force behind her words. She said that she never before realized how strongly she felt about this habit, because if she did she feared she would have to fight with him about it. Other group members concurred that sometimes it seemed easier to pretend to be less bothered rather than start an argument that might lose them a relationship. Barrett-Lennard commented on such an aspect of listening: "Just the fact that our experience has made sense to someone else can help it to make sense to us" (p. 419).

2. **Relationship enrichment** Within an established relationship among group members, reciprocal listening can enhance the quality of relationships. In experiments with age-integrated group psychotherapy, Lewis and Butler (1986) brought together elderly, adult, young adult, and teenaged members. They found that the members grew to reject stereotypes of "old" and "young" as the generations listened to each other. All the members found new kinds of relationships possible. This type of relationship is critical in the modern

world, where personal associations across age groups are often nonexistent or power-laden.

3. **Tension reduction and problem solving** The presence of good listeners can improve distressed relationships. Often, when two members are unable to listen to each other because their relationship has deteriorated, other members can take the concerns of both sides seriously and help lead the disputants to more open positions.

4. **Knowledge advancement** In-depth communication can help us all shed our presuppositions about human nature and clear the filters through which we view behavior. We usually do *closed-circuit listening* in which we pay attention to certain types of signals in a predetermined band of meanings. Sensitive listening, in contrast, promotes expansion of new understandings. For example, I have to admit that the first time I really listened to the conversation of people on the opposing end of the political spectrum from mine was in a therapy setting, where I had to! Previously, I had lumped them all together with radio and television pundits on their side. I found, naturally, that this lumping-together was erroneous.

DISCUSSION IDEAS

1. Think of a time when you noticed that you weren't really listening to what someone was saying. What were you doing instead? Why were you not listening? Come up with some ideas about what causes poor listening.

2. Discuss what one can do to become a better listener. Be as specific as you can—for example, what body posture does an intent listener have? How could you clear your mind of distracting concerns?

Nondirective Responding

The word **nondirective** describes an approach of equality and genuineness when leaders listen to group members. Person-centered therapists "tend to avoid evaluation . . . do not interpret for clients, do not question in a probing manner, and do not reassure or criticize clients" (Raskin & Rogers, 2000, p. 137). The relationship among clients and counselors, ideally, is one that the clients have probably not experienced before: it is a new type of relationship, not a repetition of old ones. People do tend to give others advice in the face of a problem, as you saw in Part I of this textbook.

Nondirective techniques create a psychological environment favorable to growth as a person. These techniques include

▪ asking of **open questions** (avoiding questions that elicit yes-or-no answers),

- reflections of emotion and meaning (often referred to as **reflection of feeling**),
- paraphrases,
- background support like *umm-hmm* and *I see*,
- and repetition of key words.

Language style is very contagious—think of how easily you pick up your close friends' patterns of talking—so your nondirective responding will be imitated by people in your therapy group. They will soon start exploring rather than fixing.

Rogerian therapy is frequently ridiculed for formulaic, superficial response patterns that are mere repetitions:

> CLIENT: I cheated on my college entrance exams.
>
> THERAPIST: So, I hear you saying that you cheated on an important exam. How did that feel?

Research shows that clients really do not like such unnatural-sounding, repetitive empathic communications (Reisman & Ribordy, 1993). These communications are found mostly in popular humor, not in group sessions.

Gendlin (1961) explained that "A good client-centered response formulates the *felt, implicit* meaning of the client's present experiencing" (p. 240). Given that there are many responses to a client statement, including silence, experienced therapists choose which response to give. Consider these two examples:

> CLIENT 1: No one likes me.
>
> THERAPIST 1: You've felt rejected lately.
>
> CLIENT 2: My parents won't let me do anything.
>
> THERAPIST 2: What would you like to do?

The counselor knows from earlier talk and from the emotion displayed in the client's nonverbal language that the client does have friends and acquaintances. In responding, Therapist 1 reflects not the actual words of the client but their meaning. He also steers the discussion toward a specific thing that happened, away from the client's overgeneral kicking of himself. Therapist 2 asks a question that brings the discussion strongly into the client's realm. This shows skill; many beginning counselors might ask about how the parents restrain Client 2 or how Client 2 has tried to solve this problem before—in both responses, letting the topic slip into the past instead of the here-and-now.

Therapist 2 chooses *which part* of a client's utterance to reflect. Leona Tyler (1969) suggested, "In making this instantaneous decision about what to respond to, one general principle is useful. Whenever the client's remarks have involved two or more persons, try to respond in terms of *his* side of the relationship rather than that of someone else" (p. 39). In the exchange above, the counselor stressed *you*, the client, rather than those people that don't like him. The counselor could choose to ask, "Who doesn't like you?" or to reassure, "Oh, surely someone likes you," but these responses are not client-centered. The client-centered remark, "You've felt rejected lately," opens the conversation to understanding the client, instead of leading to more exposition on other people's feelings. By modeling this focus on members and not on outside parties, you reinforce the here-and-now nature of the counseling group. You also keep the conversation from straying into parallel story-telling, which can be superficial.

SMALL GROUP EXERCISE

For each group member statement below, role-play three ideas for counselor's responses. Remember that you can respond by inviting other group members to react. If time permits, experiment by giving bad responses and see what happens in your mock group.

1. "My parents only care about my grades. They don't even know my friends' names. It's always grades, grades, grades."

2. "My best friend had to move 1,100 miles away. She acted like it's no big thing because we can e-mail every day, but I don't know how I can make it without seeing her every day."

3. "Things at work will be 100 percent better when we get rid of our current supervisor. He's an idiot."

Socratic Dialogue

I have been struck when listening to humanistic therapists at work by how much they use Socratic method. You may remember the question-and-answer method of Socrates that Plato recorded in *Dialogues* (c. 350 B.C.). Many people use the term **Socratic dialogue** loosely, to mean a teaching method that consists of asking students questions to assess their knowledge. Specifically, Socratic dialogue is a way of exploring, cooperatively, assumptions that lie under everyday behavior, perceptions, and judgments. Through Socratic questioning, we uncover and articulate views and knowledge we already have, knowledge bases that we usually don't recognize out loud or that we have never put into words or brought to awareness. (You have probably read the *Meno*, in which an uneducated slave boy comes up with the Pythagorean theorem under Socrates' gentle questioning.)

The Socratic method involves systematic reflection on experience, leading to insights about one's life and values. It is humanist in that truth is sought through investigating the experiences of participants, not through appeal to experts. This kind of questioning keeps turning over the assumptions and cause-and-effect reasoning behind group members' statements, fears, and anxieties.

For instance, the woman who was surprisingly angry about her boyfriend's Internet habit was pressed to investigate why she didn't let herself feel how mad she really was, and she realized that she didn't want to have a fight. Why not? Because she was afraid the fight would lead to the end of the relationship. Would it do that? Why? And so forth. This is a method of sympathetic inquiry that can be modeled by you as a counselor and learned by group members. Remember that you must take care not to interrogate harshly, which is not the style of Socrates but of professors at elite law schools.

Self-Disclosure

How much of your inner reactions do you express as the counselor in group therapy? **Self-disclosure** refers to a counselor's talk in session about her own thoughts, feelings, and experiences. Because of the **genuineness** condition of humanistic counseling, the Rogerian therapist is encouraged to self-disclose in certain contexts. Personal responses to what the clients say, for example, are considered signs of genuineness. Seligman (2001) suggests that self-disclosure should (1) serve a therapeutic purpose, (2) be short, (3) fit in smoothly with the thoughts being expressed by the client, (4) focus on the client, not the counselor, (5) provide immediate reactions to client material, not highly charged personal information like a history of sexual abuse, and (6) reflect caring and acceptance of the client. An example might occur when a group member says, "I hate myself," and the therapist responds, "I'm shocked to hear you say that. I've heard you say things you like about yourself."

Research does not support Seligman's (2001) good, clear guidelines. Knox, Hess, Petersen, and Hill (1997) analyzed thirteen clients' reports of therapist self-disclosures that they found helpful. These clients most often cited their counselors' giving personal information from the past, not reactions immediate to the therapeutic relationship at the time. The clients found helpful their counselors' talk about their own families, leisure activities, or experiences similar to the clients'. The immediate type recommended by Seligman and others was *never* cited as an example of a helpful self-disclosure in the research study. The positive consequences of the helpful self-disclosures reported by the clients were insight or a new perspective, improved or equalized therapeutic relationship,

R e f l e c t i o n

Would you tell your group clients your marital status? Your sexual orientation? Your criminal history, or your experience with mourning? What factors would go into your decisions about these disclosures, and other ones? If you have experience in group counseling, what kinds of disclosures have clients requested? What did you decide to do, and what do you think eventuated from your decisions?

and use of therapist as role model to make positive changes or increase client self-disclosure. For example, in one group for women with relationship problems, members became visibly more relaxed when the counselor disclosed that though she was happily married now, in the past she had gone through two divorces herself. The women felt that she would be less judgmental toward them because she had had her own relationship failures.

The following example comes from an adolescent group making the transition to a new high school. The humanist counselors, Dave and Ann, use several of the techniques described above as they help the teenagers explore their situations and emotions.

GROUP TRANSCRIPT: Exploration

RAMSAY [talking about having to work all the time]: Well, you've got the problem with, you feel bad that you can't hang out, you feel bad that there's like, that you're friends with someone, but you never really get to do anything with them. So like, it's kind of like a false friendship. But like, you're kind of just holding onto it.

ANN: I wonder if that happens for you Monica, too. I know you talked last week about not wanting to bring kids home because it's, you're in a foster home. Is that sort of similar to what Ramsay was saying about not bringing your friends home or . . .

MONICA: Yeah it's just . . . It's hard because I don't really like know how to introduce them to my friends and . . . like I'm worried that my friends will see . . . you know, just think that there's something wrong with my whole family just because of my parents.

ANN: Yeah.

DAVE: Yeah, like you can't even really introduce your foster mother as your mother. Just simple things, like introductions like that are hard.

ANN: Sort of where we started with you guys. Where are you guys at with this?

CHRIS: I don't know like, seems like I can get friends kind of easy. But, I don't know whether like, if I'm just going to, if they're just kind of like taking advantage of me.

Like I know that we'll go downtown and we'll get some pizza and stuff. And it seems like a lot of people, like a lot of my friends will come down with me. But like, I don't know whether they're just coming because they're just hungry and they just want to like take advantage of my money or something or . . .

DAVE: So you buy?

CHRIS: Yeah. I yeah . . . I usually just buy. Sometimes they'll chip in or they say they'll pay me back.

ANN: You know you're raising sort of an issue, Chris, not just friends but sort of depth of friends. Like, you want friends that are going to like you more that, for more not just because you're buying them pizza.

CHRIS: Yeah. Like more about my personality and stuff like that. So I don't know.

ANN: What do you think, or do you have some friends who know you well?

CHRIS: There's a couple friends that I've had since, like you know like, the first grade. But, we're splitting away now. They're meeting other kids and like I don't know, going into different groups. So . . .

ANN: That's kind of like what Ramsay was saying, I think, happens in high school is new schools combine.

DAVE: Well and you too were talking about, you're worried about your boyfriend and the fact that he's not, you know, maybe going to be around so much once high school starts.

REBECCA: Yeah. Because like there's new girls from like other schools. And I'm afraid that he's going to meet somebody else and then he'll be gone. And I don't want to lose him.

DAVE: Mmhmm.

ANN: Is it, like, what is this fear coming from? Do you have a sense of why you're afraid of that?

REBECCA: No. I just, it's just like a feeling I have.

ANN: Do you think it's because of, like what we've been saying, new kids are coming in and new groups are forming or like is it, he's told you he's going to leave you? Or what?

REBECCA: No, it's just that there's so many more people that we haven't met yet and we don't know them.

DAVE: All these unknowns, all these things that, who knows what's going to happen? Creates some, inevitably creates some fear, anxiety.

TALIA: Yes. It just seems like for most people in high school, the work seems hard, but it's more about, what you really worry about is the friends and the whole like, like . . .

RAMSAY: Too many friends, there's no time for the work. And if there's too much work, it's hard to get friends and like, like especially my situation right now, where the only reason I don't have friends, or a lot of friends, is because I have to work so much.

TALIA: Yeah. So everything is connected to the having friends.

ANN: Friendships are really big. That's what drives everything that's . . .

DAVE: Well it's kind of a, you were suggesting a doubled-edged sword to it or like a double bind. You know, on the one hand you want to have a lot of friends, so especially so you don't get picked on by upper-class people; on the other to reach out and get friends means you have to take risks, on the other hand you want to fly below the radar. So it's, it's a tricky road to negotiate.

Thinking About the Example

1. Review each of Ann and Dave's contributions to the group session, one by one. If you can, identify what humanist technique they are using in each case and what its purpose is.

2. Considering the interventions you have read about and practiced in Chapters 1 through 8, give at least two examples of other interventions that could be used in this group session. What purpose would each of your examples serve? Try to phrase each intervention in the words you would use if you were the counselor in this session.

3. In Group Transcripts from Chapters 2, 4, 5, and 7, group members were adults. What differences, if any, do you see in how Ann and Dave lead adolescents in contrast to adults? If you see differences, can you think of reasons for them? In general, how might you be different as a group counselor for adolescents in contrast to adults, and why?

Problems Addressed by Humanist Groups

Because of their focus on universal human dilemmas and the basics of therapeutic alliance, humanist counselors view their systems as applicable to all kinds of problems. Client-centered group therapy has been proven effective among alcoholics, psychiatric inpatients, cancer sufferers, and students in counseling centers (Page, Weiss, & Lietaer, 2002). Humanist groups often serve highly functioning people who wish to explore their fullest potential.

One outstanding example is humanist work with lesbian, gay, and bisexual people (LGB clients). Ruth Fassinger (2000) wrote that humanistic theory should be the basis of all counseling with LGB clients. "Through the unconditional acceptance of the therapist, clients learn self-acceptance and pride; through the congruence and genuineness of the therapist, they learn to integrate their own conflicted feelings and become more open and honest about their lifestyles and identities; and through the active listening and accurate empathy of the therapist, they learn to articulate coherent self-images and clarify their locations in both the LGB and non-LGB communities" (p. 110). My own practice was once exclusively with LGB clients, and I found the Rogerian approach both necessary and sufficient.

DISCUSSION IDEAS

1. Can you think of any psychological problems that would *not* be well addressed in humanistic therapy? Explain your reasoning.
2. Would you like to be a member of a humanistic counseling group? Why or why not?

Saving the World

Carl Rogers's belief in the goodness of human nature extended to world arenas in ways that few other psychological theories ever have. This is why he eventually called his theory *person-centered* rather than *client-centered*; the people served were not always clients. Rogers applied his theory to career counseling, management training, industry, leadership and administration, organizational development, health care, and cross-cultural understanding. He was an activist for social justice and world peace, giving workshops and lectures aimed at solving interracial and international tensions. Even shortly before his death in early 1987, Rogers organized the 1985 Vienna Peace Project where leaders from thirteen countries met, and in 1986 he organized peace workshops in Moscow.

Adaptations to Clients' Ages

Humanist therapy has been tailored for children, adolescents, and parents. These are exemplified in the following sections.

Play Therapy

One of Rogers's students and later colleagues, Virginia Axline, carried Rogers's theory into the realm of child psychology. (Rogers himself had worked extensively in child guidance settings, had written his dissertation in child psychology, and had taught psychological assessment of children before deciding to focus on adults in the 1940s.) Axline's 1947 book *Play Therapy* (revised edition, 1969) is considered a classic in the field. Client-centered (also called *relationship* and *experiential*) **play therapy** with children is especially appropriate because they may not have the words to discuss their inner lives or the abstract thinking to categorize their range of feelings (Ellinwood & Raskin, 1993). Play is also a perfect fit for Rogers's theory because play is invented by the child, not directed by an adult authority. The make-believe element of play allows children to express feelings and demonstrate events that are not allowed in their ordinary life. Instead of providing a psychologically safe place for open conversation, the play therapist provides a psychologically safe place for open self-expression through dolls, games, building blocks, doll houses, trucks, puppets, and other toys (Semrud-Clikeman, 1995). Through observing the children and interacting with them as they play, the counselor can determine the child's worries, wishes, desires, fears, and developmental struggles such as individuation, separation, and exploration.

Axline (1969) endorsed Rogerian principles in her guidelines for the play therapist, who

must work on a warm and friendly relationship with the children;

accepts the children as they are;

encourages a feeling of permission so children express themselves freely;

recognizes and reflects the feelings of individual children;

respects children's ability to solve problems and gives them opportunity to do so;

allows the children to lead the way;

does not hurry the therapy along but lets it find its own pace;

establishes only the necessary limitations for safety and makes children aware of their responsibilities.

Children, like adults, learn from the spontaneous processes of interacting with others in the atmosphere created by counselors following these guidelines. They help each other navigate the problems that arise during play. Children are able to experiment with different solutions and learn to cope with pervasive social challenges such as taking turns, sharing, winning or losing, and recognizing the pecking order. Most of them can immediately carry what they learn into interactions with children outside the counseling setting (Landreth, 2002). Many children have interactions that teach these lessons naturally outside of any counseling setting; however, when these lessons have failed or have been absent, a child's judgment, security, and social bonds in later life are weakened.

The group play therapist is not nondirective when it comes to interpretation and analysis of the children's play, though the conclusions may not be shared with the children. The counselor is alert and sensitive to signs of worry, fear, and developmental struggles. For example, a child who takes on the mommy role in playing house and proceeds to hit and berate the other children is sending a distressing message about what's bothering her.

Tyndall-Lind, Landreth, and Giordano (2001) studied the effectiveness of sibling group play therapy (brothers and sisters involved in the same play group) in comparison with individual play therapy for child witnesses of domestic violence. They found that both group and individual play therapy reduced behavior problems, aggression, depression, and anxiety, and improved self-esteem in contrast with children who had no play therapy. There was no difference in the successful outcome between individual and group play therapy.

Packman and Bratton (2003) addressed the specialized situations of preadolescents with learning disabilities and behavior problems, children who were socially isolated from both adults and peers at an age when development of social relationships is critical. The 10- to 12-year-old children participated in one-hour-a-week play activity therapy for twelve weeks, during the school day, based on humanistic principles. In comparison with a control group, the therapy group participants showed a large treatment effect in terms of overall behavior improvement, decrease in internalizing problems, and decrease in externalizing problems.

Transitions of Adolescence

In mainstream U.S. culture, adolescence is the transition between childhood and adulthood; in these years, we transfer our value system into stable relationships with people of our own age, and we separate to some extent from our parents. Both of these tasks are social, and teenagers are more or less prepared for them. The less prepared can benefit from humanistic group counseling.

As we know, the group is ideal for working out interpersonal problems and learning how to get along better. The format also works well for teenagers, who usually like to be together and who may feel even more awkward than adults in individual counseling. Furthermore, counselors are adults and can't provide the same interpersonal learning opportunities that other teens can. Holmes, Heckel, and Gordon (1991) developed a social competency group therapy program that viewed the adolescent group "as a context in which we could provide healthy parenting while simultaneously facilitating the development of meaningful peer relationships, thereby addressing the two major areas of deficit" (p. 4). In the process of their work, humanistic themes prospered:

> Within the adolescent group, we observed an intensity of affect, fluidity of defenses, and a range of behavior far greater than we had experienced in either individual psychotherapy with teenagers or in adult group psychotherapy. The adolescents pushed us to be interested in them as persons, not as patients, to respect them even when

they acted out, and to listen to their psychological suffering without taking it over. (p. 12)

Like childhood, ordinary adolescence offers plenty of opportunities for becoming socially competent. However, many preteens and teens miss these due to disorganized or pathological family and peer examples. The nondirective therapy group can provide an example of normal give-and-take among peers and models of noninterfering yet caring and accepting adults (because teen groups are usually led by co-therapists). Topics among these groups often include stances about dominance versus submission, independence versus dependence, gender and sexual identity, and vocational or educational direction. The existential dilemma of isolation also comes to the fore as a teen separates from the family nest (if there was one).

For some talented, high-achieving adolescents, a Rogerian therapy group may be their only time for hanging out with peers without an externally imposed agenda. Rosenfeld and Wise (2001) identified *The Over-Scheduled Child*, the young person whose hours are completely filled with planned, controlled activities to the detriment of free exploration of identity and relationships.

As one might expect, adolescent group members rated the curative factors of cohesiveness and universality higher than adults do (Holmes et al., 1991), though on three out of five item rankings teenagers chose the same categories as adults—catharsis, interpersonal learning, and existential awareness.

Groups for Parents and Teachers

How adults nurture children is a major concern of person-centered psychologists, and many of Rogers's followers concentrate on helping groups of parents and teachers learn to deal with children in an atmosphere of trust, genuineness, and empathy. Haim Ginott (1965) wrote a best-selling book, *Between Parent and Child*, teaching parents the basics of constructive conversation and empathic listening. Thomas Gordon, founder of **Parent Effectiveness Training** and Teacher Effectiveness Training, designed courses and books based on humanistic principles (e.g., Gordon, 1970). Although the training courses were psychoeducational groups, the families and classrooms affected by such programs took on elements of person-centered group counseling

Because the humanistic approach is not tied to graduate degrees in psychology, Rogers and his followers broadened the sphere of practitioners of empathy, congruence, and positive regard. Parents learned these principles in Child Relationship Enhancement Family Therapy, in a six-month group format or three-month single-family format. A reduction in child and parent-child problems resulted, as a number of research studies confirmed. Rogers's student and associate Thomas Gordon created a workshop for parents, intended as a preventive measure against mental health problems. The theory behind Gordon's Parent Effectiveness Training (PET) is person-centered and emphasizes the core conditions as well as democratic family organization (Gordon, 1970). PET now exists in popular workshop, self-help, and counselor training formats. The 1970 book is a classic in child-raising and was updated in 2000 (Gordon, 2000). I encourage you to sample this book; all counseling involves families, even if indirectly.

Gordon's legacy from Rogers is clear in passages about parents and children like this one:

> Why is parental acceptance such a significant positive influence on the child? This is not generally understood by parents. Most people have been brought up to believe that if you accept a child he will remain just the way he is; that the best way to help a child become something better in the future is to tell him what you *don't* accept about him now. . . .
>
> When parents learn how to demonstrate through their words an inner feeling of acceptance toward a child, they are in possession of a tool that can produce some startling effects. They can be influential in his learning to accept and like himself and to acquire a sense of his own worth. They can greatly facilitate his developing and actualizing the potential with which he was genetically endowed. They can accelerate his movement away from dependence and toward independence and self-direction. They can help him learn to solve for himself the problems that life inevitably brings, and they can give him the strength to deal constructively with the usual disappointments and pain of childhood and adolescence. (1970, pp. 31–33)

Gordon also invented a Teacher Effectiveness Training (TET) workshop that strengthened empathy, genuineness, positive regard for others, and democratic structures among child educators. A study aimed at evaluating the effectiveness of TET involved 600 teachers and 10,000 students from kindergarten to eighth grade (Ellinwood & Raskin, 1993). Students of teachers trained to high levels of TET qualities were compared with students whose teachers did not offer high levels of these qualities. Students of the high-TET teachers were found to have better attendance, more gain in academic achievement, fewer disciplinary problems, fewer acts of vandalism, increased intelligence scores in grades K through 5, higher creativity scores, and more spontaneous, higher-level thinking (Ellinwood & Raskin, 1993).

Evaluating Humanist Groups

The Ellinwood and Raskin study of the effectiveness of TET was an example of assessment used for empirical research. Structured assessment is also a tool that can be used by individual therapists to evaluate their own effectiveness. When properly employed, assessment tools can help you view your groups more objectively than your general impressions can and can assist you in improving your performance as a leader. Here and at the ends of the subsequent chapters on various types of groups, I will discuss assessment techniques relevant to each group type.

Group climate refers to interpersonal features of the therapeutic environment. Therapists find assessment of group climate valuable in thinking about the group as a whole and in analyzing the progress of the group. The Group

Climate Questionnaire (GCQ; MacKenzie, 1983) is a short questionnaire that asks each member to rate items on a scale of seven points, from "not at all" (1) to "extremely" (7), after each session. The scores can be summed as a source of information about group process and also considered individually to identify members who are experiencing the group differently from the rest. The items can be sorted into three categories: Engagement, Avoidance, and Conflict. The box lists the items and identifies which scale they belong to. This questionnaire is appropriate for humanistic groups because of its focus on the interpersonal process rather than on problems and solutions.

GROUP CLIMATE QUESTIONNAIRE

1. The members liked and cared about each other. *Engagement*
2. The members tried to understand why they do the things they do, tried to reason it out. *Engagement*
3. The members avoided looking at important issues going on between themselves. *Avoidance*
4. The members felt what was happening was important and there was a sense of participation. *Engagement*
5. The members depended on the group leader(s) for direction. *Avoidance*
6. There was friction and anger between the members. *Conflict*
7. The members were distant and withdrawn from each other. *Avoidance*
8. The members challenged and confronted each other in their efforts to sort things out. *Engagement*
9. The members appeared to do things the way they thought would be acceptable to the group. *Avoidance*
10. The members distrusted and rejected each other. *Conflict*
11. The members revealed sensitive personal information or feelings. *Engagement*

Rogers and other humanist researchers also use the **Q-sort** evaluation technique, which was developed by Stephenson (1953). In this technique, test items are written on separate cards, and the respondent is asked to sort the cards into piles according to a stated principle. To assess a client's progress in humanist therapy, for example, the cards might all have self-descriptors like "I usually like people" and "I don't trust my emotions," and the client would sort them into groups according to "This is like me" and "This is not like me." Rogers and colleagues collected Q-sorts before, during, and after therapy to see how people's self-descriptions changed. Rogers (1961) found that clients' ideal and real selves became closer during client-centered therapy. Other types of Q-sort card sets and principles exist for other types of exploration, as well.

KEY TERMS

accurate empathy   correct understanding of another's emotions

actualizing tendency   an inborn drive toward our highest potential as humans

authenticity   the quality of being trustworthy and genuine

congruence   authenticity; the opposite of presenting a facade, either knowingly or unknowingly

encounter groups   therapy groups focused on personal growth and honest relationships with others

existential encounter   a meeting between people who are behaving authentically, without pretense or power plays

facilitative conditions   same as necessary and sufficient conditions; also called *core conditions* and *conditions*; the facilitative conditions are congruence, unconditional positive regard, and empathy

fifteen-stage process   a natural course of events Rogers perceived in humanistic counseling groups

genuineness   freedom from hypocrisy, dishonesty, and poses

group climate   interpersonal features of the therapeutic environment, including engagement, avoidance, and conflict

necessary and sufficient conditions   qualities of the therapeutic relationship that must be present in order for constructive change to happen and that can enhance constructive change no matter what else occurs

nondirective   unobtrusive and noninterventionist, encouraging free expression; this term stands in contrast with directive approaches, which prescribe topics and activities and give strong guidance

open questions   queries that invite more than a yes-or-no answer

organismic valuing process   a natural sense of what is good for us and for the peace and harmony of humanity, which drives the best decision making

Parent Effectiveness Training   courses and books for adults, based on humanistic principles like constructive conversation and empathic listening

person-centered   focused on individuals rather than diagnoses, theories, or problems

phenomenological stance   a point of view that concentrates on reality according to how it is perceived and understood by human consciousness; each person has a different reality than any other

play therapy   humanistic counseling designed for children and preadolescents, in which play rather than talk is the medium of communication

Q-sort   an assessment and research technique in which test items are written on separate cards, and the respondent is asked to sort the cards into piles according to a stated principle, such as "Like me" and "Not like me"

reflection of feeling   a statement or action by one person that restates or summarizes another person's emotional state

self-actualization   fulfillment of one's highest potential

self-disclosure   openly expressing private thoughts or personal experiences

Socratic dialogue   a conversation that seeks truth through exploring people's experience rather than turning to reference works or rules

unconditional positive regard   warm acceptance and respect for the client no matter what she or he says

CHAPTER REVIEW

1. Review Rogers's fifteen-stage group process. Without looking at the text, try to explain the group process to another person. Check your accuracy and completeness with the book, and then try again with a new listener.

2. What are the three facilitative conditions? Speculate on what would happen in a group in the absence of each core condition.

3. What are four possible effects of sensitive listening? What gets in the way of sensitive listening, in your experience?

4. How are reflection of feelings and paraphrase different from mere repetition of the group member's words?

5. Describe how humanist group counseling is applied to a specific population. Think about how well it would apply to the population you serve or intend to serve.

6. Why is there a debate about the extent of counselor self-disclosure? Develop your own opinion on the topic.

FOR FURTHER READING

Rogers, C. R. (1961). *On becoming a person.* Boston: Houghton-Mifflin.

Each chapter of this classic work can stand alone as an essay about Rogers's philosophy and research. Many chapters represent lectures and research reports from his work over thirty years. You will emerge from reading this book with an extensive understanding of humanistic psychology and its applications, and probably a greater understanding of yourself. Rogers's writing style reflects his warm, empathetic personality.

REFERENCES

Axline, V. M. (1969). *Play therapy* (rev. ed.). New York: Ballantine Books.

Bachelor, A., & Horvath, A. (1999). The therapeutic relationship. In M. A. Hubble, B. L. Duncan, & S. D. Miller (Eds.), *The heart and soul of change* (pp. 133–178). Washington, DC: American Psychological Association.

Barrett-Lennard, G. T. (1988). Listening. *Person-Centered Review, 3,* 410–425.

Ellinwood, C. G., & Raskin, J. J. (1993). Client-centered/humanistic psychotherapy. In T. R. Kratochwill & R. J. Morris (Eds.), *Handbook of psychotherapy with children and adolescents* (pp. 258–287). Boston: Allyn & Bacon.

Fassinger, R. E. (2000). Applying counseling theory to lesbian, gay, and bisexual clients. In R. M. Perez, K. A. Debord, & K. J. Bieschke (Eds.), *Handbook of counseling and psychotherapy with lesbian, gay, and bisexual clients* (pp. 107–131). Washington, DC: American Psychological Association.

Gendlin, E. T. (1961). Experiencing: A variable in the process of therapeutic change. *American Journal of Psychotherapy, 15,* 233–245.

Ginott, H. G. (1965). *Between parent and child.* New York: Macmillan.

Gordon, T. (1970). *Parent effectiveness training.* New York: Wyden.

Gordon, T. (2000). *Parent effectiveness training.* New York: Random House.

Holmes, G. R., Heckel, R. V., & Gordon, L. (1991). *Adolescent group therapy: A social competency model.* New York: Praeger.

Knox, S., Hess, S. A., Petersen, D. A., & Hill, C. E. (1997). A qualitative analysis of client perceptions of the effects of helpful therapist self-disclosure in long-term therapy. *Journal of Counseling Psychology, 44,* 274–283.

Landreth, G. L. (2002). *Play therapy: The art of the relationship* (2nd ed.). New York: Brunner-Routledge.

Lewis, M. I., & Butler, R. N. (1986). Life-review therapy: Putting memories to work. In I. Burnside (Ed.), *Working with the elderly: Group process and techniques* (2nd ed., pp. 50–59). Boston: Jones & Bartlett.

MacKenzie, K. R. (1983). The clinical application of a group climate questionnaire. In R. R. Dies & K. R. MacKenzie (Eds.), *Advances in group psychotherapy: Integrating research and practice* (pp. 159–170). New York: International Universities Press.

Maslow, A. H. (1968). *Toward a psychology of being* (2nd ed.). Princeton, NJ: Van Nostrand.

Packman, J., & Bratton, S. C. (2003). A school-based group play/activity therapy intervention with learning disabled preadolescents exhibiting behavior problems. *International Journal of Play Therapy, 12,* 7–29.

Page, R. C., Weiss, J. F., & Lietaer, G. (2002). Humanistic group psychotherapy. In D. J. Cain (Ed.), *Humanistic psychotherapies: Handbook of research and practice* (pp. 339–368). Washington, DC: American Psychological Association.

Raskin, N. J., & Rogers, C. R. (2000). Person-centered therapy. In R. J. Corsini & D. Wedding (Eds.), *Current psychotherapies* (6th ed., pp. 133–167). Itasca, IL: Peacock.

Reisman, J. M., & Ribordy, S. (1993). *Principles of psychotherapy with children* (2nd ed.). New York: Lexington/Macmillan.

Rogers, C. R. (1940). The processes of therapy. *Journal of Consulting Psychology, 4,* 161–164.

Rogers, C. R. (1957). The necessary and sufficient conditions of therapeutic personality change. *Journal of Consulting Psychology, 21,* 95–103.

Rogers, C. R. (1961). *On becoming a person.* Boston: Houghton-Mifflin.

Rogers, C. R. (1967). *The process of the basic encounter group.* In J. F. T. Bugental (Ed.), *Challenges of humanistic psychology* (pp. 261–276). New York: McGraw-Hill.

Rogers, C. R. (1970). *Carl Rogers on encounter groups.* New York: Harper & Row.

Rosenfeld, A., & Wise, N. (2001). *The over-scheduled child.* New York: St. Martin's Press.

Seligman, L. (2001). Systems, strategies, and skills of counseling and psychotherapy. Upper Saddle River, NJ: Prentice-Hall.

Seligman, M. E. P., & Csikszentmihalyi, M. (2000). Positive psychology: An introduction. *American Psychologist, 55,* 5–14.

Semrud-Clikeman, M. (1995). *Child and adolescent therapy.* Needham Heights, MA: Allyn & Bacon.

Singh, J., & Tudor, K. (1997). Cultural conditions of therapy. *The Person-Centered Journal, 4,* 32–46.

Stephenson, W. U. (1953). *The study of behavior.* Chicago: University of Chicago Press.

Truax, C. B. (1966). Reinforcement and nonreinforcement in Rogerian psychotherapy. *Journal of Abnormal Psychology, 71,* 1–9.

Truax, C. B., Wargo, D. G., & Silber, L. D. (1966). Effects of group psychotherapy with high accurate empathy and nonpossessive warmth upon female institutionalized delinquents. *Journal of Abnormal Psychology, 71,* 267–274.

Tyler, L. (1969). *The work of the counselor* (3rd ed.). New York: Meredith Corp.

Tyndall-Lind, A., Landreth, G. L., & Giordano, M. A. (2001). Intensive group play therapy with child witnesses of domestic violence. *International Journal of Play Therapy, 10,* 53–83.

CHAPTER 9

Existential Group Theory and Practice

The twentieth-century existential psychologists' thoughts on meaningless-ness, freedom, isolation, and death were influenced by nineteenth-century existentialist philosophers, especially Kierkegaard (1813–1855) and Nietzsche (1844–1900). Common themes were "an emphasis on human emotions; the importance of subjective experience; a deep respect for individuality; a belief in free will; . . . [and] the importance of the individual attempting to make sense out of his or her life and freely acting upon his or her interpretations of life's meaning" (Hergenhahn, 2001, p. 198). These are themes that provide the focus of dialogue in existential group therapy. Before reading Yalom's own description of this group therapy, you may want to reread the discussion of existential factors in Chapter 6.

A Selection from

The Theory and Practice of Group Psychotherapy

By Irvin D. Yalom (1995)

[An] illustrative clinical example [of self-disclosure] occurred in the group of women incest survivors. . . . The withering anger toward me (and, to a slightly lesser degree, toward my female co-therapist) had gotten to us and, toward the end of one meeting, she and I openly discussed the nature of our experience in the group. I revealed that I felt demoralized and deskilled, that everything I tried in the group had failed to be helpful, and furthermore that I felt anxious and confused in the group. My co-leader discussed similar feelings: her discomfort about the competitive way the women related to her and about the continual pressure placed on her to reveal any abuse that she may have experienced. We told them that their relentless anger and distrust of us was fully understandable in the light of their past abuse but, nonetheless, we both wanted to shriek, "These were terrible things that happened to you, but we didn't do them."

This episode proved to be a turning point for the group. There was still one member (who had been ritually abused savagely as a child) who continued in the same vein ("Oh, you're uncomfortable and confused! What a shame! What a shame! But at least now you know how it feels"). But the others were deeply affected by our admission. They were astounded to learn of our discomfort and of their power over us, and gratified that we were willing to relinquish authority and to relate to them in an open, egalitarian fashion. From that point on, the group moved into a far more profitable work phase.

These clinical episodes illustrate some general principles that prove useful to the therapist when receiving feedback, especially negative feedback:

1. Take it seriously. Listen to it, consider it, and respond to it. Respect the patients and let their feedback matter to you; if you don't, you merely increase their sense of impotence.
2. Obtain consensual validation: find out how other members feel. Is the feedback primarily a transference reaction, or does it closely correspond to the reality about you? If it is reality, you must confirm it; otherwise, you impair rather than facilitate a patient's reality testing.
3. Check your internal experience: Does the feedback fit? Does it click with your internal experience?

With these principles as guidelines, the therapist offers such responses as: "You're right. There are times when I feel irritated with you, but at no time do I feel I want to impede your growth, seduce you, get a voyeuristic pleasure from listening to your account of your abuse, or slow your therapy so as to earn more money from you. That simply isn't part of my experience of you." Or: "It's true that I dodge some of your questions. But often I find them unanswerable. You imbue me with too much wisdom. I feel uncomfortable by your deference to me. I always feel that you've put yourself down very low, and that you're always looking up at me." Or: "I've never heard you challenge me so directly before. Even though it's a bit scary for me, it's also very refreshing." Or: "I feel restrained, very unfree with you, because you give me so much power over you. I feel I have to check every word I say because you give so much weight to all of my statements."

Note that these therapist disclosures are all part of the here-and-now of the group. I am advocating that therapists relate authentically to patients in the here-and-now of the therapy hour, not that they reveal their past and present in a detailed manner—although I have never seen harm in the therapist answering such broad personal questions as whether they are married or have children, where they are going on vacation, where they were brought up, and so on. Some therapists carry it much further and may wish to describe some similar personal problems they encountered and overcame. I personally have never found this useful or necessary. (pp. 208–209)

[A scene from a different group follows.]

Walt, who had been in the group for seven weeks, launched into a familiar, lengthy tribute to the remarkable improvement he had undergone. He described in exquisite detail how his chief problem had been that he had not understood the damaging effects his behavior had on others, and how now, having achieved such understanding, he was ready to leave the hospital.

The therapist observed that some of the members were restless. One softly pounded his fist into his palm, while others slumped back in a posture of indifference and resignation. He stopped the monopolist by asking the group members how many times they had heard Walt relate this account. All agreed they had heard it at every meeting—in fact, they had heard Walt speak this way the very first meeting. Furthermore, they had never heard him talk about anything else and knew him only as a story. The members discussed their irritation with Walt, their reluctance to attack him for fear of seriously injuring him, of losing control of themselves, or of painful retaliation. Some spoke of their hopelessness about ever reaching Walt, and of the fact that he related to them only as stick figures without flesh or depth. Still others spoke of their terror of speaking and revealing themselves in the group: therefore, they welcomed Walt's monopolization. A few members expressed their total lack of interest or faith in therapy and therefore failed to intercept Walt because of apathy.

Thus the process was overdetermined: a host of interlocking factors resulted in a dynamic equilibrium called monopolization. By halting the runaway process, uncovering and working through the underlying factors, the therapist obtained maximum therapeutic benefit from a potentially crippling group phenomenon. Each member moved closer to group involvement. Walt was no longer permitted or encouraged to participate in a fashion that could not possibly be helpful to him or the group. (p. 374)

Exploring The Theory and Practice of Group Psychotherapy

1. Why do you think there were male and female co-therapists in the first group described?

2. What had the group done to upset the therapists?

3. Why was the therapists' self-disclosure of their distress a turning point for the group?

4. What is consensual validation (paragraph 3)? Why is it important? From other reading, do you know what a transference reaction is? As a group counselor, why would it be bad to deny negative feedback about yourself when it is accurate?

5. What do you think of the responses quoted in paragraph 4? Try saying them out loud. Can you imagine saying them to a group? Why or why not?

6. Discuss with classmates the levels of disclosure mentioned in paragraph 5. What level do you think is appropriate for the types of group you lead or intend to lead? Why?

7. Why were other group members reluctant to confront Walt in the second group described? List six reasons. Have you ever seen anything like this in a group, such as a class or family? What happened?

8. What did the therapist do about the situation with Walt? Why would Walt's behavior be "a potentially crippling group phenomenon" if the counselor had not stepped in? Was the counselor's action truly nondirective? What would be a more directive intervention by the counselor?

■ ■ ■

Essential Concepts of Existential Theory

Existentialism has developed much more as a philosophical and psychological theory than as a method of counseling. Most existential counselors begin with the theory and then choose techniques that bring to light key existential themes in the counseling group.

Phenomenological Point of View

In the last chapter, you read about the **phenomenological stance** that unifies existential, humanistic, multicultural, and most modern psychological theories. Rollo May (1961) provided a useful definition:

> Phenomenology is the endeavor to take the phenomena as given. It is the disciplined effort to clear one's mind of the presuppositions that so often cause us to see in the patient only our own theories or the dogmas of our own systems, the effort to experience instead the phenomena in their full reality as they present themselves. (p. 26)

Existentialists understand people's problems as characteristics of their whole response to existence as they see it. The whole response may have adaptive as well as problematic aspects. "What looks like a minor fault may be a necessary concomitant of one of the person's most valuable traits. What looks like a sterling virtue may be a defense against anxiety destined to change its shape as anxiety diminishes" (Tyler, 1969, p. 35). For example, one group member named Alta constantly asked probing questions about other members' experiences. Her tendency to pry (a minor fault) was part of her deep caring about others and her interest in them (a virtue). At the same time, Alta's passionate interest in others (a virtue) deflected the group's attention away from her own problems, in a defense against anxiety.

Not only are our motivations for the same behavior different, but from a phenomenological stance, the same occurrence is different when perceived by different people. We attach subjective interpretations to experience, interpretations that are quite individual. A few of our group members saw Alta as irritating and intrusive, whereas most saw her as curious and caring. Researchers have discovered that different members perceive the climates of the same group quite differently (MacNair-Semands & Lese, 2000).

The existential counselor attempts to immerse herself in the client's private world of experience. "The therapist moves back and forth between noticing patterns in what a client finds happening in his world and supposing there to be some point which that pattern creatively fulfills" (Russell, 1978, p. 264). The point might be, as in Alta's case, that she manages a generally caring, positive image of herself while protecting herself from exploration. Another group member, Jim, displayed a contrasting pattern in which he became engaged only when the topic directly related to his own personal problems as he saw them. A phenomenologist would see Jim's pattern as evidence of a narrow, self-centered phenomenological experience that persists through the past and present outside the group.

R. D. Laing, a physician famous for his work with schizoid and schizophrenic people, took a phenomenological approach to even the most out-of-touch patients. "The therapist must have the plasticity to transpose himself into another strange and even alien view of the world. In this act, he draws on his own psychotic possibilities, without forgoing his sanity. Only thus can he arrive at an understanding of the patient's *existential position*" (Laing, 1969, p. 35).

DISCUSSION IDEAS

1. Tyler (1969) wrote that sometimes a minor fault can be characteristic of a major virtue and a virtue may be a defense against anxiety. Can you think of other examples? Think of the things you admire about your friends, and the things that irritate you. Is there a way you can see the faults relating to your friends' virtues or the good points relating to their anxieties?

2. Now consider the behavior of an individual in a group you've experienced, such as a class or work group. Could their habitual behavior be evidence of both a virtue and a defense? For example, what about the person who *always* volunteers in class discussions? What about the person who *never* volunteers and says he is just not comfortable in class discussions?

Basic Assumptions

Barnes (2000) outlines six assumptions of logotherapists, whose basis is existential theory:

1. Human beings comprise body, mind, and spirit. The **noetic** (spiritual) quality belongs only to humans and includes the ability to transcend one's own limited interests and to self-distance, looking at one's self objectively and often with humor. This three-part division is a critical one, because logotherapists believe that the field of medicine deals with the body, the field of psychology deals with the mind, and logotherapy deals with the *noos,* or spirit.

2. Life can have meaning under all circumstances, and people experience meaning especially in times of despair and bliss.

3. The human spirit has a **will to meaning,** which is a primary motivator. We experience a longing for meaning just as we experience longings for pleasure and for power.

4. People have freedom to change a meaningless situation into a meaningful one through action or through changing their attitudes.

5. Each situation offers a specific potential meaning that can be found and fulfilled. Though ultimate meaning is never fully reached but only approached, the meaning of the moment can be fulfilled and bring us closer to ultimate meaning.

6. Each person is unique and significant. (Adapted from pp. 24–25)

Anxiety as a Perception of Threat

The discussion of phenomenology above included several references to **anxiety.** Existentialists view anxiety holistically (as a whole), as a response to perceived threats to existence or to values we find fundamental to existence (May, 1977). In groups, you will find clients who become anxious at low levels of conflict, in circumstances where most people wouldn't be bothered—a disagreement over a popular movie, for example. From an existential point of view, the conflict-avoiding person is attempting to ward off chaos, a lack of order that threatens his position in the world. He harbors a belief that a bit of conflict will lead to a full-blown battle with destructive results. We each have a natural need to survive, to preserve our being, and to assert our being, and this need causes an unavoidable anxiety. How we deal with this anxiety varies.

Existential anxiety comes from "a deep feeling of unease that arises from our awareness of the givens: our existence is finite, we are mortal, and there is no purpose but the one we create for ourselves" (Bauman & Walso, 1998, p. 19). We must then choose to live with dread or with courage. The courageous response is to accept the facts of existence and say, "This is the way it is. Now I will live my life" (p. 20). The next step is to follow the natural search for meaning in the life we have. If the will to meaning is repressed, blocked, or minimized, a person experiences an **existential vacuum,** "a feeling of inner emptiness in which life seems boring and not worth living, and in which the person is full of doubt and despair" (Barnes, 2000, p. 27).

In this manner, you can understand the sullenness, secretiveness, and withdrawal that some parents complain of in teenagers. The adolescents are preserving and asserting their beings, when their phenomenological experience is that they fit nowhere (being between child and adult) and that their beings are threatened by adults' attempts to control them. In cultures and families that basically skip teenagehood by propelling grown children directly into adult responsibilities and roles, adolescent angst is rare. (There may, of course, be other attendant problems in those cultures.) In mainstream U.S. culture, adolescence is a period of searching for identity, which is a major form of grappling with existential issues.

Guilt as a Message

We have all felt guilty for something we have done—a small lie, a theft, a manipulative plan suited for our own advancement. However, **existential guilt** is guilt *not* for sins of commission (actions) but for sins of omission (not taking action). Knowing that we fall short of our full potential, feeling that we've acted too often out of fear, or feeling that we have failed to live life zestfully—these are the sources of existential guilt. We are denying the one inborn human impulse that we possess, the "character of self-affirmation," as May (1961) labeled it, the power of wishing, willing, decisions, and choice. Existential guilt, like Freudian anxiety, acts as a signal that all is not well. Sometimes existential guilt drives people to seek counseling, "a message from the deeper part of oneself that is seeking to take charge of one's life" (Bauman & Walso, 1998, p. 19).

Reflections

Have you ever experienced existential guilt? If so, write down what occasioned the existential guilt. Did it compel you to any action? At the time, you probably didn't identify your feeling as "existential guilt." What words did you use to describe it? If you have never experienced it, try to explain why.

Peak Experiences

Have you ever become so absorbed in an activity, sensation, or thought that you were surprised when you finally looked at the clock—you had lost track of time? In such periods, have you completely forgotten about yourself in the usual senses—like "What will I have for lunch?", "I need to buy stamps," and "It's too cold in here"? These moments of glorious loss of time and of ego Maslow called **peak experiences.**

In the 1960s, Maslow took the then-unusual route of studying healthy personality. He noticed that individuals on the road to self-actualization reported periodic episodes in which they felt wonder and awe, lost track of time and place, and were convinced that something valuable had happened.

> The B-love [nonpossessive, unselfish, I-Thou love] experience, the parental experience, the mystic, or oceanic, or nature experience, the aesthetic perception, the creative moment, the therapeutic or intellectual insight, the orgasmic experience, certain forms of athletic fulfillment, etc. These and other moments of highest happiness and fulfillment I shall call the peak-experiences. (Maslow, 1968, p. 73)

These experiences give us a sense of what existential *being* is like, and Maslow thought of them as rewards for *becoming.*

Today, Mihalyi Csikszentmihalyi (1990), in his studies of happiness and well-being, describes many of the same features as the experience of **flow,** a pleasant to ecstatic state of unselfconscious absorption during a mental or physical activity. Csikszentmihalyi identifies the state of flow as occurring at times when one is sufficiently challenged to stay engaged and yet sufficiently competent to be self-confident. An example from school might be a course that is just a bit over your head, yet you have a sense that you will master it if you try. Even children don't like games and lessons that are too easy, and they seek activities that present some challenge and take some effort. The fact that children today plow through the thick, complex Harry Potter novels with glee suggests that this reading is a flow experience for them. (My vacationing friend recently had to drag the children out of the van to look at the Grand Canyon; they wanted to sit inside and read their Harry Potter books.)

Existential Theory and Logotherapy

When asked for helpful elements of group therapy, addictions group members ranked as first or second (out of 60 items on Yalom's questionnaire), "Learning that I must take ultimate responsibility for the way I live my life no matter how much guidance and support I get from others" (Page, Weiss, & Lietaer, 2002). This high ranking is a remarkably abstract and weighty comment on the significance of existential awareness in human change.

Logotherapy is a form of existential therapy created by Victor Frankl (1946/1984). The founder originally labeled his therapy *Existenzanalyse* (existential analysis), but changed his label to logotherapy because his original term was already being used by another theorist. Frankl named the approach for his translation of the Greek word *logos* as "meaning." The setting and atmosphere of a logotherapy group are similar to any person-centered group; the difference lies in the focus on meaning in life. As the title of Frankl's book, *Man's Search for Meaning* suggests, we have an innate desire to find meaning, a desire just as strong as our drives toward pleasure and power. What a bold statement: when you look around you, you can see the intensity of human desires for pleasure and power all over the place. Is the drive for meaning equally intense? In fact, existential points of view have flourished in the midst of affluence: "The existential approach is focused on identifying the living person underneath the alienation of modern culture exemplified by compartmentalization and dehumanization" (Frankl, 2002). Most people think about meaning in life only occasionally—"Getting and spending, we lay waste our powers," as Wordsworth would say.

Why? Frankl would say that when we think about meaning in life, we are led inevitably to the topics of suffering, guilt, and death. Why do we and our fellow humans suffer? Why do we carry the burden of our own wrongdoing, failure, and neglect? Why do we live, when the end is surely death? A logotherapy group provides a place to discuss these subjects freely. Avoiding such questions takes so much psychological energy that we shut down whole aspects of ourselves and reject huge areas of experience just to protect ourselves, and end up with no real protection anyway.

Choice and responsibility are major themes in logotherapy, given its grounding in free will. Through action, inaction, or choice of interpretation, each client is responsible for his or her own distress. Meaning comes about through our own commitment, not through divine intervention, avoidance of the topic, or distraction through busy-ness. What a person does with a given situation is the important thing, not the situation itself.

Group Dynamics

"Existential psychotherapists speak of the lost person" (Rosenbaum, 1993, p. 237). Though the phrase "finding yourself" may sound laughable because it's been such an excuse for abandoning responsibility, "losing yourself" retains a poignant meaningfulness. "I feel lost" gives us a powerful image of the child among unpredictable adults, the teenager spinning out of control, the adult on the treadmill of competition. Wordsworth described this state 200 years ago:

> The world is too much with us; late and soon,
> Getting and spending, we lay waste our powers.
> Little we see in Nature that is ours;
> We have given our hearts away, a sordid boon! (1807)

The group applications that draw from existential theory are based on trust that people can get their hearts back and regain their powers, within certain settings and social atmospheres.

Ungar (1997) delineates four stages she perceived in reconstructing the lives of clients who have lost their paths to meaning:

Step 1: See life in terms of gifts received. Clients share incidents that sustained them during trying times, including meaningful encounters with others.

Step 2: Pinpoint hardships as opportunities to discover meaning that has been present all along. For example, personal tragedies are examined to define what has helped people to survive them.

Step 3: Highlight the ability to respond to an inner call. This can include a call to change attitudes, a call to be creative, and a call to deepen experience.

Step 4: Support decision making and commitment to action. Clients make personal resolutions to take responsibility for acting on their inner calls.

This process reflects the stages of group work in general in that it begins with establishing commonality among members and moves toward individual action in the outside world, with less and less dependence on the leader as the group progresses. Another phase structure for existential treatment is described by Lukas and Hirsch (2002):

> The *diagnostic phase*, in which data about the client is gathered. In many therapies, this stage is focused on pinpointing what's wrong. In existential therapy, the diagnosis must include healthy aspects of a client's functioning.

> The *therapeutic phase*, in which counselors help clients explore feelings and attitudes and use meaning-oriented techniques (as described in the next section).

> The *follow-up phase*, which involves periodic contacts to reinforce clients' new ways to enrich the meaning of life.

Leadership Skills

In logotherapy, the group leader continually brings the discussion back to existential investigation, such as "What do you really want to do, and what is preventing you from doing it?" Members learn to challenge use of the word "can't," for example, and are encouraged to try out the same statement using the word "won't." Try it yourself next time you find yourself saying that you *can't* do something; reflect on the change in meaning when you say *won't*. Ultimately, the group strives to transcend the limitations of each individual and to explore the routes toward a meaningful stance toward life's inevitable tragedies.

The selection at the beginning of this chapter from *The Theory and Practice of Group Psychotherapy* by Irvin D. Yalom (1995) highlights some of the leadership skills for the existential group. The co-leaders take the risk of exposing their honest responses to what was happening in the group, even though they took a negative tone.

Yalom (1995) has described a group approach that is **experiential,** in that the group experience itself is the active ingredient, as well as *existential*, in that existential factors are emphasized. I've also heard such groups called, plainly, *Yalom-type groups,* and in this label you can see his eminent status in the field. As with Rogers's groups, the general therapeutic factors are the basic instigators of change. However, reading Yalom's books, I see Yalom doing much more interpretation and analysis inside and outside of the group, while Rogers claims to avoid it.

The more analytical nature of existential group leadership is evident in the type of **Socratic questioning** that leaders do. Remember from Chapter 8 that Socratic dialogue is a series of questions and answers that systematically examine experience leading to insights. In logotherapy, leaders practice Socractic dialogue to illuminate five circumstances in particular (Wilson, 1997):

1. **Self-discovery** Questions that pursue a truth about self, triggered by an experience someone relates
2. **Choices** Exploring how a person is not without choice; changing either a situation or one's attitude toward it
3. **Uniqueness** Emphasizing the individual, unrepeatable situations each person has experienced
4. **Responsibility** Asking what personal commitments flow from the meaning of each new situation
5. **Self-transcendence** Probing into potentials beyond personal interests, toward service, creativity, love, and commitments (Adapted from pp. 29–30)

Techniques in Existential Group Therapy

Existentialists, like humanists, stress the unforced discussion of groups and are not fond of step-by-step technique. Existentialism began as a philosophical position, and philosophies do not require techniques. Many existential counselors adapt techniques from many other theories while keeping existential issues foremost in work with clients. May and Yalom (2000) wrote that existentialism "deals with the *presuppositions underlying therapy of any kind.* . . . There are very few adequate training courses in this kind of therapy simply because it is not a specific training in technique" (p. 282).

Focused Listening

In existential group sessions, **focused listening** is the main technique as the counselor listens for themes in the members' talk that reflect the struggles with meaning, relationships, and identity underneath the themes.

Almost any subject matter can be mined for existential ore. Lantz (1998) described a method of listening to clients' dreams: "The therapist uses personal interest, curiosity, concern, and Socratic questions to help the client focus upon the hints and clues in the dream that might help the client become more aware of repressed meaning potentials, problem solving difficulties and strengths, and forgotten meanings deposited in the past" (p. 83). Lantz, like many psychologists, believes that dreams present the dreamer with clues about meanings that have been forgotten and with problem-solving strengths and weaknesses.

Confrontation

Yalom (1980) reported a case in which a woman complained about her grown children's disrespect for her opinions and dismissal of her ideas. Yalom, tuning in to his own feelings, found that he reacted negatively to a childish whining quality of her complaints, which led him not to take her seriously. He confronted her with this feeling she engendered in him and suggested that her children might feel the same way. This confrontation helped her become aware that she acted like a child in several areas and thus was partly responsible for others' reactions to her.

May and Yalom (2000) also use confrontation to focus on each client's responsibility for his or her own distress: "When patients say they 'can't' do something, the therapist immediately comments, 'You mean you *won't* do it" (p. 289). For example, one of my group members travelled widely with her husband in the oil business. Time after time, when she came back she told us how the trip was ruined because her hair turned frizzy in the humidity, or her clothing was not warm enough, or she forgot part of an outfit she intended to wear. Incidents like these would keep her sulking in her hotel room. Other group members eventually confronted her about, first, whether anyone really cared if her hair was frizzy in a foreign country, and, second, whether she'd considered a packing plan that covered her needs in the upcoming climate. They made these confrontations with a humorous tone, and she surprised me by beginning to laugh at herself. She allowed as how she could check the weather at her destination and make a packing list to check off. This exchange, which might seem pretty superficial, led to the real issue: She wanted her husband to pay more attention to her needs and wishes when they travelled together, and seemed to sabotage herself to make him unhappy, too. An intelligent woman, she was willing to devise a plan to speak directly to him about the problem, and they were able to plan for activities and sights of interest to her while they were abroad.

The existentially oriented group is assisted to be open about the members' here-and-now process and impressions, and this often creates confrontation. Statements that would probably never surface in ordinary conversation are freely aired. For example, a group member once told another one, "You bring up your PhD all the time, and I feel about one inch tall with my high school diploma!" The educated gentleman retorted, "Oh, and you are always the voice of the working class around here." A third member chimed in, "Everyone in this group is the big expert on something, except me." The interaction provided plenty of grist for the mill.

Paradoxical Intention, Dereflection, Attitude Adjustment, and Appealing

Along with confrontation, Frankl's logotherapy made use of techniques that are also common in the practices of other theorists. True to basic interpersonal theory, group logotherapy helps clients change behavior patterns that interfere with their capacity to make the most of opportunities to ponder meaning (Lantz, 1993).

Reflections

Do you have a friend or relative who has some "can'ts" or "musts" that strike you as unreasonable and limiting? Imagine how a confrontation on this matter might run.

Why do you think everyone has some "can'ts" or "musts" that restrict their full enjoyment of life?

Frankl used **paradoxical intention** as early as 1939 (Lantz, 1986). A paradox is a seeming contradiction, like "the lonely crowd" or "sounds of silence" or, some would say, "leisure suit." In paradoxical intention, the counselor asks clients to exaggerate a symptom rather than try to suppress it or to purposely act out whatever they fear. A group member who fears taking up too much of the group's time might be ordered to talk about herself for fifteen minutes straight without interruption. The group could then process how they responded to the experiment. Paradoxical intention might be used in other ways to address a group process problem, like unequal contribution. Members who rarely speak might be prohibited from speaking for thirty minutes, for example. After this, these members are exclusively given the floor to add their commentary to the discussion and to reveal how they felt while being prohibited. Usually, this exercise increases the silent members' participation thenceforth, and it also makes the talkative members more apt to include silent members in future discussions.

Another technique of logotherapy is **dereflection.** Many clients come to therapy totally focused on themselves and their inner states. The counselor tries to counter this preoccupation by prescribing situations that encourage the client to focus on something else. That is, she tries to change the client's **hyperreflection** by suggesting a distraction, or helping the clients develop ideas for distracting activities. "Logotherapy works by enlarging the field of awareness to motivate an individual beyond immediate personal references to focus on objective, meaningful goals" (Lukas & Hirsch, 2002). Dereflection in groups often comes naturally; members focus on each other rather than themselves, responding genuinely and spontaneously rather than constantly planning their own next bid for attention. The therapeutic factor of altruism can function when a formerly self-absorbed client dereflects.

In existential groups, counselors may ask members to reflect on how others feel at the moment; "counselors may in a flowing, unstructured manner provide training in empathy for others" (Yalom, 1980, p. 474). For example, Yalom assigns extremely self-absorbed members to introduce new members to the group and help them talk to the group, a technique that obliges them to pay attention to other people's needs. This is another form of the technique of dereflection.

Changing the labels we use to describe things, we change the feelings we have about them. **Attitude adjustment** is the same thing as *cognitive reframing*, a crucial part of cognitive-behavioral therapy (Part V of this text). Sometimes, the way we phrase our behavior or feelings undermines our opinion of ourselves. In one group I co-led, a bookish 16-year-old thought of himself as a nerd and a loser because he wasn't popular with kids his age. One of the older members of the group called him an "intellectual" and pointed out that intellectuals were often "late bloomers" who could look forward to full enjoyment of life later, when their peers had peaked and were already in decline. Thinking of himself as an intellectual and a late bloomer improved the teenager's outlook on life considerably. Diversity in groups promotes attitude change, as this example shows. The older member is able to give the younger member a different perspective. Similarly, a poor person is often able to provide a new perspective for a rich person, a minority-group member is able to introduce a new attitude for a majority-group member, and men and women enrich each other's outlook.

Finally, Frankl used a technique that is rarely discussed in psychotherapy training: **appealing.** He discovered that some clients could find relief from distress when he verbally exhorted them to keep at it and try hard. Appealing to the clients to do better, pointing out the benefits of solving their problems, and reassuring the clients of their ability to persevere in improving—these homespun remedies were incorporated into a sophisticated existential framework. Encouragement and reassurance frequently come spontaneously from members of a counseling group, giving a member several sources of strength.

These logotherapy techniques are put into practice in various ways. I will describe two concrete methods that counselors have used.

The Mountain Range Exercise

In *The Doctor and the Soul* (1986), Frankl invited readers to envision their lives as a beautiful mountain range. What would they put on the peaks? A few experiences that were life-changing, people who were positive influences, individuals we love or who love us, might be peaks that make a difference in how we view life. In a group exercise, Ernzen (1990) gave participants paper and markers and time to sketch out their mountain range. Then they discussed who appeared on the peaks. Many times, the peaks represented people they hadn't thought about in years. The values or lessons or feelings kindled in this way promote attitude adjustment. This exercise has been used with groups for alcoholism, groups of psychiatric inpatients (mostly schizophrenics), classes, and personal growth groups. Group members "discover recurring values, recognize their uniqueness, and broaden their life view" (p. 134).

The Logochart

The logochart is a worksheet developed as homework and stimulus for Socratic dialogue by Khatami (1988). Each logochart is devoted to one problematic

FIGURE **9.1** Logochart

LOGOCHART

Event (Problem):

_____

_____

	Self = Automatic Self + Authentic Self		
Cognition: What do I think about the situation? How do I perceive it?	Distorted Irrational Unrealistic Rigid Learned Untrue	} thoughts {	Realistic Rational Adaptable Reasonable Valid True Chosen
Meaning: What are the values, purposes, goals in this situation?	Power Pleasure Fame Material things Unethical Selfishness	} motivation {	Love Creativity Purpose Ethical values Spiritual values Openmindedness Self-transcendence
Response/Behavior: What do I do about this situation? (Actions, Physical responses or consequences)	Passive Habitual Dependent Lazy Rigid Aimless Impulsive	} responses {	Active Unique—new Independent Positive Flexible Goal-directed Delayed gratification Responsible

What percentages do you assign to your reactions to the event evaluated in this chart?
Automatic: _____%   Authentic: _____%

situation and helps clients "see the problem in a way that shifts their response from their automatic self, which is part of their biology and psyche, to their authentic self, which is part of their noos, their spirit" (p. 67). Figure 9.1 presents a logochart with guidelines and a sample client logochart.

Clients are asked to separate their automatic and authentic reactions. Automatic reactions come from gut feelings and thoughts shaped by the past.

FIGURE 9.1   *continued*

SAMPLE LOGOCHART

Event:
Trouble with wife because I don't want to travel to
Tucson to see our stepdaughter and grandchild

Name: *xy*

Date: *10/1/088*

Self	=	Automatic Self	+	Authentic Self
Cognition:		*The baby is illegitimate* *I can't stand being around my stepdaughter* *I spent enough money supporting her drug habits*		*The baby was conceived in an illegitimate relationship but that doesn't make it illegitimate.* *No one forced me to spnd the $. I chose to do this. She has spent a year in drug treatment and is struggling to be responsible.*
Meaning:		*When things or people are "wrong" (not to my liking) they must be corrected* *(self-centeredness)*		*An opportunity to develop acceptance for someone I don't understand.* *I can go to Tucson for the sake of my wife. I can learn to care for someone other than myself (self-transcendence).*
Response/Behavior:		*Avoid stepdaughter and grandchild*		*Call today and make air travel arrangements to Tucson*

What percentages do you assign to your reactions to the event evaluated in this chart?
Automatic: *30* %   Authentic: *70* %

Authentic reactions reflect a person's essence and uniqueness, their meaning-oriented self. Filling in the authentic reactions is a springboard for Socratic exploration: What are the meaningful responses to the event? How would the client respond if he or she tapped into the noetic dimension? Khatami asserts that the longer clients do daily logochart homework, the more confident they become, with a more positive perspective on life.

SMALL GROUP EXERCISE

At home, try either the mountain range exercise or a logochart on one problem situation of your own. Bring your page to your small group and discuss the meanings you found in the activity. Discuss whether either activity would be helpful in the groups you lead or intend to lead, and why.

Problems Addressed by Existential Groups

Because they are focused on dilemmas of existence, existential groups have addressed many problems that most of us can expect in our lifetimes.

Boundary Situations

People on the verge of change need to consider the deeper meaning of the change. When people decide to change careers, they usually make a move backwards to being a trainee or student in their new career. Such changes bring one's values to the forefront, and sometimes it is not easy to acknowledge them and integrate them into the self-concept. For instance, our career counseling group included a woman who had always expected to become a physician, but her grades were not good enough for acceptance into medical school. Though she was well qualified to enter another health profession, she had never even considered any of them. She had always imagined herself with a "Dr." in front of her name and the prestige that would entail. She needed to start building a new, non-doctor identity. May and Yalom (2000) define these changes and their attendant concerns as **boundary situations,** "a type of urgent experience that propels the individual into a confrontation with an existential situation" (p. 291). Often, whole therapy groups are composed of people in boundary situations of various kinds or of the same kind (for example, groups for recent immigrants, for adults returning to college, and for the newly unemployed).

Existentialists are experts in the meaning of death, so people who are facing terminal illness and life-threatening disease or injury benefit from existential group therapy, which often includes a review of what one's life has meant. The deaths of parents, spouses, and other people who are close also bring up crises of personal meaning (Haines, 2000). Yalom and Vinogradov (1988), reporting on four bereavement therapy groups for widows and widowers, found that dwelling on loss, pain, and emotional unburdening took a smaller piece of the time than expected: "Many members struggled with complex questions of growth, identity, and responsibility for the future, questions that have not often been identified in discussions on bereavement groups as being of particular therapeutic import" (pp. 444–445). In other words, spouses' deaths brought up personal existential questions among the living. Lantz (1989) told the story of a couple he had seen in therapy who had abandoned their son when he came out as gay and then later felt guilty when he died of AIDS. The couple, in a dereflection strategy, gave presentations about their experience to families of gay men. They said, "these speeches help us turn a mistake into something meaningful" (p. 292).

Other losses, too, can be turned into occasions for existential revelations. The loss of a job, retirement from work, divorce, school failure, and infertility create boundary situations in which people need to redefine themselves. Disability incurs not only physical crises but also re-analysis of meaning in a person's life, contemplation of what to do with life from now on (Ososkie, 1998). After being released from prison, people are at a crossroads about what life path to follow and feel the pangs of isolation keenly (Henrion, 1989). These are all crises of meaning and identity for which existential group therapy is especially appropriate.

R e f l e c t i o n s

Choose one of your life's goals and imagine that something prevents you from pursuing it forever. How would you need to revise your identity? What would be your Plan B? Could a therapy group help you?

Chronic Emotional Hunger

Workaholism and shopaholism are often described as problems that elicit a certain amount of humor and envy. However, existentials believe they are surface complaints stemming from a deeper emptiness. Bugental and Bracke (1992) identified "the modern narcissistic patient who manifests few traditional symptoms but experiences a chronic aimlessness, emptiness, and lack of purpose" (p. 29). The central problem for these clients is an existential one, worsened by a widespread disintegration of community and the overvaluing of individualism and outward tokens of success. "The existential-humanist orientation is particularly suited to offer meaningful help to those who will become entangled in these problems" (p. 29) because it directly addresses the dilemmas inherent in life. Talking with others with similar feelings, which are often taboo in normal life, buttresses feelings of universality and altruism.

Heisel and Flett (2004) looked at the role of purpose in life among patients of a psychiatric hospital. These researchers found that purpose in life and satisfaction with life protected against suicidal thoughts even under the influence of neuroticism, depression, and social hopelessness. Purpose in life was more effective than satisfaction with life in their analysis, and was more effective against suicidal thought the more depressed a person was. The authors suggest that guiding a client's search for meaning and purpose in life may prevent suicide better than targeting sources of dissatisfaction with current life.

Persistent Disorders

Depression, neurotic anxiety, addictions, posttraumatic stress disorders, obsessive-compulsive disorders, and borderline and narcissistic personalities can all be conceptualized as responses to the facts of death, meaninglessness, freedom (and the accompanying responsibility), and isolation. Many problems that have lasted a long time and have taken over the sufferer's life come from a conviction that the self is an object without will (May & Yalom, 2000). I like Opalic's (1989) words, "the thematized existence of neurotic patients" (p. 400) to describe such a takeover because the phrase captures the lack of variety and richness in their experience. These problems often represent choices of security over growth, no matter how uncomfortable the security is to maintain, and choices of external control—blaming things outside the self instead of taking responsibility. Existentialist groups bring these choices up for reappraisal.

Some of the persistent disorders occur within families rather than within individuals alone. Lantz (1989) used existential family therapy to treat sexual dysfunction, anorexia nervosa, schizophrenia, and food abuse, mainly through dereflection, efforts to "redirect family focus away from its narrow and destructive range of concern" (p. 293). In treating an overweight family, Lantz refused to dwell on food, instead asking the family to "reflect upon what they were other than a group of people who shared a weight problem . . . All members of the family were surprised to notice that as they 'gained meaning' they 'lost weight' and that they were losing weight without trying to lose weight" (p. 296). The family stayed slim at one-, two-, and three-year follow-ups.

DISCUSSION IDEA

Speculate on what aided the overweight family in existential therapy. What could an existential therapist do with a family blended from two divorcees, each bringing in a 10-year-old and a 14-year-old?

Adaptations to Clients' Ages

The existential questions in life tend to be asked at different ages, so a developmental focus is often used in group counseling. Budman, Bennett, and Wisneski (1980) described short-term groups for people in their twenties to early thirties, mid-life (35–50), and post-mid-life (50–70). They found that among the youngest group, the major underlying issue was an inability to be close and intimate with others (in existential terms, the question of isolation). They used the group as a setting in which members learned how to deal with each other in an emotional and intimate manner, using a here-and-now orientation. They ran closed groups to avoid disruption of the intimacy among group members.

The mid-life group members were facing existential issues of meaninglessness, death, and isolation. Budman and colleagues (1980) speculate that these people had let many concerns fade into the background during intense career consolidation earlier, and they now felt the loss, being halfway through life. The groups were open and rotating, with each member joining for fifteen weeks. Two or three new participants rotated into a group with four to six existing members. This format "emphasizes the finitude of time, the reality and necessity of separation and loss, the possibility of forming new relationships, utilizing old social skills, and risking vulnerability in the need to trust and share with others" (p. 70). Therefore, the group became a microcosm of what the members faced in life outside. Termination was a thoroughly processed stage as each member rotated out.

Budman and colleagues (1980) found that groups of people in their fifties and sixties were grappling with existential despair—a feeling of time running out and a questioning of the meaningfulness of their lives. They set up an interesting open format, in which each participant could attend twenty sessions within one year, at any time they deemed best. Thus, the format reflected the idea that even though time is limited, one can choose how to best use it. The basic focus of this group was on the here-and-now, with a practical problem-solving orientation. "The group provides an 'undying' constant, meeting even when the therapist is on vacation" (p. 73). Personal mortality was rarely a topic of this group directly, perhaps due to shifting membership week to week.

Life Review with Elderly Clients

According to Erikson's (1950) psychosocial stage theory, our last crisis is one of integrity versus despair. As you may remember, at each of the eight stages of life we have one major developmental task, and successful handling of that task prepares the way for the next. In old age, we need to be able to look back on our lives and see them as coherent, meaningful, and satisfying. This constitutes integrity, whereas the failure to look back and frame life in this manner leads to despair. So the end of life is a time of existential concerns, perhaps more than any other (Breitbart, Gibson, Poppito, & Berg, 2004).

Old age entails many kinds of losses (Myers & Harper, 2004)—death of spouse and friends, disability, lowered income, less freedom of movement, and (in mainstream U.S. life) no well-defined, crucial, respected role in society. Needless to say, the situation calls for a questioning of life's meaning, especially with death's chariot at our backs. In the 1960s, Butler (e.g., 1963) proposed that the valued pastime of reminiscence among the elderly should not be taken lightly among counselors, that it in fact serves an existential purpose. Butler relabeled it as **life review** and began a long-lasting line of thinking among mental health professionals about how group work in the area could help old people achieve integrity over despair. Life review is natural in later life and "has emerged as the treatment of choice in virtually all settings in which older adults congregate for voluntary reasons or through institutional or group-living placements" (Myers

& Harper, 2004, p. 214). The material comes from group members exclusively. Members bring in stories, photographs, music, old clothing, catalogs, and historical objects and discuss their significance (Kiernat, 1986). A valuable advantage is that memory-impaired people can participate because they respond to these cues and are likely to have pockets of intact reminiscence to offer, bolstering their sense of identity. Cohesiveness, empathy, mutual support, and a feeling of universality are curative factors, as in any humanistic venture.

You may be thinking that regret, remorse, guilt, and sadness are inevitable in a life review and that stirring these feelings up among old people holds dangers. Life may seem a waste or shameful. However, group therapists Myrna Lewis and Robert Butler (1986) noted, "This is more likely to happen when the person makes judgments on his own, without testing or sharing them. Most people have the capacity to reconcile their lives, to confront real guilt, and to find meaning, especially in the presence of acceptance and support from others" (p. 55).

Evaluating Existential Group Therapy

On an individual level, you may want to look at each member's progress by administering tests before the group begins and again at later points, such as when a member leaves the group or when it disbands. Some of the tests designed to measure existential conditions for individuals are the Purpose in Life inventory (PIL; available from alanleak@cs.com), the Seeking of Noetic Goals test (SONG; Crumbaugh, 1977), and the Existential Vacuum Scale of the Minnesota Multiphasic Personality Inventory (EVS, a set of items from the MMPI; Hutzell & Peterson, 1985). These are described in Guttmann's (1996) *Logotherapy for the Helping Professional: Meaningful Social Work*, Chapters 9 and 10. Ernzen (1990) reported that one counselor in a psychiatric facility used the PIL in evaluating her mountain range exercise, described in this chapter. The counselor administered the twenty PIL items before the exercise and after the exercise and asked her patients to note any changes in their answers stemming from what occurred during the exercise. Five of seven psychiatric inpatients made changes in one or more items, signifying more positive thoughts about their lives.

The website *http://testcollection.ets.org* provides information on the SONG and the PIL.

KEY TERMS

anxiety emotional discomfort in response to perceived threats to existence or to values we find fundamental to existence

appealing exhortation and encouragement to improve one's situation

attitude adjustment (or *cognitive reframing*) changing one's situation by changing thoughts and feelings about it

boundary situations an identifiable experience that propels the individual into a confrontation with an existential dilemma

dereflection   a focus away from the self

existential anxiety   a feeling of fearful unease that comes from awareness of death, isolation, freedom, and meaninglessness

existential guilt   regret or remorse over sins of omission (not taking action)

existential vacuum   a feeling of inner emptiness, doubt, and despair

experiential groups   (Yalom-type) counseling groups focused on experiencing the therapeutic factors in interpersonal encounters

flow   the experience of total absorption in something outside oneself, such as work, sport, nature, and art

focused listening   paying attention, with special notice of talk that reflects the struggles with meaning, relationships, and identity as underlying themes

hyperreflection   an intense, exclusive focus on the self

life review   reminiscence therapy, in which the elderly or dying look back on their lives and identify meaningful elements

logotherapy   counseling based on existential philosophy and focused on the search for meaning

noetic   the spiritual, as opposed to bodily or mental, aspect of humans. *Noos* is the spirit

paradoxical intention   a therapeutic intervention that suggests that the client do the opposite of what is usually desirable or intensify unwanted behavior, in hopes that he or she eventually sees its folly or tires of it

peak experiences   moments of highest, transcendent happiness and fulfillment

phenomenological stance   the philosophy that we attach subjective interpretations to experience, interpretations that are quite individual; thus, reality differs for each person

self-transcendence   the human capacity to reach out beyond oneself toward people to love, causes to be served, and creative expression

Socratic questioning   give-and-take conversation seeking truth through exploring inner experiences

will to meaning   a drive to find significance in life experiences

CHAPTER REVIEW

1. Summarize the four existential themes and explain why they pose problems for humans today.

2. Develop your own opinion on the *will to meaning*. Use examples to argue for or against its validity.

3. Describe a peak experience from your own life, or as close as you have probably come to one.

4. Why do you think existential questions are avoided in most conversations? According to logotherapy, what is the value of discussing such questions?

5. In a Socratic dialogue, what are five types of question the logotherapist is likely to ask?

6. Review the techniques of paradoxical intention, dereflection, attitude adjustment, and appealing. Explain these techniques to a friend outside your class, and discuss together examples you've seen practiced informally, in your own lives.

7. Name some boundary situations other than the ones mentioned in this chapter.

8. Why is life review more effective in groups than individually? Do you think life review would be useful for younger people as well as the elderly?

FOR FURTHER READING

May, R. (1994). *The courage to create.* NY: Norton. (First published 1975)

> This is an entertaining, short (144-page) treatise that will introduce you to much existentialist thought and its applications to everyday life. May is credited with bringing existentialist psychology to America and blending it with American humanism. He studied with major figures: Alfred Adler, Paul Tillich, Henry Stack Sullivan, and Erich Fromm. For May, creativity applies to more than the creation of art; he uses the term to describe the authentic adult striving for self-actualization in the face of anxiety and uncertainty.

REFERENCES

Barnes, R. C. (2000). Viktor Frankl's logotherapy: Spirituality and meaning in the new millenium. *TCA Journal, 28,* 24–31.

Bauman, S., & Walso, M. (1998). Existential theory and mental health counseling: If it were a snake, it would have bitten! *Journal of Mental Health Counseling, 20*(19), 13–27.

Breitbart, W., Gibson, C., Poppito, S. R., & Berg, A. (2004). Psychotherapeutic interventions at the end of life: A focus on meaning and spirituality. *Canadian Journal of Psychiatry, 49,* 366–372.

Budman, S. H., Bennett, M. J., & Wisneski, M. J. (1980). Short-term group psychotherapy: An adult developmental model. *International Journal of Group Psychotherapy, 30,* 63–76.

Bugental, J. F. T., & Bracke, P. E. (1992). The future of existential-humanistic psychotherapy. *Psychotherapy, 29,* 28–33.

Butler, R. N. (1963). The life review: An interpretation of reminiscence in the aged. *Psychiatry, 26,* 65–76.

Crumbaugh, J. C. (1977). The Seeking of Noetic Goals test (SONG): A complementary scale to the Purpose-in-Life test (PIL). *Journal of Clinical Psychology, 33,* 900–907.

Csikszentmihalyi, M. (1990). *Flow: The psychology of optimal experience.* New York: Harper & Row.

Erikson, E. (1950). *Childhood and society.* New York: Norton.

Ernzen, F. I. (1990). Frankl's mountain range exercise. *The International Forum for Logotherapy, 13,* 133–134.

Frankel, B. (2002). Existential issues in group psychotherapy. *The International Journal of Group Psychotherapy, 52,* 215–231.

Frankl, V. (1984). *Man's search for meaning.* Boston: Washington Square Press. (Original work published 1946)

Frankl, V. (1986). *The doctor and the soul: From psychotherapy to logotherapy* (3rd expanded ed.). New York: Vintage.

Guttmann, D. (1996). *Logotherapy for the helping professional: Meaningful social work.* New York: Springer.

Haines, P. E. (2000). Logotherapy concepts applied to grief and mourning. *International Forum for Logotherapy, 23,* 74–80.

Heisel, M. J., & Flett, G. L. (2004). Purpose in life, satisfaction with life, and suicide ideation in a clinical sample. *Journal of Psychopathology and Behavioral Assessment, 26,* 127–135.

Henrion, R. (1989). Logotherapy for former prisoners. *International Forum for Logotherapy, 12,* 95–96.

Hergenhahn, B. R. (2001). *An introduction to the history of psychology* (4th ed.). Belmont, CA: Wadsworth.

Hutzell, R. R., & Peterson, T. J. (1985). An MMPI existential vacuum scale for logotherapy research. *The International Forum for Logotherapy, 8,* 97–100.

Khatami, M. (1988). Clinical application of the logochart. *International Forum for Logotherapy, 11,* 67–75.

Kiernat, J. M. (1986). The use of life review activity. In I. Burnside (Ed.), *Working with the elderly: Group process and techniques* (2nd ed., pp. 50–59). Boston: Jones & Bartlett.

Laing, R. D. (1969). *The divided self.* New York: Pantheon.

Lantz, J. (1998). Dream reflection in logotherapy: Facilitating the psychotherapeutic process and case studies. *Journal of Contemporary Psychotherapy, 28,* 81–89.

Lantz, J. (1986). Family logotherapy. *Contemporary Family Therapy, 8,* 124–135.

Lantz, J. (1989). Family logotherapy with an overweight family. *Contemporary Family Therapy, 11,* 287–297.

Lantz, J. (1993). Treatment modalities in logotherapy. *International Forum for Logotherapy, 16,* 65–73.

Lewis, M. I, & Butler, R. N. (1986). Life-review therapy: Putting memories to work. In I. Burnside (Ed.), *Working with the elderly: Group process and techniques* (2nd ed., pp. 50–59). Boston: Jones & Bartlett.

Lukas, E., & Hirsch, B. Z. (2002). Logotherapy. In F. W. Kaslow (Ed.), *Comprehensive Handbook of Psychotherapy* (Vol. 3, pp. 333–356). New York: Wiley.

MacNair-Semands, R. R., & Lese, K. P. (2000). Interpersonal problems and the perception of therapeutic factors in group therapy. *Small Group Research, 31,* 158–174.

Maslow, A. H. (1968). *Toward a psychology of being* (2nd ed.). Princeton, NJ: Van Nostrand.

May, R. (1961). *Existential psychology.* New York: Random House.

May, R. (1977). *The meaning of anxiety* (rev. ed.). New York: Norton. (Original work published 1950)

May, R., & Yalom, I. (2000). Existential psychotherapy. In R. J. Corsini & D. Wedding (Eds.), *Current psychotherapies* (6th ed., pp. 273–302). Itasca, IL: Peacock.

Myers, J. E., & Harper, M. C. (2004). Evidence-based effective practices with older adults. *Journal of Counseling and Development, 82,* 207–218.

Opalic, P. (1989). Existential and psychopathological evaluation of group psychotherapy of neurotic and psychotic patients. *International Journal of Group Psychotherapy, 39,* 389–411.

Ososkie, J. N. (1998). Existential perspectives in rehabilitation counseling. *Rehabilitation Education, 12,* 217–222.

Page, R. C., Weiss, J. F., & Lietaer, G. (2002). Humanistic group psychotherapy. In D. J. Cain (Ed.), *Humanistic psychotherapies: Handbook of research and practice* (pp. 339–368). Washington, DC: American Psychological Association.

Rosenbaum, M. (1993). Existential-humanistic approach to group psychotherapy. In H. I. Kaplan & B. J. Sadock (Eds.), *Comprehensive Group Psychotherapy* (3rd ed., pp. 235–243). Baltimore, MD: Williams & Wilkins.

Russell, J. M. (1978). Sartre, therapy, and expanding the concept of responsibility. *American Journal of Psychoanalysis, 38,* 258–269.

Tyler, L. (1969). *The work of the counselor* (3rd ed.). New York: Meredith Corporation.

Ungar, M. (1997). A four-step model of logotherapy. *International Forum for Logotherapy, 20,* 113–119.

Wilson, R. A. (1997). Finding meaning through Frankl's Socratic dialogue and Fromm's five needs of the human condition: A group process for school counseling. *International Forum for Logotherapy, 20,* 28–36.

Yalom, I. D. (1980). *Existential psychotherapy.* New York: Basic Books.

Yalom, I. D. (1995). *The theory and practice of group psychotherapy* (4th ed.). New York: Basic Books.

Yalom, I. D., & Vinogradov, S. C. (1988). Bereavement groups: Techniques and themes. *International Journal of Group Psychotherapy, 38,* 419–446.

The Unfolding of Awareness

In this section (Chapters 10 and 11), I will explain group therapies that have similar underlying theories. They all grow from Freudian, psychoanalytic roots, though they have strayed from the original Freudian analysis. Psychodynamic and Gestalt groups share basic assumptions. For example, they work from *universal principles* that are believed to apply to all humans, in all different settings and across the globe and through history. They also endorse the idea of the *unconscious*—an area of mental life that is outside of awareness and perception, yet still powerfully affects the way we think, feel, and behave. Furthermore, these theories concur that the past, especially experience between birth and age 6, strongly determines a person's present.

CHAPTER 10

Psychodynamic Group Theory and Practice

A Selection from "The Psychoanalysis of Groups"

Essential Concepts of Psychodynamic Theory

Life Stages ▪ *Psychological Structures* ▪ *Internal Conflicts* ▪ *Anxiety* ▪ *Resistance and Defenses* ▪ *Transference and Countertransference*

Group Dynamics

The Nature of the Group ▪ *Stages of the Group*

Leadership Skills

Investigating Transference ▪ *Promoting Insight* ▪ *Interpretation*

Techniques in Psychodynamic Group Counseling

Free Association ▪ *Dream Work*

Problems Addressed by Psychodynamic Groups

Adaptations to Clients' Ages

Evaluating Psychodynamic Groups

Psychodynamic approaches are descendants from Freudian analysis, and most psychodynamic counselors still use much Freudian language to explain the internal conflicts that express themselves in the form of life's problems. A crucial element of psychodynamic counseling involves exposing clients' unconscious drives and motives, an exposure that most clients resist in various ways. Counselors who practice individual therapy are trained to interpret the **unconscious,** the part of mental life that is outside of waking awareness, with finely-tuned timing and wording. However, in a group, the members also analyze each other's unconscious material, and they are not experts in the technique. In the following selection, Alexander Wolf, a major figure in group psychodynamic treatment, discusses the issue of whether group members are effective at unearthing unconscious material among themselves.

A Selection from

"The Psychoanalysis of Groups"

By Alexander Wolf (1949)

Unfettered expressions of feeling are one concomitant of the new permissive family that the group comes to represent for each patient. As members learn that it is safe both to give and accept spontaneous emotion, they realize that something formerly denied them in the old family has been added—tolerance. In this kind of atmosphere it becomes stimulating to plumb the causes of frustration and, communicating in a language that is dynamic, to liberate and develop resources temporarily stunted by earlier familial influence.

The naturally cautious therapist may legitimately ask: is the average precariously balanced patient safe in the clumsy hands of schizoid and neurotically aggressive patients who may expose unconscious drives too swiftly or attack too cruelly the weak and defenseless? In the group's concerted attack on the neurotic character structure, will it not be too rapidly shattered, leaving the patient dangerously insecure and with such weak ego reserves that he may be forced into psychosis? It is certainly true that the atmosphere is sometimes charged and subject to the most explosive kind of interreaction. Will these intense situations become traumatic?

The answer to this question is, indeed, reassuring. Nothing really inimical to the patient's interest ensues. If a member seems to be growing unduly anxious or overwhelmed, the analyst can return him to individual treatment for a short period. Patients are fortified against destructive attack by constant coaching from the therapist. They are cautioned to make the neat distinction between the valid and the neurotic in what is directed at them. When a member invests others with qualities they do not possess—when he projects—the therapist exposes his irrelevant and irrational distortions of reality as unreal. The patients themselves become adept at elaborating these enlightening differences between fact and fiction in every remark. Pained though a dissected member may feel, if the appraisal of him is unjust, he is usually so well fortified by well-disposed group opinion that his ego survives it substantially intact. As he progresses in treatment and learns to appreciate the neurotic character of aspects of ill-considered judgments of him, he develops an increasing immunity to them. If he had been wary of his own aggression, he learns to flail out where provocation invites it. But he educates himself best by extracting from neurotically tinged projection onto him, that kernel of information which is useful to him as insight.

The patient who is the target of free association learns why and in what ways he gladdens or irritates the group. He discovers his provocative role. He may have, up to now, always regarded himself as the victim of other people's aggression and cruelty or wondered why people fled him in distress. When they tell him face to face just how he provokes them, he develops acute insight into the way he evokes the environmental responses that in turn startle him. With an awareness of his provocative traits, both he and the group are impelled to search for the unconscious motives which arouse critical reactions in the others. Crass and unflattering as some judgment of him may be, it is always associated with an essential sympathy and friendliness from the majority of the group.

In the demonstration of a patient's provocative role the group is a natural and effective agent. In individual analysis the therapist is hardly so responsive as to clarify the patient's stimulating conduct with the same completeness as the group. The various members are each so sensitized by their particular neurotic constellations that they can more accurately discern and point up each participant's exciting peculiarities. Under individual treatment patients are impelled to review historical and present abuse at the hands of others. And the probing, sympathetic analyst is occasionally misled by the patient's complaints, unless he sees him in the animating current of the group. This has been proven to me many times after introducing a member to a group following a preliminary period of private treatment. In the social setting he often seems a quite different person. The presence of others elicits so many diverse facets of his personality that he is barely recognizable. In this regard, it is instructive to introduce a new patient following the recovery and discharge of an old one. Almost everyone shows a new aspect of himself, hitherto unseen, in response to the character structure of the newcomer. . . .

In this period the therapist urges patients to regard themselves not merely as passive recipients of insight provided by the physician, but to become adjunct analysts by actively pursuing their uncensored speculation about one another. This approach encourages them to respect their unpremeditated fantasies, expands their resources and gives them a feeling of reassurance. (pp. 547–549)

Exploring "The Psychoanalysis of Groups"

1. In the first paragraph of Wolf's explanation, how does he suggest that the group is like a family? How is it unlike members' earlier families?

2. What possible worries does Wolf bring up about bringing disturbed patients together to work on their problems?

3. What does a group member do when he or she "projects"?

4. How does the group member gain insight into how people treat him or her? Why can members accept unflattering judgments from other members?

5. Why is the therapist's opinion of a client's behavior (in individual therapy) less accurate than a group's point of view on the same client?

6. What is the role of the therapist in the group treatment Wolf describes? What is the role of the group members in relation to each other?

■ ■ ■

Reflections

1. We often use the word *unconscious* in everyday life, in statements like, "I unconsciously chose a boyfriend just like my father" or "I lost my philosophy textbook because unconsciously I didn't want to read it." Think of a time when you used the word informally, and explain what you meant (or use an example from a friend's use of it).

2. Do you think that the unconscious is a nonexistent, weak, medium, or strong influence on your behavior, feelings, and thinking? If you have never discussed this topic with your friends, do so now. Do you disagree or agree among yourselves?

Essential Concepts of Psychodynamic Theory

You have just examined a psychodynamic group explained by an expert, Alexander Wolf. Now, we will step back from this illustration while I explain some basic assumptions that are shared by the two group therapy orientations—psychodynamic and Gestalt—discussed here in Part IV. You will remember Wolf's group several times as you read through this chapter and will understand more and more elements of his discussion. Psychodynamic therapy and Gestalt therapy share similar elements derived from Freudian psychoanalysis, although they employ different terminology and put different levels of emphasis on these elements. An overall understanding of six concepts will be a good foundation for your understanding of both therapeutic orientations. These concepts are life stages, psychological structures, internal conflicts, anxiety, resistance and defenses, and transference and countertransference.

Life Stages

Psychodynamic and Gestalt therapies solidly share the idea that the past continues in the present. The experiences of our childhoods, in particular, resonate in our personalities as adults. Social and personal development occurs in identifiable stages as we go through time. At each stage, we adapt to other people and the environment in predictable patterns, and psychological problems develop when we fail to adapt as expected for some reason. We also create our own unique personalities as we face the challenges of each stage.

An example you're familiar with is Freud's Oedipal stage, in which boys between 3 and 6 years of age love their mothers and wish to possess them exclusively. A successful resolution of this stage, which presents a problem because such possession is impossible, is that the boy learns to identify with his father, who does possess the mother. Thus, the boy gets what he desires while avoiding punishment for monopolizing his mom. Freud identified the psychological components of several other stages of life, as well. Erik Erikson's psychosocial stages also follow development through life, adding a social learning element to Freud's intrapsychic stages. For Erikson (1950), the same age period (3 to 6 years of age) for boys *and* girls is a time of challenge in which they develop self-direction, purpose, and personal goals—that is, they begin to have personal initiative. A failure at this stage creates a psychological background of guilt. Each stage of life has its own challenges to be resolved: the Oedipal or personal initiative stage is only one example.

Getting stuck at one stage or failing to complete the adaptive task at one stage results in psychological distress. This distress is likely to involve repetitive, damaging, and unrealistic relationships with other people, the negative cognitive-interpersonal cycles described in Chapter 2. The distress also involves a fragmented or unstable sense of self. Psychodynamic therapists might call such problems **neuroses**. Many psychodynamic counselors believe that successful therapy includes using **regression,** going back to an earlier stage of life, to solve the problems that were not solved at the time.

Psychological Structures

Psychodynamic theories are **analytical** because they explain mental operations metaphorically as structures, with component parts that interact in a dynamic way. These parts and interactions are analyzed. Freud (1923) saw mental life divided into the **id, ego,** and **superego**, for instance. The superego carried the urges of conscience, while the id clamored for expression of primitive drives (sex and aggression), and the ego tried to balance the other two structures in ways that were consistent with outside reality. Later psychodynamic theorists, including Freud's daughter Anna Freud (1936), gave the ego a bigger role as an agent of psychological health and stability.

These are just a few examples of structural analysis common to psychodynamic thought. As I described them, you can imagine how they struggle within a single person. They affect each other and draw from the same well of psychological energy. If you are using a lot of psychological energy in one place, you don't have much left for the others. And if psychological energy is blocked in one place, it will overflow in others.

Internal Conflicts

The struggles among psychological structures are internal conflicts. These often occur outside of awareness, or unconsciously. The outward signs of these conflicts are patterns of behavior, feeling, and thought. An unrealistic, bothersome passion for tidiness may be the outgrowth of the inner conflict between messiness and order. An intense dislike for loud, boisterous people may come from keeping a close check on that side of one's self. Keeping internal conflicts from bursting forth into consciousness takes a large amount of psychological energy. As I mentioned above, this allocation of psychological energy means that somewhere else, there is a shortage of energy. Psychodynamic theorists usually adhere to this banking-type metaphor of psychic spending and debt.

Anxiety

Internal conflicts result in **anxiety.** In Freudian and psychodynamic theories, anxiety is a signal that a war between internal psychic structures is going on. One structure is threatening to overwhelm another one. For example, an inner, childish, id impulse to overeat and drink too much is nagging at the ego, which is managing the superego's insistence on perfect self-control and restriction. When this battle is at its height but out of awareness, getting hungry might be anxiety-producing. That is, the hunger sensation triggers the anxiety of the struggle between id, ego, and superego. Or one's unconscious desire to have wild sex with strangers makes one anxious when the topic comes up in a movie. The movie triggers the anxiety of the inner conflict between moral behavior and id impulses.

Resistance and Defenses

The feeling of anxiety is a signal that the war among psychological structures is escalating or that reality is threatening their balance, and something must be done. What must be done? You marshal your habitual ways of avoiding threat. These ways are often called **defense mechanisms,** and they include both fairly adaptive and severely damaging responses to threat. For example, transforming strong inner drives into acceptable social behavior such as work, humor, and creative arts is usually healthy. This is called **sublimation.** (Many of us find jokes about dentists, rabbis, psychologists, and blondes quite hilarious because these people's stereotyped roles cause anxiety.) On the other hand, **repression** and **denial,** which seek to remove pain by excluding it from awareness, and **displacement,** taking hostility out on innocent people and objects, are usually considered dangerous to mental health. Like most personality features, our patterns of defense are established early in life in response to real or perceived threats to our well-being, especially social threats such as abandonment or anger. We also tend to imitate our parents' favorite defense mechanisms and pass them along to our children. The following list describes some of the most commonly used defense mechanisms and how they might display themselves in a group:

> **Rationalization** You create a logical reason to explain a painful experience and thus remove it from the sphere of feelings. For example, a group member might go to some lengths to explain her behavior logically rather than going into her emotional motivations.

> **Reaction Formation** You act and speak in opposition to impulses you wish you didn't have. A group client might insist that he likes everyone in the group all the time because he is so threatened by negative feelings.

> **Projection** You attribute to others your own characteristic ways of being. For example, an insanely jealous person might see everyone else as driven by jealousy. Group members can project their interpretations of events,

people, and the group so strongly that others also adopt the same interpretations (Clark, 1997). When the interpretations are negative, this process undermines the whole group.

Fantasy You escape a real world that is aversive or boring by dreaming of a better situation. You might have a group member who has a rich fantasy life in sharp contrast to her real-life situation. She presents both lives as factual. Other group members and you may at first believe in the fantasy, and only later put together the facts of the situation.

Repression You forget painful experiences and situations. Trauma victims have been subjects of investigation about repression of experiences like wartime horrors and child sexual abuse.

Emotional Insulation You mask your pain by believing that you do not really care. You might see emotional insulation in a group member who describes a terrible experience with no sign of feeling or discounts the depth of his feeling by saying that he's gotten over it.

Displacement For various reasons, you cannot act out your hostility to the person you are really angry at, so you take it out on someone less threatening. In a group, members may scapegoat another member when they are actually angry at the counselor.

Denial You simply do not see the bad things that are going on. For example, there may be an angry split between subgroups in the group, but one member might not be aware of the antagonism that is obvious to others because it is so threatening to that one person.

Sublimation You transform sexual and aggressive drives into a socially acceptable form. Becoming an active leader in a group may satisfy aggressive urges.

Regression You behave as though you are at an earlier stage of development. Many psychodynamic theorists believe that group members need to revert to earlier stages to tie up unfinished business. In everyday life, you see regression when mature adults visit their parents' home and return to acting like adolescents. Groups as a whole also regress to earlier stages of group life in response to challenge or threat.

Identification You get satisfaction and overcome inferiority feelings by allying yourself psychologically with a powerful, successful entity. Group members often align themselves with their therapist.

Exploring the territory of the unknown within one's own psyche is frightening. No matter how distressing, the territory we know is less threatening than the territory we haven't explored. Psychodynamic counselors focus on **resistance** to exploration, which takes many forms:

- being late,
- missing sessions,
- refusing to speak,

- not letting anyone else speak,
- deflecting attention,
- changing the subject when a topic gets touchy, and so on.

DISCUSSION IDEAS

1. Your class includes many people who have done counseling work already. In a class discussion, give these members an opportunity to share examples of defense mechanisms and resistance that they have observed in their clients.

2. Review the above list of forms of resistance. Psychodynamic counselors are sometimes criticized for seeing resistance everywhere. Discuss how you could discern behavior that indicates resistance from the same behavior that flows from another motivation. For example, when should and shouldn't you think of lateness as resistance?

Transference and Countertransference

A great portion of our interpersonal behavior is a repetition (usually concealed) of early relationships. Consistent with cognitive-interpersonal schema theory, our current feelings and attitudes toward other people are similar to our feelings and attitudes toward significant early figures in our lives. Remember that psychodynamic thought places emphasis on the formative power of childhood experience, especially experiences with powerful authorities like mothers and fathers. Our current interpersonal behavior is a clue to what happened to us in childhood, especially when we see some resemblance—for example, men with authority remind us of fathers, and women with the power of giving and taking remind us of mothers. The current repetition of old patterns of relationships is labeled **transference** because we transfer qualities of earlier figures onto new people whom we view as similar (Foulkes, 1961). Therapy clients tend to see their counselors as parental figures and to impart their mother's or father's motivations to the counselor.

Among ourselves, we therapists often talk about cases in which clients exclaim, "I went and did just what you told me to do!" when we are quite sure that we have never given a directive at all. This kind of client *transfers* to us, as authority figures, their own expectations to be told what to do. Probably their fathers or mothers were commanding types, and they see this in other authority figures. Actually, it's highly unlikely that a counselor will single-handedly demand a specific course of action.

A significant related concept is **countertransference**—that is, how you as a counselor respond to the transference that was laid on you. For instance, as a counselor I often encounter clients who bring out a protective streak in me. This response says something about me as well as about the client. Consider that a different counselor might find the same client irritating—the client has brought out different countertransference reactions, which are based on each counselor's own interpersonal history. I respond to some clients from a side of myself that sympathizes with vulnerability. One of the ugly forms of counter-transference occurs when a counselor actively reciprocates a client's crush on him or her. Though client crushes are inevitable, counselors are trained not to take advantage of them.

Gans (1992) examined breaking the taboo of talking about money in psychoanalytic group counseling. "Interpersonal transactions around money in group highlight favoritism, sadism, masochism, secrecy, seduction, protection, and corruption. Lifting the taboo against discussing money unleashes material that may be potentially upsetting for the leader as well as group members" (p. 134). The author describes the transference and countertransference reactions to open group discussions of counseling fees, late payment, nonpayment, charges during absence, and other financial transactions involved in the therapy. Group members reenact past experiences of rivalry, rejection, idealization, and suspicion of authority figures, while the leader may feel guilty, inadequate, sadistic, worried, and wrongful depending on his or her own background experiences concerning money.

Much of traditional psychoanalysis consists of exploring transferences, countertransferences, and resistances in order to gain insight into psychological conflicts. Psychodynamic groups also concern themselves with these processes, varying group by group in how directly and deeply they do so.

Reflections

How might some of the defense mechanisms listed earlier in this chapter be enacted in a counseling group? Choose one or two, show how it would be elicited in group, and suggest how the leader and other members might respond to it. Consider whether this occurrence would be bad for the group or good for the group in some way.

Group Dynamics

Therapies based on psychodynamic theory involve insight, that is, bringing into awareness (or consciousness) processes that are out of awareness (or unconscious). A handy model for thinking about conscious and unconscious features of human interactions is the **Johari window** (Luft, 1984), which illuminates the nature of group dynamics. The term comes from combining the names of its creators, Joseph Luft and Harrington Ingham (Joe and Harry), who developed it in the 1950s. The Johari window is graphically displayed as a box divided into four quadrants, shown in Figure 10.1. Each quadrant represents a state of awareness of behavior, feeling, and motivation. Sometimes awareness is shared; sometimes it isn't. The quadrants are divided by who is aware of an act, a feeling, or a motive.

As awareness changes, the psychological state changes quadrants.

Quadrant 1, the open quadrant, refers to behavior, feelings, and motivation known to self and others [the group].

Quadrant 2, the blind quadrant, refers to behavior, feelings, and motivation known to others [the group] but not to self.

Quadrant 3, the hidden quadrant, refers to behavior, feelings, and motivation known to self but not to others [the group].

Quadrant 4, the unknown quadrant, refers to behavior, feelings, and motivation known neither to self nor to others [the group]. (Luft, 1984, pp. 60–61)

Each individual comprises all four quadrants. The first quadrant reflects a person's basic openness to the world, which varies widely from person to person. Luft believed that "knowledge, skill, awareness, and pleasure are determined by the magnitude of the first quadrant" (p. 64) and that it establishes an aspiration for change. The pattern of relationships to your self and to others is the greatest source of more openness to the world.

The blind quadrant represents the huge area of Freud's iceberg that lies below the waterline, with conscious knowledge just the small visible tip of the iceberg. Some things of which you are unaware become known to others around you. In group therapy, this is the area that can be diminished through feedback of various kinds, including **interpretation** of your behavior, feelings, and motivations by other group members and the leader. For instance, your prejudices are sometimes clear to others but not to you yourself unless they are pointed out; also, some of your rules for living are not in awareness unless someone else states them. Work in quadrant 2 involves the struggle for enlightenment and self-knowledge that we all face.

The hidden quadrant contains material that in an ongoing group is eventually shared through self-disclosure. This disclosure has an immediate effect on quadrants 1 and 2. Quadrant 1 is expanded through the growth of openness. Quadrant 2, also, is expanded, because when others see more of you openly, they also see more of your blind area. They are able to give you more accurate feedback, and this affects the diminishment of your blind area. Furthermore, self-disclosure on your part engenders self-disclosure on others' parts, leading to greater trust and lower defensiveness.

The fourth, unknown, quadrant is the realm of potential for individual and group insight into previously out-of-awareness material. Exploration of daydreams, night dreams, and experiences of altered states (fever, shock, crisis, drug reactions, hypnosis, spiritual ecstasy) provide opportunities for revealing new knowledge heretofore unknown to everyone in the group.

FIGURE 10.1   **The Johari Window**

	Known to self	Not known to self
Known to others	1. Open	2. Blind
Not known to others	3. Hidden	4. Unknown

This model of group dynamics helps us understand how feedback, self-disclosure, mutual responsiveness, trust, and interpretation work together to produce group and individual insight. It also can be used to identify in what quadrant the difficulty lies when a group bogs down and fails to progress toward its goals.

DISCUSSION IDEA

Work together to develop an elaboration of Luft's quotation concerning the first quadrant. Why is its size reflective of psychological well-being? Do you agree that being open to yourself and others reflects well-being?

The Nature of the Group

Groups based on psychodynamic theory are extremely varied, so it is difficult to make general statements about their technical set-ups. A survey of psychodynamic materials suggests that therapy groups are usually made up of seven to ten people and are heterogeneous in age, sex, and nature of problem. The recommendation for size has remained stable for more than fifty years (Rutan & Stone, 2001; Wolf, 1949). Many group leaders like heterogeneity among members because it provides a variety of opportunities for transference. Some psychodynamic groups are organized around narrower problems, such as grief and loss (Rutan & Stone, 2001).

Brief psychodynamic work can be done in twelve-week periods, with one ninety-minute session a week (Rutan & Stone, 2001). Many groups are structured to fit into another schedule; for example, college students' groups begin and end with the semester schedule. Inpatient groups run continuously, with membership changing as people come in and out of the hospital. Some groups contract to meet for a certain number of sessions and then reevaluate and integrate new members and bid farewell to others before agreeing on a new cycle of sessions. Some psychodynamically oriented groups last for years.

In comparison with the therapies explicated in Part III of this book, the humanist and existential groups, the psychodynamically based groups do focus more on individual insight and problem solving than on whole-group processes. Psychodynamically based groups had their roots in psychoanalysis, which was practiced individually: "In spite of the fact that this is a statement about psychoanalysis in groups, we wish not to ignore the truth that for each patient his own personal development is central" (Wolf, Schwartz, McCarty, & Goldberg, 1972).

Stages of the Group

Groups based on psychodynamic theory, like all groups, go through stages of development from beginning to end. A general model includes three stages and termination, assuming that individual counseling and preparation for group occurs before stage one.

In the first stage, members enter into agreements or contracts concerning the treatment and their goals. These are usually written documents (at least, parts are), and they include standard assent to attend sessions, be on time, work actively, pay for treatment, and protect the privacy of group members (Rutan & Stone, 2001). Each group leader or institutional setting may have additional items, such as promises not to socialize with fellow members outside of sessions, if that is desirable or possible. In brief psychodynamic groups, clients also identify their specific goals—what they wish to change and how they will know when they have changed. For example,

> I am suffering daily from my grief over my brother's death from cancer. I would like to come to terms with the death and move on with my life. When I achieve these goals, I will be able to keep my job and pay attention to it, and my family will also feel my attention to them and will not complain of my emotional neglect. I will be able to go twenty-four hours at a time without crying.

These contracts may be revised as the group progresses because people seeking help are frequently confused about their goals or may have difficulty imagining life without their problems.

The first stage in these groups includes a pedagogical element. Psychodynamic theory has a specialized vocabulary to describe psychological life and treatment activities, and the leader teaches this language through direct instruction, through modeling, and through example. For instance, most groups do **rounds,** an activity in which every group member is asked to respond to some cue or question (Jacobs, Masson, & Harvill, 2002). Group members learn to understand the word *rounds* in this way in the first stage. In order for sessions to progress, the members learn the vocabulary and terminology for concepts basic to the treatment. In the process, they are socialized into the treatment and develop norms. Meanwhile, the leader is asking himself or herself the question, "How can I create the conditions that will enable these people to tap into each other as resources here?" (Kepner, 1994, p.14).

In the first stage, members also develop cohesion. At this point, feeling safe and included is most crucial. Members have a tendency to emphasize the similarities among themselves, and the leader supports this inclusiveness. Exploration of members' presenting problems, and conceptualizing them in terms of the theory behind the group, is begun in this stage. For instance, inquiry into formative childhood experiences is typical, and the connection between childhood experiences and current behavior, thoughts, and feelings is a focus. Group leaders accept their role as teachers and experts in this stage and gain the trust of the group.

The second and third stages of treatment, combined, are often called the **work** of the group. This means the goal-directed activities pursued by a group that has achieved orientation, cohesion, and norms. The techniques described in this chapter are mostly used in the working stages of a group.

In the second stage, differences among the members arise, and conflicts among them are used to identify patterns of behavior, thought, and feeling that originated in early experience. The leader's job turns to supporting conflicts and modeling a permissive, calm openness to differences. Often, some of the acrimony is directed at the leader, who refuses to be defensive or retaliatory. Usually, handling conflict has been a problem for group members, and this is an opportunity to deal with disagreements and strong feelings in a safe environment. Everyone learns from here-and-now interactions that reveal attitudes and motivations. They are able to explore these interactions within the framework established in stage one. For example, the member who is stricken down with grief may benefit from hearing that others consider her immobility selfish or escapist. During this stage, each person's problems and aims become much clearer and better articulated. The idea that new options are possible blossoms.

In the third stage, these new options are explored in various ways. The leader, in this stage, hands over much of the treatment to the members, who have learned the techniques and therapist's perspective. This stage is characterized by affiliation and intimacy among group members, and conflicts are not frightening but welcome in the process. People are able to comfort each other during times of pain. Members discuss how the changes they desire will be implemented in their life outside sessions, experiment with new behaviors, and transfer their learning to everyday life. For example, the grief-stricken member could experiment with forcing herself to pay undivided attention to one person in her family fifteen minutes a day and report the experience back to the group for discussion. The outcome of the third stage is a new life, at least in some important aspects.

Termination is discussed from the beginning of the group, when the ground rules are agreed upon. The procedure of closing will vary widely. In open-ended groups, for example, a member may announce her readiness to leave in advance, and then her review of her contract and her good-byes are subjects of her last two or three sessions (Grimes, 1988). Then the group continues, with members coming in and leaving continuously. Most groups close down at once for all members, in which case the last two or three sessions involve mutual reminiscence, review of progress, and emotional leave-taking.

Remember that this division into phases is arbitrary in that most groups circle back, jump ahead, and blend among stages.

Leadership Skills

Psychodynamic groups are an outgrowth and modernization of Freudian psychoanalysis. The goal of such groups is **insight,** bringing into awareness conflicts and feelings that previously were inaccessible. According to the theory, once a client has insight, he or she will naturally move toward more adaptive behavior patterns (Pine, 1998). An intimate connection exists between insight and freedom to grow in positive directions, both as a social being and an independent entity (Wolf et al., 1972). The group leader plays a key role in this growth.

Freudian analysis, in its original form, was a one-to-one therapy that called for several sessions a week for many years. Transferring psychoanalytic theory to a group endeavor required giving up some of its old central features. One such feature was the role of the therapist. In strict Freudian analysis, the therapist attempts to be a blank slate, a figure for the client to project any significant relationship upon. This is why the cartoon depictions of analysis always have the therapist sitting out of the client's sight line. Most psychodynamic therapies today, even individual ones, do not use this arrangement. The therapist is more active than the classic Freudian analyst. This is especially true in psychodynamic group work. The selection at the opening of this chapter, by one of the early leaders of psychodynamic group theory, shows how the therapist actually has an energetic time of it. The counselor contributes to the group as a person, not as an anonymous, detached entity. As you can see from Wolf's (1949) description, the group leader is similar to the conductor of an orchestra.

The orchestra analogy holds true when you think of the highly interactive nature of the group. An advantage of a heterogeneous group is that there are many opportunities for transference and countertransference. In one-to-one therapy, the client has only one object, and the counselor only knows about how that person behaves in that particular transference relationship. For example, when a client casts me as the helpful big sister (a frequent occurrence), I have little direct reproduction of how she has related to her parents, brothers, grandparents, or others. I know much about her relationship to a sister, but not to other family members. As Wolf pointed out, he is often surprised by how different a client acts in group versus individual counseling. Each member has a "provocative role" and "stimulating conduct," eliciting more samples of how a person responds to others. In group psychodynamic therapy, the transference to the therapist or leader has a diminished role, not as intense as in individual therapy and not as taxing on the therapist (Stein, 1964). That is because there are more transferences than this one going on.

Investigating Transference

Wolf (1949), Tuttman (1986), and others point out how the family system is reproduced in psychodynamic group therapy, frequently with a male and female co-counselor team serving as parental figures and group members taking on sibling roles imported from their own histories. In other words, the group promotes **multiple transference,** which raises the likelihood that a fertile range of relationships will make itself evident. Members learn from direct instruction and modeling from the therapist and make interpretations of each other's actions (even though, as Wolf remarks, they may be off base). Each person's contributions illuminate his or her own conflicts as well as those of another person in the group. Having many members also provides more opportunities for reality testing, in that each individual can get spontaneous responses to his or her behavior, unfettered by the normal polite social limits for reacting to other people. Furthermore, the group as a whole can be an object of transference: Many group members come to see the group as a strong, accepting, benevolent mother figure, whose guidance is motivated by love.

You may wonder what is curative about the investigation of transferences, countertransferences, anxiety, and the defenses against it. According to J. Scott Rutan and Walter N. Stone (2001), both past presidents of the American Group Psychotherapy Association, vicarious learning and modeling fill an important role. Group members vary in how open they are initially to exploring hidden aspects of their psyches. Open members take readily to such exploration and expose themselves to scrutiny freely. Others, who are fearful of strong emotions, see the open members unharmed in group and even notice that they are drawn closer to their co-members through their frankness. In the process, closed-off members become willing to take emotional chances themselves. Underlying the process you see some loosening of anxiety—a feeling that it's not utterly essential to keep a tight lid on one's inner life.

Here, the factor of identification plays out. Members take on aspects or parts of others, including the counselor. Rutan and Stone (2001) note that identification can be seen early in nonverbal behavior, when members shift body positions to mirror other members' or counselors' positions. Identification with the therapist is critical so that group members can later take over roles as cotherapists for each other, a crucial part of the curative group process. The therapist serves as an example of tolerance of strong feelings, an introspective habit of mind, and an effort to understand as well as react to events. Groups strongly tend to imitate their therapists. Leaders

- who can stay calm and empathetic during emotional intensity;
- who demonstrate thoughtful, speculative searches below the surface meaning of members' statements;
- and who use analysis of historical events to understand current problems will pass on these qualities to their group members.

Identification with group norms assists in the journey toward insight. A norm of openness, demonstrated by the leader and reinforced through positive responses to the most freely expressive members, helps more reticent members to thaw emotionally. Frequently, the written information and consent document, as well as individual preparation for joining the group, emphasize the importance of this norm of openness. Group norms also develop that encourage the examination of one's own participation in any interaction. Sometimes this is the first time members have seriously considered how they are active creators of situations, not passive victims or receivers.

Promoting Insight

This consideration includes another group norm, a willingness to think about **process** elements of the conversation that are going on as well as the content. Remember that process includes group dynamics such as making alliances, scapegoating, tension and anxiety, supportiveness, power plays, conflict and resolution, elicitation of emotion, reality testing, and negotiation.

Consider the situation of three families, all of whom decide to order take-out hoagies from the local deli on Wednesday evening. The content of their decision is exactly the same, but the process could be utterly different: One family may have made the decision in a joyful, democratic way. The next family made the decision through anxiety-drenched conflict and power plays. The third family made the same boring decision they make almost every Wednesday because everyone is too depressed to think of something new.

In psychodynamic groups, processes that appear to reproduce early experiences and childhood patterns of adaptation are given particular emphasis. For instance, in groups, "members are continually feeling ignored, left out, insulted, or misunderstood" (Rutan & Stone, 2001, p. 94)—common childhood discomforts that bring forth each person's vulnerabilities and responses to injury. In contrast, a good one-to-one therapy situation offers much less of these discomforts because the counselor is focused and attentive to the client. On the positive side, the group-as-a-whole acts as an ego support for weak members (Tuttman, 1986). The curative power of altruism is available to group members as they serve this helpful function.

Insight into historical roots of problems by itself will not produce the deeper changes that psychodynamic group therapy seeks. An accompanying emotional resonance must occur to expand the sense of self, and the leader must foster affective experience. Often, this is an experience of **catharsis** (Blatner, 1985):

> If a person is yearning for something, and then receives it, or, on the other hand, if one feels burdened by something, and then is relieved of that burden, in both cases there is indeed a release of psychic energy. It is the energy of attention, and when a given task is completed, that attention is free for another task. (p. 158)

An early British theorist of psychoanalytic group work, Foulkes (1961) wrote movingly about the therapeutic process:

> [In a group analytic setting,] one is no longer dealing with patients, or cases which have a special diagnostic label, but with human beings who talk to one another about their affairs, their everyday life, their plans, their fears, their apprehensions, their worries, their pleasures, their guilt feelings, their suffering and their faith. They learn much about themselves and others which they did not know before. They act upon one another, and get to know themselves and others more frankly and more truly than ever before. Increasing understanding brings with it increasing tolerance, and the possibility of a freer development of the individual. (p. 28)

Interpretation

In *The Interpretation of Dreams* (1900/1965), Freud described interpretation as "decoding," and this is an accurate metaphor. Clients present seemingly disorganized material that the group attempts to translate into coherent, meaningful language. Interpretations aim at bringing into awareness things that clients have been unaware of most of the time (Rutan & Stone, 2001). They challenge group member's ingrained positions by offering alternative hypotheses, new frames of reference around experience and behavior (Clark, 1993). In a broad sense, interpretation attributes meaning and significance to observed phenomena (Scheidlinger, 1987). Transference, countertransference, and resistance are targets of psychodynamic interpretation. These reflect a person's habitual, unconscious responses to people, situations, and therapy.

Other sources of material for interpretation also exist. For example, Freud thought that slips of the tongue were never merely accidents. Forgetting, too, is never just an accident in Freudian terms. For example, forgetting a wedding anniversary could be interpreted as a comment on the state of the marriage. Constantly losing your car keys right before leaving for work can be interpreted as a comment on how you feel about your work. Physical symptoms can also be interpreted, especially ones that seem to have no organic explanation.

Interpretations usually include some reference to what causes the pattern that is interpreted. In psychodynamic groups, developmental experiences are common sources: "Do you think your parents' divorce when you were five is affecting how you feel about your wife's new independence?" In some groups, the causality is expressed in terms of here-and-now conflicts: "Is your laughter a defense mechanism when Joe asks you about your creative side?"

The group leader has opportunities to offer interpretations on many levels: the patterns perceived in specific individuals, the patterns perceived between individuals or subgroups in sessions, and the group as a whole, to name just three levels. Take, for example, a group which is facing the counselor's three-week vacation. When Bob relates a dream about trying to find his brother under a pile of rubble, some members respond with their own feelings of loss and helplessness. Other members ask Bob what the pile of rubble might symbolize. The leader may choose to address the whole group and their feelings about her upcoming absence (losing her). She may address Bob about whether he feels a barrier between himself and his brother; or she may point out some salient difference between the members who focused on loss and the ones who focused on the rubble.

The choice of which of hundreds of potential interpretations to offer, if any at all, demands a leader's sense of timing. You must remain aware that interpretations given to an individual affect everyone in the group (Clark, 1993; Scheidlinger, 1987). Choosing an individual interpretation that reflects a theme running through the whole group is one guideline because the group can expand on it among themselves, as they might do with Bob's dream. Judging whether the individual and group will be receptive to an interpretation is a matter of estimating the level of trust and the feeling of being understood. Therefore, some interpretations are saved for groups that have passed the initial stage of development. You don't have to worry about missing an opportunity, because meaningful patterns will offer themselves again and again in the life of a group.

"Interpretations can be too intellectual or they can be delivered in the midst of an emotional storm. There is little likelihood that interpretations at either end of this continuum will be effective" (Rutan & Stone, 2001, p. 87). You need to look for a balance of cognitive and emotional elements in the setting of an interpretation. An early interpretation may cut off emotional processes in the group by yanking the conversation into the rational world. Everyone can escape into intellectual discussion. On the other hand, lack of interpretation may leave people unaware of unconscious motivations and reasons, confused, or fearful. They may lose faith in the therapist and the treatment if they feel their strong emotions are stirred and then left hanging.

Part of the leader's task is to reinforce peer interpretations among group members. They learn from the leader's model how interpretations are given, and some members receive interpretations from peers better than from the leader. Peers will make more mistakes in timing, content, and style than therapists (Wolf, 1949); however, a well-established norm of openness allows criticism and argument about such interpretations. The leader can intervene in a clumsy peer interpretation by asking the interpreter to restate the idea in a different style, for example, supportively or phrased in a question (Clark, 1993). Sometimes, as a group leader, you hold back on an interpretation you could give, hoping that a member will come up with it instead. This encourages the group to become less dependent on you, which is an aim of the process (Foulkes, 1961).

Many of the interpretations you will observe are stated as questions. These are good models for peer interpretations as well as sound practice on the leader's part. Asking rather than declaring indicates that the interpretation is tentative and can be wrong or incomplete. It shows respect for the person or people whose behavior is being interpreted. An interpretation to the group as a whole might go thus: "I notice that you all are clamming up tonight; we've had a lot of silence here. Do you think this is happening because you are angry about the way I confronted Shirley last time, and you are trying to punish me?" In this case, the group might immediately deny being angry at you. They might inform you that they were having a heated political argument before the session and are still wincing from the sharp words exchanged then. Accepting the rejection of an interpretation sets a good example for the group. If your interpretation was actually accurate, the matter will come up again in another form, when the timing is right.

The humanist approach described in Part III of this text generally avoids interpretation, believing that it usurps the group's natural course of growth from within. Psychodynamic approaches, on the other hand, involve interpretation in some form.

A comment that points out that a pattern exists, but does not interpret it, is usually called a **confrontation.** For instance, in the above-mentioned group Ann might say to Bob, "I've noticed that you often bring up times when you were abandoned by someone important in your life." This is a confrontation. In psychodynamic groups, a series of confrontations or a confrontation that is strongly endorsed by several group members commonly leads to an interpretation.

DISCUSSION IDEA

> Will, who joined a psychodynamic group hoping to improve his
> relationships, fondly remembers his fraternity days at college, ten
> to twelve years earlier. He talks about these days at length in every
> session, nostalgically, saying that these were the best relationships
> he will ever have. He is warm and friendly to the men in the group
> and basically unresponsive to the women. He has argued against the
> rule prohibiting socializing outside the sessions, because he wants
> the guys to go to sports events together on weekends. He doesn't see
> what would be wrong with this. Will brings this issue up again the
> week before a big college football game, where he wants the other male
> football fans in the group to meet up with him.

Put together a list of possible interpretations to Will.

Feel free to be creative in constructing different scenarios for either counselor or peer interpretations. For example, what themes could be running through the group that would be relevant to Will's issue? What subgroups could be targets of interpretation? In interpreting Bob's concerns on the therapist-client level, what difference does it make whether the group leader is a man or a woman? In what situation would you choose not to interpret Bob's concerns?

_____

Techniques in Psychodynamic Group Counseling

In the Leadership Skills section, several key techniques were explained as part of the counselor's art: investigating transference, promoting insight, and interpretation. Now we will focus on the group members' participation in techniques of this therapy.

Free Association

In traditional psychoanalysis, the client's major input into the interpretive pursuit is **free association.** The client lies on the couch and is asked to say everything she is thinking and feeling, no matter what it is or whether it makes any sense or has coherence. This free flow of talk provides the analyst with material for interpretation. The client's unconscious emerges, in such an unusual discourse, encoded as choice of topic, slips of the tongue, descriptions of dreams, memories, thoughts, preoccupations, and even silences and omissions. How one subject leads to another is more grist for the mill. Disruptions and blockages in the flow of talk can also be interpreted, usually denoting some anxiety about a topic. Clients get better at free association as they become used to it. As the client talks, the analyst is conceiving of interpretations, looking for evidence or counterevidence of them, and deciding which, if any, of the acceptable interpretations should be verbalized to the client at the time.

This technique is transferred to groups in a straightforward manner. Each member is requested to free associate in rounds. Often, the prompt for association is one member's dream. Wolf (1949) suggested that after the group has become comfortable with free association, they enter a period in which each patient free associates about the next patient, in "spontaneous, uncensored speculation about other members of the group" (p. 544). From this, psychodynamic processes emerge, and the group members are invited to notice and comment upon them. Members are encouraged to respond when they feel that someone has made a particularly valid comment about them. In this way, Wolf thought, the praised member learns that his or her spontaneous, unpremeditated perceptions can be valuable—in a process of being liberated from neurotic restraint and rigidity.

Dream Work

Dreams have an important role in much psychodynamic work. A dream has **manifest content,** which is the surface action and emotion of the dream, and **latent content,** the symbolic meaning (Shapiro, 1995). Manifest content is often derived from events in recent real life, and we can often identify these easily. I might dream about catching a bus when I have thought during the day about taking a trip, for example. The manifest dream has processed unconscious meanings in several ways—in effect, disguising the latent content. Symbolism is one way—in my dream, the bus may symbolize escape from everyday life. Another is condensation, a process in which many ideas are represented with a single visual image. Thus, if I am making several changes in my life at the time, the bus I am catching may symbolize all these new journeys in life. If the bus is empty, I might be feeling quite alone on these journeys.

In groups, manifest content is used as material to associate with personality and patterns of behavior. The sleeping mind's choice of which manifest content to use is suggestive, especially when the group hears several dreams from each member. Are all the dreams full of people? Or are they devoid of anyone but the dreamer? Are they outdoors or indoors? Is the emotional tone usually positive, negative, neutral, or shifting from one to the other? Next to the dreamer, who appears most often? If there is conflict, is it resolved, and how? And so on. Discussing dreams brings the state of self to conscious awareness. In one common technique to begin dream work, all members free associate to the dream however they please. The dreamer then responds to others' associations, pondering how they fit into his or her own associations with the dream.

An additional dimension of dreams in groups is illumination of the group itself, not just the individual dreamer. Pines (2002) relates an example from a woman who was about to leave the group:

> [She] had some headaches and brought a terrifying dream: an aeroplane was taking off vertically, though its back was broken away, leaving everyone vulnerable to falling out. This dream represented both her fear of leaving the group catastrophically and being vulnerable, and the group's potential to disintegrate through a member leaving, again perhaps a fear of her underlying destructive capacities. [These had appeared in an earlier dream.] The capacity to have a horrifying dream and to have it responded to before leaving was important for her and for the group. (p. 28)

Dreams like this help the group talk about group process and group dynamics. Schlachet (2002) wrote that: "In groups, members often display an uncanny knack for understanding the communications inherent in one another's dreams. . . . It is no particular surprise, then, that patients can often communicate in dream symbols, that telling one another their dreams can become a cogent, powerful means to intimate mutual understanding, a mode of exchange which can quickly create a sense of commonality and bonding" (pp. 83–84).

SMALL GROUP EXERCISE

Explore a dream presented by one of your group members. First, take fifteen minutes or so to use the free association method. Explore manifest and latent content. Then talk about what discussing the dream meant to the whole group, not just the dreamer. If no one in your group has a dream to present, ask members to pretend that the following dream is their own and to process it in the group as if it were their own.

> I am riding on a train and getting close to my destination. There is a clock on the wall of the train, which shows that I must get my things together quickly. I have a definite meeting or appointment that I must attend on time, and I'm cutting things close. My stuff is scattered all over my train seat and the floor area, and I am trying to get it all into my tote bag. There are notebooks and pens and books and clothes and parts of sandwiches and a baby doll and lots of other objects. I can't seem to pull it together to put them all in my bag; they keep falling out and rolling away from me. I keep looking at the clock as time goes by and I am not ready to get off the train. I am very panicky, which adds to my clumsiness in collecting my stuff.

Problems Addressed by Psychodynamic Groups

Psychodynamic approaches have been used for all kinds of problems, from writer's block to criminality to headaches. Distress that is linked to anxiety is a particular focus because intrapsychic conflict produces anxiety and one foundation of psychodynamic thought is the idea of internal conflict. Clients who have benefited from psychodynamic treatment include sufferers of neurosis in general (that is, a characteristically negative response to self, others, and the world), depression, obsessive-compulsive behavior, phobias, sexual difficulties, eating disorders, hypochondria, aggressive behavior, nonorganic health problems, and, of course, anxiety. All of these disorders are believed to improve when insight into the underlying source is achieved.

When you consider the extensiveness of the six basic concepts underlying psychodynamic approaches in general—life stages, psychological structures, internal conflicts, anxiety, resistance and defenses, and transference and countertransference—the comprehensiveness of the difficulties treated is no surprise. Samples of psychodynamic research can be found in widely ranging journals, including *Alternative Therapies* (a comparison of hatha yoga and psychodynamic group therapy among heroin addicts, Shaffer, LaSalvia, & Stein, 1997); the *Nordic Journal of Psychiatry* (group psychotherapy for borderline personality disorder, Wilberg, Friis, Karterud, Mehlum, Urnes, & Vaglum, 1998); and *European Eating Disorders Review* (long-term group psychoanalysis for bulimics, Valbak, 2001).

SMALL GROUP EXERCISE

Using the PsychInfo database, find recent articles describing research using psychodynamic group therapy. Using *psychodynamic* and *group* as key terms to find in the article abstract and limiting your search to the last five years will help you handle this search. Select one of these to summarize and distribute or present to the class. Be sure to describe the group therapy treatment and relate it to concepts in this chapter.

Adaptations to Clients' Ages

Psychodynamic principles apply to children and adolescents as much as adults; however, some alterations need to be made. Traditional psychodynamic group therapy is largely based on talk. Children are less developed than adults in their ideational skill, with their thinking more concrete than abstract. They are also limited in their ability to express themselves fully in language.

An early group therapist, S. R. Slavson (1950) designed psychodynamic groups for children that made use of experiences and association more than knowledge and ideas. He wrote that for children, "Action, realistic impediments, external control, and affectionate guidance affect intrapsychic changes more than do concepts and ideas. . . . Acting out and the consequent reactions of others are more natural for these children than is talking out" (pp. 12–13). Play activities elicited opportunities for anxiety release, sublimation of primitive drives into acceptable social interactions, ego-strengthening, expression of fantasies and drives, catharsis, and feedback from other children. Slavson pointed out that the latency period (6 to puberty) is one of maximum emotional growth, when people other than one's family gain importance. Group therapy makes use of this broadening interest in others.

In adolescence, group therapy makes use of the members' preference for being together, sense of fun, and ability to influence one another more than adults usually can. In a study of 134 teenagers who continued or terminated in psychodynamic treatment, Baruch, Gerber, and Fearon (1998) found that the majority of continuers were older and internalized problems (as anxiety and depression), whereas most of the terminators were younger and externalized problems (as aggression and delinquency). They also found that both older and younger teens were more likely to continue when treated by supportive therapists. In this context, *supportive* means that the therapists focused on strengthening the client's ego and sense of self rather than interpreting transference and resistance. The researchers point out that this is an example of therapeutic success being related to developmental stage.

Holmes, Heckel, and Gordon (1991) describe their work with emotionally disturbed adolescents on an inpatient ward and how they experimented with various formats to allow for developmental stage. A psychodynamic perspective was one of several theories the therapists implemented. They found that the group tended to regress to childish and resentful behavior, which prevented exploration of matters such as defense mechanisms. The adoption of a **modified fishbowl technique** caused a dramatic, positive shift in the group's behavior. Half the group members discussed questions, while the other half sat behind a one-way mirror with a third therapist and observed. The observers joined the third therapist in the role of consultant about what was going on in the discussion group. Observers then joined the active group and shared their ideas. The group members took turns as discussants and observers. Through this approach, the teens were psychologically promoted in maturity level, rather than attending a group that, to them, appeared like any other in which adults tried to control teenagers.

SMALL GROUP EXERCISE

To get a sense of the modified fishbowl technique, try it in your small group. Have half the members discuss a common problem, such as maintaining a balance among roles in life, for ten minutes. The other members serve as observers and take notes on the discussion, focusing on both process and content. Then, observers share their ideas with the discussants. After this short practice, what do you think of the technique? Under what circumstances do you think it would be effective?

Kleinberg (1995) identified another perspective on developmental stage in an open-ended psychodynamic group of mixed ages. When adults face a midlife crisis, they undergo a period of doubt and stagnation including a sense of interpersonal impoverishment. Kleinberg discussed how only one or two members' midlife crises could infect the whole group with similar feelings and cause stagnation in the group's progress. The leader's work is to acknowledge the feelings and "try to integrate them with other aspects of the personality or attempt to master them through understanding" (p. 214) and help the group work itself out of the slump. In the process, the members in midlife crisis find their individual problems eased. This is an example of individual developmental crises being projected onto whole groups, a phenomenon counselors need to consider.

Evaluating Psychodynamic Groups

Counselors are encouraged to examine their practice, often in terms of evaluating the outcomes of treatment (e.g., Hatfield & Ogles, 2004). An additional focus of assessing treatment is exploring exactly what happens during sessions and whether the events in session are consistent with the theory supposedly being applied. For example, it is interesting to find out whether in psychodynamically oriented groups people really do zero in on the dynamics of their interactions, including transference, projection, threat, trust, collusion, conflict, and so forth. These are qualities difficult to define, let alone measure with precision (Luft, 1984). Understanding the nature of some efforts to measure group activities will help you see the complexities and purposes of such endeavors.

The Psychodynamic Work and Object Rating System (PWORS; Piper & McCallum, 2000) is a process analysis measure for psychodynamic group sessions. Raters are trained to listen to tapes of group sessions and score each statement by a member or a therapist, according to the presence of work and reference to objects (that is, references to other people). In this context, "work" means evidence of mental activity directed to the solution of a problem, either individual, interpersonal, or whole-group. The PWORS rating system codes each statement as work or nonwork, and if it is work, further codes it as belonging to different categories such as anxiety or defenses. The objects are coded as internal (the speaker, another group member, a subgroup, or the whole group) and external (people or classes of people outside the group). Higher rates of work and internal objects reflect that activities consistent with psychodynamic group theory are present, rather than other types of talk. Each statement by each person present is also timed.

This is a system that takes intensive training of the raters and many hours to code sessions. However, meaningful information can be derived from it. For example, **participation** is the ratio of a member's total statement duration over the total verbal production of the group. **Self-based work** is the ratio of a member's work statements over the member's total participation. These could be later related to outcome measures; for example, did clients with high self-based work scores have better outcomes than others? Different groups could be compared according to the distribution of various types of work; for example, do some groups gravitate toward defenses and others toward anxiety? As a counselor, you could also discover the prevailing nature of your own statements. You could explore whether types of statements changed in frequency at different stages of group process; for example, are there more anxiety-based statements in early stages than later ones?

The type of investigation done by the PWORS is valuable in discovering whether psychodynamic groups do what they purport to do, and whether it is effective. They also help counselors evaluate their own work and help agencies compare the groups they run.

SMALL GROUP EXERCISES

1. Use the PsychInfo data base to find published studies of groups using the PWORS. Choose one of the studies to read and summarize for the class. Be sure to include what questions about group therapy were investigated in the study. If PWORS studies are unavailable to you, use PsychInfo to find studies that use *group process analysis,* and select one of those to summarize.

2. Brainstorm about the psychodynamic approach and the person who leads such groups. What personality traits would be good in a psychodynamic group counselor? Why? What personal qualities or preferences would cause a person to dislike psychodynamic group counseling?

KEY TERMS

analytical   reasoning by dividing into parts and their interrelationships

anxiety   an emotional signal that conflict between psychic structures is escalating

catharsis   release of pent-up emotions

confrontation   pointing out a pattern in someone's behavior or talk

countertransference   a person's emotional response to the transference from someone else

defense mechanisms   methods of self-protection against anxiety

denial   behaving as though a conflict or bad experience does not exist

displacement   taking out anxiety on objects other than the source of anxiety

free association   a spontaneous flow of talk without regard to sense or coherence

id, ego, superego   three parts of the psyche, in analytical theory

identification   taking on aspects or parts of others, including the counselor

insight   awareness; bringing into consciousness conflicts and feelings that were previously inaccessible

interpretation   attribution of meaning and significance to observed phenomena

Johari window   a model of group dynamics based on what is known and unknown to self and others

latent content   the symbolic elements of a dream

manifest content   the features of a dream that are on the surface and usually recognizable from everyday life

modified fishbowl technique   a group arrangement using an inner and outer group; the inner group proceeds with a group session, while the outer group observes and then comments upon the inner group's process; then the placements are reversed

multiple transference   in a group, the transferences made to the leader and to all the other members

neuroses   patterns of negative thinking and emotions that are distressing and disturb personal relationships

participation   in the POWRS, the ratio of a member's total statement duration over the total verbal production of the group

process   group dynamics such as making alliances, scapegoating, tension and anxiety, supportiveness, power plays, conflict and resolution, elicitation of emotion, reality testing, and negotiation; used to refer to elements other than subject matter

regression   reentering an earlier stage of life or development

repression   forgetting of experience, with a motivation of avoiding anxiety

resistance   protection against the discomforts of insight and awareness

rounds   an activity in which every group member is asked to respond to some cue or question

self-based work   in the POWRS, the ratio of a member's work statements over the member's total participation

sublimation   protecting against anxiety through work, creativity, and humor

transference   placing qualities of important figures in the past onto figures in the present

unconscious   the part of mental life that is outside of waking awareness

work   the goal-directed activities pursued by a group that has achieved orientation, cohesion, and norms; evidence of mental activity directed to the solution of a problem, either individual, interpersonal, or whole-group

CHAPTER REVIEW

1. In psychoanalytic theory, what is the source of anxiety? Give an example of your own, from yourself or someone you know.
2. Choose five defense mechanisms and be able to define them and exemplify them without referring to the text.
3. Write a paragraph relating transference and countertransference to interpersonal theory, described in Chapter 2.
4. Think of yourself in a group such as your family, your social group, or your class. Fill in a sample Johari window as things stand today. Consider what would happen if you disclosed something specific from Quadrant 3 to this group. What quadrants would be changed?
5. If you observed an unfamiliar group in progress, what evidence might you use in guessing which stage of development the group was in? Explain your reasoning.
6. As a group counselor, how will you decide which of many possible interpretations to offer during sessions? When will you offer no interpretations, even when you privately have them?
7. Argue for or against using dreams as material in group therapy.
8. Outside of using a system like POWRS, how can you evaluate whether a psychodynamic group you lead is working satisfactorily or not?

FOR FURTHER READING

Rutan, J. S., & Stone, W. N. (2001). *Psychodynamic group psychotherapy* (3rd ed.). New York: Guilford Press.

The authors are both past presidents of the American Group Psychotherapy Association. This book goes into detail on the history of psychodynamic group therapy, methods and mechanisms of change, leadership issues, and theoretical points of view. You may find Chapter 13, The Therapeutic Process: A Clinical Illustration (pp. 259–285), especially valuable to read. This chapter includes a transcript from a session of a mature psychodynamic group, with commentary by both Rutan and Stone set off in italics and boldface type.

REFERENCES

Baruch, G., Gerber, A., & Fearon, P. (1998). Adolescents who drop out of psychotherapy at a community-based psychotherapy centre: A preliminary investigation of the characteristics of early drop-outs, late drop-outs, and those who continue treatment. *British Journal of Medical Psychology, 71,* 233–245.

Blatner, A. (1985). The dynamics of catharsis. *Journal of Group Psychotherapy, Psychodrama and Sociometry, 37,* 157–166.

Clark, A. J. (1993). Interpretation in group counseling: Theoretical and operational issues. *Journal for Specialists in Group Work, 18,* 174–181.

Clark, A. J. (1997). Projective identification as a defense mechanism in group counseling and therapy. *Journal for Specialists in Group Work, 22,* 85–96.

Erikson, E. H. (1950). *Childhood and society.* New York: Norton.

Foulkes, S. H. (1961). Group processes and the individual in the therapeutic group. *British Journal of Medical Psychology, 34,* 23–31.

Freud, A. (1936). *The ego and the mechanisms of defense.* New York: International Universities Press.

Freud, S. (1923). *The ego and the id* (Standard Edition, Vol. 19). London: Hogarth Press.

Freud, S. (1965). *The interpretation of dreams.* New York: Discus. (Original work published 1900)

Gans, J. S. (1992). Money and psychodynamic group psychotherapy. *International Journal of Group Psychotherapy, 42,* 133–152.

Grimes, J. (1988). Transactional analysis in group work. In S. Long (Ed.), *Six group therapies* (pp. 49–113).

Hatfield, D. R., & Ogles, B. M. (2004). The use of outcome measures by psychologists in clinical practice. *Professional Psychology: Research and Practice, 35,* 485–491.

Holmes, G. R., Heckel, R. V., & Gordon, L. (1991). *Adolescent group therapy: A social competency model.* New York: Praeger.

Jacobs, E. E., Masson, R. L., & Harvill, R. L. (2002). *Group counseling: Strategies and skills.* Pacific Grove, CA: Brooks/Cole.

Kepner, E. (1994). Gestalt group process. In B. Feder & R. Ronall (Eds.), *Beyond the hot seat: Gestalt approaches to group* (pp. 5–24). Highland, NY: Gestalt Journal Press.

Kleinberg, J. L. (1995). Group treatment of adults in midlife. *International Journal of Group Psychotherapy, 45,* 207–222.

Luft, J. (1984). *Group processes: An introduction to group dynamics* (3rd ed.). Mountain View, CA: Mayfield.

Pine, F. (1998). *Diversity and direction in psychoanalytic technique.* New Haven: Yale University Press.

Pines, M. (2002). The illumination of dreams. In C. Neri, M. Pines, & R. Friedman (Eds.), *Dreams in group psychotherapy: Theory and technique* (pp. 25–36). Philadelphia: Jessica Kingsley.

Piper, W. E., & McCallum, M. (2000). The Psychodynamic Work and Object Rating Scale. In A. P. Beck & C. M. Lewis (Eds.), *The process of group psychotherapy: Systems for analyzing change* (pp. 263–281). Washington, DC: American Psychological Association.

Rutan, J. S., & Stone, W. N. (2001). *Psychodynamic group psychotherapy* (3rd ed.). New York: Guilford Press.

Scheidlinger, S. (1987). On interpretation in group psychotherapy: The need for refinement. *International Journal of Group Psychotherapy, 37,* 339–352.

Schlachet, P. J. (2002). Sharing dreams in group therapy. In C. Neri, M. Pines, & R. Friedman (Eds.), *Dreams in group psychotherapy: Theory and technique* (pp. 79–97). Philadelphia: Jessica Kingsley.

Shaffer, H. J., LaSalvia, T. A., & Stein, J. P. (1997). Comparing hatha yoga with dynamic group psychotherapy for enhancing methadone maintenance treatment. *Alternative Therapies, 3,* 57–66.

Shapiro, S. (1995). *Talking with patients: A self psychological view of creative intuition and analytic discipline.* Northvale, NJ: Jason Aronson.

Slavson, S. R. (1950). *Analytic group psychotherapy with children, adolescents, and adults.* New York: Columbia University Press.

Stein, A. (1964). The nature of transference in combined therapy. *International Journal of Group Psychotherapy, 14,* 413–424.

Tuttman, S. (1986). Theoretical and technical elements which characterize the American approaches to psychoanalytic group psychotherapy. *International Journal of Group Psychotherapy, 36,* 499–515.

Valbak, K. (2001). Good outcomes for bulimic patients in long-term group analysis: A single-group study. *European Eating Disorders Review, 9,* 19–32.

Wilberg, T., Friis, S., Karterud, S., Mehlum, L., Urnes, O., & Vaglum, P. (1998). Outpatient group psychotherapy: A valuable continuation treatment for patients with borderline personality disorder treated in a day hospital? *Nordic Journal of Psychiatry, 52,* 213–221.

Wolf, A. (1949). The psychoanalysis of groups. *American Journal of Psychotherapy, 3,* 529–557.

Wolf, A., Schwartz, E. K., McCarty, G. J., & Goldberg, I. A. (1972). Psychoanalysis in groups: Contrasts with other group therapies. In C. J. Sager & S. R. Kaplan (Eds.), *Progress in group and family therapy* (pp. 47–53). New York: Brunner/Mazel.

CHAPTER **11**

Gestalt Group Theory and Practice

Gestalt is one of the few therapies that has focused on group work extensively, almost from its beginning. The best-known founder of Gestalt therapy, Fritz Perls (1893–1970), worked in short-term groups, often consisting of only one intensive two- to three-hour session. In the early part of his career, these sessions usually focused on one individual at a time, with other members representing the social environment and its feedback to the client and therapist (Frew, 1988). Later, other models of Gestalt groups were developed, making more use of the group's interpersonal dynamics. As you read the selection below, you will see how the group changes at various phases in the relationship.

A Selection from

"A Gestalt Therapy Theory Application to the Practice of Group Leadership"

By Jon E. Frew (1997)

PHASES OF GROUP DEVELOPMENT AND DOMINANT MODES OF EXPERIENCE

Although it is difficult to clearly assess the effectiveness of an intervention, there are occasions when a leader's attempt to influence a group is obviously resisted. During a first group meeting, it would be ill-advised, for example, to ask members to sing their favorite song (unless this is a theater group) or to hug a neighbor. In a conflict and differentiation phase, leaders will encounter resistance if they push for consensus on a decision. A group experiencing a high degree of cohesion may not be interested in a leader's suggestion to recognize individual accomplishments or to have a competition between subgroups.

To understand a group's opposition to certain types of interventions at different times in its life, leaders can expand their theoretical framework to include the relationship between a group's phase of development and an additional piece of Gestalt theory applied to groups, a group's "dominant mode." A group will experience a shift in the dominant mode of experience over its lifetime. Table 2 [of this article] outlines the relationship between the phase of group development and the group's dominant mode.

TABLE 2

Phases of Group Development and a Group's Dominant Mode

Phases	Dominant Mode
Orientation	Intrapersonal
Differentiation	Interpersonal
Affiliation	Group

[Next comes a discussion of the orientation phase. We skip to the section on the differentiation phase.]

THE PRACTICE: A TASK GROUP AT AN IMPASSE DURING THE DIFFERENTIATION PHASE

A cross-functional team has been formed to identify and make recommendations to rectify communication problems across departmental lines within an organization. You are appointed as team leader. You have shepherded the group through the orientation phase of development using a theoretical framework that includes an understanding of individual figure formation processes, group figures, group development theory, and levels of process and intervention.

The team is meeting for the fourth time. During the third meeting, George, who had emerged as an informal leader, had proposed that the team use a set of procedures he was familiar with to complete a set of tasks during this fourth meeting. George had pushed hard for the group to do it his way and you noticed there was no visible resistance to his ideas. As the team begins today, the following dialogue occurs:

GEORGE: Okay, is everyone ready to start with our tasks?

RANDY: I did some thinking about your procedures between meetings, George, and I have another idea about how to proceed.

GEORGE: I'm sorry, Randy. We all agreed last week to use my ideas. It's too late to change now.

RANDY: I didn't agree last week. I was silent because I felt bulldozed by your energy and rigidness.

GEORGE: Randy, you have a reputation in this company for being negative. This team won't stand for your negativity and controlling behavior.

This group is "screaming" for an intervention at this point. All eyes (except perhaps George's) will look to you hopefully. What will you say and at what level of process will you say it?

Staying at the interpersonal level you have many options. You could become actively involved in the conflict between George and Randy and serve as a conflict mediator. If you see value in shifting the conflict to another interpersonal context, you could ask if anyone else had reservations like Randy or would anyone else like to hear Randy's ideas about how to proceed. You could also decide to establish your authority and shift the focus to the interpersonal process between George and you by saying, "George, as team leader I will decide whether it is too late for new ideas." That intervention will quickly shift George's awareness from Randy to issues between the two of you.

You might encourage a shift to the intrapersonal level. "I would like each of you to take a few minutes to silently check in with what you are feeling right now." Or "Randy, I notice that you are looking at the floor. What are you experiencing?" Or, "George, instead of speaking to Randy for the whole group, take a moment and identify what your thoughts are right now."

Finally, at the group level you could say, "It is not clear in this group how decisions will be made and when those decisions are final." Or "I wonder if the communication problems in this team right now are representative of the ones organization-wide?" Or "If Randy isn't ready to move forward yet, I'll bet others are not either. I suggest we spend some time as a team brainstorming as many ideas as possible about procedures before we choose the one we will use."

As a leader your objectives during the differentiation phase are to promote the value of diversity, to reassure group members that a certain amount of conflict is necessary and normal in all human systems, and to create a culture in which differences are respected and viewed as an asset and not a liability. An approach that combines interventions that address the dominant group process mode, the interpersonal level, with interventions that shift the group's awareness to the intrapersonal and group level of process, is recommended.

THE PRACTICE: GROUP LEADERSHIP DURING THE AFFILIATION PHASE

In many ways, group leadership during the affiliation phase is like engaging the cruise control on your car as you travel down the highway. If you did your work during the orientation and differentiation phases, the group will now require little overt leadership. If the group's relationship to you during the orientation phase was dependent and during the differentiation phase counterdependent, now it is interdependent. (pp. 142–144)

Exploring "A Gestalt Therapy Theory Application to the Practice of Group Leadership"

1. Review Table 1.1 in Chapter 1. Locate the three phases Frew identifies on the table. Which stage is not included in this article, as far as you can tell from this selection?

2. Why is each activity (intervention) rejected in paragraph 1?

3. What is a "dominant mode" of experience? What three types does Frew identify?

4. What is the purpose of the group in the selection? How is its purpose different from that of counseling groups? How is its purpose the same as the purpose of counseling groups?

5. In which session does the described conflict arise? Why is conflict expected to come up at this time?

6. Why does the group look to the leader after the exchange between George and Randy?

7. Identify the interpersonal, intrapersonal, and group interventions suggested in this situation.

8. What are the goals of the differentiation phase? How do they relate to the interventions suggested?

9. Explain the metaphor Frew uses for group leadership in the affiliative phase.

10. Reread the last sentence of the selection. What is the group relationship to the leader during each phase? What changes might you expect to see if you dropped into the group three times, once at each phase (one, two, and three)?

■ ■ ■

Essential Concepts of Gestalt Theory

Now you have had a close-up view of a Gestalt group in action and the stages and focuses that inform its operation. As you read this chapter, you will look back to this selection and see more clearly the group's intricacies, but I first wanted you to plunge into Gestalt thinking for yourself. To understand the evolution of modern Gestalt therapy, we need first to briefly examine the origins of Gestalt therapy and its early relationship with Gestalt psychology.

Gestalt Therapy and Gestalt Psychology

Fritz Perls was influenced by the German Gestalt psychologists of the early 1900s. Laura Perls, Fritz's wife, contributed strongly to Gestalt therapy and had earned a degree in Gestalt psychology (Humphrey, 1986). The Gestalt psychologists studied perception, not psychotherapy. They illuminated how we create coherent, organized patterns from perceptual stimuli. As in Figure 11.1, when incomplete figures are perceived, the mind usually completes the figure. Here, you are likely to perceive a triangle rather than two rows of slashes and an underline.

Another Gestalt phenomenon is the **figure/ground relation,** in which we make sense of the complex images delivered to our brains through our eyes by organizing what we see into a shape in the foreground (the figure) and a rather formless background (the ground). Fritz Perls seized upon these and other ideas from the Gestalt perceptual psychologists and applied them to all kinds of human experience. The perceptual habit of completing figures became translated into a human drive to organize experience into coherent, organized wholes. For example, early life conflicts that were never resolved are **unfinished business** and need to be completed psychologically. In Gestalt psychotherapy, the figure and ground distinguish between important and unimportant elements of the environment (Henle, 1978). The figure in any environment is based on an individual's current needs, and when the needs are met, something in the ground may become the figure. For instance, an anxious person sees any threatening aspects of the environment as the figure, whereas a hungry person sees anything edible in the environment as the figure.

Perls's applications of ideas from the German Gestalt psychologists were loose, approximate, metaphorical, and imaginative. Although modern Gestalt therapists see little real connection between the perceptual concepts and the psychotherapeutic concepts, they still find much of Perls's terminology useful in their work.

FIGURE 11.1

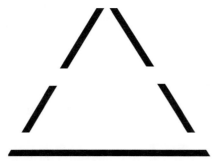

Modern Gestalt Concepts

According to Gestalt psychotherapy, people have problems because they are cut off from parts of themselves that they need for wholeness, integration, and balance. They may be alienated from their own feelings, their bodies, or other people. It is human nature to be whole, but life experience teaches us to fragment ourselves because some parts are unacceptable and will be punished. We are taught from an early age to snuff out our spontaneity. The requirements of polite and productive society include continual suppression of parts of ourselves. Gestalt therapists help clients integrate the **polarities** within themselves, such as mature/childish, loving/hateful, intellectual/emotional, wild/tame; one pole has usually been stifled and locked away and denied entrance into awareness.

The goal of Gestalt therapy is **awareness,** "the capacity to be in touch with your own existence, to notice what is happening around or inside you, to connect with the environment, other people and yourself; to know what you are feeling or sensing or thinking; how you are reacting at this very moment" (Clarkson & Mackewn, 1993). With awareness come spontaneity and intimacy. Gestalt psychologists attempt to encourage awareness rather than directly influence behavior change, on the assumption that behavior change will grow out of fuller awareness. In this, Gestalt is similar to psychoanalytic thought.

Other comparisons with Freudian theory are clear. The idea that early in life we learn to suppress impulses that are unacceptable to civilized society, and that too much of this suppression creates an emotionally damaged adult, is a common thread to the theories in this section. In Gestalt theory, **shoulds** are the rules people have learned so well that they seem natural: "You *should* earn the same or more money than your peer group"; "You *should* always put others' needs above your own"; "You *should* be married to a person of the opposite sex by the time you are thirty." These are recognizable as analogous to the Freudian superego's urgings. In Gestalt terms, unfinished business includes unresolved emotions and issues from the past, which are affecting the present. This is analogous to fixation at various stages of life and the resulting neuroses, which cause people to revisit unfinished business over and over in adult life. Gestalt therapy involves getting **unstuck** from continually reliving the past, accepting what patterns have been stuck, and moving on unburdened by them. Gestalt therapy shares this process conceptualization with psychodynamic therapy.

Gestalt theory differs from psychoanalytic theory in some significant ways that affect the course of group therapy. In psychoanalytic theory, our primitive urges (sex and aggression) and civilized life are always at odds, and an uneasy compromise between the natural person and social expectations always exists. Gestalt theory does not focus on the inevitable compromise but on the complete freeing of the natural self. It assumes that this freedom will be constructive and beautiful, whereas Freudian theory assumes that such freedom would be destructive to society. Strictly speaking, psychoanalytic practice results in healthier defense mechanisms, whereas Gestalt practice results in wholeness

and awareness that naturally lead people to good decisions and positive relationships with others (Harman, 1988). In Gestalt thinking, "breaking the mold"
is an ideal state, whereas psychoanalytic counselors prefer constructing a mold
that is more comfortable. Gestaltists also argue that they do not stress the interpretive function of therapy; that is, they don't necessarily strive to identify
childhood causes for here-and-now problems.

Reflections

A Freudian would say that to have a civilized society, primitive urges must be suppressed. A Gestaltist would say that society
is damaged by too much suppression of
natural urges. What do you think? Can you
give arguments on both sides of the issue?
How does your opinion on this matter affect
your counseling?

One reason that group therapy suits Gestalt theory is that making accurate
contact with self and others is paramount. Distortions in this contact are called
contact boundary disturbances (Harman, 1988). (The word *boundary* refers to
the line between self and others.) In group, these problems manifest themselves
in relationships with other members and with the counselors. Group therapy is
a natural setting for Gestalt work because it provides a complex brew of social
interactions. Table 11.1 describes contact boundary disturbances and how they
might manifest themselves in group work.

DISCUSSION IDEAS

1. Take turns coming up with at least one example of each contact boundary
disturbance described in Table 11.1. These can come from your experience
in groups in general, from fictional sources, or from your imagination.
2. Some discussion group members may be willing to describe situations
in which they have themselves demonstrated one or more of the contact
boundary disturbances. These are all part of normal behavior and are
harmful only in exaggerated or rigid forms.

The Gestalt therapy group serves as a setting for **experiments,** which are
here-and-now enactments designed to free up blocked aspects of the self and
to try out new behaviors. These are not interventions planned in advance by
the counselor, but come up during the course of sessions. For example, a person who continually deflects contact by turning attention to other people in the

TABLE 11.1
Contact Boundary Disturbances

Uncritical Introjection	Taking in others' views and values to the point where they seem like your own. For example, children develop a conscience through introjecting their parents' *do*s and *don't*s. As you mature, you review the opinions of others before integrating them into your own way of thinking, and you may revise the rules of your conscience as well. In introjection that is disturbed; however, you do not allow review and revision but instead embrace someone else's values completely. A group member who has introjected repeatedly will express absolute rules without being able to explain the reasoning behind them very well.
Projection	Assigning undesired parts of yourself to others, especially when you feel guilty or angry. A group member who believes everyone is obsessed with material success, for example, may harbor a guilty wish for wealth himself. Projecting feelings or motivations onto other people prevents a group member from seeing others accurately in their own right, thus creating a barrier to contact. The group can function to correct these flawed perceptions through consensual agreement that the member is off base. This type of correction is not customary in the outside society.
Retroflection	Directing a thought or action to yourself rather than toward others. For example, in Western societies, many men have a habit of rugged independence that keeps them from making emotional contact with other people. This is a quality that runs counter to group work and will almost inevitably be challenged by other members, who feel the emotional cutoff.
Deflection	Turning aside direct contact with another person or yourself. You will surely encounter a group member who deflects contact by telling long, pointless stories or, conversely, by remaining silent. Some members will deflect conversation away from a highly charged topic onto a milder one or deflect attention away from themselves onto another person or topic.
Confluence	Agreeing in opinion and feeling with someone else to the point where the boundary between self and other is blurry. This kind of merging usually involves pushing the differences between members out of awareness. Some confluence is natural in early stages of a group, when a sense of universality and cohesion are being established. However, confluence must recede to allow the group to move ahead. Awareness includes awareness of differences and of ways to embrace differences.

group might be asked to spend an hour doing the opposite—that is, verbally relating everything anyone says to herself and her own concerns. Experiments may involve body movements as well, because Gestaltists see every emotion as having a physical component. The many techniques associated with experimentation are outlined in this chapter.

Group Dynamics

Typically, in one of Perls's early intensive two- to three-hour sessions, just one person at a time sat in the **hot seat** to work with the therapist. The hot seat was the center of attention for the whole group, usually placed in the center of a circle of participants. The other group members observed and sometimes participated when called upon by the therapist. However, even this participation was focused on the hot-seat individual. This pattern was really one-to-one therapy in a group setting. Members who were silent benefited from **spectator learning** (identifying with the interaction and being aware of their own inner responses to what went on) (Frew, 1988; Korb, Gorrell, & Van de Riet, 1989; Perls, 1969b). When the group members did participate, they represented a social environment and its feedback to the client and therapist. Frew (1988) described "the absolute logic of practicing Gestalt therapy in groups (in which the individual can experience the interacting 'self' in an environment which can talk back)" (p. 78). Throughout his life as a popular psychologist and especially during his period as a guru in California at the famous Esalen Institute from 1964 to 1969, Perls used group therapy extensively. Perls's early style of group work was with individuals, with a group observing and sometimes commenting.

A later pattern, developed at the Gestalt Institute of Cleveland (Frew, 1988), involved the group members as clients more fully, because they were encouraged to express feelings of their own relevant to the central interaction or a therapist-directed theme. They each contributed as individuals rather than only as respondents to the hot-seat situation, and they built a group identity more than they did in the hot-seat pattern. Here is a snippet of Fritz Perls directing a group using a thematic approach:

> Fritz: Now I would like you, each one of you, now to tell the group how you manipulate the world. You can do it by ingratiating yourself, playing crybaby, playing tragedy queen, or whatever.
>
> Claire: I say I'm not good enough.
>
> Fritz: This is one of the famous tragedy queen plays. If you only depress yourself enough then the whole world will get depressed: we call them the gloom casters, the crepe hangers, the melancholic people. They start gloom casting; if everybody else is depressed then they go away.
>
> Mark: I think I manipulate the world by criticism. By criticizing.
>
> Fritz: By criticizing?
>
> Mark: Right. And presuming that there is a better way to do things. And perhaps my way is the better way. That's what I would probably suggest.

Fritz: These depressing games play a tremendous part in this, our social context. Not only do we depress ourselves, but many sports, for instance, and many business deals are meant to depress the other person. If I win my tennis game, then you feel depressed. Some people go to such extremes that they are real killers. They have nothing else in mind than to make themselves feel better and superior. The same goes for business deals. The rationale is forgotten as long as I get the better of the customer.

John: I manipulate the world by having accidents.

Fritz: What's the purpose of that?

John: I let someone else take care of me.

Fritz: Yes.

Jane: I manipulate the world by always trying to hide what I'm feeling and yet still expecting people to understand. Outside of the smile, I like to imply a threat, possibly a physical violence if I don't get my way.

Fritz: That is close also to a very famous way of manipulating called blackmail. (Perls & Baumgardner, 1975, pp. 109–110)

In a survey of 251 Gestalt and Gestalt-oriented therapists in the United States (Frew, 1988),

- 91 percent used groups in their practice at some time.
- 98 percent considered the group an effective technique for Gestalt therapy.
- few used the hot-seat pattern exclusively.
- 83 percent used a mixture of individual, interpersonal-dynamic, and whole-group focuses.
- 1 percent ranked spectator learning as the most important factor in group therapy.

This last point represents just one way that Gestalt psychotherapy today is different from some of Perls's original style of group work.

DISCUSSION IDEAS

1. Do you understand how each member's response is an example of "manipulation"? Is the group different from what you have seen or learned about therapy groups before? Would you like to be a member of a Gestalt therapy group?

2. Have you ever had an insight into yourself or others from watching a counseling session of someone else? Discuss examples in class. What do you think of "spectator learning" in group therapy? What are the pros and cons of having silent members in a group?

Group therapies vary on their emphasis on individual versus group interactions. Gestalt therapy, in particular, has a history of being performed with a focus on one group member in the hot seat, with other members observing and perhaps commenting. However, this practice is now a matter of the Gestalt therapist's preference, with more group-oriented work included (Korb et al., 1989). Gestalt groups are frequently demonstrated for large audiences of people, and in classrooms and workshops for people whose purpose is more educational than therapeutic. These demonstrations can be as short as half a day with no continuation. However, therapy groups are usually longer.

Stages of the Group

In the opening selection of this chapter, Frew (1997) used the terms **orientation, differentiation,** and **assimilation** to describe three phases of Gestalt group therapy. These are consistent with the general scheme of group stages, which you read about in Chapter 1. It may be helpful to see the two systems from Part IV side by side for comparative purposes.

Table 11.2 displays how experts in two types of group, psychodynamic and Gestalt, have described the stages of group process. Remember that this division into phases is arbitrary in that most groups circle back, jump ahead, and blend among stages.

TABLE 11.2
Phases of Group Process

	Stage One	Stage Two	Stage Three	Termination
Psychody-namic	Agreement. Interpretation of transference, countertransference, resistance, childhood experiences.	Working through: Further interpretation, insight, redirection of strivings, restructuring of psyche. Members take on therapeutic interventions. Personality change or (if time limited) improvement of some aspects of problem.		Reminiscence. Verbalization of gains.
Gestalt	Contract or agreement. Discovery. Identity and dependence. Orientation. Inclusion.	Differentiation. Accommodation. New choices possible. Influence and counter-dependence. Control.	Assimilation. Environmental changes for genuine self. Intimacy and interdependence. Affiliation. Affection. New life.	Reflection. Completion of contract. Acknowledgment of unfinished business.

This table is derived from Frew (1983, 1997), Horner (1991), Kepner, (1994),Oremland (1991), Polster (1987),Rutan & Stone (2001), and Winnicott (1965).

In the first Gestalt stage, members concern themselves with fitting in and establishing identity. In the second stage, they struggle for influence and question the leadership. In the third stage, members are concerned with matters of intimacy (too much and too little) and work together toward goals. (The second and third stages are both middle stages when mapped onto the psychodynamic stage model.) Members may also resist the last phase, dissolution (Frew, 1983).

Leadership Skills

The person of the therapist is paramount in Gestalt practice, as it was in Rogerian practice. However, Perls disagreed with Rogers in the positive regard area—he believed that clients should get in-the-moment feedback from counselors so that they realize how they are viewed by mature others. Thus, Perls would encourage the counselor to act bored, irritated, or impatient if that's the way she felt. In flagrant violation of some dearly held therapeutic rules, Perls (1969a) even fell asleep while clients talked. Few Gestalt counselors today would follow Perls in this extreme. The Gestalt therapist admits to being mistaken, saying the wrong thing, and using imperfect strategies in sessions and in his or her own life. The counselor is a role model of integrating polarities and remaining centered. Gestalt psychologists refrain from jumping in with interpretations because the clients need to provide their own interpretations instead of accepting expert opinion from the outside.

In light of these rather negatively phrased leadership qualities, what are the positive skills practiced by Gestalt group therapists? Feder (1998, p. 301) lists four processes that he employs (I add my own comments):

1. *Emphasize group experience over experiences outside of group.* Experiences connected to the group are more intense and productive because everyone is present for them.

2. *Attend to the balance of safety and danger in the group, and take active efforts to correct imbalance in either direction.* If the group becomes too safe, it will be boring and unproductive. If the group is too risky (that is, too threatening to some members), fright may prevent members from participating fully.

3. *Carefully develop the ground for experimentation through example and explanation.* Introduce experiments gradually from safe to risky.

4. *Attend to repetition of experiments on the same subject.* Without repetition, change and awareness can dissipate.

These are processes that the group leader must be responsible for at first because she or he can control the focus of a fledgling group. By doing so, the counselor helps set group norms of here-and-now, safety and risk, experimentation, and repetition.

Multilevel Awareness

The Gestalt group counselor develops sensitivity to three levels of dynamics occurring simultaneously: the individual level, the interpersonal level, and the group level (Frew, 1990). Interventions are available at each level. **Multilevel awareness** is exemplified in the selection you read at the beginning of this chapter.

Frew (1983) explains that the leader's work is to grasp which level dominates the group at the moment and then predict a different level and nudge it into the group's awareness. "The skill of leadership is to acknowledge and legitimize the 'what is' on the one hand, while creating opportunities for 'what else could be' on the other" (p. 178). So, for example, when a beginning group is operating on an intrapersonal (individual) level, as they usually do, the leader should support this but also use interventions that suggest the interpersonal and group levels. Thus, he or she will encourage reflection on relationships between group members in the here-and-now and will ask for discussion of the group's responses as a whole.

Techniques in Gestalt Groups

Gestaltists have embraced techniques from other approaches and redesigned them for their own purposes. They have also used their enthusiasm and creativity to welcome unexpected techniques that arise from group members.

Dream Work

Gestalt therapists incorporate role-playing into **dream work** in groups. First, the member presents the dream in detail, in the present tense. Then the dreamer plays the roles of the persons and objects in the dream, producing dialogs between different parts of the dream. Each part represents projections or aspects of the dreamer. Dreams that come back repetitively and dreams with emotional intensity make especially good material. Unusual elements and gaps in dreams are investigated as well as common contents. I dreamed recently that my friend Becky from grad school was marrying my college Shakespeare professor. They were lounging on big wicker chairs on a Caribbean beach. They were beaming at the rest of us and enjoying our surprise. When I woke up, I thought about getting in touch with Becky, who is a midwestern farm girl with a new baby. In dream work, Perls might see her as a polarity, a neglected side of my career-driven, childfree self. Other members of the group can be engaged in the dream work, with different members representing the parts of the dream and communicating in those roles. Thus, if we were working on my dream, group members might take on the roles of the wicker chairs, the pure blue sea at our feet, the Shakespeare professor, Becky, and the surprised crowd. They might suggest that I was celebrating the marriage of my two professions, literature and psychology. The point is for the group to integrate the parts of the dream so that disowned, alienated parts of the dreamer are brought together (Harman, 1988).

SMALL GROUP EXERCISE

Explore a dream presented by one of your group members. Take a Gestalt approach. Have group members help identify the parts of the dream, with the dreamer speaking the roles of the different parts or with members acting them out. If no one in your group has a dream to present, ask members to pretend that the following dream is their own and to process it in the group as if it were their own.

> I was walking several dogs that weren't mine, and trying to keep them all peaceful even though they didn't get along very well. The owners would be unhappy with me if I didn't do the job right. There were cats playing in the trees, swinging from branch to branch. When I got home, the porch steps were caving in from decay, and I wondered whether I could get some neighbors to help me fix them. Inside, the house was almost empty, including the refrigerator.

Psychodrama

When role-playing is performed by several people in a group, it is one of the most impressive therapeutic techniques, **psychodrama.** Instead of a single client acting out various parts, members of a group are assigned parts representing significant individuals in a directed re-enactment of a past experience. The client whose experience is being dramatized acts as director, along with the therapist, to inform and guide the other characters in their actions and responses. In this way the past is brought into the present (Korb et al., 1989). Often, the character of the client is played by the client, and in this role she experiments with alternative ways of behaving in the situation, while others behave in their assigned characters. For example, a person who is berating herself for being quiet in a family argument might be directed to jump in and speak her piece in a loud voice during the reproduction of the argument. Alternatively, group members might portray abstractions, such as the childish side of the actor or an imaginary monster. Such experiments are preferable to listening to a group member explain and justify behavior. In Gestalt therapy, *doing it* is always preferable to *talking about it.*

Psychodrama: An Expanded Application of Role-Playing

J. L. Moreno popularized psychodrama as a therapeutic technique, beginning with children in the parks of Vienna in the 1920s (Greenberg, 1974). Moreno coined the term *group psychotherapy* and also invented the sociogram, a graphic tool still widely used to diagram relationships of people in groups. He explained how psychodrama works:

> Psychodrama defines the drama as an extension of life and action rather than its imitation, but where there is imitation the emphasis is not on what it imitates, but upon the opportunity of recapitulation of unsolved problems within a freer, broader and more flexible social setting. . . . The patient-actor is like a refugee who suddenly shows new strength because he has set foot into a freer and broader world. Catharsis is generated by the vision of a new universe and the capability of new growth. (Moreno, 1946/1972, pp. 15–16.)

Kellerman (1984) pointed out that in Moreno's usage, catharsis is not merely release of strong emotions, but also the integration and ordering of these emotions through new coping strategies, conflict resolution, and self-regulation.

SMALL GROUP EXERCISE: A FAMILY SNAPSHOT

David Hutchinson, groups specialist, provided the following description of an introductory psychodrama exercise designed to help the group have some historical context for each member and also to help the group member with some structured self-disclosure. Try the exercise out with your small group; then follow up with the discussion ideas.

> I call this exercise, A Family Snapshot. Get someone to volunteer to go first. They invite (people can refuse) other members to play the parts of family members. Usually the director (the volunteer) chooses people who bear some resemblance (age, gender, demeanor) to the actual family, but this is not necessary. The director then comes up with a motion for each character which is symbolic of who this person is—work, disability, behavioral quirk, trait, whatever. For example, one director put his mother at the stove stirring a pot and his father in his easy chair reading the newspaper.
>
> The director poses the family in an open area, and defines their relation to each other in this space. For instance, the mother at the stove remained with her back turned to all the others, and the father was instructed not to look up from his paper. The little sister was at a distance, off in her room looking in the mirror and fiddling with her hair.
>
> Then, for only a few moments, the director puts the portrait in motion, with everyone doing their particular movement. After this, people stay in position long enough for participants and observers to share observations—trying to stay with what they see, not getting too interpretive.
>
> The timing of this is important. The group needs to be developed enough so that members feel okay with the risk of putting themselves out there, yet with enough time left to work things through. Enough time needs to be taken to debrief. Actors need to uncouple from their roles; directors need to unburden a feeling that they've been unfair to their families in how they've characterized

them. The group gives lots of support for sharing, appreciation for the inevitable differences and similarities in the portraits presented. The real work is in this process of discussion. Make sure that everyone is aware that they will have chances to go into this in more depth if they wish. (Thanks to David Hutchinson, personal communication, June 22, 2004.)

DISCUSSION IDEAS

1. Report to the class on your experience with David Hutchinson's A Family Snapshot psychodrama. What did the exercise mean to each individual? What did the exercise do for your small group as a whole?

2. Psychodrama experts include J. L. Moreno, Zerka T. Moreno (J. L.'s wife), Adam Blatner, Anne Bannister (specializing in psychodrama for children), and Jose Fonseca. Look up a work by one of these authors in the library. Report to the class on one or two applications of psychodrama.

Experimentation

Experimentation is encouraged in Gestalt therapy—Perls had a background in drama and liked improvisation. The strategy of experimentation is related to the **paradoxical theory of change** (Beisser, 1970)—*trying* to reach an ideal gets you stuck in the same patterns. You don't get anywhere. So, you should try something new just to see how it feels. Heightened emotions or awareness may result. Change occurs when something happens to bring the present situation into fuller awareness, and any new element might do this. For instance, when you add a new activity into your life, it gives you a new perspective on other, seemingly unrelated areas. When I took up watercolor painting again after a twenty-year hiatus, I found that it brought my present life situation under new scrutiny. I started to rearrange my schedule to make time for painting, found that I needed to reorganize my work space to make room, and began looking at my surroundings as potential painting subjects. If, instead, I had made a decision like, "I am going to change my life by rearranging my schedule, reorganizing my work space, and looking at things around me more closely," I might not have known exactly what to do. Paradoxically, deciding to make those changes might have stopped me from accomplishing them.

The following example shows experimentation in the Gestalt group:

Melissa was telling the group about a problem she was having at work with her secretary who consistently came late. "I've spoken to her several times about it and each time she promises to be on time, but then she comes late again. I really don't know what to do. I can't fire her because she is so competent."

After several expressions of sympathy from members of the group, John spoke up saying, "You know, Melissa, if you speak to your secretary the way you talk to us in here, I wouldn't listen very much either. Your voice is so wispy and hesitant, I don't feel there would be any consequences if I didn't listen."

"How does your voice sound to you?" the leader asked Melissa.

"Normal, like it always does," she answered.

"Can you describe it?" pursued the leader.

"Well, it is a little soft, and I do say 'er' a lot," Melissa replied.

"Would you like to make more of an impact using your voice, particularly to your secretary?" the leader asked.

"If it would get her to come in on time, I sure would."

"I can't promise that but it's worth a try, I would think," continued the leader.

Melissa nodded her head in agreement upon which the leader said, "I notice that your chest and diaphragm don't move much when you talk. Your breath doesn't support your voice. Try sitting up straight in your chair and putting your hand on your belly and see if you can move your hand with your breath. "

After several minutes of practicing this, Melissa said, "This is hard, but in some ways it feels good too. I feel fuller and bigger."

"Now could you practice telling your secretary not to come in late continuing to breathe the same way you just have been doing," the leader asked.

"Well, we've talked about this before, and you don't seem to hear me. I will not stand for your coming late one more time!" Melissa said in a loud and firm voice. With a smile on her face, she looked around the room, and turning to John said, "Well, how was that? Did I get you to listen?" (Handlon & Fredericson, 1998, pp. 286–287)

Melissa may be asked to practice speaking firmly to other members of the group, and then assigned experimental homework to try her new voice at the office.

Experiments are designed to clarify experience and to call forth awareness of how experiences are interrupted or regulated. Another experiment Perls liked was turning statements about others into statements about the self, on the premise that we are most hostile to qualities in others that remind us of our denied selves. So he might encourage the wife who says, "He never pays any attention to me," to say aloud, "I never pay any attention to me," and to see how that statement feels. Does she feel that she is not worth listening to?

Focusing on the here-and-now and intensifying present experience is another Gestalt technique: "What are you aware of now?" is a common question designed to keep the client in the moment. Instead of providing guidance or interpretation, the counselor is likely to advise the client to "Stay with that" when an emotion or intense observation emerges. In Gestalt terms, the client has not had much practice at "staying with" a strong impression until it comes into meaningful focus. More energy has been spent getting past it or pushing it away. Emotions intensify when brought into the here-and-now. For instance, if a member begins to reflect on her father, the leader suggests, "Imagine your father in the room and talk directly to him" (Barnes, 1977). The therapist acts as a supporter and a model of being able to survive experiencing fully.

The therapist makes use of the client's imagination to make experience vivid. If a patient describes his life as "rushing from place to place and not remembering why I have to rush or what to do at the place once I get there," the counselor may suggest, "Imagine you are actually rushing around, right now. Now you get to the place. What do you experience?" (cf. Yontef & Jacobs, 2000, p. 327). Other imaginative experiments include fantasizing about telling off someone you are angry with, trying something you fear, leaving your body and observing it from ceiling level, and walking slowly through a pleasant place.

In much Gestalt group therapy, the focus is on one client while other group members observe. Members take turns being in the hot seat. The observing members participate on different levels depending on the principles of the therapist. Many Gestalt group therapists use the interactions within the group as experimental laboratories (Polster & Polster, 1973); for example, a member who is fearful of conflict may be invited to take an unpopular side on an issue and argue vigorously with all the other members for a limited amount of time.

Body Awareness

Gestaltists emphasize the body as a source of information and insight. Gestaltists think that the mind versus body polarity is one of the most misleading. Perls evidently had an uncanny ability to read posture, fidgets, and other body language accurately, and this ability was a key part of his therapy technique. In later life, Perls devoted most of his time to lectures and demonstrations and "astonished his audiences by the amount of personal information he could pick up just by watching how they spoke, sat or walked" (Clarkson & Mackewn, 1993, p. 4). He believed that every emotion has a physiological component. When a client has taught herself to cut off part of her natural self, her body strains toward the cut-off impulses. "The holding back is achieved by tensing muscles which are antagonistic to those which would be involved in expressing the punishable impulse" (Perls, Hefferline, & Goodman, 1951, p. 147). For example, if a therapist notices that a group member clenches his jaw habitually, she would suspect that some impulse to speak is being repressed. A curled-in posture could indicate an attempt to protect one's vulnerable areas. Perls noted that there are conscious, rational grounds for suppressing impulses, and these were not his concern. When the holding-back is *not* under the control of awareness, it nonetheless displays itself in bodily and mental ways.

Often, **body awareness** work is done with the client on the hot seat. The therapist, meanwhile, attempts to be sensitive to body language among the other group members, which can be read as their responses to the work being done. Some Gestaltists would call on members to become aware of their own body language and what it means, as they observe work with the hot-seat client.

As you read in the case of Melissa, body work can be a focus of experimentation. A person with a habitually curled-in posture might be asked to sit in a spread-out, loose position and make exaggerated gestures while speaking. Then the member would be asked how it felt to be physically expansive rather than restricted. Did it feel scary? Heady? Uncomfortable? Such an experiment can increase awareness of self, a goal of Gestalt and other psychodynamic therapies.

SMALL GROUP EXERCISE

Go with your group to a spot on campus where people are behaving infor-mally—milling around waiting for a class to start, gathering to look at a bulletin board, waiting for the bus, standing in line at a grocery store or fast food chain. Each member of your group will target a subset of two or more people and write down your observations about the body language you see. Include in your notes your guesses about how body language reflects the dynamics among the gathering you observed. Return to your classroom to compare notes with others in your group. Discuss similarities and differ-ences in your observations and your guesses.

Empty Chair

The **empty-chair technique** is the one you see most often in depictions of Ge-stalt therapy, both fictional and real. It's also a technique frequently borrowed by counselors of other orientations, probably due to its dramatic effectiveness in helping clients and their therapists grasp an individual's unique dynamics. Two chairs are used, with each one assigned a character, attitude, emotion, or quality. The client moves back and forth between the two chairs, alternately speaking from the perspective of each. If you were a worker having trouble with a certain supervisor, you would take one chair as yourself and the other chair as the supervisor. Or, you might act out an inner conflict and let the two sides battle it out. The lazy side takes one chair, while your conscientious side takes the other. The lazy side tries to persuade you that you don't need to go visit your sick friend on this beautiful fall day, while the conscientious side argues that your sick friend needs you. The counselor sustains a here-and-now focus and cheers each chair on by acting as the director. A favorite empty-chair dialogue is the one between **top-dog and under-dog,** two polarities within one person. The top-dog is analogous to the over-critical parent, and the under-dog is analogous to the stubborn toddler. The top-dog sits in a chair and tries to persuade, bully, and threaten the under-dog to be a good person, while the under-dog occupies the other chair and pleads helplessness, using "yes, but" excuses and stubbornness to retain its power not to change. Other members of the group observe and derive personal meaning from the exercise, or are invited to comment and interact with the main event.

Leslie Greenberg and colleagues have extensively investigated the empty-chair technique (Clarke & Greenberg, 1986; Greenberg, 1979; Paivio & Green-berg, 1995). Their findings indicate that it facilitates depth of experiencing, integration of polarities, and conflict resolution. For these outcomes, the empty-chair approach held its own or had superior results in comparison with other approaches (empathic reflection of feelings and cognitive-behavioral problem solving). It appears that clients in the empty-chair approach were able to soften their inner voice of self-criticism.

DISCUSSION IDEAS

1. Imagine that you are leading a group, and you think that an empty-chair technique would be illuminating for everyone. You've never used this technique before, and it will be the fifth session. What will you do to prepare for suggesting the technique? Role-play yourself as a leader introducing the idea to your counseling group.

2. If you were a therapist suggesting an empty-chair exercise, how do you think you could encourage a hesitant group to open up to the idea?

3. Are there any multicultural points of view that you need to consider when using the empty-chair technique?

Problems Addressed in Gestalt Groups

Gestalt therapy's underlying theory predicts the type of client it has most often assisted: People who are too well socialized, rigid, subdued, and inhibited. These clients benefit from working with their polarities and integrating the wild, free, flexible sides of themselves with the surface complaisance they have cultivated so far. Gestaltists also treat anxiety and depression, though, unlike the DSM and many theories, they do not view these problems as categories of mental disorder. Depression, according to Gestalt thinking, is just a sign of unresolved anger and sadness, treatable as "unfinished business." And anxiety is a sign of over-preoccupation with the unforeseeable future and the bad things it possibly holds, relieved by Gestalt emphasis on the here-and-now.

Gendered Lives

In Gestalt experimentation, men and women are often encouraged to practice behaviors with the other-sex members within the group. Earley (2000) gives an example of Hank, a member who says that certain kinds of women intimidate him. He is asked to identify women within the group who intimidate him and to pay attention to interactions that intimidate him during sessions. Hank might later be asked to role-play a situation with a woman in the group, asserting himself in a setting where he might usually be intimidated and retreat.

Gestalt is one of the few theories that involved strong women in its development from the very beginning (publicly, that is—women have contributed to most famous psychological theories, even Freudianism, but rarely got credit till recently). The inclusion of women in theorizing may have led to Gestalt's success with problems that are associated with conventional womanhood (Sharf, 2000). Social demands for politeness, unselfishness, submissiveness, pleasantness, and compliance are more strongly felt by women; for one example, women are often told to smile by strangers, whereas this is an unheard-of request toward men. Women's identities are more wrapped up in their children and spouses than men's are. Women physically take care of aging parents, even their husbands' parents. They suffer keenly when children grow up and when marriages fail. These conditions create women who have denied their own leanings so often that they need awareness exercises even to identify their own desires, separate from the desires of others. They are at increased risk of low self-esteem, ineffectuality, and depression (Enns, 1987). Enns suggests a feminist version of Gestalt therapy, including "(a) creating self-definitions and owning personal power, (b) developing awareness of unexpressed anger and using it constructively, and (c) expanding personal options by incorporating behavioral alternatives that have been previously unconsidered" (p. 93).

Men also suffer from restricted sex roles and the splitting-off that fulfilling the sex role entails. Historically, men have felt pressured to make major decisions for the family, drive in heavy traffic, advance in income level, and be handymen, as well as to interrupt their lives and put themselves in terrible danger serving in the military. The strain of stringent standards of being a man can cause gender role conflict and "increases in depression, anxiety, anger, substance abuse, loneliness, and other interpersonal problems" (Blazina, 2002, p. 24). These gendered polarities harm men's contact with other people and the environment, especially in the form of "a fragmented and unintegrated perspective of the world of relationships, that of our partners, and ourselves. This often includes an inability to move beyond splitting the world and significant others into artificial dichotomies of gratifying or ungratifying" (p. 27). Obviously, Gestalt therapy's focus on integration is appropriate for such problems.

Psychosomatic Complaints

Because Gestaltists reject the idea of a clear mind/body split, they view symptoms of psychopathology as appearing in emotion, thought, behavior, and body. Their investigation of posture, gesture, and other nonverbal features reflects this idea. Illnesses, too, are part of a client's psychological makeup. "We describe a psychosomatic event as one in which the gross physical disturbances are more impressive than the ones that occur on a mental or emotional level" (Perls, 1973, p. 55). Headaches, for example, were viewed as "excuses for withdrawal in thousands of cases in daily life" (p. 56) when direct withdrawal is too frightening or impolite. Cohn (1970) provides an account of curing a 9-year-old's constant severe stomachaches using techniques of Gestalt therapy. She encouraged awareness of body and feeling by placing her hand on the girl's stomach and asking questions like: "Where and how does it hurt?" "How does my hand feel?" "Is the pain usually the same, or does it get worse at times?" "What does the pain say?"

Couples and Families

Many of the problems experienced by couples are within the realm of Gestalt theory because such intimate relationships are often vexed by contact boundary disturbances, especially when complicated by sex role demands and social expectations, as heterosexual marriage is. Some of the boundary problems Gestalt techniques investigate in couples are these:

- **Introjection**   June has been with Steve since they were in high school, and now that she's 40 years old, she automatically agrees with his opinion on everything from world politics to loud plaids. This agreement isn't just to keep the peace; June has taken on Steve's values herself. The couple suffers from lack of the give-and-take of ideas that keeps relationships vital.

- **Projection**   Whenever Ann is quiet and pensive, Loren treats her as though she is depressed, because that's what it means when *he* is quiet and pensive. This causes problems. Ann doesn't like to be treated like a depressed person when she's merely thinking, and Loren gets upset when Ann is quiet and won't believe that she is not depressed.

- **Retroflection**   Jana kicks herself for not being able to live up to Dan's fastidious demands around the house. She may be avoiding the truth that she is really angry with Dan, not herself, for being so fussy. Thus, she is unable to talk with him about the problem and provide the reality check that partners usually give each other.

- **Deflection**   One or both partners may avoid touchy subjects between them by deflecting attention to something else. Many couples use their children as an outside focus that helps them remain unified (at least on one level). It may not be a problem until the children rebel or grow up.

- **Confluence**   In a close relationship, it's a virtue to feel the other partner's joys and pains. However, each person needs to maintain some separation from the other's emotional state. For example, Ken was unable to help Mary when her parents died because he was so devastated by her sadness. Similarly, the partners of depressed people have difficulty in maintaining their own joys in life.

A Gestalt therapy perspective on the family "focuses on the configural patterns that structure the interactions among family members and greatly characterize the family as a unit. Such configural patterns form social Gestalten" (Lawe & Smith, 1986). In therapy, once a family has identified the patterns that govern their interactions (often driven by contact boundary problems as exemplified above), they experiment with changes in the patterns, first in therapy sessions and then at home. For example, an overbearing father might experiment with letting everyone else in the family speak before he does.

Traumatized Clients

While Gestalt psychotherapists serve traumatized clients, they refuse to *explain* current problems by past traumas. If past trauma is still very active in a person's identity and daily decisions, it stifles growth. Almost any psychologist acknowledges that the source of current emotional problems can be past traumas, even from the distant past. Gestalt theory would place past trauma that is still active in the category of unfinished business. The goal of therapy is not to forget the trauma but to integrate it into a complete current self, usually not by talking *about* it but by reexperiencing it.

Holman and Silver (1998) studied incest survivors, Vietnam veterans, and firestorm survivors, and the research findings support the Gestalt perspective. People who were "focused on a distressing and seemingly unresolvable past" (p. 1159) were significantly more psychologically disturbed than others with the same experiences behind them. People who were able to weave the past into an integrated life story were able to live with it. Other ways of being stuck in the past are to negate or deny negative experiences, through suppression, repression, or motivated forgetting. Gestalt techniques designed to make contact with split-off aspects of the self are used in these situations.

Physical trauma has psychological effects that respond to Gestalt therapy as well. Livneh and Sherwood (1991) related Gestalt principles to the psychological struggles of disabled people. The discordant poles of experience in these cases are victim versus oppressor, healthy versus sick, independent versus dependent, coping versus succumbing, and disabled versus intact. Disability disrupts the homeostasis, and people with disabilities are faced with restoring equilibrium to their lives. Livneh and Sherwood suggest techniques such as role-playing (including empty-wheelchair) and self-awareness exercises to help clients come to terms with their losses and the implications.

Early, repetitive trauma in relationships with parents often underlies personality disorders, which are usually considered quite difficult to treat. People with borderline personality disorder, for example, usually had parents who failed to nurture them well enough, and the children suppressed the development of their natural selves (for example, they persisted in seeking parental attention when they ordinarily would be branching out into the world). They grow up into people who have chronically troubled relationships with other people, continually seek the perfect person and continually are disappointed, and paradoxically fear and desire closeness. Greenberg (1989) explained how Gestalt therapy can address borderline features. *Splitting* occurs when a client can only see others (including the therapist) as all good or all bad, and obviously this is a polarity in Gestalt terms. *Awareness* of one's own feelings and preferences is lacking in the borderline, who needs to learn to feel and want without reference to someone else. Finally, borderline clients are often full of rage and terrified that they will let it loose and never get it back under control again. The setting of Gestalt group sessions allows experimentation with expressing strong feelings in an atmosphere where they will have no awful repercussions.

DISCUSSION IDEA

As you have read, Gestalt group therapy helps people find their spontaneous impulses. Group members become less stuck in negative thoughts and behavior and more open to experience. Imagine that you are putting together a Gestalt-oriented group for self-discovery among heterogeneous adults. Are there certain kinds of people who would be poor candidates for a Gestalt group? Describe them. Discuss why the Gestalt approach would not be the best choice for them.

Adaptations to Clients' Ages

Because Gestalt groups encourage movement, drama, and experimentation, their active nature can be appealing to children. Children experience contact boundary disturbances such as projecting blame onto others, deflecting or turning away from deep feelings, and confluence, blending into the feelings of attractive others (Oaklander, 1999). Presented with a variety of experiences in group therapy, "the child may become more aware of himself: who he is, what he feels, what he likes and doesn't like, what he needs, what he wants, what he does, and how he does it—he finds that he has choices he can make—choices for expression, getting needs met, and exploring new behaviors. The self becomes stronger as he defines himself" (p. 165). Oaklander provides several case examples, including this one:

> A group of children, all with fathers in an alcoholic treatment center, were asked to share their dreams. This group ranged in age from eight to sixteen and included several sets of siblings. At the time in question, this unorthodox group had been meeting for most of a year, and the members were quite comfortable with each other in spite of the age differences. They had discovered that they shared many common experiences. One girl, age twelve, described a dream in which she is in a car driven by her father going down a steep hill. At the bottom of the hill there is a lake. The car is going very fast and she is screaming at her father to slow down. She fears the car will go right into the lake. Her father ignores her, and just as the car is about to take its plunge, she wakes up. The other children listened intently to this dream. As soon as she stopped speaking, an eight-year-old boy said, "I have a road in my life just like that." (p. 170)

Oaklander advises that groups comprise six to eight children over 8 years old, and three to six children under 8. A co-therapist is important because at times a child needs individual attention during group sessions. The groups are more structured than adult Gestalt therapy groups, with the counselors planning the activity for each one and one-half to two-hour session. Each group begins with rounds and closes with the children cleaning up and taking their seats for a final round of closing comments, critiques of the activity, and communications to each other. It takes four to six sessions for children to feel safe and get to know each other, so counselors need to plan noninvasive, nonthreatening activities for the first phase.

Evaluating Gestalt Groups

In general, Gestaltists resist quantitative measurement of results because usually such measurement cannot reflect humans holistically. However, in today's atmosphere of accountability and empirical evidence, you may want to pursue proof of the effectiveness of any group you lead. I will introduce you to two instruments that have been used to assess outcomes of Gestalt groups.

O'Leary, Sheedy, O'Sullivan, and Thoresen (2003) used the **Profile of Mood States** to assess both negative and positive moods before and after a Gestalt therapy group with older adults. This self-report measure, now available in a brief thirty-question form, assesses positive and negative items on six subscales: Anger-Hostility, Vigor-Activity, Fatigue-Inertia, Confusion-Bewilderment, Tension-Anxiety, and Depression-Dejection (POMS; Lorr, McNair, & Heuchert, 2003). The POMS may be administered to a group weekly or further apart to gauge changes in affective states, which theoretically should alter with Gestalt awareness. O'Leary and her team found that their Gestalt group significantly reduced levels of hostility and confusion. In using the POMS, remember that changes in positive directions are not always expected during Gestalt counseling. Growth of awareness can create *more* distress when people begin to think and feel in previously suppressed ways. However, we hope that by the close of counseling, most changes have turned in a positive direction.

Interpersonal aspects of life should also reflect the effects of Gestalt groups, so Paivio and Greenberg (1995) used the **Inventory of Interpersonal Problems** (IIP, also now available in a short form; Barkham, Hardy, & Startup, 1996). The researchers were studying the effectiveness of empty-chair dialogue. This thirty-two-item self-report survey derives scores on eight interpersonal difficulties: hard to be sociable, hard to be assertive, too aggressive, too caring, hard to be supportive, hard to be involved, too intrusive, and too dependent. In Paivio and Greenberg's research, the empty-chair group reported significantly greater reductions in interpersonal distress than a psychoeducational group. The IIP can be given to groups pre- and posttreatment, or used to compare types of groups as the empty-chair study did.

In research studies like these, it is important to be able to link the instruments you use (for instance, the POMS and IIP) to the theoretical bases for your counseling approach. The researchers considered that these measures would show changes consistent with improvement from a Gestalt point of view. For client groups emphasizing body awareness, a reduction in pain and health complaints may also be a valid measure of improvement.

KEY TERMS

assimilation a middle stage of group process in which members become interdependent and intimate in efforts to reach goals

awareness the capacity to be in touch with one's inner self, to notice one's surroundings, to feel related to the environment, other people, and self, all in the present moment; the goal of Gestalt counseling

body awareness use of physical sensations and nonverbal behavior as sources of insight and information

contact boundary disturbances distortions in accurate distinctions between self and others; confusing self and others as sources of thought and feeling

differentiation a middle stage of group process in which members see their differences and experience conflict

dream work analysis of dreams, often starting from the assumption that each part represents projections or aspects of the dreamer

empty-chair technique a role-playing technique in which a member splits two aspects of his or her self and stages a dialogue between them, moving between two chairs and speaking for each aspect in turn

experiments trials of new behavior that arise from occurrences within group sessions

figure/ground relation the way in which we organize what we see into a shape in the foreground (the figure) and a rather formless background (the ground); Gestalt therapy uses the figure/ground relation to describe what is important in consciousness at the moment (figure) versus unimportant aspects (the ground); the contents of figure and ground shift with needs

hot seat the spot in which an individual sits when he or she is the focus of a Gestalt group session

Inventory of Interpersonal Problems a self-report measure that evaluates eight sources of distress in relationships with other people

multilevel awareness a sensitivity to individual, interpersonal, and group aspects of episodes within sessions

orientation an early stage of group process in which members become socialized to counseling processes and discover similarities among themselves

paradoxical theory of change the idea that seeking change directly usually doesn't work; change occurs when a person is seeking something different, and usually eventuates when novelty is invited into life

polarities opposing forces and tendencies, which do battle within one person

Profile of Mood States a self-report measure that provides scores on six affective categories

psychodrama multimember role-plays in which members take parts to act out a situation, story, or inner conflict belonging to one member

shoulds rules of behavior, usually in moralistic and judgmental terms

spectator learning vicarious learning that group members experience while observing the person in the hot seat and the Gestalt therapist

top-dog and under-dog the over-critical parent and the stubborn toddler within each of us; often, these are aspects used in the empty-chair dialogue

unfinished business unresolved emotional dilemmas from a person's past that cause distress in the present; equivalent to neurosis in psychodynamic terminology

unstuck loosened from patterns determined by past experiences and habits

CHAPTER REVIEW

1. If you dropped into a group without foreknowledge, what might clue you in to the fact that it was a Gestalt group?

2. Explain three techniques of Gestalt therapy, and make up your own applications of these techniques to groups you lead or intend to lead.

3. Develop your own opinion on the hot seat/spectator learning model of group therapy. Explain your reasoning.

4. Try an experiment in multilevel awareness next time you are in a group of three or more people. Take notes on what happened on individual, interpersonal, and group levels.

5. Review the table of contact boundary disturbances (Table 11.1). Use one or more of these concepts to explain a problem you have experienced, have observed, or have seen in a fictional account.

6. List three or four problem situations that would be good material for a psychodrama exercise in group counseling. Explain why these situations lend themselves to psychodrama.

7. Think about a dyad or group you belong to (or belonged to in the past). Can you see yourselves going through stages of orientation, differentiation, and assimilation? Explain.

8. What relationship should there be between theory and outcome assessment in group counseling?

FOR FURTHER READING

Feder, B., & Ronall, R. (Eds.). (2000). *Beyond the hot seat: Gestalt applications to group.* Montclair, NJ: Beefeeder Press.

First published in 1980, this classic collection includes chapters by many of the leading practitioners of Gestalt group therapy. It was the first book devoted entirely to group practice of Gestalt. The chapters are divided among four areas: theory, clinical applications, educational applications, and community applications. Therefore, you can probably find a chapter that is directly relevant to your area of practice.

REFERENCES

Barkham, M., Hardy, G. E., & Startup, M. (1996). The IIP-32: A short version of the Inventory of Interpersonal Problems. *British Journal of Clinical Psychology, 35,* 21–35.

Barnes, G. (1977). *Tranactional Analysis after Eric Berne: Teachings and practices of three TA schools.* NY: Harper & Row.

Beisser, A. (1970). The paradoxical theory of change. In J. Fagan & I. L. Shepherd (Eds.), *Gestalt therapy now* (pp. 77–80). New York: Harper & Row.

Blazina, C. (2002). The fragile masculine self model: Implications for clinical use. *Texas Psychologist, 52*(3), 24–27.

Clarke, K. M., & Greenberg, L. S. (1986). Differential effects of the Gestalt two-chair intervention and problem solving in resolving decisional conflict. *Journal of Counseling Psychology, 33,* 11–15.

Clarkson, P., & Mackewn, J. (1993). *Fritz Perls.* London: Sage.

Cohn, R. C. (1970). A child with a stomachache: Fusion of psychoanalytic concepts and Gestalt techniques. In J. Fagan & I. L. Shepherd (Eds.), *Gestalt therapy now* (pp. 197–203). New York: Harper & Row.

Earley, J. (2000). A practical guide to fostering interpersonal norms in a Gestalt group. *Gestalt Review, 4,* 138–151.

Enns, C. Z. (1987). Gestalt therapy and feminist therapy: A proposed integration. *Journal of Counseling and Development, 66,* 93–95.

Feder, B. (1998). Models for understanding individuals changing through participation in Gestalt therapy groups. *Gestalt Review, 2,* 295–301.

Frew, J. (1983). Encouraging what is not figural in the Gestalt group. *Journal for Specialists in Group Work, 8,* 175–181.

Frew, J. (1988). The practice of Gestalt therapy in groups. *Gestalt Journal, 11,* 77–96.

Frew, J. (1990). Analysis of transference in Gestalt therapy. *International Journal of Group Psychotherapy, 40,* 189–202.

Frew, J. (1997). A Gestalt therapy theory application to the practice of group leadership. *Gestalt Review, 1,* 131–149.

Greenberg, E. (1989). Healing the borderline. *Gestalt Journal, 12*, 11–56.

Greenberg, I. A. (1974). Moreno: Psychodrama and the group process. In I. A. Greenberg (Ed.), *Psychodrama: Theory and therapy* (pp. 11–28). New York: Behavioral Publications.

Greenberg, L. S. (1979). Resolving splits: Use of the two chair technique. *Psychotherapy: Theory, Research, and Practice, 16*, 316–324.

Handlon, J. H., & Fredericson, I. (1998). What changes the individual in Gestalt groups? *Gestalt Review, 2*, 275–294.

Harman, R. L. (1988). Gestalt group therapy. In S. Long (Ed.), *Six group therapies* (pp. 217–255). New York: Plenum Press.

Henle, M. (1978). Gestalt psychology and Gestalt therapy. *Journal of the History of the Behavioral Sciences, 14*, 23–32.

Holman, E. A., & Silver, R. C. (1998). Getting "stuck" in the past: Temporal orientation and coping with trauma. *Journal of Personality and Social Psychology, 74*, 1146–1163.

Horner, A. J. (1991). *Psychoanalytic object relations therapy*. Northvale, NJ: Jason Aronson. (Original work published 1980)

Humphrey, K. (1986). Laura Perls: A biographical sketch. *Gestalt Journal, 10*, 5–11.

Kellerman, P. F. (1984). The place of catharsis in psychodrama. *Journal of Group Psychotherapy, Psychodrama and Sociometry, 37*, 1–13.

Kepner, E. (1994). Gestalt group process. In B. Feder & R. Ronall (Eds.), *Beyond the hot seat: Gestalt approaches to group* (pp. 5–24). Highland, NY: Gestalt Journal Press.

Korb, M. P., Gorrell, J., & Van de Riet, V. (1989). *Gestalt therapy: Practice and theory* (2nd ed.). Boston: Allyn & Bacon.

Lawe, C. F., & Smith, E. W. (1986). Gestalt processes and family therapy. *Individual psychology, 42*, 537–544.

Livneh, H., & Sherwood, A. (1991). Application of personality theories and counseling strategies to clients with physical disabilities. *Journal of Counseling & Development, 69*, 525–538.

Lorr, M., McNair, D. M., & Heuchert, J. W. (2003). *POMS-Brief*. North Tonawanda, NY: Multi-Health Systems.

Moreno, J. L. (1972). *Psychodrama* (4th ed.). Beacon, NY: Beacon House. (Originally published in 1946)

O'Leary, E., Sheedy, G., O'Sullivan, K., & Thoresen, C. (2003). Cork Older Adult Intervention Project: Outcomes of a Gestalt therapy group with older adults. *Counselling Psychology Quarterly, 16*, 131–143.

Oaklander, V. (1999). Group play therapy from a Gestalt therapy perspective. In D. S. Sweeney & L. E. Homeyer (Eds.), *The handbook of group play therapy* (pp. 162–175). San Francisco: Jossey-Bass.

Oremland, J. D. (1991). *Interpretation and interaction: Psychoanalysis or psychotherapy?* (Hillsdale, NJ: Analytic Press).

Paivio, S. C., & Greenberg, L. S. (1995). Resolving "unfinished business": Efficacy of experiential therapy using empty-chair dialogue. *Journal of Consulting and Clinical Psychology, 63*, 419–425.

Perls, F. (1969a). *Gestalt therapy verbatim*. Lafayette, CA: Real People Press.

Perls, F. (1969b). *In and out the garbage pail.* Lafayette, CA: Real People Press.

Perls, F. (1973). *The Gestalt approach & eyewitness to therapy.* Palo Alto, CA: Science & Behavior Books.

Perls, F., & Baumgardner, P. (1975). *Gifts from Lake Cowichan and Legacy from Fritz.* Palo Alto, CA: Science & Behavior Books.

Perls, F., Hefferline, R. F., & Goodman, P. (1951). *Gestalt therapy.* New York: Julian Press.

Polster, E., & Polster, M. (1973). *Gestalt therapy integrated.* New York: Brunner/Mazel.

Polster, M. (1987). Gestalt therapy: Evolution and application. In J. K. Zeig (Ed.), *The evolution of psychotherapy* (pp. 312–325). New York: Brunner/Mazel.

Rutan, J. S., & Stone, W. N. (2001). *Psychodynamic group psychotherapy* (3rd ed.). New York: Guilford Press.

Sharf, R. S. (2000). *Theories of psychotherapy and counseling* (2nd ed.). Belmont, CA: Brooks/Cole.

Winnicott, D. W. (1965). *The maturational processes and the facilitating environment.* New York: International Universities Press.

Yontef, G., & Jacobs, L. (2000). Gestalt therapy. In R. J. Corsini & D. Wedding, (Eds.), *Current psychotherapies* (6th ed., pp. 303–339). Itasca, IL: Peacock.

PART V

A Life of Learning

In this section (Chapters 12 and 13), I explain group therapies based on learning theories, both behavioral learning and intellectual (cognitive) learning. These therapies, in contrast with the therapies in Part IV, do not focus on unconscious processes, nor do they usually have a goal of illuminating early childhood experiences. The learning theories focus instead on how current thoughts and behavior influence mental health. Because we live among others, we learn in a social context, so what we learn from people around us is also explored and used therapeutically.

One way to look at the distinctions among approaches in Parts III, IV, and V is to consider where the counselor turns first in conceptualizing cases. Existential humanists turn first to emotions and meaning; psychodynamic and Gestalt therapists turn first to inner conflicts; and learning-based counselors turn first to knowledge, thoughts, and actions.

CHAPTER 12

Cognitive-Behavioral Group Theory and Practice

Behavioral and cognitive therapies apply to life's demands in a broad way because they are based on *learning,* the process by which all organisms acquire new behaviors through experience. **Behavioral learning theory** emphasizes the role of reinforcement, punishment, observation, and similar environmental processes in what we learn. **Cognitive learning theory** emphasizes the role of our thinking processes in what we learn. When you look at things from either theoretical viewpoint, both healthy and unhealthy behaviors come from the same learning processes. Sometimes what we learn serves us well, and sometimes we learn things that hold us back from our best performance and our most fulfilling relationships.

In the following excerpt from a classic book on the treatment of depression, Beck, Rush, Shaw, and Emery (1979) explain how the group assists in changing the thought processes (cognitions) of depressed members. The first author, Aaron Beck, is a pioneer in cognitive learning theory.

 A Selection from

Cognitive Therapy of Depression

By Aaron T. Beck, A. John Rush, Brian F. Shaw, and Gary Emery (1979)

A patient's invidious comparisons of himself with other group members can provide special opportunities for therapeutic intervention. In [one] instance, a male group member, a carpenter, expressed a strong concern that he was far less competent than another male group member, a financier, who was temporarily unemployed due to his ongoing depression. The former patient, who had been progressing steadily during his first three weeks in treatment, became profoundly discouraged when the latter patient began to show marked therapeutic improvement. Sample cognitions, once their expression was encouraged, were "I've been working at this for weeks longer than G., yet he's catching on much faster than I am; I'll never get better," or "He's doing this much better than me, I never do anything right." Once identified, these automatic thoughts were then explored and related to similar processes (for example, unwarranted generalizations with respect to time, all-or-none thinking, and selective abstraction) which the patient frequently manifested in his everyday concerns.

In both instances, the group format not only provided situations which brought to light the misinterpretations derived from depressogenic cognitive sets, but also served as an immediate, available context for systematically examining and correcting those negative inferences. As in individual cognitive therapy, while the focus is on events and the cognitions about events that occur outside of therapy, the cognitions that are revealed during the session are often the ones which provide the most compelling demonstrations of both the crucial role of idiosyncratic thinking in depression and the potency of therapeutic techniques in attenuating such dysfunctional thoughts. Group sessions increase the likelihood that negative social comparisons will be triggered. If unattended to, such ideation can undermine the progress of treatment. If identified, such ideation provides opportunities for change which might never arise in the course of individual treatment.

NEGATIVE EFFECTS ON OTHER GROUP MEMBERS

Coyne (1976 a,b) has presented evidence suggesting that the presence of a depressed individual in a group can in itself increase dysphoria among those who interact with him and can lead to the rejection of the depressed individual. While these studies have involved the effects of depressed individuals' interaction with nondepressed individuals, the dynamics of the phenomenon, if applicable to interactions between depressed pairs, might serve as the basis for a prediction that depressed patients in homogeneous groups raise one another's levels of dysphoria.

Our clinical experience suggests that this is not a major concern. Simply talking about problems or symptoms is, by itself, unlikely to have any tangible effects except perhaps to increase dysphoria—one possible explanation for the fact that traditional expressive psychotherapies have fared so poorly in controlled studies. However, in group cognitive therapy, the therapist works actively to focus attention on the examination and reevaluation of these idiosyncratic perceptions as he maintains considerable structure within the sessions. Our experience has been that the behavior of homogeneously depressed groups can be kept task-relevant, and under these circumstances they appear strikingly animated, spontaneous, and active. As in individual cognitive therapy, it is important to realize that many depressions appear "realistic" to the depressed patient. In group cognitive therapy, it appears that focusing on the process by which systematic misconstructions and distortions in information processing combine to make troublesome—but workable—situations appear unresolvable can, with the assistance of other group participants, forestall the type of "contagious" negative affective slide which is apparently attributable to the group's unquestioned acceptance of the depressed patient's pessimistic evaluations.

UNIVERSAL VERSUS PERSONAL DISTORTIONS

While depressed patients appear prone to negative thinking about themselves, their worlds, and their futures, there is evidence suggesting that such distortions are curiously limited to information concerning the depressed individual himself. It appears that depressives apply to themselves rules quite different from those they apply to others, or, stated another way, that errors in inference and thinking are most evident when the depressed patient is thinking about himself, not when he is thinking about others.

The greater objectivity and flexibility in judging people other than themselves is borne out in our clinical experience with therapy groups. First, a depressed patient generally finds that the recognition of errors in the negative cognitions of other patients and the reevaluation of their thoughts and assumptions is less difficult than the recognition and reevaluation of his own cognitions. Secondly, and of utmost importance, the patient's recognition of the cognitive distortions of others, and his experience with reevaluating them, appear to facilitate the recognition and reevaluation of his own idiosyncratic cognitive sets. Thus, the members of the group reality-test assumptions, and in so doing, increase their skills in correcting their own maladaptive reactions.

In summary, depressed patients appear capable of functioning within a group format and deriving specific benefits from their group experiences. (pp. 332–335)

Exploring Cognitive Therapy of Depression

1. What does *invidious* mean? Why did the authors use this word to describe the patient's comparisons of self with others?
2. What type of thinking was habitual for the carpenter? Why do you think the authors describe this thinking as "automatic"?
3. In paragraph 2, what distinction is made between cognitions occurring outside of sessions and cognitions occurring during sessions?
4. In group therapy, how can negative social comparisons be explored better than in individual therapy?
5. What did Coyne's evidence suggest about putting a group of depressed patients together for therapy? Did Beck and colleagues find that Coyne's dynamic was a major concern in depressed groups?
6. In paragraph 4, the authors write, "It is important to realize that many depressions appear 'realistic' to the depressed patient." What does this mean? Can you think of an example?
7. How can contagious negative affect be avoided in a group of depressed people?
8. What difference is there in how depressed individuals think of themselves and how they think of others? How can this difference be useful in group therapy?

▪ ▪ ▪

Essential Concepts of Cognitive-Behavioral Theory

In the selection you just read and discussed, you saw how the group challenged each others' thoughts, which will in turn change behaviors. Now I will give you an example starting with a group member's behaviors. Fredo, a group member, is full of confidence about every subject, including his co-members' problems, and dominates them with pronouncements on what they should do. The group considers him a know-it-all and discounts his statements. They don't like to talk when he's around. Neither he nor they benefit.

Fredo needs to back off. Therefore, there's a *behavior* that needs change. Both maladaptive and adaptive behaviors are learned the same way, through reward and punishment (and related processes). Fredo learned somewhere that being knowledgeable and intimidating was the best way to function in a group. He learned that silence or uncertainty would indicate his weakness, and no one would respect him.

Notice that I said, "Fredo learned somewhere. . . ." When I act as a behavior therapist, where and when and why the learning occurred is not the main issue. If I were acting as a psychodynamic counselor, I'd investigate the family roots of this internal demand for perfection. (Perhaps Fredo grew up in a household where he had to stand up against domineering parents and siblings.) But for a behaviorist, if the therapeutic goal is to help Fredo change this maladaptive behavior, delving into its history is a means to that end, not an end in itself. The historical antecedents are helpful in understanding what keeps the problematic behavior going, currently, but we don't need to know the origins of the problem in order to change it. Systematically changing the consequences of the behavior can alter it, or learning a substitute behavior can replace it.

As you read about learning theory and how it relates to your thinking, feeling, and behavior, you'll find that you have been applying the principles to your own and others' lives for a long time.

- For example, after you've studied a certain amount you promise yourself a treat, like a snack or a session of e-mailing. If you've cared for children, you may have used Time Out to interrupt and control bad behavior. In both of these cases, you controlled what *followed* the behavior. You were applying principles of *operant conditioning*.

- You also control your actions by controlling what *precedes* a behavior, for example, if you want to become a writer, by creating a comfy setting for writing and carrying a notebook all the time (Skinner, 1981). This is called *contingency management*.

- You've changed your behavior by changing the way you *think* about things, as well. How many times do you "talk yourself into" doing a chore, or being patient, or paying attention? You put yourself in a constructive frame of mind through *cognitive* activity.

- Finally, you have probably chosen to hang around people who succeed in meeting goals like yours; for instance, being in a social group with good study habits enhances your own academic behavior. This social component of behavior control is called *modeling*, because you look at other people as models to imitate.

Notice again that regulating the preceding, following, cognitive, and social contexts of behavior can occur without an analysis of the history behind why you act in certain ways.

SMALL GROUP EXERCISE

Think of other behavioral control examples from everyday life. You have lived in groups, like families, dorms, or apartment complexes; you have probably tried to change a family member's or roommate's behavior through behavioral control. What did you try, and how did it work out?

Being depressed is certainly a feeling, but it involves negative thinking and a lack of energy for action. On the brighter side, love is an emotion tied to positive thinking and boundless energy. Actions, feelings, and thoughts are all interrelated. Fredo's behavior is related to a set of beliefs he holds, such as that he will gain respect through strongly authoritative pronouncements. And longing for respect, in turn, is an emotion. So his thoughts and feelings need to change, as well as his behavior, if we want an alteration that's more than skin deep. The interaction of behavior, emotion, and cognition presents a problem for practitioners who want to make a division between behavioral therapy and cognitive therapy. The division isn't really clear. Most behaviorist practitioners use cognitive approaches, and vice versa. The following explanations of essential concepts move from behavioral principles to cognitivist principles, in the order they developed historically.

Classical Conditioning

You have probably already heard of Pavlov's famous dogs. At the dawn of the twentieth century, the physiologist Ivan Pavlov in Russia first described **classical conditioning.** In his work with the digestive processes of dogs, Pavlov discovered that a light caused dogs to salivate if the light had repeatedly indicated they were about to be fed. Eventually, the light brought out the same response even when no food was presented.

John B. Watson, an American psychologist who is called the father of behaviorism, followed Pavlov's line of thought. He believed that psychologists could discover what stimuli predict what responses in individuals, with *stimulus* meaning an outer or inner condition, and *response* meaning anything a person did. Watson eventually became wildly successful in the advertising business by applying these principles. He realized that people buy a product not only because of its performance but also because of the other stimuli associated with it, and so he manipulated the images connected to each brand name.

In Pavlov's laboratory, it became clear that the stimulus-response pattern could be changed once established. A bell could become associated with feeding and eventually could call forth salivation in dogs. When the bell rang with no presentation of food, the response still occurred. But eventually, as the bell continued to ring with no presentation of food, it stopped calling forth salivation. This process is called **extinction.** The response is extinguished; it disappears.

A child who never has tantrums may spend hours alone playing Legos. Her parents are delighted that they have some private time for themselves, and they never interrupt her play. Soon, she plays less and less and comes in to bug her parents more and more because she is getting no reinforcement for playing quietly. Unfortunately, sometimes extinction happens to positive behaviors. Behavioral principles don't work according to values automatically. The parents could have saved their treasured time alone if they had just once in a while paid attention to their angelic Legos fan.

Operant Conditioning

In the early twentieth century in the United States, psychologist Edward Thorndike (1911) investigated how behavior is changed by what comes after it, a process called **operant conditioning** or **instrumental conditioning.** (A *stimulus* comes before a behavior, whereas a *reinforcer* comes after it.) Thorndike devel-

Reflections

Think about Watson's assertion that we buy products based on images associated with them, not on their relative performance. Peruse magazine or television advertisements. List what images are associated with products to make them attractive, and list as well the kinds of people who would be most attracted by these images. (All advertisers know how to choose images that will attract their "target markets." Sometimes the images are not even relevant or realistic; a popular wine commercial on television these days associates wine drinking with slenderness and athletic skill.) Finally, consider the kinds of images to which you tend to respond. What is it about yourself that makes you vulnerable to such images?

oped two laws of learning. One, the *law of exercise*, says that the more often a connection between a behavior and its consequence is made, the stronger the connection becomes (and conversely, with disuse the connection becomes weaker). The *law of effect* says that if a connection is followed by a "satisfying state of affairs," it will be strengthened (and conversely if it is followed by an "annoying state of affairs," it will be weakened). So, the more often parents give in to children's demands during tantrums, the more tantrums they can expect.

Beginning in the 1930s, B. F. Skinner did research on operant conditioning. Skinner eventually applied learning principles to individual human behavior, as well as animals. (Thorndike also went on to apply the psychology of learning to humans and made many suggestions for changing the educational system.) Skinner used the word **reinforcement** to apply to anything that changed the frequency of a response. Reinforcers increase the likelihood of a response, and punishments decrease the likelihood of a response. Two kinds of reinforcers are *positive reinforcers* like treats, money, and praise and *negative reinforcers* like relief from pain or release from distress.

Skinner focused on reinforcement as a learning tool because punishment involves many negative byproducts. A key concept of reinforcement theory is *contingency*, which means that to be effective, a reinforcement must occur after a certain, identifiable response, not just any response. That is, the reinforcement is contingent upon the behavior. Reward alone does not work—this is the principle behind giving salespeople commissions. If each salesperson got the same paycheck no matter what, you can imagine that some sales clerks would not work very hard.

If you are rewarded every single time you do something, you will probably learn it fast, but as soon as rewards stop coming, you will start stopping the behavior. The behavior will be extinguished through lack of reward. According to Skinner (1974), how much you repeat a behavior depends on more than the nature of the reinforcer. It depends on the **schedule of reinforcement.** If Skinner's pigeons got a food pellet every time they pecked a bar, they stopped pecking soon after the pellets stopped coming. Most of us don't learn through continuous reinforcement, though. We learn through *intermittent reinforcement*—sometimes we get the reward, and sometimes we don't. Intermittent reinforcement creates behavior that is more difficult to extinguish than continuous reinforcement. This principle is what keeps people gambling even though they lose much more often than they win. Much foolish or useless behavior that mysteriously continues has probably been intermittently reinforced.

Like Skinner, Dollard and Miller perceived in the 1950s that cues evoke responses, and responses are strengthened under certain conditions. Furthermore, they studied *counterconditioning*, in which one response to a cue is replaced by another. For example, enough pleasant experiences (or lack of unpleasant ones) after a cue can make you change your previously negative response to the cue. Two or three drives to the park instead of the vet can change your dog's response to car rides from whimpering and shivering to joyous tail-wagging. One of the behavioral exercises for a group of alcoholics is to identify nondrinking activities that they formerly avoided because they did not involve alcohol or because they couldn't be done while drunk. Group members are encouraged to try some of these activities so that they can find pleasure in sobriety. They become counterconditioned.

Dollard and Miller's assertion that humans are reaction systems, responding to external stimuli, turned out to be oversimplified (Patterson, 1980). Humans are more complex than this. However, Dollard and Miller's integration of learning theory into counseling theory was a significant step in the growing cognitive-behavioral approach.

DISCUSSION IDEA

Remember how you were taught proper behavior in elementary school. Give some examples of conditioning and counterconditioning, positive reinforcement, and punishment.

Generalization and Discrimination   We are not classically conditioned to respond only to exact stimuli but to other stimuli that remind us in some way of the original one(s). This is **generalization.** Animals fear humans who remind them of individuals who have harmed them; you probably know dogs who recoil from children's advances. Humans often fear humans who remind them of bad experiences. Some people fear women who act like intrusive mothers or men who act like abusive fathers.

In the process of learning, we start out with generalized responses and then fine-tune them as we see the results of our behavior. Children's language development shows this stimulus **discrimination;** for example, toddlers who have begun to use the -ed past tense often use words like "getted" instead of "got" and "goed" instead of "went." They have generalized the -ed ending even to words that have irregular past tenses. Later, they discriminate between regular and irregular verbs. In similar ways, we learn how to discriminate appropriate behaviors according to our surroundings; for example, you use different words when you describe your Saturday night date to your friends and then to your parents. Stimulus discrimination works *against* behavior therapy when people learn something in one setting but can't generalize it to another setting. For instance, this happens when alcoholics are able to refrain from drinking except when they are in a bar with old pals.

The Role of Meaning: Cognitive Theory

How many times have you heard comments like these?

"You got me all wrong! I didn't mean that you overprotect your children!"

"When I told you to dress informally, you took it the wrong way."

"All I said was, Isn't that your fifth cookie?"

Clearly, our words do not always communicate what we intended, or they communicate *more* than we intended, or at least more than we wanted brought out in the open. When Susan says to Patrick, "Isn't that your fifth cookie?" it would be hard *not* to get the message behind the words.

In behaviorist terms, therapy focuses on measurable, observable stimuli and responses, and in cognitivist terms, therapy focuses on the element of the *meanings* behind stimuli and responses. Making a meaning out of a behavior is something done inside our heads, something not observable. Most behavioral therapies today integrate cognitive components. Cognitions include inner processes like interpretations (as in the examples above), wishes, plans, motivations, fantasies, problem solving, hopes, expectations, reasoning, attention, imagery, judgments, doubts, and daydreams. We say, "I told myself that I had to stay home," and "I argued with myself over that," showing that we experience something like inner speech, which is not observable but still drives our actions. Inner talk and intentions make behavior changes last over time and transfer to new situations. As a resident of Illinois, if you've really given up smoking pot, you are not likely to suddenly fire up a joint in Iowa.

The cognitive-behavioral approaches I introduce in this chapter share the **mediational position** (Dobson & Block, 1988), which is "that cognitive activity mediates the responses the individual has to his or her environment, and to some extent dictates the degree of adjustment or maladjustment of the individual" (p. 29). Albert Bandura went beyond straight stimulus-response learning theory when he investigated the effects of what we expect, how competent we feel, who we see as models, and what we observe vicariously—none of which are behaviors. The field of cognitive psychology blossomed in the 1960s, with Ulrich Neisser's *Cognitive Psychology* (1967) presenting research on "all the processes by which . . . sensory input is transformed, reduced, elaborated, stored, recovered, and used" (p. 4), emphasizing the ways we process information (sensory input), in a stage between stimulus and outward response. Human behavior is more complex than most animals' behavior, and understanding humans requires investigating their inner workings. There really are people who've given up buying lottery tickets except when they cross a state line, and I have two friends who are complete vegetarians except when they are on airplanes.

Two pioneers of cognitive behavior theory and therapy, Albert Ellis and Aaron Beck, independently theorized that most psychological distress stemmed from faulty or damaging mental processing of experience, rather than from "esoteric themes such as castration anxiety or psychosexual fixations" (Beck, 1991, p. 369). They also questioned the constraints of psychoanalytic therapy. Ellis thought:

> Why, when I seemed to know perfectly well what was troubling a patient, did I have to wait passively, perhaps for a few weeks, perhaps for months, until he, by his own interpretive initiative, showed that he was fully "ready" to accept my own insight? Why, when patients bitterly struggled to continue to associate freely, and ended up by saying only a few words in an entire session, was it improper for me to help them with several pointed questions or remarks? (Ellis, 1962, p. 7)

Connection Among Behavior, Emotion, and Cognition

In changing the name of his main theory from social learning theory to social cognitive theory, Albert Bandura focused on how "the human mind is generative, creative, proactive, reflective, not just reactive" (2001, p. 4). Albert Ellis, too, promoted name changes for his system, from *rational therapy* (in 1955); to *rational emotive therapy* (in 1961), to include the emotional aspect in the title; to *rational emotive behavior therapy* (in 1993), to stress that behavior change is an integral part of the treatment.

Aaron Beck wrote that early in his career as a psychoanalyst, he noticed the connection among behavior, emotion, and cognition: "I was struck by how ascertaining the idiosyncratic or special meanings people attached to events helped to explain what might otherwise have represented quite inexplicable affective and behavioral reactions" (1991, p. 369).

Private experience provides us with interpretations of incoming information. We have personal ways of processing events, on a more individual level than our cultural and subcultural tendencies. A person who grew up in a home where the father suddenly disappeared for weeks at a time may become nervous when a loved one runs out for a bottle of scotch, even as an adult. Such individual response tendencies become part of our personalities, or what George Kelly (1955) called our set of **personal constructs.** These are our characteristic ways of viewing the world around us: what catches our attention, what we think is important, what we remember for a long time, what touches us emotionally, and so on. In a group therapy setting, people become aware of their idiosyncratic ways of processing information in comparison to the ways of other members. Members are able to challenge each other on the accuracy and suitability of their individual response tendencies.

DISCUSSION IDEA

Take a vote in your class about who likes heartwarming family movies and who dislikes heartwarming family movies. See how people can explain the differing learning histories that created various responses to these films.

Automaticity   When Aaron Beck was treating clients from a traditional psychoanalytic stance, he began to notice the influence of cognition in the workings of psychology. Beck (1991) summarized the experience:

> At one point I observed to my surprise that my patients experienced specific types of thoughts of which they were only dimly aware and that they did not report during their free associations. In fact, unless they were directed to focus their attention on these thoughts, they were not likely to be very aware of them. Although these thoughts seemed to be on the periphery of the patients' stream of consciousness, they appeared to play an important role in the psychic life of these patients. . . . These thoughts (cognitions) tended to arise quickly and automatically, as though by reflex; they were not subject to volition or conscious control and seemed perfectly plausible to the individual. They were frequently followed by an unpleasant affect (in the case of the depressed patients) that the patients were very much aware of, even though they were unaware of, or barely aware of, the preceding automatic thoughts.
>
> When I directed the patients to focus their attention on these "automatic thoughts," they began to report a string of them, particularly in response to a cognitive probe, "What are you thinking right now?" Connecting these thoughts brought out certain negative themes such as deprivation, disease, or defeat. Grouped together they fell into the category of a negative view of the present, past, and future experiences. Later, in working with more severely depressed patients, I noted that these types of thoughts were no longer peripheral but occupied a dominant position in consciousness and were repetitive. (p. 368)

In coining the term **automatic thoughts,** Beck was identifying a level of thought that occurs beyond voluntary thoughts, which are usually quite accessible. **Automaticity** was operating, that is, the thoughts spontaneously occurred without beckoning. We have automaticity in our behavior, too, as you know from your habits when driving a car, taking a shower, and going through other daily routines. We even call it "being on automatic pilot," when we accidentally drive toward work on our day off or write the wrong year on checks during the month of January. Our minds have an automatic pilot that steers us in habitual directions without much attention.

Automatic thoughts control a disturbed person's response to the outside world, giving their minds a **systematic bias.** These habitual inclinations usually come with an emotional component and seem believable to the person who holds them. For example, depression can be seen as a pattern of negative thoughts about self, experience, and the future (Beck & Weishaar, 2000).

Through practice, conscious control can be applied to systematic biases, overcoming maladaptive responses to people and situations.

Group Dynamics

Groups that focus on cognitive-behavioral learning follow predictable courses through their lifetimes, though some processes are repeated over and over within this lifetime. For instance, the processes of checking in or review of the last session may be repeated in each session. Learning-based groups are often brief, with an upper limit of twenty-eight sessions (Koss & Schiang, 1994). Rose and LeCroy (1991) propose thinking of cognitive and behavioral groups on a continuum: on the short-term end are highly specific psychoeducational groups with a restricted number of sessions and a defined agenda at each session. You will read about such groups in Chapter 13. On the long-term end are learning groups based on complex, varied problems that make more use of group processes as learning experiences and invent agendas according to common needs that arise in the group. Between four and ten members is usually a size that makes best use of the activity and practice orientation of these groups.

The Stages in Cognitive-Behavioral Groups

Beginning Stage

The beginning stage of cognitive-behavioral groups is similar to that stage in other groups, but with a special emphasis on educating members about the process and establishing clear goals.

Intake and Establishment Usually, a counselor schedules individual interviews with potential group members. The members are often self-referred through public announcements (like leaflets, newspaper ads) or through recommendation by other counselors or members. As a counselor, you want to be sure that each person understands the basic practice of group work and the goals of the group. The details of when and for how long the group will meet, how much it will cost, and guidelines about attendance and participation are included in this interview. An informed consent document is discussed and signed, with copies for the client and the counselor. In the intake interview, the counselor emphasizes the commonalities among group members and presents an optimistic view of their ability to help each other. Clients whose goals do not fit into the group's purpose are referred to more appropriate treatment forms. For example, when I began a social skills group for graduate students, one potential member struck me as markedly distressed globally and severely depressed. I persuaded him to make individual appointments with another therapist at the counseling center instead of joining the group at this point. He feared individual therapy and had thought of group work as a watered-down version that was not as threatening; most experienced group members would agree that this is probably exactly opposite from the truth! Several misconceptions about group work can be headed off in the intake interview (see Chapter 3).

Hollander and Kazaoka (1988) advise exclusion of clients with severe antisocial problems, such as rape or child abuse, from a heterogeneous group (a group of people with various problems). They also discourage including involuntary referrals, such as court-ordered clients, in voluntary groups because of motivational problems. However, groups composed homogeneously of criminals or involuntary referrals have met with some success (e.g., Schwartz & Waldo, 2004), especially when they focus on cognitive distortions that arouse anger and provide behavioral practice at impulse control.

Assessment   Most people enter the group with a fairly broad description of the problem they wish to work on, usually one that fits the way the group was described to them. For example, people who respond to a leaflet promoting a social skills group believe that they have problems in interpersonal areas. One of the first tasks of the group is to help each member explain the specific, concrete problems they experience. Group discussion helps by providing diverse examples that each member can see as similar or different from his or her own. I have found that almost everyone says that they suffer from procrastination, but what they mean is widely different. In my writer's block group, one person said that she procrastinated: "Sometimes I mess around and listen to the radio for twenty minutes or so before I get down to work." Another member had quite a contrasting definition: "Procrastination means that every college grade on my transcript was once an Incomplete."

In the process of assessment, group members are encouraged to break down broad descriptions into smaller components, because in cognitive and behavioral treatments these components will be targets of change. In a group for relationship improvement, Marina, who wants to stop fighting with her spouse, would enlist the group's help in identifying the topics or settings of the fights. She might decide that the fights they have about differing attitudes toward work are the worst ones. Meanwhile, other members, who are thinking about their own fights in comparison, might point out that attitudes toward money or child-raising are hot topics for them. In such ways, the group provides a context for defining problems.

Generally, in an assessment we want to discover

- when the problem (a behavior, feeling, thought, or combination) occurs;
- how frequently it occurs;
- what usually comes before and after it occurs;
- how behavior, thoughts, and feelings are all involved during the problem;
- what the client has already tried in order to solve the problem.

In keeping with the scientific basis of the therapy, members are taught to keep records related to their problems, usually in paper-and-pencil form. These include records like food or exercise logs; tallies of drinks, cigarettes, or social contacts; diaries of conflicts; notes on thought processes; and ratings of urges, cravings, and moods. The record-keeping serves many purposes, including making the group more aware of each member's problems. Also, the initial records serve as baselines for comparison later. Most groups involve ongoing record-keeping, so members can see whether the interventions they try are working. The rate of problem occurrence and its intensity should decrease with treatment.

Several printed (and, now, computerized) methods of collecting information by inventories and questionnaires are used in cognitive and behavioral therapies. For instance, rational emotive behavior therapy groups are given lists of irrational beliefs and asked to identify the ones they fall prey to. Glynn and Ruderman (1986) developed a questionnaire to measure a person's perceived self-efficacy in coping with a variety of tempting eating situations, rating how difficult eating is to control "when you feel restless," "when you want to cheer up," "around holiday time," and so forth. Use of this questionnaire allows people who want to develop greater self-control over eating to see that there are a number of causes of overeating and to realize which situations are easiest or most difficult to deal with.

Psychoeducational Component   During the beginning stage of the group, the leader presents the learning theory that will be used to promote change. This psychoeducational component is included in all cognitive-behavioral treatment. A basic learning point of view, that problems arise in the context of antecedents and consequences—what comes before and after them—is infused in the way the leader elicits information. This gives members a frame of reference that they will use throughout the group. Here is an example from a group of caregivers of the elderly:

MRS. W.: My husband has had it with my mother. I can understand his feelings. She is hard to live with. But I'm caught in the middle. I'm the only daughter she has.

MRS. Y.: I'm in the same situation. You know, my mother has Alzheimer's disease. In the past two years it's gotten a lot worse. My husband says I should find a good place to put Mom, a nursing home, but I just can't bring myself to do it!

MRS. W.: [Looking at Mrs. T, the counselor] What can I do?

MRS. T.: Both of you are in a difficult situation. [Looking at Mrs. W.] Is there one thing that your mother does that is particularly bothersome?

MRS. W.: [pause] When mom refuses to take her medication her mood swings really get out of hand. At that point, even I have trouble with her.

MRS. T: Is there any pattern to your mom's refusal to take her medication?

MRS. W. It seems she does it when we try to get away for the weekend. . . . (Toseland, 1995, p. 239)

Notice that the counselor requests a specific example. She follows up by asking for patterns, encouraging the idea that behavior occurs in a context. Speaking in specifics and seeking patterns are both aspects of the general frame of reference the group will use.

Goal Setting   Hollander and Kazaoka (1988) list some general interpersonal goals for groups based on learning:

(a) feeling more secure,

(b) reducing dependencies on others,

(c) expressing genuine affection,

(d) letting go or holding on to relationships, and

(e) reducing emotions that interfere with sound interpersonal relations (social anxiety, explosive anger, depression). (pp. 304–305)

There are also personal, behavioral goals, such as quitting smoking or drinking or eating too much, overcoming hypochondria, and overcoming stage fright.

Group members create specific goals for themselves, often expressing these in written contracts. Marina, who wishes to stop her marital fights, might devise a goal of reducing arguments about work to once a week over the course of six weeks. Many goals have step-down (or step-up) plans, with gradual reduction or increase of episodes. The episodes could be instances of behavior, emotion, or thought processes.

SMALL GROUP EXERCISE

In your group, choose one of the five general interpersonal goals from the Goal Setting list. Brainstorm about what specific behaviors would be associated with this goal. For example, how does being insecure manifest itself in everyday behavior? After you have brainstormed, discuss which of these behaviors you might start with as targets in a counseling group, and why.

Middle Stage

In the middle stage of cognitive-behavioral groups, the emphasis of the work is on using the approaches learned in the beginning stage to alter members' thinking and behavior and on evaluating each individual's progress as they go along.

Treatment   True to the experimental nature of cognitive-behavioral therapies, treatments are usually exercises practiced in sessions and given as homework outside. They are targeted to members' specific situations and goals. The power of the group to brainstorm for exercises and to use the learning theory they have learned from the leader is harnessed in the process. For example, in a group going over responses to Glynn and Ruderman's (1986) eating self-efficacy scale, which helps people identify problem overeating habits, members will naturally help each other with ideas about how they control overeating in various situations. One person may have a trick for avoiding overeating at parties, while another knows alternatives to eating when upset. Exercises are derived from behavioral and cognitive learning theories, as you will see in the section on techniques.

Evaluation   Because cognitive-behavioral group members have a clear understanding of their goals, whether they are unitary (like smoking cessation) or various (each person having a separate target of change), evaluation is woven into treatment. Each session usually begins with a check-in, which is a brief evaluation of the homework. If something didn't pan out the way the group expected, they brainstorm about why. For example, an apple as a planned reward for staying on task while studying might turn out to be too weak of a reward, in the face of distractions. Psychoeducation, which continues as long as necessary, perhaps being part of each session, is evaluated often by asking group members to summarize main points or define terms in their own words, to make sure the information got through accurately.

Contracts, a common feature of cognitive-behavioral therapies, also help group members evaluate their progress. If they wish, for example, to decrease family conflicts to fewer than one a week, they write this down and discuss it with the group. At regular check-ins, everyone can tell from record-keeping evidence whether the goal (or a step toward it) has been met. In this way, the outcomes of cognitive-behavioral groups are easier to evaluate than those of other groups, which hold goals of happiness or self-actualization or authenticity.

Ending Stage

Generalization and Maintenance   Treatment is considered successful when the group members can transfer functions the group performed for them into their everyday life outside therapy. For example, successful members of social skills groups eventually make their own circle of friends, get along with others on the job, and may establish a romantic attachment. In the closing sessions of the group, clients plan for activities independent of counseling, such as joining nontherapeutic groups (Rose & LeCroy, 1991). They also discuss how to deal with times when they are tempted to revert to their old ways or when they do in fact revert. A systematic plan for predicting and acting in stressful situations will certainly help prevent relapse. For example, in a group of adult survivors of childhood abuse, each member wrote five healthy strategies for coping with stress onto note cards to carry with them (Choate & Henson, 2003).

Post-Group Support   Many times, cognitive-behavioral groups terminate through a **fading system,** in which they space meetings farther and farther apart, finally only holding quarterly booster sessions. Others wean themselves from the counselor and continue to meet occasionally without professional guidance. At this point, they act as a **support group,** a voluntary self-help group with a focus on some feature they hold in common—in this case, following the learning model they acquired in group counseling. Another common procedure is the **buddy system,** in which each member is paired with another to call on in times of need.

SMALL GROUP EXERCISE

Imagine yourselves as leaders of smoking cessation groups (or choose another specific cognitive-behavioral group). What barriers to generalization and maintenance do you predict for your group? Make up at least three strategies to enhance generalization and maintenance for your group. Ask one or more volunteers to role-play, introducing a strategy to the group members.

Leadership Skills

The leader of a cognitive-behavioral group is not neutral or detached, even when he or she is following a manual or defined agenda for treatment. The therapist must gain the clients' trust and must present the treatment as credible, or the clients will not cooperate with the many efforts they will be asked to make outside the session. The fact that this kind of therapy often follows a step-by-step manual makes some people think that it is a cold, mechanical approach. In truth, encouragement and hopefulness are critical features when group members are practicing thoughts and behaviors that are difficult for them. In a study of ninety-four clients with various problems, clients who received behavioral therapy rated their counselors higher on accurate empathy, self-congruence, and interpersonal contact than clients who received psychoanalytical insight-oriented therapy rated their therapists (Sloane, Staples, Cristol, Yorkston, & Whipple, 1975).

The counselor in behavior therapy lends expertise in identifying goals and planning treatments with the clients. The clients' input is crucial, because no one will follow a plan that they feel is forced upon them as long as they are free to quit. Gazda, Ginter, and Horne (2001) describe the group leader's role as shifting from teacher to coach to consultant as the group progresses. As teacher, the leader explains the learning theory involved, socializes members into the behavior expected in the group, demonstrates tracking of target behavior or thoughts, and takes responsibility for most content and process of sessions. As coach, the leader helps members practice new behaviors or thoughts, brainstorms for practice ideas, encourages and suggests ideas (but from the sidelines), and cheers the team on. And finally, as consultant, the leader offers ideas and assistance when asked, although group members take most responsibility for change, and orchestrates termination and booster sessions in the future.

This succession of roles reflects a major theme of cognitive-behavioral groups: the members eventually operate independently according to the information, principles, and practices they learn in group. Smokenders is a good illustration; members are expected to be able to maintain abstinence from nicotine after the seminars have ended.

Cognitive-behavioral therapy (CBT) is a persuasive methodology, in that the counselor works to convince the client that his or her way of viewing the world is not the only one or, in fact, the most correct one. The role of the therapist is one of teacher or guide, a catalyst through which educational and corrective experiences come about. The counselor must have the qualities important to any helping professional, such as being trustworthy and inspiring confidence. In addition, many such counselors seek (or already have) training as teachers to enhance the psychoeducational component of their practice.

In cognitive-behavioral treatment particularly, the counselor verbally challenges the client's systems of belief. Thus, she must possess sharp reasoning herself and a good rhetorical ability to present her arguments. If you are a person known for your powers of persuasion, you are well suited for the verbal aspect of cognitive-behavioral therapy. Well-honed analytical abilities are needed to infer the schemas from which clients are working and devise dialogues and experiments to disconfirm biases.

The therapist does not present himself as a blank slate because transference is not important therapeutically. Instead, modeling has a place in the relationship, and often cognitive-behavioral therapists admit their own imperfections, beliefs, and values so that clients can observe that a person does not have to be superhuman to deal effectively with life's challenges.

Reflections

Look back on your experience in terms of leading or teaching others. You might think of organizations or committees you have led, teams you have been important to, or even group vacations you have organized. Do you like the role? Which of the roles described above—teacher, coach, or consultant—do you enjoy the most? What qualities do you have that make you effective in one or more of these roles? Do you have qualities you will have to overcome or downplay in one or more of these roles should you choose to become a cognitive-behavioral counselor?

Techniques in Cognitive-Behavioral Groups

Cognitive-behavioral group workers often flexibly choose among techniques based on behavioral and cognitive learning theories. In the following sections, I describe a few of the standard techniques and encourage you to practice some of them on a limited basis to get a feeling for them.

Behavioral Interventions and Homework

As I have emphasized, in today's world of group therapy, it would be hard to completely separate behavioral and cognitive approaches, because they usually occur together. For the pedagogical purposes of this textbook, I will describe first techniques that originated from behavioral principles and then those that originated from cognitivists, but remember that you will usually encounter them mixed together and adapted for the group's goals. Remember as well that because of the experimental nature of cognitive-behavioral therapies, techniques are tried, altered, strengthened, and discarded according to their results in practice.

Fear Reduction If you think of the things that make you anxious, you can see how anxiety is related to fear. Wolpe (1990) believed that anxiety was the basis of most neuroses. If I have test anxiety, it means that I fear taking tests, due to something in my learning history. My friend Anita is anxious when she thinks she may be the center of attention, which keeps her from making presentations that would advance her career. This anxiety also makes her avoid talking much at social gatherings, and therefore she rarely makes new friends outside of work. Fear reduction is one of the most solidly proven uses of behavior therapy (Barlow, 1993; Emmelkamp, 1994).

I once received a practicum assignment to a hospital. The first day, the atmosphere, smells, and sounds of the hospital drained me of my composure because my last experiences of the hospital world were dreadful. My work at the practicum was highly absorbing, and my supervisor was a kind, humorous fellow. By the fourth day or so, the hospital setting didn't faze me a bit. My anxiety reactions to the setting abated in just a few days. This is an example of *desensitization*. By repeated exposure to the feared stimuli, with no bad consequences and good new experiences, I lost my learned association of hospital sights and smells with pain and hopelessness. Desensitization is necessary all the time in everyday life. If we were sensitive to all suffering, we would never even be able to watch the evening news.

Anxiety has a physiological basis, as you know if you have given a performance and felt your heart race and your palms sweat. Relaxation, which also has a physiological basis, is a competing emotion, and according to the principle of counterconditioning, anxiety and relaxation cannot co-exist for long. The trick is to make relaxation win out. The *systematic* part of **systematic desensitization** involves a careful sequencing of anxiety and relaxation to ensure that anxiety loses. The technique was developed by Joseph Wolpe (1958), who saw anxiety as avoidance-based and worked to help patients reduce avoidance. Take a look at how Foa and Kozak (1986) conceptualize the process:

> Fear is evoked by information that activates an existing fear structure containing propositions about stimuli, responses, and their meaning. Changes in such a structure, we have proposed, require the integration of information that is incompatible with some elements of the fear structure. (p. 27)

The "existing fear structure" is what your history has taught you about a situation. This structure kicks in when you perceive similar conditions. For example, one hospital smells pretty much like another one and brings out the same responses (stimulus generalization). When you have new experiences under similar stimulus conditions with new nonthreatening information coming in, the old fear structure loses its sting. If I had carefully avoided hospital work consistently, I would still have the old responses; this is probably the basis for folk wisdom about "getting back on the horse" after falling off. One psychoeducational aspect of systematic desensitization involves teaching group members about anxiety, avoidance as a response that strengthens anxiety, and relaxation as a response that competes with anxiety.

When you use systematic desensitization in group therapy, you work with the clients to prepare in two ways:

▪ The clients learn deep muscle relaxation. A **progressive relaxation** technique codified more than seventy years ago (Jacobson, 1938/1929) still prevails. It instructs clients to tense and relax various skeletal muscle groups until they are able to create deep states of relaxation. It is efficient to teach this technique to groups. It is time-consuming, and members often feel more comfortable learning it in a group, similar to a yoga class, than by themselves in a counselor's office.

▪ With the group's help, each client draws up a list of anxiety-causing events and organizes these events according to how anxiety-producing they are. Spiegler and Guevremont (1998) give an example from a client who was anxious about dating. From most to least, the **anxiety hierarchy** looked like this:

10. Initially greeting date
 9. Saying goodnight
 8. Being on the date
 7. Driving to pick up date
 6. Getting ready to go on date
 5. Calling someone for date
 4. Asking for potential date's telephone number
 3. Talking to potential date in class
 2. Meeting an attractive member of the opposite sex
 1. Thinking about going on date next weekend (p. 207)

When the client has learned to relax at will, the client is led through imagining the anxiety-evoking events, from the least to the most anxiety promoting, while practicing relaxation. When the client is able to imagine "thinking about going on date next weekend" without any anxiety, he moves on to "meeting an attractive member of the opposite sex" and on up the hierarchy. When completed, the client will be able to date in the real world with little or no anxiety.

This technique is called **imaginal** because the events are images in the client's mind. A similar desensitization technique can operate as **in vivo exposure;**

that is, it happens in real life. A friend with agoraphobia (fear of going out in public) went to a therapy group and made a hierarchy that began with walking out onto the porch to check the mail and ended with going to the shopping mall. Two other group members visited him at home and accompanied him out onto the porch repeatedly, slowly hanging back until my friend could go out onto the porch while they stayed inside the front door, and then could go out on the porch while they were not present. They practiced each step of the anxiety hierarchy, ending up at the mall shopping.

This *in vivo* procedure is called **exposure and response prevention,** because the client is exposed to a feared situation and then prevented from performing a fearful response (in my friend's case, fleeing back into the house immediately). Exposure and response prevention is usually successful for phobias and obsessive-compulsive behaviors like hand-washing and checking. The other members' comforting and supporting presence acts as the relaxation response competing with the fear response. Each client assists in systematic in vivo treatment of other members' fearful habits. The availability of several group members (with different fears) is especially helpful because this technique is very time-intensive, often with daily practice sessions. When feasible, family members are recruited to help with the daily practice, too.

Systematic desensitization is most frequently used for serious problems such as panic attacks, phobias, and eating disorders. Usually, groups are composed of people who share the same problem, so the treatment can be specifically targeted.

Contingency Management Behavioral homework frequently involves managing the conditions that make a desired action more or less likely—the contingencies. Contingencies can operate at two times: before a behavior and after it. Many behavioral treatments consist of **contingency management**—manipulating the situation that precedes a behavior and the state of affairs after a behavior. Examples of frequently used contingency management systems in groups are described below:

■ **Stimulus Control** Dieters are encouraged to keep only low-calorie snacks in their cupboards. This is an example of *stimulus control*, analyzing and manipulating preceding contingencies. In behavioral treatment for insomnia, clients are encouraged to control sleep-related stimuli by only using the bed for sleeping, regularizing bedtimes, darkening the room, and avoiding certain foods and excitement before bed. The group helps the client to identify conditions that encourage desirable behavior and to create these conditions. Brainstorming with other people creates many more possibilities than lonely musings. We help each other learn to avoid doing things that seem to sabotage our efforts.

■ **Pleasant Activities Planning** Many cognitive-behavioral groups assist each other in drawing up lists of pleasant events to reward themselves after they comply with some part of the treatment plan. Purposeful use of rewards is a contingency management of what happens after a behavior. Many times, distressed people neglect not only the daily necessities of life but also overlook things they once enjoyed. Lewinsohn and MacPhillamy (1971) created the Pleasant Events Schedule, which lists 320 possibilities from "listening to the sounds of nature" to "thinking about sex." This list is handy for people who seem unable to originate their own lists, and it is an interesting exercise for the group to compare and contrast their choices from the list. For some members, it's been a long time since they had a talk focused on the positive rather than the negative.

Shaping A gradual approach to behavior change is exemplified by *shaping*. When the behavior that is desired doesn't occur naturally, there is no opportunity to reward it. So we reward behaviors that come closer and closer to the desired goal, in a process of *successive approximations*. In groups, successive approximations can be acted out within the safety of the session. For example, a person who is too shy to make routine phone calls can enlist the help of other members. First, they might take turns modeling ordinary telephone calls for her and then including her as a caller, within the session. Then they might make up a schedule of times that she agrees to call each member with a very limited script. She might just have to identify herself, say hello, and ask one question about the other member's day. She is reinforced by her fellow members at the time and again by the group in the next session. Shaping involves, then, designing ever more challenging and realistic phone calls to make, such as asking theaters for film times or asking a government body to mail her some information. The idea is that these phone calls become closer and closer to the desired goal, while being systematically reinforced.

Differential Reinforcement Rewards can be used to ensure that certain desirable behaviors become more frequent while other undesirable behaviors fade away (become extinct). In *differential reinforcement*, rewards are delivered when the client is *not* performing an undesirable behavior. Weight Watchers, a highly successful behavior control organization, rewards group members enthusiastically and publicly for not overeating. Kazdin (1994) gives examples from institutions in which patients reduced self-injuries and even seizures through being rewarded for problem-free intervals.

Response Withdrawal Another way to ensure that undesirable behaviors fade away is to withdraw responses when the undesirable behaviors occur. When a group member comes in with a highly dramatic problem every week, the attention and excitement he creates are often rewarding in themselves and perpetuate the problems. A group counselor may divert the group's attention to another topic instead of focusing on the drama, in a *response withdrawal* technique. Deprived of the center of attention and distracted with other topics, the dramatic member can calm down mentally and physiologically. In a similar way, a group leader responds at more length and more positively to members who are reporting successful thought or behavior control, while downplaying unsuccessful reports.

SMALL GROUP EXERCISE

Individually, work on designing a small change that would improve your living situation—apartment house, family home, dormitory, or neighborhood. Focus on a specific, limited improvement. What would all the members of the living situation have to do to make the first step toward the improvement? Role-play as a therapy group and discuss and revise the plans together. Your instructor may ask you to choose a good example, prepare it, and distribute it to the class as a whole, on paper or electronically.

Modeling Behavioral therapy frequently draws upon the strong effects of watching others behave, both positive and negative (Bandura, 1986). Parents are well aware that children use them as models of behavior, sometimes disconcertingly so. We purposely model skills for others when we teach activities like doing the foxtrot, making bread, and hitting a golf ball. We also get our ideas about what is fun, what is frightening, what is socially acceptable, and what is punishable by watching how others behave.

In *covert modeling*, the model exists within the client's imagination and is called upon when the client chooses how to behave. The group helps the client develop an imaginative character who can act as a reference point when the client is under stress. Sometimes clients choose people in their groups as covert models of desirable behavior; for example, Jan admires Brian's ability to stand up for himself under pressure, and she asks herself what Brian would do when she is put in that kind of spot. Some covert models are fictional characters with admirable qualities. When I was growing up, girls were encouraged to model ourselves on one of the four sisters in *Little Women*, a novel by Louisa May Alcott. Each sister demonstrated virtuous behavior that fit her personality type—artistic, intellectual, fun-loving, or domestic—and we chose to emulate the sister most like ourselves.

Sometimes cognitive-behavioral groups use *negative* modeling (also sometimes called contrast modeling or stressful modeling). For example, a counselor might ask people to act out a situation in which the character is so self-effacing and submissive that she gets brutally taken advantage of in order to spur a client's assertiveness in reaction to the model (Rosenthal & Steffek, 1991). Sometimes a group member is influenced by negative models among themselves when observing the effects of each other's problematic thinking. For example, in one group Maurice had insisted on his wife's repeated pregnancies in an effort to produce a son after a string of daughters, against her physician's warnings about her increasing frailty and burdens. Other group members were reminded of their own selfish attempts to control people they supposedly loved. These negative models can be effective when the client makes an emotional identification with them.

DISCUSSION IDEAS

1. Have you seen examples of modeling in children's and teenager's social groups? Discuss both positive and negative modeling among young people.

2. What are some covert, fictional models for young people today?

3. How could you make use of real-life and fictional models in talking with a group of adolescents about a specific problem or situation? Such situations might include adjustment to a new school or neighborhood, sexuality, conformity, parental discord, and romantic attachments.

Techniques from Cognitive Approaches

Couples therapist R. B. Stuart (1980) views cognitive and behavioral interventions contributing to different stages of therapy. Each intervention supports the improvements achieved by the other:

1. Cognitive change to potentiate new action.
2. Behavior change to potentiate new experience.
3. Cognitive change to potentiate the repeat of the desired actions by conceptualizing their effects. (p. 49)

In my work with delinquent adolescents, I find that much of their behavior is driven by a core of hopelessness, a belief that nothing in their miserable lives will get better no matter what they do. They have no connection to the future because they don't really believe that they will live to adulthood. This belief has to be challenged and modified in order for the teens to have any motivation for change at all. When they are able to make a good-faith effort to change their behavior, even in small ways, they have new experiences, such as freedom from punishment and the pleasure of good grades. The relief from this threat of punishment needs to be cognitively processed thoroughly so that the individuals substitute more hopeful automatic thoughts for the defeated ones.

■ Defeated thought pattern: "Everyone is out to get me; it doesn't matter what I do."

■ Substitute, adaptive thought pattern: "I can act in a way that doesn't get me in trouble all the time."

Rational Emotive Behavior Therapy Albert Ellis's rational emotive behavior therapy **(REBT),** is a specific brand of cognitive behavioral treatment. Trained as a psychoanalyst, Ellis (1992) found in his early practice that his patients did not make as much progress as he suspected they could. He wrote that "most of them felt better but rarely got better in the sense of making a profound philosophic change that would allow them to lose their symptoms and be less disturbable for the rest of their lives" (p. 9). He became interested in identifying the irrational beliefs that were driving his clients' behavior and developed a style of confronting and arguing against these irrational beliefs. In the end, he founded a treatment that is active, directive, and persuasive, in stark contrast with psychoanalysis. A basic tenet of REBT is that people have the capability to be happy and productive, but also have a tendency to embrace disturbing irrational thoughts that hamper them. These beliefs are the source of unhappiness, panic, anxiety, and depression, and furthermore, they block the solutions to life's problems. Ziegler and Leslie (2003) tested the tenet experimentally by giving 192 college students the Survey of Personal Beliefs and the Hassles Scale. Students who had more irrational thinking, as reflected on the Survey of Personal Beliefs, also reported significantly more practical and interpersonal hassles in daily life. This finding supports Ellis's theory that people who respond to situations irrationally are more distressed. Irrational beliefs were probably picked up in childhood from parents and culture, but tracing the origin is not important in REBT. Reforming the damaging thought process and substituting rational processes *is* important.

The theory behind REBT is embodied in the A-B-C-D-E-F model (Ellis, 1994). The mnemonic starts with A, B, C (the examples are mine):

A—activating event An episode of new information or interaction coming in from outside, or a thought coming from within. A poorer than hoped-for grade on an exam is an example of an activating event.

B—belief The often spontaneous, often irrational perception or thought within a client's mind in response to A. These are based on irrational beliefs that are sometimes dysfunctional, leading to unhappiness and neurosis. They are often encoded in statements using *must* and *should*, such as (in the case of a poor grade) "A person must be perfectly competent to be considered worthwhile," or "A person should worry deeply about dangerous or fearsome things," or "Life should be fair." An irrational belief in response to the poor grade might be, "I'll never be able to pass this kind of test. My grade point average is doomed."

C—consequence Emotional and behavioral outcomes arising from B. If B was irrational, C is likely to be rigid, demanding, and absolutist behavior and feeling. An irrational B might lead to our example student's rage over the unfairness of the test, or miserable evaluation of his or her own abilities in the subject, or a long period of worry.

The D, E, F part of the mnemonic represents what will happen due to therapy:

D—disputing intervention The therapist (and later, the clients themselves) asks questions about the B that came between A and C. These questions dispute the rationality of B and suggest alternative beliefs. Another group member might dispute the disappointed student's beliefs by saying, "It's not too late to improve your course grade. The counseling center has college skills groups to help us with test-taking; maybe you should join one."

E—effective new philosophy Clients learn to substitute more adaptive thoughts in place of the beliefs that are unrealistic and overgeneralized. For our student, that might be, "I need to learn to study in a different way for the next test! This grade is disappointing, but I can handle it."

F—feelings (new) More effective, flexible, and rational behavior comes from more realistic thoughts, and distress is eased. The student calls the counseling center and signs up for the college skills group, thinking, "At least I can do *something* about future tests."

Behavioral exercises, direct persuasion, and psychoeducational materials are part of REBT's war on irrational beliefs.

DISCUSSION IDEAS

1. Start with an activating event that could stir powerful feelings, and write it on the board. Suggestions: You get a C- on a midterm exam you thought you were prepared for; Your parents decide to move to a different state; You are offered a job that is better than you ever expected to get. Create a story line that takes this A and follows it through a sample irrational B, then C-D-E-F. If time permits, make up more than one story to show how different irrational beliefs lead to different consequences.

2. Have you ever been accused of having an irrational reaction to an activating event? Or, have you accused someone else of reacting irrationally? Describe the situation in Ellis's A, B, C terms. Were other people ever able to convince you that you were being unreasonable? How does this experience relate to REBT practice in group therapy?

Ellis is known for being directive and confrontational with his clients. He sees little purpose in fulfilling clients' need to be loved because he believes "I absolutely need to be loved" is an irrational belief. And, Ellis disagreed with the practice of letting clients dwell on their pasts—he called it "indulgence therapy." Therefore, an REBT session looks different from other group counseling sessions. The therapist may be seen actively arguing with the clients and calling their beliefs ridiculous. Though many REBT practitioners are gentler than Ellis, they are always more active and talkative participants than most group counselors are. Humor is a hallmark of REBT; people can often see the funny side of their exaggerated, childlike beliefs. They are often able to see the irrationality of other people's beliefs, which makes group work a powerful setting and the one Ellis prefers.

The techniques of REBT group counseling are education about the A-B-C model and energetic processing of the D-E-F part as it applies to situation after situation presented by the group members. Besides questioning and reasoning, REBT counselors prescribe behavioral exercises within the group setting and outside as homework to combat irrational beliefs. In the group setting, a woman who believes that men find her stupid and dull is assigned to engage a man in the group in a discussion of a subject she is interested in, such as the environment or a currently popular movie. The group members observe the interaction. Afterwards the woman shares with the group the thoughts she was having during the discussion. Group members give her frank feedback on how the interaction went and apply the A-B-C-D-E-F method together to discover alternative ways to think and feel in the situation. As homework, an extremely self-conscious person might be assigned to wear a silly outfit to work or burst into song in a public place, in order to see that most bystanders are only mildly interested if they even notice at all. Clients also receive reading and listening assignments from the many REBT books, articles, worksheets, and audiotapes available at bookstores and through the Albert Ellis Institute in New York City (*http://www.rebt.org*). A list of eleven **irrational beliefs** often published by Ellis follows:

1. It is essential that a person be loved or approved by virtually everyone in the community.

2. A person must be perfectly competent, adequate, and achieving to be considered worthwhile.

3. Some people are bad, wicked, or villainous and therefore should be blamed and punished.

4. It is a terrible catastrophe when things are not as a person wants them to be.

5. Unhappiness is caused by outside circumstances, and a person has no control over it.

6. Dangerous or fearsome things are cause for great concern, and their possibility must be continually dwelt upon.

7. It is easier to avoid certain difficulties and self-responsibilities than to face them.

8. A person should be dependent on others and should have someone stronger on whom to rely.

9. Past experiences and events are the determinants of present behavior; the influence of the past cannot be eradicated.

10. A person should be quite upset over other people's problems and disturbances.

11. There is always a right or perfect solution to every problem, and it must be found or the results will be catastrophic. (Adapted from *Reason and Emotion in Psychotherapy*, 1962)

SMALL GROUP EXERCISE

Review Ellis's list in your small group. Let each person identify an irrational belief that they sometimes find themselves invoking. Notice that even highly functioning, normal people hold some of these at some times. Practice disputing these beliefs among yourselves as though you were in a counseling group, using logical argument and examples.
Ellis wrote:

> I am really an optimist about mental health. I have written hundreds of articles, chapters, and books and have recorded scores of cassettes on how people have enormous power to think about their thinking, to use rationality and the scientific method, and to radically control and change their emotional destiny—providing they really work at doing so. . . . I believe that, along with their powerful self-defeating and self-destructive tendencies, humans also have great self-changing and self-actualizing powers. (1987, p. 374)

Cognitive Therapy Beck's cognitive therapy **(CT)** is another treatment based on the **cognitive model** (J. S. Beck, 1995), which depicts thoughts occurring on various levels. Clients work together with their group leader to identify automatic thoughts. Deeper levels of cognition operate beneath automatic thoughts.

■ *Intermediate beliefs* are rules, attitudes, and assumptions about if-then relationships (that is, *conditional beliefs*), from which many different automatic thoughts are generated. The intermediate beliefs are harder to bring into awareness than automatic thoughts. Intermediate beliefs (sometimes called *schemas*) lead people to perceive situations in habitual, internally consistent ways. Psychologically distressed people have schemas that bias them toward seeing the potential for loss, danger, and threat in new situations.

■ The deepest level consists of *core beliefs*, which are broad tendencies toward certain ways of perceiving, like "The world is a threatening place." The core beliefs and the schema that flow from them are established from early childhood interactions with the world and people. The child makes sense of these interactions by creating general rules that seem to fit, and of course, these rules are often distorted. Subsequently, they distort adult perceptions.

Cognitive therapy (CT) consists of identifying and modifying beliefs at all three levels (automatic thoughts, intermediate beliefs, and core beliefs).

Parallel to Ellis's irrational beliefs, Beck created a list of **faults in information processing.** These are flaws in perception and interpretation that maintain negative beliefs even when evidence is scant or absent.

1. **Arbitrary inference**   Drawing a specific conclusion in the absence of supporting evidence or in the presence of contrary evidence

2. **Selective abstraction**   Focusing on a detail taken out of context, ignoring other meaningful features of the situation, and labeling the whole experience on the basis of this fragment.

3. **Overgeneralization**   Drawing a general rule or conclusion on the basis of one or more isolated incidents and applying the concept across the board to related and unrelated situations.

4. **Magnification and minimization**   Errors in evaluating the significance or magnitude of an event. These errors are so gross that they distort the event.

5. **Personalization**   A tendency to relate external events to yourself when there is no basis for making such a connection.

6. **Absolutistic, dichotomous thinking**   Placing all experiences in one of two opposite categories: flawless or defective, immaculate or filthy, saint or sinner. (Adapted from Beck et al., 1979, p. 14)

Beck thinks that we all operate from systems of beliefs that are related in a network and give us consistent ways of looking at situations. These schemas develop from past experiences, like our upbringing and particular traumas. Thus, Beck remains closer to the psychodynamic tradition than Ellis does. We may have a negative core belief that usually lies dormant, but becomes activated by some outer or inner situation that resembles its psychodynamic source. For example, my friend Amy was raised by a strict, cruel father, and years later when a college professor handed out a rigorous and imperious syllabus, she found herself having rebellious and angry thoughts about the course. Though the syllabus was merely rhetorically flawed, Amy responded as though she was personally insulted.

The techniques used in CT are similar to those in REBT: "to identify maladaptive automatic thoughts, evaluate and (usually) modify these thoughts, uncover dysfunctional beliefs, and modify beliefs" (Haaga & Davison, 1991, p. 261). This is done through questioning and disputation, along with thought experiments and homework testing alternative interpretations of reality. "What's the evidence for and against the way you are thinking (or were thinking)?"; "What are some other ways of looking at the situation?"; and "How useful is your way of thinking about it?" are common questions heard in CT groups. Lang and Craske (2000) point out several ways in which the group setting is appropriate for this type of **cognitive restructuring** (changing beliefs):

- Watching other members in the process of identifying and changing thoughts provides vicarious learning.

- Challenges and suggestions for restructuring coming from other members may be more effective than coming from a therapist because people affiliate more with those who have similar experiences.

▪ Helping other group members assists each person to practice the model repeatedly.

▪ The group can be a resource for testing hypotheses, brainstorming for evidence, and role-playing.

For example, in Lang and Craske's group for panic and phobia, one client lies down on the floor as though she has fainted (a common fear of agoraphobics), and the other group members respond as they would in outside life. This practice episode helps the clients see that other people are likely to help them, not step over them or react cruelly, even if the fainting really happened. The catastrophic belief that fainting in public would be unbearable weakens its hold.

In CT, a relapse prevention stage at the end of therapy identifies early maladaptive schemas, emphasizing developmental patterns and long-term interpersonal difficulties that may signify dangerous relapse situations (Young, Beck, & Weinberger, 1993). An important distinction between approaches is that Beck does not apply the same set of irrational beliefs to all disorders, whereas Ellis does. Beck has identified core beliefs that underpin specific clinical problems.

Adaptations to Clients' Ages

Learning theory informs many of the practices counselors use with children and adolescents. The developmental stage of the clients in the group helps determine how the therapy is administered most effectively and palatably (Ivey, Ivey, Myers, & Sweeney, 2005). Children are amenable to active exercises that make use of their senses and the here-and-now, so behaviors like complimenting others in the group and saying thank-you to compliments are used in structured behavioral groups to improve social skills, and drawing, painting, and role playing in sessions are common (e.g., Khalsa, 1996). At a very young age, though, children would not be able to tell coherent stories from daily life and relate them to their social skills or reflect upon patterns in them. Preadolescents and beyond are able to do this with structured help, and more talk-oriented work and behavior homework can succeed. Word choice with children, as usual, needs to be modified. For example, in REBT with young people (Ellis & Wilde, 2002) therapists use different language in psychoeducation; instead of "irrational beliefs" and "rational coping statements" they talk with the children about "hot and cool thoughts." With both children and adolescents, the counselor can expect lower frustration tolerance than most adults have, and so should be ready to discuss repeatedly beliefs about change like, "It will take too long," "I can't stand it," and "I already tried that and it didn't work."

Ellis and Wilde (2002) also point out that adolescents usually desire some time to discuss things that are outside the main goals of the group and the session. Though most cognitive-behavioral counseling is goal-directed on principle, with young people often the goal was originally someone else's (the parents' or school's). When groups of young people are allowed to spend part of the session discussing their other concerns, there are still opportunities to reinforce REBT concepts in how they handle these other complaints. The curative factors of commonality, cohesiveness, and altruism operate to help the members feel valued as people, not merely as problems. During the transition from childhood to maturity, adolescents are beginning to grapple with the truth that adults are fallible people who sometimes make mistakes and act wrongly. Cognitive-behavioral approaches help the group members realize that though adults do sometimes act unjustly, selfishly, or stupidly, the members can learn to handle their own reactions.

A convincing body of research supports cognitive-behavioral therapy for older adults (Gallagher-Thompson, McKibbin, Koonce-Volwiler, Menendez, Steward, & Thompson, 2000). Late-life depression and late-life anxiety are two targets, and even more severe psychological problems are amenable (Hyer, Kramer, & Sohnle, 2004). However, Hyer, Kramer, and Sohnle suggest that integration of therapeutic-factors sensitivity into CBT is especially crucial in working with the elderly population (see Chapters 4 through 7). They particularly emphasize the role of the therapeutic alliance in individual therapy. In group therapy, you may remember from Chapter 4, the analog of the therapeutic alliance is cohesiveness (Budman et al., 1989; Yalom, 1995). Focusing on group members' emotions and interpersonal relationships may be more important in an older group than CBT's usual directive education, especially in the early sessions when cohesiveness is built. Older people who have experienced loss and displacement need pressingly to form the dependable attachment the group offers. Education and socialization into the cognitive-behavioral thinking style may, therefore, go more slowly in early sessions with older adults, making room for activities that enhance cohesion (see Chapter 4 for ideas).

Hyer and colleagues (2004) also suggest presenting the ideas of CBT in the context of aging successfully, which comprises selection of alternative goals, optimization of energy allocation, and compensation for deficiencies (Baltes & Baltes, 1990). This "doing the best with what you've got" approach gives validation to the realistic point of view toward functional decline, rather than the "Anything is possible!" approach counselors might take with younger CBT groups. Fortunately, older people use emotions in more complex and adaptive ways than they did when younger; have goals that are more based on collecting good feelings than collecting knowledge; and function better in emotionally charged situations (Carstensen, Isaacowitz, & Charles, 1999). Therapists can work such ideas into the educational part of group CBT, showing respect and hope (another important therapeutic factor).

Problems Addressed by Cognitive-Behavioral Groups

Cognitive-behavioral strategies powerfully dominate the lists of empirically supported treatments (ESTs) approved by the American Psychological Association. These treatments are chosen using rigorous standards of inclusion, a continuing effort that began in 1995 (see, for example, Nathan & Gorman, 1998). Cognitive therapy began in an effort to treat depression, and it is now considered the most effective treatment (Young et al., 1993). Behavior therapy originated largely from efforts to rid people of crippling fears and phobias, and it has been proven effective repeatedly (Emmelkamp, 2004). Of the twenty-seven disorders with empirically supported treatments discussed in Nathan and Gorman, sixteen of the treatments involve behavioral, cognitive, or cognitive-behavioral therapy.

These therapies have lent themselves well to the group setting. White and Freeman (2000) explained the advantage of cognitive-behavioral therapy in groups in the following manner:

> In these group therapy settings, conditional beliefs naturally rose to the surface, providing multiple opportunities to identify, test, and revise those underlying rules that govern social behavior. There was immediate activation of automatic thoughts without having to resort to "out of group experience" to find clinically relevant material. The single best advantage of CBT delivered in group settings seems to be the fundamental fact that it is the group itself that generates its own adaptive response. Members gain immeasurably in acquiring this skill through social modeling with each other. . . . We have seen over and over that a group's capacity for adaptive response usually exceeds the ability of those same individuals to undertake adaptation while by themselves. (p. xi)

Common therapeutic factors of the group, such as cohesiveness and universality, boost the power of cognitive and behavioral interventions.

A survey of the literature reveals that cognitive-behavioral groups have been formed for stress management, eating disorders, parent effectiveness, obesity, drug abuse, dissociative disorders, social skills improvement, posttraumatic stress disorder, pain, schizophrenia, borderline personality disorder, and attention deficit disorders (Burlingame, MacKenzie, & Strauss, 2004; White & Freeman, 2000). CBT groups convened over the Internet have assuaged loneliness among people with physical disabilities (Hopps, Pepin, & Boisvert, 2003). In a comparison study, group CBT for social phobia was compared with psychoeducational group work for social phobia (Heimberg, Juster, Hope, & Mattia, 1995). After 12 weeks of treatment, 75 percent of the CBT group members were judged clinically improved, compared to 40 percent of the psychoeducational group. Followed up about five years later, CBT group members were functioning better in several ways than psychoeducational group members were. White and Freeman predicted that CBT group therapy will constitute half to three quarters of mental health treatment in the future because its records of empirical proof and cost effectiveness fit in with the direction of our country's public policy.

SMALL GROUP EXERCISES

1. From the list of uses for CBT, choose a problem your group members find interesting. Using "cognitive behavioral" (or "cognitive" or "behavioral" separately), "group," and the name of the problem as keywords, search PsychInfo to find an article or book chapter about applying treatment in groups to this problem. Read the selection, get together, and discuss what aspects of learning theory are relevant to the treatment described.

2. On *www.rebt.org,* the website for the Albert Ellis Institute, click the "REBT research" button, and you will be directed to a list of recent studies (updated quarterly) with summaries. From this list, you can see the wide variety of applications for REBT and the research being done currently. In your small group, discuss applications that pertain to your probable counseling settings.

Evaluating Cognitive-Behavioral Groups

The nature of these therapies allows for frequent and informative assessment of the group because the goals are often measurable. Did the clients in a smoking cessation program quit smoking or not? Was the husband able to lower the number of marital disputes to one a week? Does a graph of anxiety ratings at the end of each day show a declining slope? Was group attendance and participation regular, with a low dropout rate? Did Barry finally get a date, and did Mary resist adopting another stray dog?

Even cognitive change, an inner shift, is reflected in overt changes. Children whose parents are divorcing may be angry and anxious and feel they are to blame for the schism. A cognitive-behavioral group may address their irrational thoughts and inaccurate beliefs about the situation. Their behavior at home, their grades at school, and even their physical health, can serve as indicators of whether the group was successful. Thus, even though we can't look into the child's heart, we can see the outward signs of change.

Another way of evaluating your group's effectiveness is to use standardized measures relevant to the group's purpose. There are several instruments designed to measure depression, anxiety, children's behaviors, fears, marital happiness, and symptoms of emotional distress. One advantage of using these is that they have been *normed;* that is, a user's manual will let you inspect the scores of large numbers of other people like your group members and see how your group compares. When you look at an individual member's pretreatment and posttreatment scores on such a measure, you can see improvement, decline, or no change.

One normed measure designed specifically for use in REBT is the Survey of Personal Beliefs (Demaria, Kassinove, & Dill, 1989). This is a measure of irrational thinking based on rational-emotive theory. A group member who takes this survey receives scores on overall rationality and five categories of beliefs: awfulizing, self-directed shoulds, other-directed shoulds, low frustration tolerance, and self-worth. Giving this survey to members before the group begins and again later will help you gauge whether their beliefs have changed over the course of the group.

In assessing client change, many times you can use the **Jacobson-Truax Clinically Significant Change Tables.** These tables, using statistical analysis of large samples of scores, help you decide whether a change is reliable (that is, not just due to chance), and whether the change brings the client into the score range of normal, nondistressed people (Beal & Duckro, 2003). That is, you can judge whether your group members have joined the ranks of ordinary people, with usual ups and downs. Ogles, Lambert, and Masters (1996) have compiled these tables for a number of commonly used clinical instruments. Using these, you can aggregate data from groups you lead over time and evaluate your success with various approaches and with experience. This practice is not only good for your self-evaluation but can also serve as a way of collecting data for research. Most individuals do not lead enough groups at once to collect large data sets, but over time it can be done. Our field is in need of research done in the real world of counseling practice, and your contribution could be considerable.

KEY TERMS

anxiety hierarchy   a list of situations organized in the order of how anxious they make a client

automatic thoughts   inner statements or evaluations that occur without effort and form a person's viewpoints on self and experience; these are associated with Beck's CT

automaticity   a mental phenomenon beyond voluntary thought, in which thoughts spontaneously occur without beckoning

behavioral learning theory   emphasizes the role of reinforcement, punishment, observation, and similar environmental processes in what we learn

buddy system   pairing up group members for purposes of mutual support outside sessions, especially in the termination stage of a group

classical conditioning   the process whereby a response becomes associated with a stimulus through experience that connects them psychologically

cognitive learning theory   emphasizes the role of our thinking processes in what we learn

cognitive model   a layout of mental activity that places thoughts on different levels of depth and generality

cognitive restructuring   changing beliefs on a deep and lasting level—rebuilding thought processes

contingency management   manipulating the conditions that make a desired action more or less likely; these conditions can occur before or after the desired action

CT   acronym for cognitive therapy, the approach designed by Aaron Beck

discrimination   responding to exact stimuli and not to others that resemble it

exposure and response prevention   exposure to a feared stimulus, without recourse to one's usual avoidance actions

extinction   the disappearance of a response when an associated result stops being paired with it

fading system   spacing group sessions farther and farther apart in time in the termination stage

faults in information processing   flaws in perception and interpretation that maintain negative beliefs even when evidence is scant or absent

generalization   responding similarly to stimuli that resemble one another

imaginal exposure   exposure to a feared stimulus in the imagination

in vivo exposure   exposure to a feared stimulus in reality

irrational beliefs   disturbing illogical thoughts that are the source of unhappiness, panic, anxiety, and depression and, furthermore, block the solutions to life's problems, according to REBT doctrine; these beliefs were probably picked up in childhood from parents and culture

Jacobson-Truax Clinically Significant Change Tables   statistically derived charts to help you decide whether a measured change in a client is reliable (that is, not just due to chance) and whether the change brings the client into the score range of normal, nondistressed people

mediational position the belief that mental operations intervene between stimulus and response. Judgment, evaluation, and belief, for example, can determine how we react to a stimulus

operant conditioning (instrumental conditioning) the process in which behavior is changed by what comes after it—for example, by reward or punishment

personal constructs our characteristic ways of viewing the world around us: what catches our attention, what we think is important, what we remember for a long time, what touches us emotionally, and so on

progressive relaxation a system of muscle tightening and loosening, moving through the parts of the body in sequence

REBT acronym for rational emotive behavior therapy, the approach designed by Albert Ellis

reinforcement anything that raises the likelihood that a behavior will be repeated; it could be positive, such as food, or negative, such as relief from pain

schedule of reinforcement the spacing and frequency of reward for a certain behavior

support group a voluntary self-help group with a focus on some feature they hold in common; in some CBT approaches, the support group takes over after termination of the professionally led group; support groups may or may not have trained leaders

systematic bias a pattern of automatic thoughts that control a person's response to the outside world. These habitual inclinations usually come with an emotional component and seem believable to the person who holds them

systematic desensitization the gradual sequencing of anxiety and relaxation to ensure that anxiety fades out

CHAPTER REVIEW

1. Explain why Bandura and Ellis made changes in the labels for their theories.

2. What are the similarities between psychoeducational groups and cognitive-behavioral groups? Name a group that you would classify as both, and explain why. Write your own rule for making a distinction between the two types of group.

3. Name the six stages of cognitive-behavioral group counseling. Write one or two sentences summarizing the main task of each stage (a total of twelve or fewer sentences).

4. Review the four contingency management strategies. Make up your own example of how each one could be applied in your own life or in the life of someone you know.

5. Discuss the idea of modeling with a friend or relative outside of class. Explain modeling to this person. Together, think of times you have benefited from or used modeling. What makes modeling effective? What might work against the effectiveness of modeling?

6. For each of the six faults in information processing listed in this chapter, describe a sample scene in which a character uses the faulty processing and maintains negative beliefs about self, others, or the world.

FOR FURTHER READING

White, J. R., & Freeman, A. S. (2000). *Cognitive-behavioral group therapy for specific problems and populations.* Washington, DC: American Psychological Association.

Step-by-step protocols for group counseling are described in the chapters of this book, covering thirteen different problems (such as obesity), populations (e.g., parents), and settings (e.g., hospitals). The authors of each chapter are practitioners of empirically supported cognitive-behavioral treatments in groups. You will read about specific applications of many of the techniques in these chapters as well as learn about the problems that may come up in each type of group.

REFERENCES

Baltes, P. B., & Baltes, M. (1990). Psychological perspectives on successful aging : The model of selective optimization with compensation. In P. B. Baltes & M. Baltes (Eds.), *Longitudinal research and the study of successful (optimal) aging* (pp. 1–49). Cambridge, England: Cambridge University Press.

Bandura, A. (1986). *Social foundations of thought and action.* Englewood Cliffs, NJ: Prentice-Hall.

Bandura, A. (2001). Social cognitive theory: An agentic perspective. *Annual Review of Psychology, 52,* 1–26.

Barlow, D. H. (1993). *Clinical handbook of psychological disorders* (2nd ed.). New York: Guilford.

Beal, D., & Duckro, P. (2003). Empirically documenting clinically significant change in rational emotive behavior therapy. *Journal of Rational-Emotive & Cognitive-Behavior Therapy, 21,* 75–88.

Beck, A. T. (1991). Cognitive therapy: A 30-year perspective. *American Psychologist, 46,* 368–375.

Beck, A. T., & Weishaar, M. E. (2000). Cognitive therapy. In R. J. Corsini & D. Wedding, *Current psychotherapies* (6th ed., pp. 241–271). Itasca, IL: Peacock.

Beck, A. T., Rush, A. J., Shaw, B. F, & Emery, G. (1979). *Cognitive therapy of depression.* New York: Guilford Press.

Beck, J. S. (1995). *Cognitive therapy: Basics and beyond.* New York: Guilford Press.

Budman, S. H., Soldz, S., Demby, A., Feldstein, M., Springer, T., & Davis, S. (1989). Cohesion, alliance and outcome in group psychotherapy. *Psychiatry, 52,* 339–350.

Burlingame, G.M., MacKenzie, K.R., & Strauss, B. (2004). Small-group treatment: Evidence for effectiveness and mechanisms of change. In M. J. Lambert (Ed.), *Bergin and Garfield's handbook of psychotherapy and behavior change* (pp. 647–696). New York: Wiley.

Carstensen, L. L., Isaacowitz, D. M., & Charles, S. T. (1999). Taking time seriously: A theory of socioemotional selectivity. *American Psychologist, 54,* 165–181.

Choate, L. H., & Henson, A. (2003). Group work with adult survivors of childhood abuse and neglect : A psychoeducational approach. *The Journal for Specialists in Group Work, 28,* 106–121.

Coyne, J. C. (1976a). Depression and the response of others. *Journal of Abnormal Psychology, 85,* 186–193.

Coyne, J. C. (1976b). Toward an interactional description of depression. *Psychiatry, 39,* 28–40.

Demaria, T. P., Kassinove, H., & Dill, C. A. (1989). Psychometric properties of the Survey of Personal Beliefs: A rational-emotive measure of irrational thinking. *Journal of Personality Assessment, 53,* 329–341.

Dobson, K. S., & Block, L. (1988). Historical and philosophical bases of the cognitive-behavioral therapies. In K. S. Dobson (Ed.), *Handbook of cognitive-behavioral therapies* (pp. 3–35). New York: Guilford Press.

Dollard, J., & Miller, N. E. *Personality and psychotherapy.* New York: McGraw-Hill, 1950.

Ellis, A. (1962). *Reason and emotion in psychotherapy.* New York: Lyle Stuart.

Ellis, A. (1987). The impossibility of achieving consistently good mental health. *American Psychologist, 42,* 364–375.

Ellis, A. (1992). My early experiences in developing the practice of psychology. *Professional Psychology: Research and Practice, 23,* 7–10.

Ellis, A. (1994). *Reason and emotion in psychotherapy* (rev. ed.). New York: Kensington.

Ellis, A., & Wilde, J. (2002). *Case studies in Rational Emotive Behavior Therapy with children and adolescents.* Upper Saddle River, NJ: Merrill Prentice Hall.

Emmelkamp, P. M. G. (2004). Behavior therapy with adults. In M. J. Lambert (Ed.), *Bergin and Garfield's handbook of psychotherapy and behavior change* (pp. 393–446). New York: Wiley.

Emmelkamp, P. M. G. (1994). Behavior therapy with adults. In A. E. Bergin & S. L. Garfield, (Eds.), *Handbook of psychotherapy and behavior change* (4th ed., pp. 379–427). New York: Wiley.

Foa, E. A., & Kozak, M. J. (1986). Emotional processing of fear: Exposure to corrective information. *Psychological Bulletin, 99,* 20–35.

Gallagher-Thompson, D., McKibbin, C., Koonce-Volwiler, D., Menendez, A., Steward, D., & Thompson, L. W. (2000). Psychotherapy with older adults. In C. R. Snyder & R. E. Ingram (Eds.), *Handbook of psychological change: Psychotherapy processes and practices for the 21st century* (pp. 614–637). New York: John Wiley & Sons.

Gazda, G. M., Ginter, E. J., & Horne, A. M. (2001). *Group counseling and group psychotherapy.* Boston: Allyn & Bacon.

Glynn, S. M., & Ruderman, A. (1986). The development and validation of an Eating Self-Efficacy Scale. *Cognitive Therapy and Research, 10,* 403–420.

Haaga, D. A. F., & Davison, G. C. (1991). Cognitive change methods. In F. H. Kanfer & A. P. Goldstein (Eds.), *Helping people change: A textbook of methods* (4th ed., pp. 248–304). New York: Pergamon Press.

Heimberg, R. G., Juster, H. R., Hope, D. A., & Mattia, J. I. (1995). Cognitive behavioral group treatment for social phobia. In M. B. Stein (Ed.), *Social phobia: clinical and research perspectives* (pp. 293–321). Washington, DC: American Psychiatric Press.

Hollander, M., & Kazaoka, K. (1988). Behavior therapy groups. In S. Long (Ed.), *Six group therapies* (pp. 257–326). New York: Plenum Press.

Hopps, S. L., Pepin, M., & Boisvert, J.-M. (2003). The effectiveness of cognitive-behavioral group therapy for loneliness via Inter-relay-chat among people with physical disabilities. *Psychotherapy: Theory, Research, Practice, Training, 40,* 136–147.

Hyer, L., Kramer, D., & Sohnle, S. (2004). CBT with older people: Alterations and the value of the therapeutic alliance. *Psychotherapy: Theory, Research, Practice, Training, 41,* 276–291.

Ivey, A., Ivey, M., Myers, J., & Sweeney, T. (2005). *Developmental counseling and therapy.* Boston: Lahaska/Houghton Mifflin.

Jacobson, E. (1938). *Progressive relaxation.* Chicago: University of Illinois Press. (Original work published in 1929.)

Kazdin, A. E. (1994). *Behavior modification in applied settings* (5th ed.). Pacific Grove, CA: Brooks/Cole.

Kelly, G. A. (1955). *The psychology of personal constructs* (Vol. 2). New York: Wadsworth.

Khalsa, S. S. (1996). *Group exercises for enhancing social skills and self-esteem.* Sarasota, FL: Professional Resource Press.

Koss, M. P., & Shiang, J. (1994). Research on brief psychotherapy. In A. E. Bergin & S. L. Garfield (Eds.), *Handbook of psychotherapy and behavior change* (4th ed., pp. 664–700). New York: Wiley.

Lang, A. J., & Craske, M. G. (2000). Panic and phobia. In J. R. White & A. S. Freeman (Eds.), *Cognitive-behavioral group therapy* (pp. 63–97). Washington, DC: American Psychological Association.

Lewinsohn, P. M., & MacPhillamy, D. J. (1971). *Pleasant Events Schedule.* (Available from Peter M. Lewinsohn, Department of Psychology, Straub Hall, University of Oregon, Eugene, OR 97411.)

Nathan, P. E., & J. M. Gorman, (Eds.) (1998). *A guide to treatments that work.* New York: Oxford University Press.

Neisser, U. (1967). *Cognitive psychology.* New York: Appleton-Century-Croft.

Ogles, B. M., Lambert, M. J., & Masters, K. (1996). *Assessing outcome in clinical practice.* New York: Allyn & Bacon.

Patterson, C. H. (1980). *Theories of counseling and psychotherapy* (3rd ed.). New York: Harper & Row.

Rose, S. D., & LeCroy, C. W. (1991). Group methods. In F. H. Kanfer & A. P. Goldstein (Eds.), *Helping people change: A textbook of methods* (4th ed., pp. 422–453). New York: Pergamon Press.

Rosenthal, T. L., & Steffek, B. D. (1991). Modeling methods. In F. H. Kanfer & A. P. Goldstein (Eds.), *Helping people change: A textbook of methods* (4th ed., pp. 70–121). New York: Pergamon Press.

Schwartz, J. P., & Waldo, M. (2004). Group work with men who have committed partner abuse. In J. L. DeLucia-Waack, D. A. Gerrity, C. R. Kalodner, & M. T. Riva (Eds.), *Handbook of group counseling and psychotherapy* (pp. 576–592). Thousand Oaks, CA: Sage.

Skinner, B. F. (1974). *About behaviorism.* New York: Vintage.

Skinner, B. F. (1981). How to discover what you have to say—a talk to students. *Behavior Analyst, 4,* 1–7.

Sloane, R. B., Staples, F. R., Cristol, A. H., Yorkston, N. J., Whipple, K. (1975). *Psychotherapy versus behavior therapy*. Cambridge, MA: Harvard University Press.

Spiegler, M.D., & Guevremont, D. C. (1998). *Contemporary behavior therapy* (3rd ed.). Pacific Grove, CA: Brooks/Cole.

Stuart, R. B. (1980). *Helping couples change*: *A social learning approach to marital therapy*. New York: Guilford Press.

Thorndike, E. L. (1911). *Animal intelligence*. New York: Macmillan.

Toseland, R. W. (1995). *Group work with the elderly*. New York: Springer.

White, J. R., & Freeman, A. S. (2000). *Cognitive-behavioral group therapy for specific problems and populations*. Washington, DC: American Psychological Association.

Wolpe, J. (1990). *The practice of behavior therapy* (4th ed.). New York: Pergamon.

Wolpe, J. (1958). *Psychotherapy by reciprocal inhibition*. Stanford, CA: Stanford University Press.

Yalom, I. D. (1995). *The theory and practice of group psychotherapy*. New York: Basic Books.

Young, J. E., Beck, A. T., & Weinberger, A. (1993). Depression. In D. H. Barlow (Ed.), *Clinical Handbook of Psychological Disorders* (2nd ed., pp. 240–277). New York: Guilford Press.

Ziegler, D. J., & Leslie, Y. M. (2003). A test of the ABC model underlying rational emotive behavior therapy. *Psychological Reports, 92*, 235–240.

CHAPTER 13

Psychoeducational Group Theory and Practice

A Selection from "A Group Counseling Intervention for Children with Attention Deficit Hyperactivity Disorder"

Essential Concepts of Psychoeducational Group Theory

Concepts Derived from Learning Theory ■ *Concepts Derived from Social Learning Theory* ■ *Problem Solving*

Group Dynamics

Stages of the Group ■ *Structured and Unstructured Components* ■ *Multiple Relationships in Groups*

Leadership Skills

Clarity ■ *Communication Skills* ■ *Creativity* ■ *Knowledge of Process* ■ *Personality*

Techniques in Psychoeducational Group Counseling

Modeling and Coaching ■ *Role-Playing* ■ *Homework* ■ *Classroom Strategies*

Problems Addressed by Psychoeducational Groups

Knowledge and Skill Deficits ■ *Assertiveness Training* ■ *Self-Management*

Adaptations to Clients' Ages

Evaluating Psychoeducational Groups

In all likelihood, as a counselor you will lead psychoeducational groups. They enjoy great popularity, and conditions are ripe for their further growth. Managed care organizations and mental health providers predict a significant increase in the use of psychoeducational groups in the future (Taylor,

Burlingame, Kristensen, Fuhriman, Johansen, & Dahl, 2001). "Short-term, highly structured groups are receiving strong endorsement from managed care companies, and are predicted to grow faster than traditional process-oriented groups" (p. 261).

Psychoeducational groups, which include more teaching and coaching than others, owe their development to the field of counseling psychology (Gelso & Fretz, 2001). The Association for Specialists in Group Work (2000) includes psychoeducational group work as a specialization area, and it provides a useful definition:

- The application of principles of normal human development and functioning
- through group-based educational and developmental strategies
- applied in the context of here-and-now interaction
- that promote personal and interpersonal growth and development and the prevention of future difficulties
- among people who may be at risk for the development of personal or interpersonal problems or who seek enhancement of personal qualities and abilities.

You can see by comparison with these five points of definition that the ADHD intervention described in the selection below is a good instance of psychoeducation. Notice, in particular, the emphasis on prevention of future difficulties; this is a major, positive force in psychoeducational groups. The ADHD group aims to help students manage their situations *before* they have school problems.

A Selection from

"A Group Counseling Intervention for Children with Attention Deficit Hyperactivity Disorder"

By Linda D. Webb and Robert D. Myrick (2003)

A recent study sponsored by the National Institute of Mental Health reported that a carefully managed protocol of stimulant medication and behavioral intervention was effective in treating ADHD symptoms. The combination resulted in improved social skills, parent-child relations, and academic achievement. It was also reported that in some circumstances, behavioral/psychosocial interventions alone produced these same results. While school counselors often help to identify behaviors symptomatic of ADHD, diagnosing and medically treating ADHD are not school counselor functions. However, helping students understand and manage their behavior and their relationships with others to maximize their learning potential is an important school counselor function.

The widespread use of stimulant medication and the emphasis on behavioral modification by teachers and parents raises another question. Should ADHD students feel less responsibility for the outcomes of their behavior? They may falsely conclude that what happens during the school day is the result of their medication and teachers' efforts, rather than their own choices and actions. This external locus of control can lead students to disclaim personal responsibility for what they do and lay a foundation for making excuses when problems or difficulties arise. Research findings support this external locus-of-control finding for ADHD students along with the need for explicit external cues. . . .

THE JOURNEY: A GROUP COUNSELING INTERVENTION

What follows is a description of a small group counseling intervention that has been used with ADHD students. The intervention focuses on increased understanding of the disorder and how it affects school performance. It was assumed that students needed to face their disorders and recognize that it is part of who they are. Further, the disorder by itself will not keep them from their personal, academic, or career goals. To the contrary, many individuals who have ADHD have made valuable and significant contributions to society. The secret to success is being able to manage one's thoughts, feelings, and behaviors.

Fourteen elementary school counselors from one school district delivered the intervention consisting of six small group sessions designed for about six students per group. Each session had a specific objective related to thoughts, behaviors, and skills that focused on school and personal achievement and began with a review of the previous session and a check on application of skills. Sessions ended with tasks for practice and an encouraging summary statement. The unit culminated with snacks, juice, and talk about the group experience as well as a review of plans for utilizing strategies.

The sessions were based on the theme of a journey that students might imagine they were taking. Of course, the journey required preparation and the ability to recognize certain road signs and to manage the vehicle in such a way that the students would arrive safely at their final destination. Because the students had ADHD, they would be a different kind of traveler and, at times, take a different route than others, although they would eventually arrive at the same destination. The metaphor of a journey provided opportunities to construct group activities that were fun and enabled participants to reflect on goals and goal setting, the influence of personal characteristics on achieving goals, and personal management skills. As they considered skills needed to move them along on their imaginary journey, they also thought about how the skills were related to the academic, personal, social, and career goals shared by all students their age.

PREPARING FOR THE JOURNEY

The counselor begins the unit by telling students that they have been selected for the group because they have been identified as different kind of learners: They have ADHD. They are asked, "What do you know about ADHD?"

Discussion and clarification help the students identify ADHD symptoms and how the symptoms are manifested in school, which often makes them learn in different ways than others. They are, in one sense, a different traveler in the education world. It is explained that sometimes they take the same road as others while learning things and then, at other times, they will go another way, perhaps taking some detours, even though everyone is trying to get to the same place. The counselor leads the participants through a series of structured learning activities. Special efforts are made to focus on what students experience (their feelings) and how those feelings are related to behaviors (their actions). Students discuss what they believe to be true about themselves and others, and how they can manage their thoughts, feelings, and behaviors. Once introductory activities are completed, the journey begins.

Session One: Our Journey

Participants begin their journey as they explore a variety of paths to reach a single destination in Map Quest [an interactive website used to find directions and maps]; they talk about goals and places to go. As they discover the link between an objective and school success, students realize that not all students must take the same journey through school; however, they can each achieve success and arrive at the same destination. Summary statements include: "Having ADHD doesn't mean you can't be successful as a student; however, it does mean that you might have to find some ways to get there (success) that will be a little different than the routes others take. You will need to learn to be a different kind of traveler and do some things to help yourself become successful. If you do, you will have more control over where you are going and how you will get there."

Session Two: Pack It Up

Students experience the "messy bag." The counselor begins the session by rummaging through a bag or backpack, throwing things left and right and creating havoc. It is a demonstration of the chaos that comes from being cluttered and disorganized. Students explore their own bags and the need for organization. Being orderly will probably remain a difficult task to learn, but students may have more insight as to why others are continually trying to organize them. Organizational skills are introduced, demonstrated, and practiced. The session closes with a brief summary statement: "Keeping things organized is important. It is one way for you to help yourself on your journey to school success."

Session Three: Stop Lights and Traffic Cops

Students embark on an imaginary "car ride" to heighten their awareness of the need to attend and pay attention to the signs around them. As they pretend to drive a car, signs are flashed in front of them, and they have to navigate obstacles in the room. They then play the "paying attention" game. A participant wins the game by keeping his or her eyes focused on an object, a book, or perhaps a person who is walking around the room such as a teacher might do for various time intervals. Time intervals are increased from a few seconds until a one-minute interval is reached. The counselor summarizes by saying, "Having ADHD makes paying attention and listening more difficult, but it can be done. Learning and remembering strategies like we practiced today help us notice important things along the way and let us take control during our journey."

Session Four: Using Road Signs as a Guide

Students identify familiar road signs (cards) that cue behavior on the road before they identify signs in their classroom that may help to cue behavior or remember something. Students each develop their own cue to support increased success in the classroom. Summarizing remarks include, "Students with ADHD can be successful in school and get things done—using cues and reminders in your classroom and making up your own are ways to do it."

Session Five: Road Holes and Detours

Students imagine things that could go wrong on a road trip, including obstacles to getting to their destination (construction, detours, holes in the road, etc.). Students generate school situations (many times generated by their own behavior) that create obstacles to success in school. The counselor teaches and demonstrates selected cognitive behavioral strategies before giving students an opportunity for practice. The counselor closes with, "We know there will be holes in the road for ADHD students. There are holes in the road for all students, but your map is marked and you can expect them. You are learning ways to get around obstacles and difficult situations at school and go on with your journey."

Session Six: Roadside Help and Being Your Own Mechanic

Students explore the idea of breaking down on the road and becoming their own mechanic. Previously learned skills and attitudes are reviewed as tools they will need to get back on the road. Sometimes one has to ask for assistance from someone else when necessary tools are not in the toolbox. However, most of the time, students will have the tools they need to stay or get back on track. Knowing that they can fix things and be their own mechanic is an empowering experience. They are more responsible for managing their own vehicle. The topic of medication is introduced. Doctors and parents usually determine if medication is an appropriate intervention. If students have been prescribed medication, they are encouraged to help themselves by taking the medication, as if it were a tool, and working on the self-management strategies.

The final session summary includes, "We know that all students can be successful in school and that not everyone must be the same kind of traveler or learner. During our sessions we have learned about ADHD and some of the skills and attitudes that will help us in our travels as we journey through school. We have talked about the value of being organized, using cues and strategies to help us remember things, paying attention, and thinking before we act. We also practiced some skills and tried using them in school and at home. With the right kind of attitudes and skills, we can reach our destination—school success." (pp. 108–112)

Exploring "A Group Counseling Intervention for Children with Attention Deficit Hyperactivity Disorder"

1. What do you know about ADHD? Discuss your experience with this condition and how you have seen it handled.
2. What is the problem with the external locus of control, mentioned in paragraph two, among children with ADHD?
3. What thoughts (cognitions) about ADHD are targeted in the intervention? What feelings are targeted? What behaviors are targeted?
4. Paragraph four outlines the structure of sessions. Can you explain the reasoning behind each part of the session?
5. What is the imaginative comparison used throughout the intervention? Did you like this comparison for use with the children? Why or why not?
6. What props are used in this treatment? The authors don't tell us their group's ages; can you suggest what age groups would find the props appealing? What props might you use with an adult ADHD group, if any?
7. In sessions 5 and 6, students are encouraged to think about problems that might come up. Given that psychoeducational groups are focused on the positive, why do these counselors include problems in the intervention?
8. What is "an empowering experience"? Why is this experience important for group members?
9. The authors write that they give "tasks for practice" at the end of each session, but don't describe what these are. Choose one of the six sessions and make up a take-home task for the children to do.
10. Do you think this intervention would work in individual counseling for a child with ADHD? What does the group setting add to the treatment, beyond what would happen in individual counseling?

■ ■ ■

Essential Concepts of Psychoeducational Group Theory

In the ADHD group, the educational function of the group is in the foreground, giving students information about their condition and what it does and does not mean. Notice that self-disclosure by the attendees is not the focus of this type of group. The amount of personal material disclosed in counseling varies among psychoeducational groups. It is usually not a crucial element in success or failure, as it may be in the other groups described so far.

Sometimes psychoeducational techniques are used in the beginning stage of counseling groups to prepare members for the group work that lies ahead. As Chapter 2 suggested, clients should be educated about what they will be doing in group work, told what will be expected of them, disabused of some of the common myths about group counseling, and reassured about the process. The psychoeducational format is ideal for this preparation.

The final point in the ASGW definition in this chapter's opening deserves note, too. Psychoeducation includes people who seek personal enhancement, not only those at risk. So, for example, many of the workshops you will attend as a counselor are psychoeducational; they will enhance your counseling skills by introducing you to new knowledge, techniques, and theories. In the past year, I have attended psychoeducational seminars on the insanity defense, leading reality-therapy groups, and cross-cultural views on suicide, to name a few.

SMALL GROUP EXERCISE

Outline a one-session psychoeducational presentation to prepare potential members for one type of group you lead or intend to lead. Your instructor may want you to exchange your plan with the other small groups in class.

Because psychoeducational groups emphasize content and instruction, there's a much wider range in psychoeducational groups as far as size (from two people to a large lecture hall full) and length (from one hour to six months) than in other counseling groups. The main goals are clearly set by the leaders, or institutions (schools, clinics, hospitals, workplaces), whereas in other group counseling, members set the goals. Self-disclosure is not a major therapeutic factor in most psychoeducational groups.

One way to classify psychoeducational groups is by their goals.

■ **Preventive groups** convene to avoid foreseeable problems. For example, before puberty most American girls attend a psychoeducational group session about menstruation, which attempts to avert ugly surprises and to debunk popular myths. These provide accurate information and reassurance. As this example indicates, psychoeducational group members need not be in distress to find the group helpful. Orientation groups prepare well functioning people to handle potentially troublesome aspects of a new life situation, such as preschool, parenthood, retirement, college, or a complex work setting.

■ **Remedial groups** intervene to solve an existing problem and keep it from getting worse. Middle schools, for instance, sometimes try to identify children headed for delinquent behavior and build psychoeducational groups intended to steer them in more fruitful directions. Remedial psychoeducational groups help people adjust to existing problems like cancer, divorce, grief, early parenthood, and caregiving pressures.

■ **Developmental groups** teach people skills that are useful for their age and situation, yet were missed somehow in the course of their ordinary life. Social skills are taught in psychoeducational groups at every age level, for example. In work settings, people's leadership skills may be developed through psychoeducational interventions so that they can move up in the organization.

Concepts Derived from Learning Theory

Because of their educational component, psychoeducational groups depend on the principles of learning theory that address the ways in which people acquire and maintain knowledge. From your own many years in school, you know that some learning experiences were more effective than others. Think about an excellent course and a sorry course from your own life as a student as you read the following principles of learning effectiveness enhancement.

Active Participation Optimal learning occurs when group members are active rather than passive. Discussing, practicing, role-playing, and movement are active ways of learning, whereas listening to a lecture is usually passive. Even when your material is best presented in a lecture, you can encourage mental activity by having group members jot down responses, engage in a show of hands on some question, and think of their own examples (as I did above). In the Small Group Exercises, Discussion Ideas, and Chapter Reviews in this textbook, I make use of this learning principle.

Self-Referential Learning People learn material that relates to themselves. This may seem overobvious, but some educators neglect the principle. Applying knowledge to one's own present or past experience entrenches that knowledge in the mind. When I run groups for dissertation writers, I lecture on two opposite sources of writer's block: underarousal and overarousal. As I talk about these, I encourage students to think about writing projects during which they suffered from either an under- or over-supply of excitement. **Self-referential learning** imbues the information with a personal meaning. In the Reflections in this textbook, I make use of this learning principle.

Organization In psychoeducational groups more than others, group leaders control the order of the sessions. This means that we can take advantage of learning principles that concern the advantageous organization of material. Learners do best when they have an overview of the topics for the session. Usually, a single session deals with a whole concept and its component parts. The most effective structure is to introduce the whole, or the big picture, and then to present the parts. Show how each one relates to the whole and to the other parts. Organized material is more easily grasped and more memorable than jumbled material. That is why I begin each chapter of this textbook with an outline of the chapter content.

Variety In organizing a session, make use of the human zest for variety. I once attended a day-long workshop for counselors, in which we were told that we would listen to lectures all morning, break for lunch, and then in the afternoon we would do small-group exercises based on the lecture material. Of course, we were nearly zombies by lunchtime. The day would have been more productive if we had had a short lecture followed by a related exercise, then another short lecture, and so forth. Activity itself can be varied, mixing talk, writing, movement, drama, and artistic modes.

Concreteness People learn abstract principles through concrete examples and details. They also tend to remember the concrete material and then call forth the abstract idea from that. When I taught the history of psychology, I noticed that my students always remembered theories that I had illustrated with a good lively story. You yourself may remember Clever Hans, the horse that wowed audiences in the early 1900s by doing math, telling time, spelling, and performing other mental feats, communicating through tapping his hoof. This classic story is used to illustrate the power of conditioning, and sticks in almost every student's mind.

Feedback Learning is enhanced when the learner receives feedback on how well he or she is grasping the material. In school, tests give students feedback. In groups, members engage in role-plays and in summarizing concepts out loud for the purposes of feedback. Therefore, instruction in giving each other honest feedback without being hurtful is an important part of psychoeducational work.

Transfer of Training Our main goal in psychoeducational work is **transfer of training**—that is, the broad, productive use of knowledge and skills applied to situations other than the original learning context (De Corte, 2003). If group members don't apply outside what they learn inside the group, the group has largely failed. For this reason, psychoeducational groups almost always include practice in everyday life outside the sessions, reports on how the practice worked out, and analysis of what succeeds and fails. So, a group working on shyness would include specific instructions to try to speak up in daily life, and members would share the results of their efforts in the next session.

Adapting Group Strategies to Client Characteristics Psychoeducators often don't know their clients before the group convenes, so we must make educated guesses about how to tailor our sessions for the people we expect will attend. One obvious characteristic is age group—we use different activities and language for children, teens, and adults, and adaptation by age is a topic discussed later in this chapter. It's also good to ponder the motivations that bring people to group. Best of all are inner motivations—shy people wanting to be more outgoing, fat people wanting to be thinner, smokers wanting to stop the habit. But some group members are extrinsically motivated—that is, the courts, schools, families, bosses, or spouses have insisted that they attend the group. When we lead groups made up totally or partly of coerced members, we need to put early efforts into igniting some inner motivations as well, such as emphasizing the better quality of life members will enjoy through learning from the group. Often, the group is at least better than the alternative (like jail or divorce).

Leaders need to consider the probable backgrounds members bring into the group with them. How much do they already know about the subject? When I go to a session at a counseling conference, I am put off when the presenter dwells too long on information that is thoroughly taught in standard counselor training—I want to hear something new. Alternatively, you may have an audience that knows very little about your subject matter, and you need a method to gauge where to begin. Group leaders often collect questionnaires for this purpose at the first session, so that from the second session on they can adjust their level of presentation.

We also need to find out what needs to be *unlearned* among our group members. Many people have misconceptions about the problem they are experiencing. For instance, the children in the ADHD group in the selection you read might have thought that their disorder would impair them in school and work life, and much of the psychoeducation consisted of proving that this notion is not necessarily true. Like members joining any counseling group, yours bring with them some anxieties and defenses. If you can determine in advance what these might be, you can address them early and make learning more effective. For example, people coming to an anger management group can be expected to have more hostility than others, on average. How can you prepare to deal with this?

DISCUSSION IDEA

Assume that you are a school counselor planning a self-control group for adolescents with behavior problems in school. Their teachers have encouraged, but not required, these teens to come to your group. What knowledge, background, and attitudes can you reasonably predict? Discuss some tactics that you might use to increase your members' acceptance of the group they have joined.

Concepts Derived from Social Learning Theory

Mary Cover Jones, under John Watson's supervision in 1924, is known for the first experimental use of modeling in the removal of anxiety. The researchers worked with a child named Peter who had many objects of fear including white rats, rabbits, and fur coats. Jones had Peter observe other children playing happily with rabbits; they served as models and showed that there was nothing to fear from bunnies. Jones later added counterconditioning to the systematic program, and Peter was freed from most of his fears. Modeling—watching others perform a feared act comfortably—is still a major technique of psychoeducational group counseling, used not only in eliminating phobias but in assertiveness training and social skills improvement, too.

Modeling is also a major force in the natural learning process. Albert Bandura (1986) described **social learning theory,** which adds the influence of thought processes to stimulus-response-reinforcement theory. He emphasized, for example, that to learn something, it helps

- ▪ if you are paying attention,
- ▪ if you are able to remember it,
- ▪ if you have some motivation to learn it,
- ▪ if you believe you are capable of learning it (self-efficacy),
- ▪ and if you have some reason to believe you will benefit from learning it (outcome expectations).

Notice that these are not strictly observable behaviors. They mostly seem to take place within an individual. Bandura later (2001) changed the name of his theory to **social cognitive theory,** further emphasizing the mental activities involved, such as attention and motivation. From a social cognitive point of view, successful modeling also involves other inner factors, like whether you admire the person who serves as a model and whether you perceive her as similar to you. Social cognitive theory holds true not only for specific skills like driving a car and baking bread, but for learning complex, unstated rules. Bandura (1974) noted that people change "their judgmental orientations, conceptual schemes, linguistic styles, information-processing strategies, as well as other forms of cognitive functioning" based on observing other people (p. 864). The changes a person undergoes in joining a cult are dramatic examples. On the positive side, healthy changes after joining a counseling group can stem from modeling after other members and following group norms. Bandura's quotation underlines the fact that these changes are far more than skin deep.

When you review the basic dynamics of group counseling in Chapter 2 of this text, you will see that social cognitive theory informs group work from the ground up.

Reflections

All of us have experienced modeling in the groups we belong to. Describe a time when you found a model in an educational setting, a person or set of persons who altered your behavior, thoughts, or learning through your observation of them rather than through direct instruction. I have a friend who recounts big changes in his personality and point of view when he joined a set-building crew and began to hang around with the theater crowd in high school, for instance. Unfortunately, we don't always adopt positive models. Have you ever found yourself following the patterns of a negative model? What happened?

Problem Solving

Many psychoeducational therapies can be seen as *problem-solving* enhancements, if we define *problem* as a situation or set of situations "which, by virtue of their novel aspects, complexities, ambiguities, or conflicting stimulus demands, present circumstances that involve the failure of 'automatic' effective action" (D'Zurilla & Goldfried, 1971). Psychological distress decreases a person's ability to concentrate, recall, and reason (Beck, Rush, Shaw, & Emery, 1979), which are all needed to define a problem and think up a variety of potentially effective responses to choose from. Furthermore, some people have developed their approaches to problems in a faulty way, according to social information-processing theory (Foster & Crain, 2002). Faulty processing leads to deviant or maladaptive social behaviors, including aggression.

Problem-solving groups teach people a thoughtful, step-by-step way to approach situations. Foster and Crain (2002) describe a children's group that teaches members to

(1) identify problem situations;

(2) stop and think when confronted by a problem situation;

(3) define the nature of the problem;

(4) generate ideas for how to solve the problem;

(5) evaluate the ideas and pick the idea most likely to produce positive outcomes and minimize negative outcomes; and

(6) plan and implement the idea behaviorally. (p. 40)

Adult problem-solving models are similar. Systematic problem solving is taught in cutting-edge treatments of eating disorders, following the same six steps as above (Agras & Apple, 2002).

When I first learned this approach in my counselor training, I thought it seemed blatantly obvious to anyone. However, in my years of practice, I have seen a surprising number of people who lack any logical system when confronted with problems. Learning such a system is life-changing for many kinds of troubled people. O'Donohue and Noll (1995) list twenty-eight published applications of problem-solving skills with a wide range of problems, including depression, headaches, obesity, classroom management, and closed-head injuries.

A psychoeducational group seeks to prepare a person to deal with day-to-day problems in general (D'Zurilla & Goldfried, 1971). This means that the members are prepared with a course of action when they meet new problems and challenges. Because of transfer of training, even specifically targeted groups (like smoking cessation) can engender improved handling of a variety of other situations (De Corte, 2003). You can imagine the children in the ADHD group applying the strategies from the group at home, even though the focus was on the school setting.

Group Dynamics

Many accounts of the stages of psychoeducational group development and the dynamics associated with each stage follow the process I have described for groups in general (e.g., Brown, 1998; Rodway, 1992).

Stages of the Group

In early stages, the leader takes responsibility for explaining what is expected from the group, providing instruction, and helping build cohesion. In middle stages, the group takes on an active role and has meaningful relationships within it. Members cooperate and are supportive. In the middle stages of some groups, interpersonal conflicts and anger toward the leader arise. (However, in psychoeducational groups the conflictual elements may be muted or absent; the ADHD group you read about is an example.) Finally, every group goes through termination. Psychoeducational groups usually include some evaluation activities during termination, which help bring closure through reflection on what happened. The leader plans ahead for the last stage, even in a one-day workshop, and attempts to make sure that members don't feel suddenly booted out.

Structured and Unstructured Components

A major distinction of psychoeducational groups is that they are structured by some external content, which the leader brings in. These groups often move from highly structured, leader-centered beginnings to less structured, member-centered endings. A good example comes from a men's group at a campus–community counseling center (Hetzel, Barton, & Davenport, 1994). The group ran for ten two-hour sessions, one a week. The first six sessions consisted of presentations and exercises, each week on a single theme: masculinity, emotions, work and identity, sexuality and intimacy, and family of origin (two sessions). In the last four sessions, the focus was on issues raised by the members and on their relationships with each other. They experimented with giving and receiving feedback on how others perceived them. In other words, the second set of sessions was like the humanist groups discussed in Part III of this textbook. The themes from the first six meetings were developed by the leaders, from reading literature about men's issues and from topics that came up while screening members for the group. The structured nature of the first part of the group helped the men get to know each other in a safe, managed setting so that they could later take the risks of a more open, uncontrollable setting.

In this example, two thirds of the sessions were externally structured, whereas one third were internally driven. Other psychoeducational groups have different proportions. Some never have the unstructured component, such as the ADHD group you are now familiar with. Some devote more time to interpersonal sharing and self-disclosure, as a twelve-session group for chronically lonely people did (Rodway, 1992). This group used their answers to a questionnaire about loneliness as a springboard for writing and discussing life areas where social interactions occurred, brainstorming about tactics to increase social interaction, and reporting the results of their efforts outside of the group. Thus, the fifty-five-item questionnaire was the sole educational device. A group for families of Alzheimer's sufferers split each session in half, with 50 percent structured didactic presentations and 50 percent open discussion of participants' experiences and problems (Glosser & Wexler, 1985).

Multiple Relationships in Groups

Counselman and Weber (1994) consider the problematic group dynamics that occur when an outsider leads a psychoeducational group within an institution, like a school or corporation. Some natural suspicion is aroused, as members wonder whether there is an organizational agenda being engineered. Furthermore, a group in which the members see each other all week in other settings will have different dynamics than one is which their only contact is the group. Brown (1998) discusses these concerns as **boundary issues** and suggests the following topics be included in early sessions:

- What topics members and the leader can discuss with people not in the group, and under what conditions.
- What material should not be discussed with people not in the group.
- What group content can be talked about between members in the group when they are outside the group (i.e., socializing).
- What data the leader has to share with other professionals, and in what form (i.e., with or without personal identifying data).
- What use will be made of the information shared by the members. (p. 66)

Note that you have come across the concept of boundaries twice before: in the description of various intragroup boundaries (Chapter 1, Figure 1.1), and in the Gestalt concept of boundary disturbances (Chapter 11). In all these senses, boundaries give us a useful image of where and how lines are drawn around individuals and groups, distinguishing them from surrounding environments just as boundaries on a map distinguish geographical areas from their surroundings.

Leadership Skills

Psychoeducational groups resemble coursework, with more than the usual dose of attention to feelings and self-expression. So, the good teacher and the good psychoeducational group leader have many qualities and skills in common. One prerequisite is a solid grasp of the target content, whether it be male socialization, nicotine addiction, or child aggression. As the leader, you need to know the content beyond what you plan to teach so that you can answer questions with confidence, change track when necessary, and feel comfortable in all discussions. Many organizations provide prepackaged psychoeducational materials and plans, but merely knowing what is in the package, such as a workbook, is not enough and leaves you on shaky ground. As an analogy, think of all the knowledge you use when you follow a recipe, knowledge that isn't included in the recipe's instructions. Measurement of ingredients, choosing kitchen utensils, timing of operations, and organizing your process are background skills you need for confidence and success.

Clarity

Clear presentation will never lose its charm. William Blake, the eighteenth-century poet, wrote that if the truth is told clearly, it will be believed. I agree. First, clear goals and objectives for psychoeducational groups come from you, the leader. Group members suffer when what they expected to gain is not what they got, as researchers found in unsuccessful marital enrichment groups that did not have the expected focus (Ripley & Worthington, 2002). Though you will solicit individual members' goals and accommodate all that you can, your main concern is eliciting agreement about the original objectives and how they will be met. This includes technical matters like promptness and attendance rules, number and length of sessions, amount of outside work, and bringing in food and drinks.

Making the educational material clear is your teaching task. This includes knowing the content, organizing it so that it's easily followed, and having plenty of examples and illustrations on hand. Papers that you hand out and images you project on a screen should be understandable, not confusing. For many psychoeducational groups, materials will come to you already designed with educational principles taken into account. Still, you need to be able to evaluate their instructional quality and correctness. For instance, providing children with handouts containing spelling errors is a serious disservice.

You also need to be clear when giving instructions for the exercises and activities you ask your group to do. For instance, if I were to say, "In your small group, come up with an example of a parent-toddler conflict," some members might think that each person in the group should come up with an example, and some might think that the whole group has to think of only one example. Test-drive your instructions on a friend or family member to see whether there is any ambiguity in them. Giving clear corrections while group members are actively practicing, such as reminding someone to make eye contact, requires your keen attention (Shean, 1985).

Finally, develop a clear closing summary of the session. Members should leave with a satisfying sense of accomplishment and direction.

Communication Skills

Brown (1998) suggests that you use a checklist to consider your communication style. See the box "Effective Verbal Communication Behavior" for his list (Communication Checklist from Brown, 1998, p. 48). Record your own ratings

Effective Verbal Communication Behavior

Directions: Rate yourself on the items below using the following scale:

5 = I do this most of the time or all the time.
4 = I do this often.
3 = I do this sometimes; more often than not.
2 = I seldom do this.
1 = I do this little or not at all.

1. Restate what others say without parroting	5	4	3	2	1
2. Restate what others say without adding to the meaning	5	4	3	2	1
3. Make clearer what others mean in what they say	5	4	3	2	1
4. Check with others to ensure clear understanding	5	4	3	2	1
5. Focus on underlying feelings	5	4	3	2	1
6. Focus on underlying issues	5	4	3	2	1
7. Bring conflicting thoughts/feelings into focus	5	4	3	2	1
8. Identify commonalities between self and others	5	4	3	2	1
9. Combine, tie together or identify themes in verbal interactions	5	4	3	2	1
10. Ask questions only for information, not to get my point across	5	4	3	2	1
11. Seek not to bombard others with questions	5	4	3	2	1
12. Make more statements than questions in conversations	5	4	3	2	1
13. Focus my questions on "what" and "how," rather than on "why"	5	4	3	2	1
14. Allow others to express difficult feelings without interrupting	5	4	3	2	1
15. Let others interpret their behavior	5	4	3	2	1
16. Reflect feelings accurately	5	4	3	2	1
17. Sense what feelings others are trying to express	5	4	3	2	1
18. Refrain from giving advice	5	4	3	2	1
19. Provide concrete feedback to others they can use	5	4	3	2	1
20. Am comfortable with silence	5	4	3	2	1

of each item, and ask someone who knows your interaction style well to rate you independently. The answers will make you aware of habits you want to keep, increase, or change, as well as whether others see you the same way you see yourself when you communicate.

Give some thought to how you ask and receive questions because these will be major communication skills in your group. Let your group know that you welcome questions and make a point of demonstrating this early, or they will not believe it. Identify a spot in your presentation that involves opinions, personal experiences, definitions, or making distinctions between one thing and another.

Invite questions and comments and wait for one to come—it will, though it may seem like forever to you. Pause before answering a question, and repeat it if it's complex, to be sure you're answering what was asked. If you can't answer, say so, and indicate how you or the group member can find the answer. If you don't want to answer because it would take too long or divert focus, indicate when you will be able to discuss the matter in the future. For instance, you might say, "I was hoping someone would bring that up. It's an important topic we'll take it up in depth next week," and give a very brief preview.

DISCUSSION IDEA

Observe instances in which your professors field questions from students in all your classes for a few days. Take notes on how they do this. Discuss with the class some of the teachers' methods for dealing with questions and whether they are well received by students.

Creativity

Good educators are creative. They think of unusual and varied ways to get across their points. They find connections that reverberate with their audience's experience. For instance, those of you who cook probably responded well to my connection between wide background knowledge and following a recipe.

Even when your curriculum is prepackaged, things don't always go as planned. Projector bulbs burn out, the copier eats the originals, no one has their homework, you forget something you need, the energy level hits a new low. Your creativity comes in at these times, when you have to shift activities and still achieve the goals for the day. A sense of humor comes in handy. So does a grab-bag of substitute activities that can be done with few or no props.

One aspect of creative effort that is rarely acknowledged is research ability. Do you know how to use the Internet to find information and teaching tips on your topics? Where is your closest library, and what kind of materials relevant to your groups are held there? What are the major reference works in your topic's general area? Finally, who might you call or e-mail that can give you an authoritative answer to a question? These are all creative approaches to developing your group work.

SMALL GROUP EXERCISE

Pretend that your discussion group has been assigned to collect materials for a psychoeducational group on one of the following topics:

Masculinity

Menopause

School-to-work transitions for graduating high school seniors

Shyness

Career choice

Brainstorm about how you will go about developing a body of information and resources about your topic, then divvy up the tasks and do the research. Work together to organize the materials into a psychoeducational group plan. Present your plan to other discussion groups or the class as a whole, or send it around through e-mail.

_____

Knowledge of Process

A psychoeducational group is still a group, and your knowledge of group process will be valuable. Understanding how the group is feeling through interpreting their body language, comments, and silences is crucial. You will be practicing the following skills, in particular:

Linking Drawing together several comments by group members to show their commonalities

Blocking Protecting one or more group members through stopping some damaging behavior in group (such as monopolizing the floor or insisting on misinformation)

Supporting Encouraging, reinforcing, and affirming group members; assisting members when they need it and cheering them on when they can succeed without the assistance

Evaluating Letting group members know how well they are doing and specifying what could be improved

Personality

Some skills in leading psychoeducational groups, as with humanistic groups, are matters of personal traits as much as anything else. A rigid, authoritarian streak tends to turn off psychoeducational group members as well as to hinder leaders when the unexpected occurs, as it is bound to do. Extroversion helps a leader enjoy participating in the psychoeducational process. However, many introverts are also successful in the endeavor and blossom within the structured process, finding it more comfortable than an unstructured interpersonal situation. Openness to experience allows counselors to relish the process of learning new content material and developing resources on the topic.

Fiedler (1972), in a **contingency model,** postulated that the effectiveness of a group or organization depended on two variables, which interact: the motivation system of the leader and the favorableness of the group situation.

- Leaders are divided into task-motivated and relationship-motivated types, according to whether task accomplishment or relationships with people are their main source of satisfaction.

▣ Groups are most favorable when the task is structured, the leader–member relations are good, and the leader's position is strong, and groups are least favorable when the task is unstructured, the leader–member relations are poor, and the leader's position is weak. By "position," Fiedler meant the amount of power and influence the leader holds from the beginning. A well-known community figure has more position power than a graduate-student counseling trainee.

Task-motivated leaders perform best in either most favorable or least favorable situations. At the unfavorable extreme, at least the task gets done quickly. At the favorable extreme, relationships are already affable, and the group needs help staying on task. Relationship-motivated leaders perform best in the intermediate ranges of favorableness. They build the team cohesiveness necessary to deal with the ambiguities of the situation. Therefore, Fiedler thought it inaccurate to think of good leaders and bad leaders, and better to consider what leaders perform well under what circumstances. Using the contingency model, you can estimate when you will be at your best as a leader, by analyzing where the group falls on continuums of task structure, leader–member relations, and leader's strength of position. If you are a well-liked clinic supervisor leading a psychoeducational group on time management, being task-motivated suits the situation, which is highly favorable. If you are a new colleague leading a psychoeducational group on work styles, this is an intermediately favorable situation, and being relationship-motivated suits the setting.

Techniques in Psychoeducational Group Counseling

Psychoeducational group counseling is distinctive in that process and content are so closely entwined that they are often indistinguishable. In fact, eight group work experts diverged in their definitions of process and content in the psychoeducational setting, and they also failed to agree when coding process and content episodes in tapes of children's psychoeducational groups in school (Geroski & Kraus, 2002). Thus, techniques blend process and content as well.

Modeling and Coaching

Through modeling, we acquire new behaviors by observing and imitating others (Borgen & Rudner, 1981). This happens naturally and coincidentally in everyday life, but counselors make planned applications of the principle. Counselors use live models, sometimes themselves, in teaching skills (like assertiveness) and reducing fears. Modeling is used extensively in behavior therapy groups. For example, Ost, Stridh, and Wolf (1998) devised a group treatment for spider phobia in which the therapist approaches and handles spiders, assists a group member in doing the same with her spiders while the others watch, and then instructs all the members to approach and handle their spiders with the assistance of other members and the therapist. In this way, clients at lower levels of anxiety can act as models for more anxious clients. This is called **participant modeling.** In pyschoeducational groups, when live models are not possible, **symbolic**

models may be used, such as characters in films, cartoons, and books. Children going through parents' divorces are given books that portray how child characters cope with the situation. We use symbolic models with adults, too, when we recommend novels or films with characters who cope with a problem similar to our clients'. Joshua and DiMenna's (2000) *Read Two Books and Let's Talk Next Week: Using Bibliotherapy in Clinical Practice* is a good source.

Coaching is a direct teaching technique that includes modeling (Elliott, Gresham, & Heffer, 1987). The leader presents the rationale and rules for an appropriate behavior. Then, the behavior is practiced with the coach and with other group members. The coach-leader provides feedback during and after the practice. You can see why this method is named after sports training. (*Coaching* is also a term for a specific type of counseling that resembles sports training. The clients determine the goals of the counseling, and coaches help them pursue those goals. Interpretation, confrontation, and character change are not emphasized. See *www.lifecoachtraining.com* for information on this type of counseling).

Role-Playing

Practicing behavior in sessions, as in the coaching process described above, is **role-playing.** Shean (1985) describes it as "having a person step into a role or situation which requires use of the skill being studied" (p. 27) within the group session. The principle behind role-playing is that merely understanding a skill is not enough; practice is what makes a skill our own. Like any technique, role-playing needs to be introduced early in the group's life, with easy, nonthreatening assignments. For instance, I was in a training group once in which we interviewed the member next to us and then role-played introducing them to the group as though we were talk show hosts introducing them on television. This simple, humorous role-play prepared us for enacting more serious roles later in the group.

DISCUSSION IDEA

Take five minutes to jot down an example of something you have learned through participant modeling, symbolic modeling, coaching, or role playing. Why was the technique effective in your case? Were there other learners who did not learn from the technique? Why not? Participate as volunteers share their examples and thoughts.

Homework

After successful activities within the group session, members are prepared to transfer their learning to everyday life outside. Thus, they are given homework assignments, usually requiring that they practice at home, school, or work. Exactly when it is appropriate to apply a new skill or enact a new behavior is a

An Example Rationale for Saying "Thank You"

1. It tells others you appreciate their behavior.
2. It makes others want to say or to do nice things for you again.
3. Adults are happy with you because you were polite.
4. You are proud of yourself for "doing the right thing."

Steps	Remarks
Knowing if someone has done something to deserve a "thank-you"	When someone gives you a compliment, gift, or favor
Knowing the right time and place to say "thank you"	Usually right after someone gives you a compliment, gift, or favor
Knowing the right way to say "thank you" to someone	Use words and, maybe, give them a compliment, gift, or favor later, and/or write them a thank-you note
Knowing how to say "thank you" to someone	Sound friendly, smile, use words that indicate you are sincere, and tell them why you appreciate what they did for you

Role-Play Situations
1. At school when a classmate likes your drawings.
2. On the playground when a friend helps you carry the equipment.
3. At home when a neighbor comes to visit you (because you are ill or just to play).
4. At home when a family member gives you a gift.

Homework Assignments
1. Say "thank you" to your neighborhood friends and family members.
2. Notice what people do when you say "thank you" to them.

judgment call that can only be learned through experience in the real world. The leader can prepare members to choose appropriate timing, but their successes and failures in everyday life will fine-tune their sense of rightness (Shean, 1985). For example, shy people who have learned self-disclosure with humor within the group might attempt this tactic outside when other people are busy or preoccupied, which would not occur within sessions. Assessment of the homework experience back in the group will help them adapt the tactic to the situation.

"Thank you!": A Sample Intervention An example of an intervention for children appears in the box "An Example Rationale for Saying 'Thank You'" (Elliott, Gresham, & Heffer, 1987, p. 155). This plan shows how rationale, modeling, coaching, role-playing, and homework can be integrated.

Looking at Happiness

Directions: Please read each question and give yourself a few minutes to think about your response before writing it down.

1. Think about your parents or guardians. How do you know when they are feeling happy?

   _____

2. What are some specific things that (you think) make them happy?

   _____

3. How do you feel when they are feeling good? Why?

   _____

4. Think about other people in your life: friends, siblings, or relatives. How do you know when they are happy?

   _____

5. List ways these people have positively affected the way you think and act.

   _____

Classroom Strategies

Not all psychoeducational material can be taught through modeling, coaching, and role-plays (Shean, 1985). For instance, some content involves thinking and remembering and analyzing, not behavior, and it cannot be acted out. Techniques from classroom learning are integrated into psychoeducational groups for this material. They include written exercises, games, structured discussions, drawing, and movement activities. All are designed to clarify a concept or consolidate memory of a concept.

The Activity Sheet "Looking at Happiness" from *Group Exercises for Enhancing Social Skills and Self-Esteem* (Khalsa, 1996, p. 34) exemplifies a classroom strategy for preparing young people to have a structured discussion. The goals are "to increase awareness of role models for personal happiness, to gain an understanding of what makes people feel happy, and to explore how people can positively affect each other" (p. 33). After filling out the sheet, volunteers read their answers and the group discusses them.

Another technique, especially useful during a lecture, is to provide a printed main-topic outline of the lecture, with spaces for group members to take notes below each topic. This helps them grasp the organization of the material and relationships among the topics. Think about appealing to various learning styles and skills, not depending completely on verbal modes. In a leadership training day I attended, we were put in groups of four or five people, given markers and shelf paper, and asked to make a group drawing that represented the ideal leader. Then we displayed our drawings and explained them to the other groups. Psychodrama, explained in Part VI, can make use of the acting skills of group members in portraying the situation of one member, who serves as the director of the drama. These can be done in charades if you want to deemphasize verbal agility.

In the next section, you will read about more specific classroom techniques used for targeted problems.

Problems Addressed by Psychoeducational Groups

Psychoeducational groups address such a wide range of problems that they are difficult to corral in one short discussion. You have read about several examples so far. I have chosen a few broad categories (which unavoidably overlap) in the following sections: correction of knowledge and skill deficits; fear reduction, including systematic desensitization and assertiveness training; and self-management.

Knowledge and Skill Deficits

One theoretical basis for psychoeducational interventions goes this way: Social situations arise regularly in life in which an individual must be able to respond in a competent manner, if he or she is to achieve some goal (maintaining good health, raising normal children, keeping a job). Some individuals are deficient in the knowledge and skills necessary to respond competently, and this failure has various negative outcomes (depression, frustration, loneliness, illness, violence). These individuals can profit from an educational experience in which their deficits are directly addressed and remediated (O'Donohue & Krasner, 1995). Competence includes both declarative knowledge (accurate information) and procedural knowledge (how-tos).

Babies' healthy cognitive and emotional development hinges on appropriate responsiveness by their caregivers, usually their parents. Many psychoeducational interventions aim to teach parents about infant development (declarative knowledge) and to train them in behaving responsively (procedural knowledge) (Barclay & Houts, 1995). The facts taught concern how babies grow through interchanges with their parents and caregivers. The actions practiced include maintaining eye contact, face-to-face positioning with the baby, and vocal imitations. Most families can benefit from this kind of psychoeducation. A more intensive form is helpful for parents who need to reduce their use of verbal and corporal punishment, because this punishment has proven links to child behavior problems (e.g., Nicholson, Anderson, Fox, & Brenner, 2002).

Many other social skills are targets of psychoeducational groups, assisting people who want to maintain or improve their love relationships (Halford,

2002), veterans who need to develop good support networks (Greene et al., 2004), and children whose peers reject them (Foster & Crain, 2002).

Reaching personal goals often requires accruing accurate facts. Healthy lifestyles involve wisdom about nutrition, eating habits, and activity levels, and smokers are helped to quit by understanding health risks and the nature of addiction (Greene et al., 2004). Coping with illnesses like diabetes, multiple sclerosis, and arthritis can be promoted through education about what to expect and what other people with the disease have done to achieve full lives (Elliott, Rivera, & Tucker, 2004).

Assertiveness Training

As we discussed in Chapter 12, relaxation is a good counterconditioner for anxiety about objects and situations that are difficult or damaging to avoid, such as riding in elevators, going out in public, and visiting the dentist. The situations remain the same after therapy, only the client doesn't find them as distressing. But some anxiety-producing situations *can* be changed by the client's activity, especially interpersonal situations. In these situations, *assertiveness* rather than relaxation acts as a counterconditioner to anxiety. "Actively expressing admiration, irritation, and appropriate anger can inhibit anxieties over rejection, embarrassment, and possible failure" (Prochaska & Norcross, 1999, p. 281). Here are some occasions that call for assertiveness:

A friend asks you to do a favor that will be a big burden for you.

Your dinner guests keep staying long after you are ready to go to bed.

At a restaurant, your food is served cold when it should be hot.

You feel a surge of affection for your best friend.

Your doctor ends the appointment before you've asked all your questions.

You hold an opinion different from everyone else's in the room, while everyone acts as though you agree with them.

Your adult daughter house-sits while you are on vacation and buys $300 worth of clothes on your credit card.

What would you do in these cases? Chances are, in some cases you would *assert* yourself by expressing your feelings; and in some cases you would feel uncomfortable asserting yourself but do it anyway; and in some you would not assert yourself at all. Some of you might even respond aggressively in some cases, such as yelling at the waitress, writing a nasty note to your daughter, or saying something sarcastic to your friend. Most people vary between situations in their level of assertiveness.

Be sure to think about a client's cultural status in terms of the level and context of assertiveness. Many Asian-American women wish to shake off the deference that keeps them from asserting themselves in the Western world, whereas others see it as essential to their femininity. People who work under White male authority, such as women and minorities, must learn very sophisticated modes of assertiveness to avoid being labeled pushy or considered threatening.

Reflections

In what situations do you feel perfectly confident asserting yourself? Do you have more trouble expressing negative or positive feelings? Can you think of a situation in which you wish you had asserted yourself more? Why did you choose not to at the time? Do you ever pattern your behavior after someone else's when you are feeling unconfident in a certain situation?

When a person's work life, relationships, or leisure time is undermined because he or she is not assertive enough, group therapy can help. **Assertiveness training** helps clients learn social skills they need to express themselves appropriately, neither submissively nor aggressively. It assists them in untangling themselves from overdependent and exploitive relationships.

Assertion training often proceeds by role-playing in therapy groups and getting feedback on one's behavior. Suggestions on how to phrase a strong feeling and how to persist in the face of discouragement come from other members of the group or the therapist, and the practice sessions serve as desensitizers. As in other desensitization procedures, often a client works through a hierarchy of assertive behaviors, from the most difficult to the least, in a certain area. For example, a woman who has trouble refusing time with her boyfriend might start with "Telling my boyfriend I need to be home by midnight on Saturday night" as the easiest task and "Telling my boyfriend I want to go out with my girlfriends on Saturday night" as the hardest. Another member of the group would play the boyfriend, with some direction about how the real person might act.

A cognitive component of assertiveness training is crucial, though it is behavior that must change ultimately. Frequently we hold beliefs that make us unassertive, and these need to be challenged. In the best-selling self-help assertiveness book *When I Say No, I Feel Guilty* (Smith, 1975), the reader is encouraged to adopt a "Bill of Assertive Rights," including "You have the right to judge your own behavior, thoughts, and emotions, and to take the responsibility for their initiation and consequences upon yourself" and "You have the right to change your mind." Assertiveness training is used in combination with other group treatments for depression, eating disorders, agoraphobia, obsessive-compulsive disorders, and sexual problems (Bergin & Garfield, 1994) because these problems often have a component of conflict avoidance.

Self-Management

Sometimes a goal of a group is to achieve specific kinds of **self-management,** so that the therapy sessions are no longer needed. Hospital nurses, school counselors, and psychologists advise patients in groups in how to comply with medical directions, control pain, cope with dietary restrictions, and stick to exercise programs. People who have suffered heart attacks, for example, always go through a course of group therapy that helps them maintain heart-healthy lifestyles. This type of approach is often very brief, including as few as one to five sessions. Frequently, these groups grow emotionally close and act as support systems far longer than the brief psychoeducational treatment lasts. Groups of students first attending college are offered brief orientation courses or study skills workshops that give them tips for developing good habits at school. These are interventions with self-management goals.

As school counselors know, the classroom lends itself to self-management strategies because the students learn to administer the intervention to themselves (Mace, Brown, & West, 1987). For example, when I was in grade school we learned the SQ3R method of studying (survey, question, read, review, recite), which was a way of directing our own textbook learning. With this method, the teacher was freed from leading the class through each of the steps. Students can also learn to reward themselves for good class performance, again easing the teacher's load. Research supports the effectiveness of self-management interventions in schools for improving spelling, handwriting, and mathematics; decreasing aggression, disruption, tardiness, and anxiety; increasing positive social behavior; and improving the performance of teachers and administrators (Mace et al., 1987).

As rehabilitation counselors know, clients with substantial learning disabilities can hold down mainstream jobs if they learn self-management skills to regulate their work performance (Rusch, Hughes, & Wilson, 1995). For example, workers who can't tell time can learn to use pictures of clock faces to match to the workplace clock so they can take their breaks and lunch at the right times without being told. They can also learn self-talk methods of leading themselves through a series of steps in job tasks, learn how to keep records of their production, and learn the procedures for handling unexpected situations and emotions. Through psychoeducation, these people can function in a range of jobs, when without it they would require sheltered work settings.

Self-management in the form of anger control has helped men reduce or eliminate violence toward their partners (Brownlee & Chlebovec, 2004). Group members learned skills like identifying their "red flags," listening better, stress reduction, taking "time out," and positive self-talk. These skills helped men maintain relationships and keep out of jail, and they most likely generalize to other settings like work and friendships.

Though many of us are able to learn self-management skills on our own, many people benefit from having a counselor and group guide them at first. The fact that we are responsible for almost all of our own behavior is scary, and the belief that we are capable of controlling our situations and actions must be instilled for behavior therapy to work (Kanfer & Gaelick-Buys, 1991). Psychoeducational group leaders are careful to discourage being seen as miracle workers because that just fosters the dependency they are trying to eliminate. A conviction of self-efficacy (that is, capability to organize one's behavior and perform adequately) is the best guarantee of ongoing ability "to manage ever changing circumstances, most of which contain ambiguous, unpredictable, and often stressful elements" (Bandura, 1986, p. 391) and may be the best predictor of happiness (Day & Rottinghaus, 2004). The support and examples that groups provide help reassure each member that they can attain self-efficacy.

R e f l e c t i o n s

Consider a content area within your own expertise that could be applied to a psychoeducational group intervention. For instance, I used my experience as a writer when I designed my group for blocked dissertation writers. Be creative; your special skills could come in at any level of the intervention. If you are good at arts and crafts, you could integrate them into exercises for a children's social skills group.

Adaptations to Clients' Ages

Psychoeducational groups were originally designed primarily for school-age children, though now they have been extended to the full range of ages (Gelso & Fretz, 2001). A 1990s survey reported the most frequent group topics in each school setting (Dansby, 1996):

> Elementary school: Self-Concept/Self-Esteem, Behavior (including conflict resolution and anger control), Friendship, Study Skills, and Single Parent/Divorce.

> Middle school: Decision Making, Self-Concept/Self-Esteem, Career, Study Skills, Behavior, and Transition to New School or Grade.

> High school: Planning for College, Career, Decision-Making, Self-Concept/Self-Esteem, Study Skills.

Life Skills Training for seventh graders is a popular preventive group intervention, which teaches decision making, coping, self-management, communication, assertiveness, and resisting peer and media pressures (Foster & Crain, 2002). Research indicates that this type of psychoeducation lowers the use of tobacco, alcohol, and illegal drugs, whereas most programs directly targeted at curtailing drug use, such as D.A.R.E., have been ineffective.

Psychoeducational groups are also gaining popularity at the other end of the life span. This approach has been used to support psychological well-being in the elderly in spite of physical degeneration, through education about how to increase rewarding life events while minimizing aversive ones (Housley, 1992). A program for depressed and anxious elderly inpatients in Australia aimed to help group members identify and label their feelings, and included progressive muscle relaxation, meditation, guided imagery, and breathing techniques (Moffatt, Mohr, & Ames, 1995). Instruction in increasing pleasant events and positive, rational thinking was also given.

Another group intervention actually reversed age-related declines in pro-spective memory (remembering to carry out planned activities) (Villa & Abeles, 2000). Prospective memory improvement has a definite positive effect on daily functioning for the elderly, enabling them to follow medication regimens, keep appointments, pay their bills, make plans with friends, and so forth. A seven-session psychoeducational workshop included lessons on the impact of mood on memory, mnemonics, relaxation training, self-management, and rational thinking, with significant pre- to post-test improvement on the Prospective Memory Screening Test (PROMS). Clearly, psychoeducational groups for the elderly focus on enhancing the quality of life in the present, in contrast with school-age groups that are more concerned with preparation for the future.

Besides addressing homogeneous age groups, psychoeducation brings different generations together for a common cause. Families with physically and psychologically distressed members participate in programs teaching about the disorder, its course, the medicines involved, and management. In a notable intervention for families of mood-disordered children and adolescents, families learn to be the patient's support and therapy team (Fristad, Gavazzi, Centolella, & Soldano, 1996). Single- or multiple-family groups are taught to reduce the levels of stress, tension, and distraught emotionality in their homes through didactic sessions. Because children with distressed mood are at large risk of developing adult psychopathology and substance abuse, these psychoeducational interventions are meaningful preventive efforts.

Evaluating Psychoeducational Groups

Reviewing research on similar interventions, Fristad and colleagues (1996) proposed evaluating the effectiveness of pyschoeducational interventions with families of hospitalized patients by comparing how many patients are rehospitalized for the disorder, with or without the family program, at a given follow-up point (like two years). If the patients with families in the program have significantly fewer relapses than the patients whose families are not in the program, the program can be considered effective. This is an example of evaluation tied to external evidence. Many psychoeducational groups have measurable goals that serve as evaluation benchmarks: rates of recidivism for violent spouses, episodes of class disruption for children, pounds gained or lost, or percentages of people who quit smoking or drinking.

Especially when you need to report the amount of change your groups produce, you will want to use standardized tests and rating scales before and after group intervention. These have the advantage of being normed, so that you can compare your group, both at beginning and end, to the average for similar people or for the general population. At *www.uhl.edu/buros/*, you will find the Buros Institute for Mental Measurement, which provides links to test reviews online. You can ask for a list of tests by category (like "personality") or by key words (like "child depression"). Each test in the list is linked to a description of the test and a reference to reviews of the test, which appear in the *Mental Measurement Yearbook* (MMY), available in your library's reference section. In today's atmosphere of accountability, being able to present evidence from standardized testing is a boon.

On top of these external and standardized methods, you probably want to add some method of evaluating your intervention in particular. You may want to write an instrument tailored to your psychoeducational program. Brown (1998) advises starting from your original goals and objectives and writing ten to fifteen items asking members to rate the group in terms of structure, content, and leadership. The most common rating scale goes from 1 (poor) to 5 (excellent). You are familiar with this type of evaluation form from teacher evaluations in school. It's best to work from examples from other group workers who have refined their instruments. Many times, these are included in published treatment planners for your specific type of group (for example, *The Addiction Treatment Planner* [Perkinson & Jongsma, 2001]).

Rose (1988) summarized the methods of systematic data collection in groups as follows:

A. pre- and post-tests, self-rating scales, and inventories,

B. post-session and post-group questionnaires to be filled in by clients at the end of every session,

C. systematic observations of individuals in groups by trained observers,

D. post-session questionnaire for leaders,

E. homework assignments given and completed,

F. attendance and promptness records, and

G. self-monitoring recordings of clients' own behavior or cognitions. (p. 44)

SMALL GROUP EXERCISE

Choose a psychoeducational intervention that one (or more) members of your small group would like to facilitate. Using the suggestions above, locate three or four relevant evaluation methods. Brainstorm about the pros and cons of each one.

KEY TERMS

assertiveness training psychoeducation aimed at overcoming the fear of being outspoken in social situations

boundary issues concerns about what agendas are being pursued through the group, including who will have access to information shared in the group

coaching directly teaching a skill of the client's choice through demonstration, practice, and feedback

contingency model the leadership theory of Fiedler, which classifies leaders into task-motivated and relationship-motivated

developmental groups psychoeducational groups that teach people skills that are useful for their age and situation, yet missed somehow in their ordinary life

evaluating letting group members know how well they are doing and specifying what could be improved

participant modeling observation and imitation of other group members as they perform a task

preventive groups psychoeducational groups convened to avoid foreseeable problems

remedial groups psychoeducational groups that intervene to solve an existing problem and keep it from getting worse

role playing dramatic recreation of situations during group sessions, with members taking on assigned parts

self-management the ability to regulate and reward one's own behavior

self-referential learning applying knowledge to one's own present or past experience

social cognitive theory (formerly, social learning theory) Bandura's theory of the learning process, which adds the influence of thinking to stimulus-response-reinforcement theory

supporting encouraging, reinforcing, and affirming group members; assisting members when they need it and cheering them on when they can succeed without the assistance

symbolic modeling observation and imitation of people portrayed in films or books

transfer of training the ability to use knowledge and skills in settings other than the one they were learned in

CHAPTER REVIEW

1. How are psychoeducational groups similar to other counseling groups? How are they different?

2. Find at least three resources on Life Skills Training.

3. Review the six basic steps in problem solving. With a friend or classmate, think of a problem one of you now has, and practice going through the steps.

4. Why are people suspicious or wary when an outsider is brought in to lead a psychoeducational group? What could you do, as the outsider, to address these feelings?

5. Think of a great course you have taken. Jot down how the teaching of this course included active participation, self-referential learning, organization, variety, concreteness, and/or feedback.

6. Ask a person who knows you to fill out the ratings in the "Effective Verbal Communication Behavior" box as they apply to you. At the same time, make a copy of the rating sheet and fill it out for yourself. Are there differences between your ratings and your confederate's? Discuss your answers.

7. Pretend that you are leading a psychoeducational group and give a homework exercise. At the next session, no one has completed the homework. What do you do? Explain your reasoning.

8. Using PsycInfo or other research tools, find examples of psychoeducational interventions that fall under each of three goals: correction of knowledge and skill deficits, fear reduction, and self-management. Were the examples

you found directed at specified age groups? If so, how were they designed appropriately for these age groups?

FOR FURTHER READING

Brown, N. W. (1998). *Psychoeducational groups.* New York: Brunner-Routledge.

This short, easy-to-read volume covers principles and strategies of psychoeducational group leadership, using lists, tables, and brief discussions. Brown includes sample handouts and exercises for school success, social skills, and work-related groups. The handouts include statements of permission to photocopy for use in your groups.

REFERENCES

Agras, W. S., & Apple, R. F. (2002). Understanding and treating eating disorders. In F. W. Kaslow & T. Patterson (Eds.), *Comprehensive handbook of psychotherapy* (Vol. 2, pp. 189–212). New York: Wiley.

Association for Specialists in Group Work. (2000). *ASGW professional standards for group counseling.* Alexandria, VA: Author.

Bandura, A. (1974). Behavior theory and the models of man. *American Psychologist, 29,* 859–869.

Bandura, A. (1986). *Social foundations of thought and action.* Englewood Cliffs, NJ: Prentice-Hall.

Bandura, A. (2001). Social cognitive theory: An agentic perspective. *Annual Review of Psychology, 52,* 1–26.

Barclay, D. R., & Houts, A. C. (1995). Parenting skills: A review and developmental analysis of training content. In W. O'Donohue & L. Krasner (Eds.), *Handbook of psychological skills training* (pp. 195–228). Boston: Allyn & Bacon.

Beck, A. T., Rush, A. J., Shaw, B. F., & Emery, G. (1979). *Cognitive therapy of depression.* New York: Guilford Press.

Bergin, A. E., & Garfield, S. L. (1994). *Handbook of psychotherapy and behavior change* (4th ed.). New York: Wiley.

Brown, N. W. (1998). *Psychoeducational groups.* New York: Brunner-Routledge.

Brownlee, K., & Chlebovec, L. (2004). A group for men who abuse their partners: Participant perceptions of what was helpful. *American Journal of Orthopsychiatry, 74,* 209–213.

Counselman, E. R., & Weber, R. L. (1994). Leadership of mental health consultation groups: A model for group therapists. *International Journal of Group Psychotherapy, 44,* 349–360.

Dansby, V. S. (1996). Group work within the school system: Survey of implementation and leadership role issues. *Journal for Specialists in Group Work, 21,* 232–242.

Day, S. X, & Rottinghaus, P. (2004). The healthy personality. In B. Walsh (Ed.), *Counseling psychology and optimal human functioning* (pp. 1–25). Mahwah, NJ: Lawrence Erlbaum Associates.

Day, S. X, & Rottinghaus, P. (1998). The healthy personality. In B. Walsh (Ed.), *Counseling psychology and optimal human functioning* (pp. 1–23). Mahwah, NJ: Erlbaum.

De Corte, E. (2003). Transfer as the productive use of acquired knowledge, skills, and motivations. *Current Directions in Psychological Science, 12,* 142–150.

D'Zurilla, T. J., & Goldfried, M. R. (1971). Problem solving and behavior modification. *Journal of Abnormal Psychology, 78,* 107–126.

Elliot, T. R., Rivera, P., & Tucker, E. (2004). Groups in behavioral health and medical settings. In J. L. DeLucia-Waack, D. A. Gerrity, C. R. Kalodner, & M. T. Riva (Eds.), *Handbook of group counseling and psychotherapy* (pp. 338–350). Thousand Oaks, CA: Sage.

Elliott, S. N., Gresham, F. M., & Heffer, R. W. (1987). Social-skills interventions: Research findings and training techniques. In C. A. Maher & J. E. Zins (Eds.), *Psychoeducational interventions in the schools* (pp. 141–159). New York: Pergamon Press.

Fiedler, F. E. (1972). The effects of leadership training and experience: A contingency model interpretation. *Administrative Science Quarterly, 17,* 453–470.

Foster, S. L., & Crain, M. M. (2002). Social skills and problem-solving training. In F. W. Kaslow & T. Patterson (Eds.), *Comprehensive handbook of psychotherapy* (Vol. 2, pp. 31–50). New York: Wiley.

Fristad, M. A., Gavazzi, S. M., Centolella, D. M., & Soldano, K. W. (1996). Psychoeducation: A promising intervention strategy for families of children and adolescents with mood disorders. *Contemporary Family Therapy, 20,* 385–402.

Gelso, C., & Fretz, B. (2001). *Counseling psychology* (2nd ed.). Fort Worth, TX: Harcourt.

Geroski, A. M., & Kraus, K. L. (2002). Process and content in school psychoeducational groups: Either, both, or none? *Journal for Specialists in Group Work, 27,* 233–245.

Glosser, G., & Wexler, D. (1985). Participants' evaluation of educational/support groups for families of patients with Alzheimer's Disease and other dementias. *Gerontologist, 25,* 232–236.

Greene, L. R., Meisler, A. W., Pilkey, D., Alexander, G., Cardella, L. A., Sirois, B. C., et al., (2004). Psychological work with groups in the Veterans Administration. In J. L. DeLucia-Waack, D. A. Gerrity, C. R. Kalodner, & M. T. Riva (Eds.), *Handbook of group counseling and psychotherapy* (pp. 322–337). Thousand Oaks, CA: Sage.

Halford, W. K. (2002). A skills-training approach to relationship education in groups. In F. W. Kaslow, & T. Patterson (Eds.), *Comprehensive handbook of psychotherapy* (Vol. 2, pp. 495–518). New York: Wiley.

Hetzel, R. D., Barton, D. A., & Davenport, D. S. (1994). Helping men change: A group counseling model for male clients. *Journal for Specialists in Group Work, 19,* 52–64.

Housley, W. F. (1992). Psychoeducation for personal control: A key to psychological well-being of the elderly. *Educational Gerontology, 18,* 785–794.

Joshua, J. M., & DiMenna, D. (2000). *Read two books and let's talk next week: Using bibliotherapy in clinical practice.* New York: Wiley.

Kanfer, F. H., & Gaelick-Buys, L. (1991). Self-management methods. In F. H. Kanfer & A. P. Goldstein (Eds.), *Helping people change: A textbook of methods* (4th ed., pp. 305–360). New York: Pergamon Press.

Khalsa, S. S. (1996). *Group exercises for enhancing social skills and self-esteem*. Sarasota, FL: Professional Resource Press.

Mace, F. C., Brown, D. K., & West, B. J. (1987). Behavioral self-management in education. In C. A. Maher & J. E. Zins (Eds.), *Psychoeducational interventions in the schools* (pp. 160–176). New York: Pergamon Press.

Moffatt, F., Mohr, C., & Ames, D. (1995). A group therapy programme for depressed and anxious elderly inpatients. *International Journal of Geriatric Psychiatry, 10,* 37–40.

Nicholson, B., Anderson, M., Fox, R., & Brenner, V. (2002). One family at a time: A prevention program for at-risk parents. *Journal of Counseling & Development, 80,* 362–371.

O'Donohue, W., & Noll, J. (1995). Problem-solving skills. In W. O'Donohue & L. Krasner (Eds.), *Handbook of psychological skills training* (pp. 144–160). Boston: Allyn & Bacon.

O'Donohue, W., & Krasner, L. (1995). Psychological skills training. In W. O'Donohue & L. Krasner (Eds.), *Handbook of psychological skills training* (pp. 1–19). Boston: Allyn & Bacon.

Ost, L., Stridh, B., & Wolf, M. (1998). A clinical study of spider phobia: Prediction of outcome after self-help and therapist-directed treatments. *Behavior Research and Therapy, 36,* 17–35.

Perkinson, R. R., & Jongsma, A. E. (2001). *The addiction treatment planner* (2nd ed.). New York: Wiley.

Prochaska, J. O., & Norcross, J. C. (1999). *Systems of psychotherapy: A transtheoretical analysis* (4th ed.). Pacific Grove, CA: Brooks/Cole.

Ripley, J. S., & Worthington, E. L. (2002). Hope-focused and forgiveness-based interventions to promote marital enrichment. *Journal of Counseling & Development, 80,* 452–463.

Rodway, M. R. (1992). Self-examination of loneliness: A group approach. *Social Work with Groups, 15,* 69–80.

Rose, S. D. (1988). Training for empirical group work. *Social Work with Groups, 11,* 43–51.

Rusch, F. R., Hughes, C., & Wilson, P. G. (1995). Utilizing cognitive strategies in the acquisition of employment skills. In W. O'Donohue & L. Krasner (Eds.), *Handbook of psychological skills training* (pp. 363–382). Boston: Allyn & Bacon.

Shean, G. D. (1985). Rehabilitation: Social skills groups. In R. K. Conyne (Ed.), *The group workers' handbook: Varieties of group experience* (pp. 23–41). Springfield, IL: Charles Thomas.

Smith, M. J. (1975). *When I say no, I feel guilty*. New York: Bantam Books.

Spiegler, M. D., & Guevremont, D. C. (1998). *Contemporary behavior therapy* (3rd ed.). Pacific Grove, CA: Brooks/Cole.

Taylor, N. T., Burlingame, G. M., Kristensen, K. B., Fuhriman, A., Johansen, J., & Dahl, D. (2001). A survey of mental health care providers' and managed care organization attitudes toward, familiarity with, and use of group interventions. *International Journal of Group Psychotherapy, 51,* 243–263.

Villa, K. K., & Abeles, N. (2000). Broad spectrum intervention and the remediation of prospective memory declines in the able elderly. *Aging & Mental Health, 4,* 21–29.

Webb, L. D., & Myrick, R. D. (2003). A group counseling intervention for children with attention deficit-hyperactivity disorder. *Professional School Counseling, 7,* 108–116.

PART VI

On Becoming a Citizen

The two approaches in this section have much in common. They both emphasize that each of us is a part of a large social sphere. Through our own choices, we either contribute to the well-being of the larger world, or we damage it. Adlerian individual psychology and choice theory define positive emotional adjustment by how well a person fulfills her or his needs within the context of a civilized society. Meanwhile, society ideally promotes the well-being of its individual members. This is why I label this section "On Becoming a Citizen," reflecting an emphasis different from Carl Rogers's "On Becoming a Person."

CHAPTER 14

Adlerian Group Theory and Practice

A Selection from "Group Psychotherapy from the Point of View of Adlerian Psychology"

Essential Concepts of Adlerian Theory

Style of Life ■ *Social Interest* ■ *Encouragement*

Group Dynamics

Stages of Group Development

Leadership Skills

Role Modeling ■ *Providing Early Guidance* ■ *Sense of Humor*

Techniques of Adlerian Group Counseling

Early Childhood Recollections ■ *Dream Analysis* ■ *Family Photos* ■ *Samples of Adlerian Interventions*

Problems Addressed by Adlerian Groups

Perfectionism ■ *Alienation: Adventure-Based Therapy*

Adaptations to Clients' Ages

Child and School Problems ■ *Groups for Parents*

Evaluating Adlerian Groups

Alfred Adler (1870–1939) labeled his theory *Individual Psychology*. The emphasis was on the word *individual*, a mark of breaking away from Freud's point of view. Adler, once a member of Freud's inner circle, thought that Freud overgeneralized about how people develop. Freud believed that we are all motivated in the same way, spending our lives fending off anxiety (successfully or not, mostly in methods we are not aware of), and that we all have the same sources of anxiety determined by id impulses and superego demands. Adler's disagreement with Freud finally drove them apart. Adler, in naming his theory, wanted to stress that people can be better understood as integrated individuals. Each individual has a social history that fashions his or her personality in a unique way, and that personality is a complete whole. People who become aberrant and distressed do so through taking their own individual paths, in contrast with the Freudian belief in a common road to madness. People who turn out fine also have their own unique paths. Thus, Adler's theory is a **holistic** one, a theory that views each person as unified rather than as a collection of symptoms or a battlefield where psychic structures struggle with each other.

 A Selection from

"Group Psychotherapy from the Point of View of Adlerian Psychology"

By Rudolf Dreikurs (1957)

[Note: Rudolf Dreikurs, one of Alfred Adler's students and fellow physicians in Vienna, came to the United States in 1939 and popularized the group procedures of Adler in this country (Corsini, 1988). You will often find his name associated with Adlerian theory and practice.]

In individual therapy it is relatively difficult to provide insight for the patient, particularly in regard to his goals. We are so used to rationalizing, that we all find it difficult to recognize our own goals and true intentions. This is the more so when the patient is ambitious and overconscientious, as many neurotics are. The group facilitates the process of gaining insight; for many, it is almost a prerequisite without which they never are able to learn about themselves what they need to know. How is this greater ability to understand oneself achieved in the group?

Interestingly enough, the individual patient may show the same blocking to interpretations in the group as in private consultation. What helps him to overcome his resistance is the similar resistance observed in his fellow patients. There he can clearly see the validity of the psychological interpretation and the difficulties of the patient to recognize the obvious. Most psychological disclosures and interpretations in the group are not for the benefit of the patient to whom they are directed, but for the benefit of the others who learn from it. There is sufficient fundamental similarity in faulty motivations and mistaken approaches among all participants so that each one can, time and again, recognize himself in others. This is particularly true if the members of the group are selected because of their similar problems, a group of mothers, of teenagers, of obese women, of executives, of patients with depression, etc. We try to arrange our groups in such a way that some common element of either personalities, psychopathology, interests, age or education is evident. After all, patients learn from each other. This seems to be a fundamental principle, explaining the therapeutic efficiency of group psychotherapy.

In this sense, it is characteristic for all group psychotherapy that the patients help each other. What they tell each other is often much more significant to them than what the therapist has to say. They accept each other more in their corrective endeavors, because they feel equal to each other. This is the reason why some patients can only benefit from group psychotherapy and less so from individual therapy, like juvenile delinquents, alcoholics, drug addicts, the crippled and the blind and other groups which perceive themselves as a minority. The therapist, regardless of how acceptable he may be to them, is still a member of the hostile or at least different majority. His influence depends on his ability to win the active support of some group members.

Insight is not necessarily a strictly personal matter. Certain psychological dynamics, which operate in all of us alike, are hardly known. While man probably never will be able to understand himself, he will, before long, learn a great deal more about human nature. The significance of inferiority feelings, of guilt feelings, the fallacy of prestige and of the desire for self-elevation, they all are still unknown to most. The patients in the group learn not only about themselves, but about people. As they begin to understand people, they begin to understand themselves. Psychotherapy, as we understand it, is primarily an educational process, the intellectual stimulation being supported by strong and impressive emotional experiences. It seems that the group as such facilitates all learning. A seasoned teacher often prefers a small group to individual instruction. Similarly, the learning process called psychotherapy is greatly facilitated by the group. . . .

The most important therapeutic factor in our concept of psychotherapy is the removal of inferiority feelings, or to say it in a positive way, the increase in self-respect. This process can justifiably be called encouragement. It is our contention that the effectiveness of any corrective procedure, be it called analytic, therapeutic or educational, rests with the degree of encouragement which it entailed. Without increased self-confidence, without restored faith in his own worth and ability, the patient cannot improve and grow. This aspect of therapy may not be recognized by the therapist, or be minimized by him as constituting mere "supportive" assistance; however, it seems to be the essential factor in all cure and improvement.

In which way does the group contribute to the encouragement of each of its members? To understand this all-important aspect of group psychotherapy, one must take into consideration the peculiar social structure of the therapy group. It is quite unique and different from any other group found in our society. It is characterized by a status of social equality which each member enjoys. Unlike any other group, here, individual differences and particularly deficiencies do not lower the patient's status. Conversely, leadership qualities and personal assets do not necessarily give the patient a status of superiority or envy, since this very envy can be openly expressed by less fortunate members of the group who then see to it that the patient's attempts to achieve elevation are thwarted.

It is this social atmosphere of equality which characterizes a therapy group and which exerts one of the most effective therapeutic influences on each one of its members. First of all, it removes the need for distance. The highly competitive atmosphere of our civilization produces a state of emotional isolation for everybody; revealing oneself as one is entails the danger of ridicule and contempt. In the therapy group this danger is eliminated. For the first time the individual can be himself without fear and danger. This is an utterly new experience, and counteracts the basic fears and anxiety which are usually concerned with possible personal failure and defeat.

In this sense, the group provides subtle but all-persuasive encouragement for each member. It permits an unrestricted feeling of belonging without necessary personal bonds or attachments. Unlike personal and close relationships based on friendship or love, the feeling of solidarity is not based here on a union of personal aspirations. It is truly a feeling of human fellowship without any ulterior motives of personal benefits or advantages, which characterize the relationship of friends and lovers. Accordingly, the desire to help each other in the group springs from the deepest source of human empathy and fellowship, from a feeling of solidarity, of genuine humaneness. We have seen patients who never concerned themselves with anyone's interests or needs, and who were moved in the group to give assistance and support without any one of the attributes which those acts usually have in our society, namely the demonstration of personal superiority. (pp. 371–374)

Exploring "Group Psychotherapy from the Point of View of Adlerian Psychology"

1. What is the educational value of the group, in comparison with individual therapy?
2. Why does Dreikurs endorse some homogeneity in group membership?
3. Why do some people benefit more from group counseling than they do from individual therapy?
4. In paragraph 4, Dreikurs wrote about "the fallacy of prestige and of the desire for self-elevation." How can prestige and the desire for self-elevation be considered fallacies?
5. What is the essential factor in psychotherapy, according to Dreikurs? If you had to name an essential factor, what might you say?
6. Why is the atmosphere of equality in the group positively therapeutic?
7. In paragraph 7, Dreikurs described "the highly competitive atmosphere of our civilization." Do you think this description is accurate today?
8. How is the relationship among group members different from friendships and love relationships?
9. This article was published in 1957. Did it seem old-fashioned to you in any way? Why?

▪ ▪ ▪

Essential Concepts of Adlerian Theory

Adler felt that the unity of personality was ignored in case conceptualization; too often, one symptom or manifestation was singled out for scrutiny. He used a musical metaphor to explain:

> Sometimes such a manifestation is called a complex, and the assumption is that it is possible to separate it from the rest of an individual's activity. But such a procedure

is comparable to singling out one note from an entire melody and attempting to understand the significance of this one note apart from the string of notes which make up the melody. (1930, p. 24)

Freud's psychoanalytic theory assumes that gratification is our central need, whereas Adler assumed that there are countless motivating factors besides gratification. Needs for power, security, self-esteem, achievement, and social welfare are other central motivators in people's lives. And, though we may not be in control of our needs, we can choose how to express them. For example, a need for achievement could create a popular movie star or an unknown inventor. A need for security could be expressed by a husband who calls home every hour on the hour, or it could manifest itself in years of loyal service to the same company. In groups, one member's need for power could result in bullying, or it could operate through quick mastery of the group's theoretical principles.

Therefore, personal choice plays an important role in Adlerian psychology. While this is a hopeful stance because it offers the possibility of behavior change, it also places an uncomfortable burden on the individual. Freedom of choice includes responsibility for our own actions, and we aren't always happy to take on such responsibility. This idea explains why Adlerian psychology is called **existential;** it deals with the dilemmas of existence such as freedom, choice, responsibility, and the meaning of life. Adlerian group counseling is a setting where these topics are openly discussed, whereas they are relatively rare in daily life. Many widely endorsed psychotherapies today have at least some existentialist underpinning, as you saw in Chapters 8 and 9. In fact, the spirit of Adler hovers near many of the group approaches in this book (Watts, 2000; Watts & Pietrzak, 2000).

SMALL GROUP EXERCISE

In your discussion group, review the following motivations, and list at least four different ways each one could manifest itself interpersonally, as it would in a group setting. Try to list both good and bad expressions of the motivation. Here are some motivations that can be considered from an Adlerian point of view:

Attention (An example would be: A group member could monopolize discussions, dress inappropriately for the situation, enjoy role-playing techniques, take the lead in bringing up topics.)

Achievement

Control

Security

Power

Self-esteem

Social welfare

Comfort

Pleasing others

Affiliation

_____

Style of Life

Adler's **style of life,** the mosaic of life's pattern, is an essential concept of his theory. In computer parlance, you might think of style of life as the default settings of your character. According to Adler, these defaults were set by the time you were about six years old, and they remain fairly constant throughout life. They are the internal sources of your values, beliefs, goals, and interests. Most important, your style of life determines how you perceive your own experiences: It is the eyeglasses through which you see the world. Like your computer defaults, your style of life and its expression can be changed, but only through very purposeful efforts. Adler believed that changing one's style of life was much more difficult than making changes *within* one's style of life. A change within the style of life might involve, for example, changing from expressing your need for safety through avoiding conflictual topics in a group to embracing the norms of the group faithfully. In contrast, a total change in style of life would entail giving up the need for safety altogether and becoming a member willing to take risks. (Either type of change might entail an improvement.) Style of life is very similar to personality in that it persists over various situations and through time.

Adler places less influence at the door of biology than Freud did. Instead, Adler believed that the main influence on your style of life is your social world as a child, mostly your family constellation. As a small child, you are aware of your limitations and weaknesses in comparison to parents and siblings, an awareness that Adler labels a **sense of inferiority.** In response to these feelings, you develop physical and psychological ways to overcome them, in Adler's terms, your **strivings for superiority.** So, even though in everyday speech we use terms like *superiority complex* or *acting superior* in a negative way, meaning snobby or pretentious, that is not the way Adler meant it. Strivings for superiority can be negative, positive, anywhere in between, or mixed. Adler believed that his own nearly fatal illnesses and accidents in early childhood provided the basis for his goal of becoming a doctor and foiling death. Discouraging reports from his school teachers propelled him to study harder and prove his potential for the medical profession. We all strive to make up for the inferiority we felt in childhood, though not all as successfully as Adler. As adults, we respond to problems and unfamiliar situations by using psychological patterns we learned in childhood. You can see how Adler's early thinking was psychoanalytic (see Chapter 10).

The Adlerian view is also labeled **socioteleological.** Teleology is belief in a purposeful development toward an end; human impulses are not random but goal-oriented. The prefix *socio* emphasizes the major influence of social systems on this development, rather than biological or theological systems. A modern practitioner of Alderian group therapy puts together the socioteleological point of view in this way:

> A goal or a purpose makes sense out of what otherwise seems incomprehensible. Goals and purposes to which the individual attaches great significance lead to the development of patterns that both reinforce the motivation and its necessity in the person's life. Repeated patterns and motivation are always interwoven. Unlock one, and the other is merely a step away. (Sonstegard, 1998)

Contributions of Birth Order to Style of Life The psychological make-up of the family as a whole affects the style of life established by each child. In a family of my acquaintance, the oldest son tends to be gloomy and works in a challenging but underpaid job organizing efforts toward world peace The next son is relentlessly cheerful and works various jobs in the casinos of Las Vegas. The last child, a daughter, still lives at home at the age of 35 and works part time as a receptionist. It's easy to look at the situation from an Adlerian point of view. The first brother cornered the market in seriousness and responsibility. Instead of trying to equal or surpass him, the second brother chose a different path, devoted to an easy and colorful life. The daughter, protected by parents and both brothers as the baby sister, continued to need protection and made a life centered at her lifelong home. These roles were consistent not only with the siblings' birth order but with the gender roles of the time. It is more socially acceptable for a woman to live with her parents and work part time than it is for a man of the same age. Throughout their lives, one brother was the dedicated do-gooder, one was a party animal, and the sister was the quiet homebody.

Adler formulated **birth order analysis,** a typological system that assigns personality characteristics according to chronological place in the family. This typology is prominent in popular psychology. Research studies support the idea that the first-born is often dominant, most responsible, most conservative, and achievement-oriented. The last child tends to be more dependent, less responsible, and socially apprehensive. Like the family described above, the second child is more carefree than the first. This is probably because most parents are more relaxed in caring for their second infant than their first, whose addition to the household brought out self-doubts and alarms.

To explain a person's character wholly in terms of birth order is inadequate. What about a last child who is born after older children have left home? Will she be like a last child who shares a home with four older siblings? What about the situation of a second child among three versus a second child among seven? Or a second child who got most of her care from a devoted grandmother? Though some popular books take a simplistic view of birth order typology, Adler did not. He emphasized the importance of *psychological* birth order, or position in the **family constellation.** Like a constellation of stars, the family as a whole takes on a form with each member anchoring a definite spot. Often the roles we take on in the family are complementary or compensatory—for example, a fun-loving child balances out a studious sibling or a rebellious adolescent serves as a cautionary model for a conformist younger family member. Many of us try to take on roles that aren't already mastered by some other family member, or else we face a lifetime of competition. The family constellation also configures the roles assigned to each sex in the family, the atmosphere and mood that prevails in the home, the relationship between the parents, the values that are outwardly espoused, and the values that are truly enacted. Adler's thoughts on family constellation still inform family therapy systems of all sorts today. Powers (1973) connects the family constellation to the style of life:

> It is as if the situation of each child were that of being born into the middle of the second act of a play, and having to ad lib his way into the action. To do this, he has to "size up" the situation and his place in it (his "role" in the "play") by asking (and deciding), "What's going on here? What kind of a world is this? What kind of person am I? What must I do, and what must I become in order to get in on things?" Neither the questions nor his answers take this explicit form, however. They are played out in movement amongst the others, first by trial and error, later in a more finished performance to which he adheres as to a well-rehearsed role. (p. 275)

This description also applies to a person entering group therapy, sizing up the situation and finding his place in it. Each group member develops a well-rehearsed role, and it often mirrors his or her role in the family constellation.

DISCUSSION IDEAS

1. Do you think that your spot in the family constellation affects your behavior in groups? How? Give some examples.
2. If you have led groups of some kind, can you perceive a family constellation acted out? Explain your example to the class.

Social Constructivism Adler wrote that "any experience may have many interpretations. We will find that there are no two people who will draw the same conclusion from a similar experience." The idea that reality is not objective but subjective, not public but personal, is a **constructivist** attitude (Watts & Pietrzak, 2000). The world is the way that you see it and interpret it, according to your style of life. Your experience may not be shared by others. Think about courses in which you receive assignments to complete in groups. You may look forward to this as fun, whereas a friend may groan with misery at the prospect. A constructivist attitude, therefore, requires a phenomenological method of exploring reality—that is, it uses human experience as raw material (rather than, say, statistical norms, moral touchstones, or general categories of diagnosis). Watts (2003) suggests that Adlerian theory is *social constructivist*, meaning that our subjective interpretations of reality are built through a social process.

We each have a cognitive map of the world and its inhabitants, and we place events on this map. What we pay attention to and what we ignore is determined by whether it fits the geography of our maps. This is clear in the circumstances of a depressed person, who walks down the street noticing the trash in the gutter rather than the brilliant sunrise. You have probably had the phenomenological experience of seeing a film or reading a book in a different way than your friends and classmates do.

The way that we perceive and interpret the world determines how we behave. If you see the world as hostile and yourself as never quite adequate, your main goal is to protect yourself from blows to your self-esteem. This stance, according to Adler, makes you avoid risk-taking, because you might look like a fool and will probably fail anyway. Because the pursuit of a meaningful, happy life always involves risk-taking, avoiding risks completely is a no-win strategy. Consider your own situation: Every time you sign up for a class, you risk failure or disappointment. Yet, obviously you consider your goals as worth the risk, and you expect that you are capable of passing. Adlerians define mentally healthy people as those who see the world as friendly and themselves as competent. They will see opportunity where others see risk. According to Adlerian theory, these qualities lead naturally to social interest, expressing love of humanity through good works.

Adler enthusiastically embraced the ideas of philosopher Hans Vaihinger, whose book *The Philosophy of "As If"* (1911/1925) came out the same year that Adler left Freud's inner circle of psychoanalytic theorists. Adler found Vaihinger's term *fictions* a good way to describe people's cognitive maps because they are not reality but constructed out of inner experience, like fictional writing is. So Adler saw each of us as having a **fictional self** to whom we conform our behavior (to clarify Vaihinger's title, we behave "as if" we were that self), and we choose goals that also conform to the fictional self, in what he called **fictional finalism.** We have a **private logic** that determines our interpretations of experience and a **life script** that is like a play in which we direct our own character. Adler provides a good series of examples in *What Life Should Mean to You* (1931):

> Unhappy experiences in childhood may be given quite opposite meanings. One man with unhappy experiences behind him will not dwell on them except as they show him something which can be remedied for the future. He will feel, "We must work to remove such unfortunate situations and make sure that our children are better placed." Another man will feel, "Life is unfair. Other people always have the best of it. If the world treated me like that, why should I treat the world any better?" It is in this way that some parents say of their children, "I had to suffer just as much when I was a child, and I came through it. Why shouldn't they?" A third man will feel, "Everything should be forgiven me because of my unhappy childhood." In the actions of all three men, their interpretations will be evident. They will never change their actions unless they change their interpretations. (p. 209)

Each of the three men deals with his experience according to his private logic. Adler clearly thinks that the first man's fiction is best. All three private logic premises are untrue: (1) "We can remove our children from all harm," (2) "Unfairness dominates the world," and (3) "Bad experiences excuse bad behavior." However, the first one leads to goals of social welfare, whereas the others do not. And as you will soon see, social feeling is a major element in Adler's ideal style of life.

In group counseling, people will reveal their life scripts by the stories they tell about themselves. In one college student social skills group, a member acted seductively and mysteriously. Her situation as she described it was very hard and unhappy, and she believed that she needed to find a prince on a white horse to whisk her away from all that. She played a charming damsel in distress, but her co-members in group were quick to point out that fairy tales don't really come true in this world.

It may be hard to accept that many of our well-loved assumptions are fictions, despite plenty of evidence disproving them. But remember that they may still be socially and personally beneficial. "All humans are created equal," "It takes all kinds to make a world," "Good deeds are rewarded." These are fictions that promote civilized society.

SMALL GROUP EXERCISE

Imagine that you studied for an important exam and took it with some confidence. In a few days, you go to the bulletin board where scores are posted, and you discover that you have received a C- on the test. Jot down quickly what you would think, feel, and do immediately upon getting this news.

Now, share your reactions with your small group. What different ways do you see among yourselves of dealing with the same experience? What is revealed about your fictional selves and your private logic? Were your reactions more similar or more different from each other? Why is this so?

Within your group, are there members whose responses could be changed for the better? As a group, try to persuade one of these members to respond to the situation differently. Then analyze why your persuasion worked or did not work.

Basic Mistakes According to Adler, many of us embrace **basic mistakes** as we develop our style of life in childhood. As children, we make up principles to explain what we perceive, and because children are naïve, the principles are sketchy and erroneous. These errors continue into adulthood as firm convictions about ourselves, others, and the world, and they lie behind how we interpret experience and how we choose to behave. An example you have no doubt seen occurs when a child's parents divorce, and the child wrongly decides that if he or she had behaved better, the marriage would have stayed intact. One (among many) mistaken convictions carried into adulthood from this experience might be, "I need to please everyone to maintain harmony in my world."

What a stressful belief this is! You can see how the person holding it would suffer. An Adlerian group would seek to substitute a different conviction for this damaging one: "You can never please everyone, and trying makes you look like a phony." Though most of our lifestyle convictions are fictions, some promote well-being in community, work, and love, whereas others toss up wall after insurmountable wall around us. The walls around us are breached by the close, equal, and straightforward relationships built in group counseling. Groups learn to identify statements that sound like basic mistakes, and the norms of the group allow members to call each other on them.

SMALL GROUP EXERCISE

Here is a list of basic mistakes compiled by a modern Adlerian, H. H. Mosak (2000). Mosak provides examples of statements exemplifying each one. Role-play what a group leader could do when a member makes one of these statements. How could a group leader include other members in the discussion?

1. **Overgeneralizations** "People are hostile." "Life is dangerous."
2. **False or impossible goals of "security"** "One false step and you're dead." "I have to please everybody."
3. **Misperceptions of life and life's demands** "Life never gives me any breaks." "Life is so hard."
4. **Minimization or denial of one's worth** "I'm stupid." "I'm undeserving." "I'm just a housewife."
5. **Faulty values** "Be first even if you have to climb over others."

Social Interest

Adler believed in the purposeful nature of behavior. Obviously, the style of life has a purpose: to compensate or overcome a sense of inferiority and to meet one's needs. As he wrote in *Understanding Human Nature* (1927/1957), "a human being always employs his experiences to the same end" (p. 20). The assertion that we are goal-driven sets Adler apart again from the Freudians, who saw us driven by the past, not the future. For Adler, goals, plans, ideals, and self-determination were very real forces in human behavior, while Freud would say that these concepts are rationalizations for behavior that is actually propelled by unconscious conflicts. If you are an Adlerian, you have a more positive view of human nature than a strict Freudian would. An Adlerian allows that a great artist may be motivated by desire to touch or amuse an audience, while a Freudian would insist that the artist is motivated by sexual repressions (Adler, 1929).

Even though Adler saw no inherent meaning in life, he strongly believed that the psychologically healthy "fiction" lay in *social interest*. This concept covers cooperation with other people, concern for their welfare, contribution to society, and value placed on humanity. Social interest is an innate aptitude that develops with life experience, if everything goes well. As adults, we have three arenas for expressing social interest: community, work, and love (sometimes Adlerians label these society, work, and sex). Our lives are interwoven with other people's by living cooperatively among others, pursuing a useful occupation, and being part of a loving couple. The three areas overlap, and an improvement in one area is likely to result in an improvement in the others. As I near retirement, I still plan to take on graduate students to help with their research, to keep a small private counseling practice, and to attend professional meetings. My style of life is imbued with social interest to the point that I will continue in that vein when I no longer need to financially.

In the selection that begins this chapter, Dreikurs explained social interest within counseling groups. People with underdeveloped social interest may exploit others through crime, bullying, political clout, physical strength, or economic power; or they may be loners, avoiding involvement with other people in all three arenas. Adler placed such a value on social interest that he equated it with psychological well-being. He even wrote, "A man of genius is primarily a man of supreme usefulness" (Adler, 1929, p. 35), and placed social interest above intelligence: "In our over-intellectualised civilisation especially, practically everyone is wonderfully adept in the use of his own individual tricks: The really important differences of conduct are not those of individual cleverness but of usefulness or uselessness" (p. 78). In group counseling, social interest can blossom through therapeutic factors like universality, cohesion, and altruism. Members have the opportunity to feel themselves part of a community of value and to want the best for this small community.

SMALL GROUP EXERCISE

In a round-robin discussion, each member briefly states one or more ways in which they demonstrate social interest. Then, each person imagines what would be different in their life if they lost their expressions of social interest. In this way, you each can glimpse the emptiness and fear counseling group members may be experiencing when they join the group.

Encouragement

Adler clearly believed that change was difficult for us—in fact, "The hardest thing for human beings to do is to know themselves and to change themselves" (1927/1957, p. 21). Think for a moment about the hard things you have had to do. Did they entail knowing yourself and changing yourself? Career counselors frequently encounter clients who must face the fact that they don't have the natural skills, physical abilities, intellectual capacity, or financial backing to pursue the vocation they have always dreamed of. These can be heartrending professional efforts, as we strive to help these clients change longstanding visions of their future.

We cling to the mental, emotional, and behavioral habits that we developed in childhood, even when they are clearly not working toward the best outcome in adult life. Adler wrote that people insist that they cannot change these habits because they are too longstanding. Certain habits of thought provide us with excuses or alibis for not changing. Because we interpret experience however it suits our style, we can come up with plenty of evidence for ideas like, "Nothing ever works out for me." "I never get the love and support I need." As Dreikurs (1957) pointed out, in group counseling people are able to recognize these habits in others better than in themselves. (Remember that the very same background of experience could provide evidence for a person who thinks, "Things usually work out for the best." "I can get love and support when I need it.") For Adler, psychopathology equals a feeling of **discouragement,** a feeling that you and the world are not going to change, and why try? Therefore, a major goal of group therapy is the **encouragement** of clients. They must feel that change is possible and worth the effort. Making the effort is what takes courage.

R e f l e c t i o n s

Think about a time you became truly discouraged. Write down the situation that made you discouraged, and describe as accurately as you can what your feelings were.

Do you remember what eventually encouraged you? How can you apply your experience to working with a group of discouraged people?

Group Dynamics

The therapeutic processes in an Adlerian group are emotional, cognitive, and behavioral. These are very familiar to you from your study of group process in general. I will summarize Dinkmeyer's (1975, pp. 222–223) overview of these processes:

- **Emotional** Acceptance of, empathy with, and involvement with others. An opportunity for each member to find his or her place. Altruism and social interest. Transference, meaning strong emotional attachments to the leader and other members, both positive and negative.

- **Cognitive** Spectator therapy, meaning the opportunity to observe and learn from others' transactions in group. Universalization, realizing that one's concerns can be shared. Intellectualization, learning about feelings, purposes, values, and perceptions.

■ **Actional (behavioral)** Reality testing, the chance to test behavior and ideas in a safe atmosphere. Ventilation, expressing negative or positive feedback without holding it in. Interaction, seeing how goals and purposes are revealed in the transactions among group members.

DISCUSSION IDEA

Review the list of therapeutic factors covered in Chapters 4 through 7. Link each factor with one or more of Dinkmeyer's therapeutic processes.

Stages of Group Development

Like most group therapies, Adlerian therapy doesn't progress through a series of distinct stages, though it does move toward an overall goal, which might be expressed as "becoming decent human beings." The therapeutic process in Adlerian groups can be divided into four elements, all of which are ongoing throughout. These elements are

■ forming a group relationship,

■ psychological investigation,

■ psychological disclosure [interpretation and insight], and

■ reorientation. (Dreikurs, 1957)

In some cases, all four elements occur within one counseling session (see Sonstegard & Bitter, 1998, for a detailed example). The next sections explain the four elements in more detail.

Forming a Group Relationship The proper group relationship is one of equality and respect. More important, the members' confidence in the counselor's ability must be developed, or they will not be able to overcome the inevitable disturbances that come up. A distrustful client will be influenced by other members who have faith in group counseling, which can make the group setting effective when individual counseling wouldn't be. Unlike most other approaches, Adlerians do not always advise careful screening of members for potential disruptiveness or self-absorption, in the belief that prescreening might eliminate the very people who could most benefit from the experience (Sonstegard & Bitter, 1998). However, members who share similar problems and situations are often recruited. Corsini (1988) prefers groups to be relatively homogeneous in terms of age, socioeconomic level, and intelligence. However, he warns against groups who are uniformly passive and hostile, who include no influential positive models among themselves.

A democratic, nonauthoritarian relationship is set by the counselor's soliciting of **agreements** rather than setting forth rules. The therapist might begin by asking, "What agreements do we need in this group?" Ideas about how often to meet, whether to require attendance and promptness, what to do about quitting, and where to draw lines of confidentiality are topics decided by the group. It's preferable for members to bring up the topics necessary, but our ethical codes demand that some topics need to be aired one way or another, such as confidentiality and fee plans (see Chapter 3).

Psychological Investigation The Adlerian group seeks to understand each client's style of life, including how it originally developed in the family and other social settings, what basic convictions are operating, and how the style of life is hampering participation in community, work, and love. The search for understanding is called a *lifestyle investigation* or *lifestyle assessment,* and it typically includes both free-form and structured exercises. An Adlerian will often simply ask each client to tell his or her life story. Because we can never capture our whole life story, the events and people we dwell on in our summary are those that we are now considering important. A listener can also discern themes in the life story, such as abandonment or achievement, and can label the overall emotional tone of the story. These are the themes and tone of the person's style of life. In the group setting, each client's style of life becomes more obvious in interaction with other group members than with an individual therapist (Dreikurs, 1957).

Because people may talk for widely different times on their life stories, many leaders structure the opening investigation. For example, Dinkmeyer (1975) gives each person a prearranged, limited amount of time to address the three main tasks of life (community, work, and love):

1. Socially with friends, acquaintances, or strangers. The members address themselves to the question of how they get along with people, whether they feel they have enough friends, and what sense of belonging and acceptance they experience.

2. In terms of earning a living and dealing with the work task, are they satisfied with their accomplishments and their position? How involved are they in their work? What kind of co-worker are they?

3. In respect to love and sexual identification, do they feel loved and do they give love? How do they view themselves as either a man or a woman? Are they comfortable with this view? (p. 224)

At the end of each member's time, the group responds for ten or fifteen minutes in terms of ideas and feelings they had while listening. The group leader observes and begins hypothesizing about the members from their interactions during this discussion.

Usually, the first part of group counseling also investigates the *family constellation,* the particular social arrangement of each individual's family (like an arrangement of stars in a constellation). The techniques of early childhood recollections and dream analysis, which will be described later in this chapter, are key assessments here. Members are encouraged to comment on patterns of feelings and beliefs they see in each other's discourse.

Interpretation and Insight In an Adlerian group, the counselor and clients build interpretations together from the evidence gathered in the course of investigation. While part of lifestyle investigation involves pondering childhood roots, more attention is paid to the clients' current and future patterns of thought, emotion, and behavior. Insight may concurrently involve an analysis of one's *basic mistakes* and how they are affecting one's life. For a worthwhile interpretation, the client needs to answer the questions: "What life task is my symptom allowing me to avoid?" "What price am I paying for this?" Adler was sure that each symptom had an underlying purpose, often serving as an excuse to retreat from life's demands.

Nira Kefir (1981), who devised a system of therapy based on Adlerian principles, interprets clients' styles of life in terms of four **personal priorities,** each of which is designed to avoid a frightening outcome:

1. **Control** Controlling every situation in order to avoid being ridiculed or embarrassed.
2. **Superiority** Seeking achievement, fame, and advancement in order to avoid insignificance and meaninglessness.
3. **Pleasing** Looking for affection and approval in order to avoid rejection.
4. **Comfort** Refusing to take risks or make commitments in order to avoid any kind of stress.

We all share these priorities to some extent; you probably recognized your favorite right away. Problems arise when the price of the avoidance is too high. An Adlerian insight might be just that—a realization that the effort to avoid something produces worse results than the bad thing itself would. For example, a group could help a shy person see that by refusing invitations, he creates a loneliness worse than making the effort to socialize.

Regardless of how much insight group members gain, for Adler insight was never enough. While Freud believed that bringing unconscious motivations into consciousness was curative in itself, Adler thought that such insight was superficial if it did not lead to a change in motivation, and from there to a change in behavior.

Reorientation Each client needs to gain (or regain) the courage to face life's demands. This probably involves giving up long-ingrained convictions that produce avoidant behavior and pursuit of impossible goals. **Reorientation** turns insight into action. Clients discover that taking the risks they once avoided is not as bad as they'd expected.

A focus on assets is another reorientation task. Many clients have come to dwell on their problems so deeply that they forget to develop their strong points. Accepting a weakness may be necessary, but a compensating strength should be cultivated. For example, if a group member has been distressed by having only two intimate friends, he could look at the depth of those friend-ships as his asset. He could also decide to develop several friendships that are not very intense—for example, having a tennis pal, a moviegoing companion, a lunchroom buddy—and realize that limited friendships hold their own charms. Such a decision would entail throwing off some of the values of the external culture—like its assumption that a likable person has lots of close relationships. Dreikurs (1957) said that the counseling experience "induce[s] the patient to consider self-evaluation as most important. . . . Counseling and psychotherapy lead the patient to a sounder approach to social living, enable him to cooperate, and provide him with healthier and more practical sources of satisfaction and security than those which he previously had considered necessary" (p. 373). Paradoxically, throwing off society's definitions makes the client a better mem-ber of the same society. Being a valued member of a counseling group is a reori-entation to accepting a small corner of life's demands.

Leadership Skills

Adler was an early popularizer of psychoeducation (see Chapter 13). Adler-ian alliances often take on a teacher-student flavor, because psychoeducation is part of the process. For example, Adlerians doing family therapy teach the family about how its constellation gives each member a distinct role to play. An Adlerian counseling a group of alcoholics would explain the principle of self-distraction from life's tasks, and how drinking is a form of self-distraction. Unlike most theories of psychotherapy, Adler's condones advice-giving in cer-tain circumstances, just as equals give each other advice when they can. The Adlerian group counselor, when he or she wants to contribute wisdom from education and experience, does not withhold it in the guise of being nonauthor-itarian. The leader knows more about motivations and goals than other group members, and withholding knowledge is a pretense and cover-up (Dreikurs, 1951). Sonstegard and Bitter (1998) suggest offering an interpretation or insight with a question like, "Would you like to hear what I think?" Thus, the Adlerian group leader possesses good teaching skills such as confidence, clarity, audi-ence awareness, listening talent, and organization.

Role Modeling

The counselor also serves as a role model of social interest and vigor. The client may never have observed such a model closely before. The therapist clearly cares about people and acts on the feeling through his or her choice of occupa-tion. Most important, the counselor admits to being fallible and flawed, and models a healthy response to failings, for example, being able to laugh at oneself or to shrug off minor mistakes as an expected part of living. Thus, the counselor is not a blank slate upon which the client inscribes transference. In Adlerian therapy, transference and countertransference are considered evidence of the client's typical interpersonal patterns, because the same dynamics will oper-ate in session as well as outside. For instance, a client whose basic mistake is

"I have to please people in authority" will try to figure out what the therapist wants and then to provide it. As a result, the therapist will feel courted rather than trusted, and the other group members feel rivalry for approval. The counselor then uses these feelings to demonstrate to the individual how his mask of congeniality affects others.

Corsini (1988) emphasizes the leader's personality characteristics more than his or her specific skills. He lists intelligence, ability to act decisively, compassion, kindness, concern, and most important, courage, as qualities he finds ideal in a group leader of any stripe. Sonstegard (1998) produces much the same list of qualities, and adds the element of faith in the group process. The leader who believes that the group will work out well displays a calm relaxation impossible to fake.

Providing Early Guidance

As the group progresses, it will find its own natural leadership and will be able to apply Adlerian process without much counselor directiveness. In early days, though, members can use specific help in fundamentals of group discussion. Many people have rarely participated in a meaningful, personal discussion amongst equals. Sweeney (1998) lists seven skills that the leader models for participants early on. (Though his list is directed to leaders of Adlerian children's groups, I think it pertains across all ages):

1. **Helping establish ground rules**
2. **Ensuring total group participation** Include silent members by asking them to comment on a topic, question, or issue that anyone would feel safe expressing an opinion upon.
3. **Modeling through initial leadership** Show how members can think through experiences, question and evaluate what they have heard, and reach a conclusion.
4. **Handling touchy problems** Intervene when derogatory and meaningless discourse occurs by returning the focus to constructive thinking.
5. **Stimulating ideas** Anticipate topics that will motivate people to talk meaningfully and build their confidence in discussing things.
6. **Encouraging group decisions and avoiding premature interventions** Allow the consequences of group agreements to unfold without pointing out the problems yourself. Failed courses of action can be discussed as learning experiences.
7. **Summarizing and evaluating progress made** Periodically make statements that wrap things up and look ahead to the future: "What have we done?" "In what ways has it been of value?" "What other things might we do that could be helpful or needed?" (summarized from pp. 437–439)

Though most Adlerian therapists seek to achieve nondirectiveness (Corsini, 1988), we shouldn't shy away from preparing the group to function effectively.

Sense of Humor

The counselor models laughing at oneself and seeing the funny side of human frailty, another way of subverting the painful struggle for dignity and prestige. Because the winter holidays are often stressful for people of any religion in the United States, beforehand I like to share with my group some of the horrific stories from my own family holidays, emphasizing the humor of how even grown adults revert to childish patterns at these times. When the group reconvenes after the holidays, members usually have had their own tales to swap. They often say how thinking of how the group will enjoy the story defuses their distress at the time of the episode. One client made a list ahead of time of all the insulting remarks she could expect her mother and sister to make over Thanksgiving, and returned to group having kept score of each one as it flowed from their lips. Though the family members were not about to change their patterns, the client was able to change hers—she stuck to evaluating herself by her own standards and seeing theirs as silly.

Techniques of Adlerian Group Counseling

Adlerian counselors are free to choose any ethical techniques that work toward encouraging and revitalizing their group members. Three stand out as part of the psychological investigation stage, when assessment is the focus.

Early Childhood Recollections

An Adlerian will usually ask clients to describe in detail their earliest childhood recollection. These are specific scenes, not general memories, often called up from age four or five. It makes little difference whether the client remembers correctly or whether the client could come up with a different recollection given enough time. The memory recounted will reveal the client's current style of life. Let me give you an example:

> I was about three or four. I was lying on the daybed and my parents were watching television. My father came over and placed a sofa pillow beside me so that I wouldn't roll off it accidentally. He patted me on the head and said I was a good boy. Then they went back to watching TV. I felt happy surrounded with the sofa cushions, hearing my parents murmur in the room.

The client, Sam, didn't realize at the moment how much his early childhood recollection reflected him as the group had come to know him, as an adult. For one thing, Sam loved to nap and was often found catching a quick snooze in the counselor's waiting room before a group session. Also, there was something about him that brought out protectiveness in others. Because they knew he came to group directly from work, members often picked up a snack for him to munch before going into the session. As they shared their own early childhood recollections, the seeds of their current selves were discernible in their stories.

The early childhood recollection, like the life story, exposes the style, themes, core conflicts, and tone of the personality. Adlerians look at polarities that reflect one's habitual way of organizing the world. Is the situation dangerous or safe? Social or solitary? Active or subdued? Is the child helpless or competent? Trusting or mistrusting? Participant or observer?

SMALL GROUP EXERCISE

In your small group, do a round in which each member relates his or her earliest childhood recollection. By this time, you know each other fairly well and can discuss whether each recollection reflects the person you know today. Then discuss whether you edited your recollection before telling it to the group. What are some reasons people edited? Do you think the early recollection exercise is useful even if most people edit their stories? Why or why not?

Dream Analysis

Adler wrote, "Freud has claimed from the first that dreams are fulfillments of infantile sexual wishes. On the basis of actual experience this appears to assign to dreams a too limited scope" (1929/1956, p. 358). Adler assessed clients' dreams in much the same way as their early childhood recollections, as a source of speculation about their style of life. He did not assign fixed meanings to objects and events in dreams, as Freudians tend to do. The meaning of each dream element is specific to the dreamer. The interpretation should be reconcilable with other evidence, such as early recollections, current problems, and usual tendencies. In dreams, we experiment with possible actions that we might never consider in waking life. According to Adler, a forgotten dream means that we reject or postpone the action it suggested, whereas a nightmare discourages us from a contemplated action (Mosak, 2000). Dream analysis is used as a psychological disclosure technique as well as an investigation technique. In group counseling, dreams sometimes seem a safer way to reveal one's self than direct exposition. In groups, members often bring up a comparable dream of their own and can engage in exploration together.

Dreams, according to Adler, rehearse possible actions. These may be actions that our style of life excludes from waking thoughts. Dreams can be used for solving problems we are having at the time. Consider the dream Gregor relayed to his men's group. As you read it, try to interpret it in Adlerian terms.

> I was supervising moving a whole house down the road on a trailer pulled by a semi cab. The house was creaking and groaning but everything looked like it was going to be okay. A man watching the house go by asked me why I was moving my whole house rather than just choosing a new one in the de-

sired location, and moving my belongings. I remember saying in the dream, "Well, I just thought it was about time I did the whole thing."

You will immediately see the significance of Gregor's dream when you know the situation in which he told it to the group.

Gregor was a city police officer in his late thirties, who had moved up the ladder of responsibility quickly and single-mindedly in his years on the force. Attending a high school class reunion threw him into a state of questioning what he'd missed on his way up. He didn't have much fun in life, and his job acquainted him mostly with the negative parts of human nature. He had made resolutions to change his life in several ways, like taking ballroom dancing, signing up for an Internet dating service, and joining a men's counseling group. The moving house seemed to portray himself, and the road suggests his journey to a new life. The creaking and groaning were the discomfort he felt making life changes. Gregor's statement in the dream summarizes what he'd decided to do with his life. Gregor had also cut down on his heavy drinking in his new lifestyle, and the group joked about whether the house in the dream was going to "fall off the wagon." Do you think that moving the whole house means that Gregor didn't want to change completely—just to be himself in a better place? In this men's group, members were able to tell each other their feelings and perceptions through discussing their dreams, better than through ordinary conversation.

Family Photos

In the psychological investigation stage, remember that family constellation is a critical clue. Some Adlerians have each group member select three to six family photographs to bring to the group to discuss (Sherman & Dinkmeyer, 1987). Members each have a time period in which to explain why they chose the pictures, who is in them, when they were taken, and so forth. The group involves itself in asking questions and giving their reactions.

Samples of Adlerian Interventions

Therapists are encouraged to be creative, so you will see Adler's followers prescribing outdoor adventures or encouraging clients to stay awake and worry all night. Techniques can be divided into three categories: reframing, behavior experiments, and resource development.

Reframing As discussed earlier, clients need to change their cognitive map of the world and self. This requires alteration of old, habitual ways of thinking and the substitution of new ways, which is labeled **reframing.** (You have probably noticed how the same picture looks quite different when you put it into a new frame.) Groups learn to help each other look at things in alternative manners.

The Question Adler (1929) advised asking clients **The Question,** which goes something like this: "If I could magically eliminate your symptom immediately and completely, what would be different in your life?" The client's answer may lead directly to an understanding of what he or she fears most, or what is being avoided. An agoraphobic client might answer, "I'd be able to do my own grocery shopping." This might indicate that the client fears the burden of self-sufficiency. In groups, clients can learn to ask each other The Question and discuss the answer among themselves.

The Push-Button Adler asked group members to imagine pushing a button and then picturing a pleasant experience they'd had, in as much detail and vividness as possible. He exhorted them to notice how the memory made them feel good in the present moment as they imagined it. Then he would have them do the same with the memory of an unpleasant event and notice how it made them feel bad in the present. He repeated this technique, asking clients to switch back and forth, to get them to realize that they have inner control of how they feel at the moment, through control over what they think about.

Role-Playing The client acts out a distressing encounter but must take the character of a different person. For example, a teenager might act out a scene of his father picking on him, taking the role of the father. Another group member would act out the teen's role, with advice from the others to make it realistic. In role-plays, the client is able to reframe the situation from a different point of view, and perhaps break the mold of his habitual ways of construing it. In a group I co-led, a teenager in a role-play like the one above realized how unpleasant his father felt when criticizing him, something he'd never considered before.

Brainstorming After identifying some basic mistakes in thinking, counselor and members brainstorm alternative convictions that could be substituted and discuss the implications of adopting those instead. For "I never get what I need," try out "I usually get what I need." Evidence can be found on both sides, but one conviction promotes healthy behavior. The group can assign homework to each member, substituting a new conviction for an old one for a week, and report back to the group next session. I used to be easily unhorsed by bad news breaking, with inner convictions like, "This is awful! Fixing this will take hours and hours of work, if it can be fixed at all! And meanwhile it's my turn to make dinner! I'm so overloaded!" and so on. Now I have a friend who often says, "Things are never as bad as you think they're going to be." I've adopted her conviction instead and saved myself many a tizzy.

Behavior Experiments Because Adlerian counseling is action oriented, cognitive reframing alone is not enough. Adlerians suggest active experiments inside and outside the counseling session. Kefir (1981) noted that clients often come equipped with a narrow repertoire of behaviors and therefore have limited choices when faced with unfamiliar or threatening situations. Broadening this repertoire is a goal of therapy. In these experiments, the stress is not upon a perfect outcome, but on the effort and process. Adlerians frequently use contracts to solidify the agreements made within group about what each member will do in the real world between sessions. A contract makes it more likely that the client will not avoid or forget the homework. The group discussions when the member reports back on the experiment often serve all the members.

Behaving "As If" The client tries out behaving "as if" he or she were psychologically better. You have probably done this exercise yourself—for example, forcing yourself to go to a social gathering even though you feel sluggish, knowing that you will feel lively once you are there. Pam, who has trouble walking into a room of people and introducing herself, notices that Ann finds this easy and does it nicely. Pam practices behaving "as if" she were Ann when walking into meetings. She can practice this within a group session, with tips from Ann and others, before trying it in the outside world.

Task Setting An Adlerian group might have given a homework task to Pam. She might be asked to force herself to walk into one room and introduce herself each day, no matter what. The group would help her make a list of some easy tasks to start with, such as telling her name to people in her building's elevator. Threatening situations become less and less scary with more exposure, usually. Otherwise, people would never stay in counseling groups!

Because social interest is so critical in Adlerian philosophy, clients are often assigned to do community service homework, like volunteering in a soup kitchen or literacy brigade. This type of useful work reorients clients away from the self-centeredness that usually comes along with psychological distress, especially depression. It also spurs activity rather than passivity. Adlerian group members find social interest in helping each other, something they may have been too self-involved to try for a long time. When the whole group performs a community service together, such as acting as flood relief volunteers, they build a life history together, strengthening cohesiveness.

Catching Yourself Because your habitual ways of thinking and acting have become so automatic, if you want to change them you need to become more aware of when they kick in. Counselors who help people quit smoking or overeating usually ask them to keep records of their cigarettes or food. The very act of writing down each instance increases their awareness of the behavior and helps them see what spurs them to overindulge. In the same way, you can "catch yourself" about to respond to a situation in an old maladaptive way and choose to respond otherwise. In group counseling sessions, often the conversation floats on a superficial level, sounding like dinner-table talk. Members must learn a signal to "catch themselves" at this and discuss why they are reluctant to go deeper at this time. They may want to brainstorm about what they could habitually do when their discussions linger on a surface level.

Adlerians help their groups identify other habits and short-circuit them, even emotional habits. For example, a husband who doesn't make much money feels that he is being criticized whenever his wife admires a beautiful, expensive item. When he talks about this in group, other members who window-shop point out that his wife may not have a critical intention at all. She is just sharing her enjoyment of window-shopping. The group reminds the husband of other evidence that his wife is more artistic than acquisitive. He could "catch himself" feeling belittled next time and choose instead to look for the item's beauty.

Countersuggestions In Adlerian therapy, countersuggestion may take the form of asking an insomniac to stay awake all night or telling a worrier to try to worry about everything continually and avoid any nonworrying thoughts. If a client's basic mistake was a conviction that life was unfair, Adler might ask him or her to whine about every grievance, no matter how small. The mechanisms that make countersuggestions work are complex. Probably, many habits become boring, painful, ridiculous, or humorous when intensified. There may be relief in giving up the fight and finding that the result is not so bad after all, or not so satisfying, or self-limiting (as in the insomniac's efforts to stay awake).

Intensifying a habit within the group leads to immediate reactions from other members, and in this setting the reactions are not masked as they are in polite society. A member who is set loose to whine about everything soon feels the disgust, ridicule, amusement, and boredom of people he or she has come to care about. Their reactions hold up a mirror that may inspire change.

Resource Development In times of psychological distress, people often let the positive side of their lives wither on the vine. A physically fit person who becomes depressed is likely to stop working out, even though the exercise would surely be a boon. An anxious person who enjoys reading novels may forget to pick one up at the library. Adler encouraged clients to develop the neglected healthy aspects of life. In a long-term women's group I joined, we knew each other's strengths and interests well. When a member was focusing on negatives, another member countered her with a dare to do one of her positive activities within the next week and report on it next session.

Compensation In many areas, we accept our weaknesses rather than try to cure them. Through **compensation,** we make the most of our strengths. But when discouragement prevails, assets are neglected as well. An Adlerian counselor asks clients to inventory their strong points and skills, and the group investigates what can be done with those. Let's say that Stan, a job-hopping academic, is a very good teacher but realizes in group that many conditions of work in a college setting are distasteful to him. His group could help him to think about other ways in which he could use his talents—for example, organizing and giving workshops for business firms or doing industrial training. A job has much more to it than one activity, and people with the right skill frequently find that they are mismatched with the job in most other ways. This mismatch is a source of deep unhappiness, yet if a person is too discouraged to take risks, she or he feels stuck.

In another type of compensation, Adler would ask how a depressed client could use his or her strengths in a socially useful way to balance an unsatisfactory personal life. Many clients find that helping others within group counseling adds satisfaction to a dreary life situation.

DISCUSSION IDEA

Adler's customary techniques are often used without a therapist. Sometimes groups of close friends or family groups suggest Adlerian techniques when you are out of sorts. Look back over the list of techniques, and see whether you can think of a time when you or someone you know used one of them. Discuss the examples and the results people found from using the techniques. The fact that non-psychologists come up with these techniques highlights Adler's common sense point of view.

Problems Addressed by Adlerian Groups

Adler was ahead of his time, as a psychologist, in seeing the individual embedded in a broad social context. Because of his vision of each of us functioning in a network of other people and institutions, some beneficent and some hostile, many ideas of today's theorists are identical to his. He contributed to the systemic approaches of family counseling, to the establishment of group therapy, and to the vision of social constructions of reality, all of which are integral in contemporary theories.

The challenges of friendship, work, and love are usually concerns of people who seek therapy (Dinkmeyer, 1975), and Alderian approaches have addressed these challenges in most of their forms. "Much of Adlerian group therapy is preventive, educational, and developmental in nature, as maladjustment is usually considered to be closely related to faulty interpretations of one's environment, misguided or distorted forms of compensation for feelings of inferiority, and goals inappropriate to social living" (Donigian & Hulse-Killacky, 1999, p. 43).

Adler would be happy to see that counselors in training are now exhorted to investigate the categorical identity of each client and whether the client embraces or rejects this identity. As I have said earlier, this is not a matter of making generalizations based on visible differences like skin color. Instead, it is an exploration of the values, worldview, and practices dominant in the world of each client. Adler would say that these are *always* relevant to the client's problems. Adlerian therapy in this way is tailored for working with clients who belong to minority groups.

Adler was aware that many of women's problems and marital problems stemmed from women's inferior status in society. He felt that they suffered not from some primal penis envy, but from envy of the real power and privilege that men hold. Men, on the other hand, found it too easy to translate their strivings for superiority into towering above women. Marital discord, he felt, was not merely a private matter but a symptom of social inequality between the sexes, often exacerbated by the tendency of insecure men to marry women whom they considered their inferiors. Adler's thoughts were a precursor of feminist theory in many ways. He would have been pleased with the proclamation, "The personal is political." Problems between ethnic and racial groups, too, can be considered in the light of struggles to gain power or maintain privilege. Hawes (1985) described the development of an Adlerian personal growth group for women, which avoided any underlying assumption of psychopathology among the members.

Dreikurs (1956), along with several other historians, conceptualized psychiatry as having three revolutions: the first, in the eighteenth century, when insanity became a topic of medicine rather than religion (previously, insanity was largely considered the result of demons and witchcraft). The second revolution occurred when ideas about personality development and psychological mechanisms gave rise to psychoanalysis, at the turn of the twentieth century. The third, in the 1920s, recognizing the social factors in psychiatric disorders, created methods such as psychodrama and group work based on the basic social nature of humanity. Adler was a critical figure in the third revolution. Dreikurs wrote that each revolution put the psychiatrist (we would say, the counselor or therapist) in a different setting:

> The first put him into mental hospitals; the second removed him from the hospital and put him in private practice; the third removes him from the confines of his office and puts him right in the community . . . in industry, in schools, in community centers, in churches, anywhere in the community where problems of inter-relationships arise. (p. 124)

Perfectionism

Though we often look at perfectionism as a *symptom* of a disorder, like obsessive compulsive disorder or body dysmorphic disorder, Adler saw psychopathology as a *response* to perfectionism (Lombardi, Florentino, & Lombardi, 1998). Perfectionism is striving for superiority gone amuck. General anxiety disorder, eating disorders, somatoform disorders, alcoholism, and drug addiction are some of the problems addressed through the basic mistake, "I must be perfect." Less severe but nonetheless self-destructive habits also stem from perfectionism: wanting to excel no matter what the price, concealing and denying one's emotions, doing nothing if it can't be done flawlessly. Adler encouraged such clients to give up ideal perfection and strive for "normal perfection," which includes striving for improvement through taking risks and making mistakes, the "courage to be imperfect."

Joining a counseling group is itself showing the "courage to be imperfect." Members learn to admire and even love others whose flaws are known, and feel the acceptance of their own flaws by other group members. To happily belong in a group where you don't hide your imperfections is a new and curative experience for many clients.

Alienation: Adventure-Based Therapy

Adlerian techniques do not all require high levels of verbal or cognitive skill, so they are applicable to a broader population than many talk therapies. **Adventure-based therapy** often involves cooperative tasks like building a bridge with a limited set of materials, blindfolded trust walks, and mountain climbing (Wick, Wick, & Peterson, 1997). These activities build legitimate self-esteem through problem solving and actions that benefit each participant and the group they belong to. Errors have natural consequences that the whole group must deal with—for example, breaking a piece of the bridge material means that the group has to come up with a plan to fix it or build without it. This demonstrates the difference between punishment and natural consequences. Adventure programs have been especially effective with delinquent youth (Glass & Myers, 2001).

People who are not strong in verbal expression or academics may find themselves leaders in adventure therapy groups. The charm of an unfamiliar task, like those designed in adventure therapy, is that the individuals cannot fall back on *private logic* habits, and they often discover unexplored parts of themselves. Adler and his followers saw the group as a natural basis for individual change because it is a social setting that can reenact the family constellation with a better outcome. The 1985 film *The Breakfast Club,* which was wildly popular among teenagers, exemplified Adlerian adventure therapy principles (the adventure was enduring a day-long school detention). You might enjoy renting the film and looking at it as an Adlerian.

Wilderness group therapy is a contemporary application of Adlerian principles. For example, Passages to Recovery (PTR) is a program for addicts ages 18 to 50 (Kennedy, 2003). The participants camp in nature, moving every day, for at least thirty-five days. They learn survival skills such as starting fires without matches, cooking, creating shelters, choosing campsites, and dealing with nature's surprises. In the process of staying alive, they learn to get along with each other, make decisions, and work as a team. The self-esteem and social skills they develop protect them against relapse into addiction and resumption of their addictive thought patterns. A similar program for school dropouts in Israel (Romi & Kohan, 2004) resulted in improvements in happiness and satisfaction, behavior, looks and abilities, popularity, and belief in success through personal initiative. The report of this wilderness program mentioned the advantage of counselors' access to teens who were tired and hungry, "thus ill-equipped to hide their emotions" (p. 117).

Adaptations to Clients' Ages

Like psychoeducational approaches (Chapter 12), Adlerian group approaches are unusual in that they were originally intended for children rather than adults. The approaches were then extended to adults, especially parents and teachers.

Child and School Problems

Because of Adler's positive view of humanity and the ability to change, he and his followers practiced among the general population, giving lectures and parenting workshops and consulting with schools. Their focus was upon designing social settings in which neurosis would *not* develop. Adler believed that children's behavior, like adults', is purposive and can be understood by its function in the family or classroom constellation. Children's problems stemmed from "inability to cooperate with society, feeling inferior, and lack of a life goal" (Utay & Utay, 1996), the same sources of adult problems. Therefore, his work with schools and parents emphasized orienting or reorienting the children toward successful and satisfying group activity. If the children had developed lonely, discouraged, and isolated styles, they could gain encouragement through participation in teams that made use of their skills in ways that were challenging but within reach. Rudolf Dreikurs made Adlerian educational principles popular in the United States. These principles included democratic rules, individual responsibility, encouragement, social awareness, and natural consequences rather than punishment (Pryor & Tollerud, 1999). Modern school-based interventions for attention deficit hyperactivity disorder (Edwards & Gfroerer, 2001), raising self-esteem through adventure therapy (Wick, Wick, & Peterson, 1997), counseling for ridiculed children (Utay & Utay, 1996), and motivating defiant children (Pryor & Tollerud, 1999) are firmly based in Adlerian thought.

Groups for Parents

The same democratic principles inform Adlerian practices in child-raising, evidenced in popular books like *Discipline Without Tears* (Dreikurs & Cassel, 1990) and in the choice theory of Glasser (Chapter 15).

Parent study groups convene as educational courses, not considering themselves therapy groups (McKay & McKay, 1993). They read and discuss Adlerian materials, practice the principles between sessions, and use the group setting to exchange ideas and receive encouragement. These groups have been sponsored by churches, social service agencies, school counselors, and colleges. Systematic Training for Effective Parenting (STEP) programs can be ordered as multimedia packages ready to be used, with leader's guides, video and audio cassettes, parents' books, and other materials. Separate programs are available for parents of children, parents of teens, stepparents, and parents who want more advanced training after graduating from the first program. Consistent with the Adlerian philosophy, these do not request that licensed counselors or psychologists serve as group leaders.

Evaluating Adlerian Groups

How can you tell whether your Adlerian group is working? Hawes (1985) evaluated her women's personal growth groups through taped discussions with members two to six months after the twentieth session. She evaluated responses in terms of reported improvements in work and social situations. The fact that all her groups maintained either regular meetings together or informal networking structures, three years after the experimental groups closed, also serves as positive evidence about the groups.

You may wish for more quantitative, pre–post treatment results, for your own or agency reasons. Three different scales are available and relevant. Considering that the Adlerian concept of social interest is the opposite of loneliness, Brough (1994) used pre and post scores on the UCLA Loneliness Scale (Russell, Peplau, & Ferguson, 1978), finding highly significant improvement after a ten-session group program. The UCLA Loneliness Scale has the advantage of being very widely used, so you will be able to compare your results with the results of many other research programs.

Two scales to measure social interest exist. The Social Interest Index (SII; Greever, Tseng, & Friedland, 1973) asks members to rate endorsement of thirty-two items that concern equality of all humanity, acceptance of self and others, responsibility for self, sense of having a place in the world, and so forth. The items form subscales on topics of work, friendship, love, and self-significance. Crandall's Social Interest Scale (SIS; Crandall, 1975) asks participants to underline from paired adjectives which they value more highly, such as forgiving-gentle, efficient-respectful. A twenty-four-item test, including nine dummy items unrelated to social interest, the SIS is easily scored by counting up the number of underlines of choices keyed as relevant to social interest (in the example pairs, *forgiving* and *respectful*). The entire SIS is available in Crandall's article, making it free for your use (with appropriate credit given) as well as easy to administer.

KEY TERMS

adventure-based therapy   a mode of group work in which members attempt a cooperative task; the activities build legitimate self-esteem through problem solving and actions that benefit each participant and the group they belong to

agreements   in Adlerian groups, guidelines developed by group discussion (in contrast with rules given by authority)

basic mistakes   convictions based on wrong impressions developed from the limited perceptions of childhood

birth order analysis   looking at the family position, such as first child, as a generator of patterns of behavior

compensation   making use of one's strengths to balance out weaknesses

constructivist   a description of a theory that emphasizes the subjective nature of reality—how it is constructed by the individual

discouragement   the emotional component of psychological distress, including a sense of futility and low energy

encouragement   finding or reviving a sense of hope and efficacy

existential   having to do with the basic dilemmas of human existence

family constellation   the group formed by parents, siblings, and other influential adults; a new child attempts to find a meaningful spot in this constellation

fictional finalism   the choice of goals and hopes that are consistent with the fictional self

fictional self   the self-concept built from observations and interpretations of others' reactions to one's self; it is fictional in that it is made up in the imagination

holistic   a description of the belief that feelings, thinking, and behavior are a unified whole, and that something is lost by analyzing one element in isolation from the others

life script   the story or drama associated with the fictional self—for example, a damsel in distress will be rescued by a dashing prince, or a life of good deeds will reap spiritual rewards

personal priorities   control, superiority, pleasure, comfort—four driving goals; individuals are usually primarily driven by one of them

private logic   a way of reasoning that is consistent with the fictional self

reframing   instead of changing reality, changing the way one perceives it

reorientation   the stage of counseling or of a counseling session in which insight is put into action or plans are made to put insight into action

sense of inferiority   a feeling at the beginning of life that parents and older siblings function better and know more

socioteleological   belief in a purposeful development toward an end; human impulses are not random but goal-oriented; the prefix *socio* emphasizes the major influence of social systems on this development, rather than biological or theological systems

strivings for superiority   attempts to cope with a sense of inferiority; these can be positive (applying oneself in school) and negative (putting on a false front)

style of life   the unifying motivations, goals, and beliefs that pervade a person's behavior and life course

The Question   "If I could magically eliminate your symptom immediately and completely, what would be different in your life?"; the client's answer may lead directly to an understanding of what he or she fears most, or what is being avoided

CHAPTER REVIEW

1. Explain Adler's concept of social interest to a friend or family member. Can you agree on a person you both know who demonstrates this concept—or a lack of it? Discuss how you evaluate someone's level of social interest.

2. Why is the group setting ideal for Adlerian counseling?

3. After a successful Adlerian group counseling experience, do you think a person's early childhood recollection would be different than before? Explain why you think it would or would not change.

4. Pretend you are in a group and must present your responses to Dinkmeyer's three prompts (page 383). Formulate what you would say. What do you think your group members could tell about you from your answers? Reflect on the experience of formulating your presentation: What emotions did it bring up, for example?

5. Get together with classmates or friends to discuss your fictional selves and life scripts. Can you identify one that you seem to be following? For instance, I like "Bad girl makes good." There are also scripts for "Overcoming all odds," "Born loser," "Knight in shining armor," "Favorite son," "Golden girl," "Thwarted genius," and so forth. If you have trouble, think of films

and stories with which you strongly identify. Are there characters that might represent your fictional self?

6. What do you think of the idea of sense of inferiority and the resulting strivings for superiority? Do you think these concepts apply to everyone? Form an opinion and defend it. For the best review, find a classmate who disagrees with your opinion and discuss the issue.

7. Because of Adler's interest in schools, many of the references to his work are published in education journals rather than psychology journals. Look in your education database and ask for "Adler" and "Adlerian" in the titles of articles published in the last two years. Do the titles of the articles make sense to you after reading this chapter? Be sure to save any citations that appeal to your interests.

FOR FURTHER READING

Online, at *http://ourworld.compuserve.com/homepages/hstein*, you will find a wealth of Adlerian information. This site has video clips of Adler and Adlerians (including a newsreel of Adler in Vienna in 1929), a question-and-answer page, quotations, concept maps, and references. At *http://www.alfredadler.org*, the North American Society of Adlerian Psychology displays its web page with news about the national organization's meetings and links to Adlerian schools and other organizations.

REFERENCES

Adler, A. (1929*). Problems of neurosis*. London: Kegan Paul.

Adler, A. (1930). *The education of children* (E. Jensen & F. Jensen, Trans.). South Bend, IN: Gateway.

Adler, A. (1931). Extract from *What life should mean to you*. In H. L. Ansbacher & R. R. Ansbacher (Eds.), *The individual psychology of Alfred Adler: A systematic presentation in selections from his writings* (p. 209). (Reprinted from *What life should mean to you*, 1931, Boston: Little-Brown)

Adler, A. (1956). Extracts from *The science of living*. In H. L. Ansbacher & R. R. Ansbacher (Eds.), *The individual psychology of Alfred Adler: A systematic presentation in selections from his writings* (pp. 357–358). New York: Harper Torchbooks. (Reprinted from *The science of living*, 1929, New York: Greenburg)

Adler, A. (1957*). Understanding human nature* (W. Beran Wolfe, Trans.). New York: Fawcett. (Original work published 1927)

Brough, M. F. (1994). Alleviation of loneliness: Evaluation of an Adlerian-based group therapy program. *Individual Psychology, 50,* 40–51.

Corsini, R. J. (1988). Adlerian groups. In S. Long (Ed.), *Six Group Therapies* (pp. 1–48). New York: Plenum Press.

Crandall, J. E. (1975). A scale for social interest. *Journal of Individual Psychology, 31,* 187–195.

Dinkmeyer, D. (1975). Adlerian group psychotherapy. *International Journal of Group Psychotherapy, 25,* 219–226.

Donigian, J., & Hulse-Killacky, D. (1999). *Critical incidents in group therapy* (2nd ed.). Belmont, CA: Brooks/Cole.

Dreikurs, R. (1951). The unique social climate experienced in group psychotherapy. *Group Psychotherapy: Journal of Sociopsychopathology and Sociatry, 3,* 292–299.

Dreikurs, R. (1956). Contribution of group psychotherapy to psychiatry. *Group Psychotherapy: Journal of Sociopsychopathology and Sociatry, 9,* 115–125.

Dreikurs, R. (1957). Group psychotherapy from the point of view of Adlerian psychology. *International Journal of Group Psychotherapy, 7,* 363–375.

Dreikurs, R., & Cassel, P. (1990). *Discipline without tears.* NY: Dutton.

Edwards, D. L., & Gfroerer, K. P. (2001). Adlerian school-based interventions for children with attention-deficit/hyperactivity disorder. *Journal of Individual Psychology, 57,* 210–223.

Glass, J. S., & Myers, J. E. (2001). Combining the old and the new to help adolescents: Individual psychology and adventure-based counseling. *Journal of Mental Health Counseling, 23,* 104–114.

Greever, K. B., Tseng, M. S., & Friedland, B. U. (1973). *Journal of Consulting and Clinical Psychology, 41,* 454–458.

Hawes, E. C. (1985). Personal growth groups for women: An Adlerian approach. *Journal for Specialists in Group Work, 10,* 19–27.

Kefir, N. (1981). Impasse/priority therapy. In R. J. Corsini (Ed.), *Handbook of innovative psychotherapies* (pp. 401–415). New York: Wiley.

Kennedy, A. (2003, November). Roughing it to recovery: Wilderness therapy an option for substance abusers. *Counseling Today,* 8–9.

Lombardi, D. N., Florentino, M., & Lombardi, A. J. (1998). Perfectionism and abnormal behavior. *Journal of Individual Psychology, 54,* 61–71.

McKay, G. D., & McKay, J. (1993). Parent study groups. In O. C. Christensen (Ed.), *Adlerian family counseling* (rev. ed., pp. 165–186). Minneapolis, MN: Educational Media Corp.

Mosak, H. H. (2000). Adlerian psychotherapy. In R. J. Corsini & D. Wedding (Eds.), *Current psychotherapies* (6th ed., pp. 54–98). Itasca, IL: Peacock.

Powers, R. L. (1973). Myth and memory. In H. H. Mosak (Ed.), *Alfred Adler: His influence on psychology today* (pp. 271–290). Park Ridge, NJ: Noyes Press.

Pryor, D. B., & Tollerud, T. R. (1999). Applications of Adlerian principles in school settings. *Professional School Counseling, 2,* 299–304.

Romi, S., & Kohan, E. (2004). Wilderness programs: Principles, possibilities and opportunities for intervention with dropout adolescents. *Child & Youth Care Forum, 33,* 115–136.

Russell, D., Peplau, L. A., & Ferguson, M. L. (1978). Developing a measure of loneliness. *Journal of Personality Assessment, 42,* 290–294.

Sherman, R., & Dinkmeyer, D. (1987). *Systems of family therapy: An Adlerian integration.* New York: Brunner/Mazel.

Sonstegard, M. A. (1998). The theory and practice of Adlerian group counseling and psychotherapy. *Journal of Individual Psychology, 54,* 217–250.

Sonstegard, M. A., & Bitter, J. R. (1998). Adlerian group counseling: Step by step. *Journal of Individual Psychology, 54,* 176–216.

Sweeney, T. J. (1998). *Adlerian counseling: A practitioner's approach* (4th ed.). Philadelphia, PA: Accelerated Development.

Utay, J., & Utay, C. (1996). Applications of Adler's theory in counseling and education. *Journal of Instructional Psychology, 23,* 251–256.

Vaihinger, H. (1925). *The philosophy of "as if": A system of the theoretical, practical, and religious fictions of mankind.* New York: Harcourt, Brace. (Original work published 1911)

Watts, R. E. (2000). Adlerian counseling: A viable approach for contemporary practice. *TCA Journal, 28,* 11–23.

Watts, R. E. (2003). Adlerian therapy as a relational constructivist approach. *Family Journal, 11,* 139–147.

Watts, R. E., & Pietrzak, D. (2000). Adlerian "encouragement" and the therapeutic process of solution-focused brief therapy. *Journal of Counseling and Development, 78,* 442–447.

Wick, D. T., Wick, J. K., & Peterson, N. (1997). Improving self-esteem with Adlerian adventure therapy. *Professional School Counseling, 1,* 53–56.

CHAPTER 15

Choice Theory and Reality Therapy

William Glasser, the author of the selection below, began his practice of reality therapy after being disappointed with the failures of psychoanalytical practice, in which he was formally trained. Reality therapy, unlike many other therapies, originated as a group approach designed to be useful in tough settings such as prisons and dangerous schools. In the 1980s, Glasser identified **control theory** as a sensible basis for his therapy. Control theory came from physical sciences and cybernetics, explaining how systems regulate themselves internally. Glasser liked the idea that people, too, are controlled internally rather than by external demands. Later, he changed the label of his theory to **choice theory**, emphasizing the freedom of choice we all have in controlling our lives.

A Selection from

"School Violence from the Perspective of William Glasser"

By William Glasser (2000)

Even though statistics show that school violence is diminishing, it is still a threat no school can afford to dismiss. To make schools safer requires the effort of staff, students, and parents. But it is the skill of counselors that can provide what may be most needed, an effective violence prevention program. From my long experience working with students, I believe such a program is neither difficult to explain nor expensive to put into place.

Unhappiness, combined with the strong feeling in the perpetrator that others should be punished for the way he feels, is by far the main reason that anyone strikes out at another human being. Why the unhappy boy or man lashes out at the particular time he does, however, cannot be predicted. What can be predicted is that almost all unhappy boys and men carry within them the potential for violence, and in our schools there are many unhappy students. Therefore, the key to reducing violence is to do what I believe can be done in every school—reduce the number of unhappy students. The fewer there are, the fewer school problems including violence. . . .

In retrospect, a lot of information about the unhappiness of Harris and Klebold has been made public. But prior to the violence it is doubtful that anyone at Columbine, or any other similar high school, could have picked up enough information to predict any violence, much less that it would have been committed by these young men. What was needed then and is still needed is a violence-prevention program (VPP), not only in Columbine, but in every school in the United States. Such programs would not only reduce the incidence of violence, they would reduce the incidence of all behavior problems in school. The cost of violence far exceeds the cost of an effective VPP.

What is being done now in Columbine and almost every school in the country is to enhance security. This step—security guards, X-ray machines, and restricted entrances and exits—is being taken because everyone can see it. It also gives administrators and school boards the sense that something visible is being done. But short of what is done in airports, the chance of enhanced security preventing much violence is small for the amount of money it costs. I'm not saying it shouldn't be done if there is plenty of money available, but if money is short, it will be much more effective to spend it on a VPP run by well-trained counselors who have no responsibilities other than this program.

I would estimate one such counselor for every 1,000 students would be a good number to start. In Columbine this would have meant two full-time counselors with no other responsibility except the VPP. I recognize that in a time when most school boards are reducing the number of counselors, this may seem to be a large increase. But compared with the cost of even average security, the salaries of two counselors would not be out of line. Well-trained counselors can reduce the number of unhappy students significantly. In fact, the sight of more security personnel and equipment may become an attractive challenge to violence-prone students.

During 11 years at the beginning of my career, I worked as the psychiatrist for a California Youth Authority facility for 400 adolescent and young adult delinquent women. I became personally involved with reducing the unhappiness of what I was sure were some of the unhappiest young women in the school. Then, as now, I did not prescribe psychiatric drugs. I only counseled and supervised other counselors. I realized that girls were not as violent as boys, but our girls had a much higher rate of unhappiness than the girls found in any public school. Nevertheless, during my 11-year tenure at this school there were many fewer "girl-fights" than occurred in most public high schools.

What I did, which the counselors in a violence-prevention program would need to do if the program were to be successful, was I made it my business to get to know two specific groups of girls. The first group was obvious; it included the girls we knew from their records had a history of violence or had a way of dressing or wearing their hair that provoked negative attention in our school. That would be similar to the obvious trench coat Mafia group at Columbine.

But it was the much less obvious second group that was the key to the success we had in preventing violence. This group was made up of girls who were most in touch with what was going on in the school. They knew who was unhappy and what the unhappiness was about. Such a group exists in every high school, it just takes time to determine who comprises it.

These girls for the most part liked the reform school. They appreciated what we were trying to do, and they did not want our school marred with violence any more than we did. To find out who they were, I spent a lot of time hanging out in the cottages or in the school. I ate lunch with the girls and talked to the housemothers and teachers to get suggestions of whom I should see. When I found one and talked to her enough so she began to trust me, she usually directed me to others. After a while I developed a reputation at the school for helping the girls that they suggested to me. Very often when I would call a girl to my office, that same girl had heard about what I did and wanted to talk with me.

I did not even have to guarantee that I would keep what the girls told me confidential. In fact, I told them not to tell me anything that could get them into serious trouble with any girl or her friends that she recommended to me. But, they still told me because they knew that if someone was a danger to herself or others, I would try to handle it without telling more than I had to. But that did not mean that I kept anything that was potentially harmful away from the superintendent. Basically, the girls trusted the superintendent and me to never use their information to get anyone punished or in trouble. Occasionally, a girl had to be segregated for a short time until we could resolve the problem. It was a narrow line to walk, but mostly I was able to stay on it.

The violence-prevention counselor is not a police officer who seeks out and punishes wrongdoers. Even in the girls' school, none of the girls I dealt with was involved in a serious crime. They might be planning to do something wrong, or they may have done something wrong, but to find this out was not my role. My role was prevention, and the only way I can prevent violence or any other undesirable behavior is to build a strong satisfying relationship with the unhappiest students and with the students who can help me find them. A few students played both roles, the source of information and also the subject of a problem.

I cannot overestimate the importance of doing this. In Columbine, the trench coat Mafia were well known. That at least two of them were potentially violent was learned too late. What seemed to render them less dangerous was they were good students. But that is no protection against their being violent; I'm sure the Unabomber was a very good student. What all these violent students share is exactly what the violence-prevention program is designed to address. They lack good relationships with warm, caring responsible adults. The job of the VPP counselor is to be that adult for these students. The success of the program will be directly related to how well the counselors can do this. . . .

At the Ventura School, many of these unhappy girls became my biggest successes. I succeeded because I was able to convince them that I did not want to punish them, I only wanted to get to know them and to help them. The idea that an adult authority figure would deal with them when they were unhappy and not try to blame, punish, or even excuse them for what they were doing was an approach that very few adolescents had experienced. Klebold and Harris did not have this kind of relationship with their parents or with any teacher in school. Most adults look at young people in trouble as if they are guilty, and if the adult is to relate to them, they have to prove their innocence.

In *Choice Theory* (1998), I contend that because of the psychology that 99% of the people in the world use—what I call external control psychology—it would be difficult to reduce any of the human problems such as violence, unloving sex, mental illness, or addiction. To have any chance of solving these problems, it is important to give up external control and replace it with choice theory. While the details of choice theory are too much to explain in this brief article, it is what I did at the Ventura School and exactly what I recommend that the VPP counselors do. . . .

The world is dominated by what I call the seven deadly habits of external control psychology—criticizing, blaming, complaining, nagging, threatening, punishing, and bribing. A bribe is a reward with the aim to control. These habits destroy relationships and, in doing so, cause almost all the problems with which people struggle. In actual fact, the problems such as mental illnesses are the way people choose to resist the control of others or keep their own anger in check.

Choice theory contends that whenever people have difficulty with others, they should never use the deadly habits. Instead, they should choose only to do what could bring them closer or keep them closer. Doing this is not difficult. In fact, whenever we have any problem with our long-term good friends, we do this all the time. We do not use the seven deadly habits because we don't want to lose our friends. Unfortunately, when we have difficulty with almost everyone else, we immediately put the seven habits into practice and make things worse.

Finally, although I can only touch on it here, we will never have the kind of success in school that we so desperately want until we can get external control out of the classroom and replace it with choice theory. (pp. 77–80)

Exploring "School Violence from the Perspective of William Glasser"

1. According to Glasser, what is the key to reducing school violence?
2. What does Glasser think about enhancing security measures in schools? What effects may this course of action have?
3. The author, a physician, emphasizes that he did not use psychiatric drugs or punishment at the reform school. Why do you think he chose not to use these methods?
4. In paragraph 10, Glasser wrote, "It was a narrow line to walk." What is the narrow line he refers to?
5. What key relationships do violence-prone students lack?
6. What is external control psychology? How is it different from choice theory?
7. Have you ever been in an institution, organization, or situation dominated by the seven deadly habits of external control? Did these lead to the outcomes Glasser predicts?
8. Glasser claims that his strategies reduced the number of girl-fights at the reform school. Do you find this believable? If not, what further evidence would convince you? Where can you look for this evidence?
9. Do you think that violent teens can be calmed by good relationships with good adults? Why or why not?

■ ■ ■

Essential Concepts of Choice Theory

Robert Wubbolding, Glasser's associate, has elaborated on choice theory and has codified the techniques of reality therapy. I will draw on both Glasser and Wubbolding to explain basic concepts.

Pragmatism

If Carl Rogers's approach (the warm, accepting humanist) reminds you of the perfect daddy you never had, William Glasser's approach reminds you of the smart, tough-but-fair uncle you never had. From Glasser's point of view, how the world treats you is a reflection of how well you are doing psychologically; reality is the test. He explained his terminology in *Reality Therapy: A New Approach to Psychiatry* (1965):

> All patients have a common characteristic: they all deny the reality of the world around them . . . . Whether it is a partial denial or the total blotting out of all reality of the chronic backward patient in the state hospital, the denial of some or all of reality

is common to all patients. Therapy will be successful when they are able to give up denying the world and recognize that reality not only exists but that they must fulfill their needs within its framework. (p. 6)

The underlying philosophy harks back to the turn of the 20th century, when the Americans William James and John Dewey put forward the point of view that what makes an action or thought right or wrong is whether it yields satisfactory results in resolving a difficulty, in both the short and long runs. Each person's universe is made up of items and thoughts related to our needs to deal with obstacles to successful action. This is philosophical **pragmatism.**

Glasser's focus on the demands of external reality makes reality therapy a natural choice for clients who are acting out or delinquent, and the approach is most frequently used in schools and other settings that focus on behavior control. Often, reality therapy clients are in trouble with society—in jail, in mental hospitals, on probation, in halfway houses or foster homes, or unemployed. They are frequently "addicts, child abusers, psychotics, criminals, school failures, sex deviants, and the many others who do not come for counseling voluntarily" (Glasser, 1992). The techniques of the treatment accommodate short, irregular, emergency contacts between the counselor and clients if necessary, and the language of the treatment is that of common-sense advice. Its down-to-earth, friendly style appeals to people who would be put off by fancy psychological lingo.

Control Theory, Choice Theory, and Human Behavior

Glasser did not originate control theory. Control theory existed separately as part of cybernetics, an explanation of dynamic systems. Glasser uses metaphors and terms from control theory to explain his approach (1981). Cybernetics, the understanding of self-regulating systems, applies to physics, engineering, mathematics, economics, and medicine, as well as to human systems like bureaucracies, governments, schools, and businesses. The key idea is that the ideal system regulates itself toward a given desired state by sensing the present condition and making adjustments to it, bringing it closer to the goal state. A common mechanical example is a thermostat, which senses the temperature in the room (the present condition), compares it to a reference point (the desired temperature), and automatically makes the required adjustment (doing nothing, turning on heat, or turning on air conditioning).

The same principles serve as models for individual human functioning (Carver & Scheier, 1982). Our behaviors can be seen as adjustments that we make when there is a discrepancy between a desired state (a reference value, in cybernetic terms) and a present condition. A good example comes from a transition-to-work group I once co-led in a veterans' hospital. One patient, Manny, believed that he was destined to be a smart, successful businessman, and he constantly asserted that he was a better caliber human than his fellow group members. Yet, the other disgruntled men were quick to point out that Manny was stuck in the same dreary situation they were: sad, unemployed residents of the VA with nowhere else to go. If he was so great, why was he there? They tried to convince him that he'd just have to take a job that he considered beneath him, if he were to fulfill his glittering promise eventually. They were acting on principles of control theory; Manny needed to make an adjustment between his desired state and his current one. The adjustment that he was presently trying, talking big and setting himself above other men, was obviously not working.

In the psychological arena, the process of self-regulation involves setting desired states for ourselves, observing our actions, and evaluating the actions by comparing their outcomes with the desired states (Carver & Scheier, 1982). We make attempts to match the reference value with the present state. Neurotic or maladaptive behavior comes from flaws in these matching attempts. First, we may not see how to get to the desired state: "many people want to be 'fulfilled,' or 'likable,' or 'successful' but have no idea what actions will move them in the direction of those superordinate goals. Indeed, they often do not know where to begin in *determining* what concrete steps will provide such superordinate discrepancy reduction" (p. 125). Second, if we have continually failed at reaching desired states, we expect future failure and refuse to exert sustained effort toward our higher goals. Third, we may have developed faulty ideas about what will get us from a present state to a desired state. (For example, throwing lavish parties does not get you a devoted circle of friends, and a series of successful heists doesn't gain you financial security. In Manny's case, bragging about his superiority was not moving him toward a superior position.) On top of these difficulties, throw in the facts that our desired states sometimes change and that external conditions are always tossing in an unexpected twist, and it's no wonder so many people go off track.

Because the term *control theory* applies to so many different systems, in the 1990s Glasser changed to using *choice theory* to describe self-regulatory behavior in human beings.

DISCUSSION IDEA

List four or five ways in which human errors occur in the process of matching the reference value with the present state. Give some examples from your own life or other lives you know of to illustrate each of the errors. Which flaw in the matching attempts do you think is most common among your peers? Why?

Five Human Needs

Understanding **five universal needs** is fundamental to choice theory and reality therapy (Glasser, 1998). Every course of reality therapy includes instruction in these needs.

1. **Survival** This covers physiological needs, what we need to remain healthy and safe. Most survival needs are driven biologically, such as thirst, hunger, breathing, and movement.

2. **Belonging (including love)**   Most people need to be part of society and to give and receive love within a social group, family, and couple. Most of us also derive satisfaction from fitting in with others at our chosen workplace.

3. **Power (including achievement, self-worth, recognition)**   We need to feel effective, influential, and important in some way. For many people, competition serves a need for power, whereas for others, being able to help or create serves the need just as well.

4. **Fun** Playing, laughing, having a good time socially, and forgetting our troubles while engaged in hobbies (or even enjoyable work) are expressions of real needs. Glasser and his followers are special in including fun as a critical need; this wisdom may stem from their close association with children and teens, whose need for fun is so dynamic.

5. **Freedom** We need the opportunity to make choices. A comfortable life is a prison if we never get to decide what to do next. Most of us even long for the freedom to make our own mistakes and learn from them, and we would never agree to someone else's directing our lives no matter how much we trusted them.

Through exploring these five needs and how they rank in importance, we can go a long way toward understanding any person, of any age and situation. This straightforward formula is one of the charms of choice theory and reality therapy.

The need list probably reminds you of Maslow's (1968) hierarchy of needs: physiological, safety, belonging/love, respect, self-esteem, and self-actualization. However, Wubbolding (2000) points out the distinction: Whereas Maslow's needs are arranged in a hierarchy, from the most fundamental to the loftiest, Glasser's needs are all in operation at different intensities at all times. People even give up survival, or risk it, in the service of other needs sometimes (for love, power, freedom, or fun).

Reflections

How are the five needs balanced in your own life right now? Distribute 100 points among the five needs, with more points given to more proponent needs. This is your current profile of needs.

Needs and Responsibility

According to choice theory, we all share this set of universal needs: survival, belonging, power, freedom, and fun. From these needs, we devise a personal vision of what we want, images of what will satisfy our needs. This vision is called our **quality world.** Behavior consists of the choices we make in trying to get this satisfaction. The quality world contains mental pictures of people, material things, achievements, and emotional states we treasure. It can be compared to a personal photo album of prized images. One of the counselor's first and main jobs is to become part of each client's quality world. In reality therapy, the concept of individual choice and responsibility is critical (Glasser, 1998). We choose our thoughts, emotions, and behaviors, and these choices make up the quality of our lives. The goal of reality therapy is to help people make better choices and have more control over their lives, within the constraints of the outside world (reality). While other approaches focus on identifying problems, reality therapy focuses on each group member's quality world (Stehno, 1995) and the gap between what each person wants and what each is getting.

An individual's **total behavior** is made up of four elements: actions, thinking, feeling, and physiology (Wubbolding, 2000). We have the most direct control over our actions and thinking. These are the elements reality therapy focuses upon, in the conviction that changes in emotion and physiology will follow. Let me give you a clear example from a group. My friend Alice leads groups for men who have been violent at home. The most important first thing these men need to do is to control their actions—that is, refrain from violence. In a group, the men brainstorm about ways to exercise self-control. They can walk out of the room when angry, controlling their overt action. Meanwhile, it helps them if they start to think differently at the same time. For example, they can tell themselves to stop and count to ten, taking a deep breath, when they feel the anger rising. They can ask themselves to come up with explanations for the situation that don't induce their anger. They can remind themselves that they will end up in jail if they lash out. By the time they have held back their action and rehearsed some of these thoughts, their physiological arousal has calmed and their anger is no longer raging. In this way, their control over actions and thoughts leads to controlled emotions and physiology.

In reality therapy, assigning blame to external events such as abusive upbringing or bad company is discouraged as excuse-making. "Expending time and energy to discuss the reasons that underlie ineffective behavior serves only to reinforce clients' belief that they are only minimally capable of making changes" (Wubbolding, 1996, p. 9–8). Similarly, emotions are not highlighted; feelings are discussed "in connection with the actions involved, but as infrequently as possible in isolation" (p. 9–12). When Glasser consults with schools, parents, and institutions, he encourages them to avoid blame and recrimination but to emphasize **natural consequences** of a person's actions. For example, grounding a teenager for staying out past curfew is a punishment; however, if the teenager has to complete chores at home or school at the usual times no matter how tired he is from staying out late, that is a natural consequence. If another teenager can't pay for a school field trip because she has already spent her whole allowance on yet another new belly shirt, this is a natural consequence. These teens are learning the effect their behavior has in reality, not in an artificial reward and punishment system.

DISCUSSION IDEAS

1. How much control over your behavior has come from blame, recrimination, and punishment, and how much from natural consequences? Discuss examples of both types of behavior control with your discussion group. Can you evaluate how effective other people's efforts to control your behavior have been?
2. Argue the case that in some instances, people should be protected from the natural consequences of their actions through external control.

Rejection of Mental Illness

Among the theorists you have studied, William Glasser is the most militant in rejecting the concept of mental illness as a disease, especially one that could be effectively treated with psychiatric drugs. In a 2004 article, he wrote:

> Right now in America there are more people diagnosed by psychiatrists, psychologists, and social workers as mentally ill than at any other time in psychiatric history. Almost all of these people are being treated with brain drugs for nonexistent mental illnesses that can often harm and sometimes lead to death, suicide, and murder. The people who prescribe these drugs or support this practice seem to have no concept of the existence of mental health. (p. 339)

Glasser (2003) titled one of his latest books *Warning: Psychiatry Can Be Hazardous to Your Mental Health*. He believes that just as couch potatoes can regain physical health through eating better and exercising more, unhappy people are mentally out of shape and can regain mental health through vigorous practice of choice theory. This extreme position, though arousing controversy, makes Glasser a stimulating and delightful figure on the affably moderate counseling landscape.

DISCUSSION IDEA

In our field, we often take for granted that our practices are generally beneficial. Instead, try arguing for the idea that "psychiatry can be hazardous to your mental health." Collaborate with your discussion group to develop three convincing points against the concept of mental illness, the use of psychoactive drugs, or the benefits of psychological analysis. Do you think that your points also apply to group counseling? Explain why or why not.

Teaching Orientation

Teaching the concepts and applications of choice theory is the main therapeutic intervention of reality therapy. Group therapy resembles a highly interactive class, in which students help each other learn principles and critique each other's mastery of the material. Epstein and Maragos (1983) note that the delinquent adolescents in their program do not even perceive the reality-group discussions as therapy, which is an advantage because many are jaded veterans of traditional office-based therapy. A similar advantage holds for many of the other target groups of reality therapy, who hold conventional psychiatry in disdain or find it embarrassing to seek psychological help.

Choice theory and reality therapy should strongly remind you of Adlerian individual psychology. In theory, two differences are choice theory's disregard for insight and birth order, which are venerated in Adlerian theory (Wubbolding, 2000). In practice, reality therapy follows a more defined set of procedures than Adlerian therapy. In most other ways, the two approaches here in Part VI are strongly compatible.

Group Dynamics

Reality group leaders do not ordinarily use assessment instruments to diagnose clients; assessment of self is an integral part of the entire process. However, Harvey and Retter (1995) developed a **Basic Needs Survey** for use with children in grades three through six. This is a twenty-item survey, with each item including four possible answers, each reflecting one of the four psychological needs (deleting survival needs). The number of responses for each basic need is tallied, creating a profile of the relative salience of needs at that time. The authors have found the Basic Needs Survey especially useful for understanding the motives behind disruptive students' behavior. Adults are able to view the disruptions not as malicious or deficient, but as efforts to meet legitimate, universal needs. I can imagine that an adult version of the Basic Needs Survey would be a valuable tool in group discussions investigating members' quality worlds.

Wubbolding (2000) links the developmental stages of reality therapy groups with the basic needs of choice theory. In the initial stage, the need for belonging dominates, as the group leader works to make everyone feel included and to enhance cohesion. This stage is a psychoeducational stage, in which learning the terminology they will share increases group identity. The leader helps create an environment of openness and cooperation.

In the second, transitional stage, we expect for conflict and questioning to arise, reflecting group members' needs for power. The leader tolerates anxiety and resistance, attempting to convey that each member does have influence within the group.

In the third, working stage, power and achievement come to the fore as members become committed to change and realize that they are able to help each other. Self-evaluation is checked against other members' perceptions, and plans are brainstormed and critiqued collectively.

In the final stage, the need for belonging is further addressed as the group readies for termination. Activities that fulfill a need for fun may be foregrounded here. Freedom, in the form of autonomy from the group, is discussed as members ponder how to keep applying the system they have learned, outside the group format.

This description of the life course of a group is very general. The distinctive group dynamic in reality therapy is not linear, but cyclical. The group continually cycles through the system explained in the next section.

The WDEP System

The reality therapist makes use of a cycle based on the concepts of control theory, needs, and choice. The acronym for the four modes of intervention is **WDEP,** for Wants, Direction and Doing, Evaluation, and Planning.

Wants A client's understanding of his or her wants is a major step in reality therapy. Friendly, fair-minded questioning by the counselor and the group helps clarify what a client wants from him- or herself, family, friends, job, coworkers, teachers, bosses, children, society in general, and counseling. Each person gets a picture of each other member's quality world, which will assist in the next part of the system.

Direction and Doing In a popular television talk show, psychologist Dr. Phil repeatedly asks his guests the classic question, "How's that workin' for ya?" This question addresses the topic of direction—where is a client's behavior taking her? Is it toward one of her wants, or away? A reality counselor uses *time projection questions* such as, "If you continue in the same way, where will you be in five years? One year? Where will your family be? How will you look at this situation in one year?" and so on. The counselor and group encourage vivid and specific details in the answers, which will help the client see consequences.

Evaluation of Self Client's self-evaluations are "the cornerstone of reality therapy" (Wubbolding, 1996, pp. 9–13). In this intervention, they look at their behavior in terms of its impact on other people and on their own satisfaction. They also are asked to state how their behavior is evaluated by external rules, like whether it is against the law, against company policy, against school rules, or against probation requirements. Furthermore, they evaluate their actions based on unwritten norms of acceptability. Whether their wants are realistic, appropriate, and worthwhile, and whether getting what they want is worth what they must do to get it, are questions of evaluation.

Planning The thorough evaluation should lead to formulation of a plan for action. Reality therapists encourage a plan that is simple, realistic, measurable,

TABLE 15.1
Six-Session Reality Therapy Group

Session	Objective	Procedure
		Reality Therapy Group
1	Introduce facilitator, participants and group purpose.	Discuss purpose of the group.
		Discuss ground rules including the importance of maintaining confidentiality within the group.
		Group exercise: "Who am I?" Facilitator will ask participants to share something most people know about them.
2	Participants will become better acquainted with each other and will be able to state the "five basic needs."	Group exercise: "Get Better Acquainted Activity." Facilitator will ask participants to share something about them that few people know, i.e., a favorite hobby.
		Group exercise: Present and discuss five basic needs:
		a. Survival,
		b. Love/belonging
		c. Power
		d. Freedom
		e. Fun (Glasser, 1998).
3	Participants will be able to state the five basic needs, will be able to state four aspects of "Total Behavior," and will understand how they are responsible for their behavior.	Review previous sessions
		Introduce "Total Behavior Model," Acting, Thinking, Feeling, and Physiology (Glasser, 1998).
		Group Exercise: "Who is in Charge?" Facilitator will ask participants "who controls their life and what direction are they heading."

Source: Lawrence, 2004, p. 13.

immediate, involved, committed, continuous, and within the client's powers (not dependent on other people's efforts).

After the planning step is complete, the group member commits himself or herself to carrying it out, often in a written document. Next, the member returns with a report on progress. If the plan didn't work out or if the member didn't carry it through, the leader and group do not take a stance of blame, and they don't allow the member to punish him or herself. Neither are excuses acceptable. Instead, they return to the WDEP system to devise a more reasonable plan. A major tenet of the process is "Never give up!"

Table 15.1 describes a six-session reality therapy group used for adults with mental retardation in an effort to promote self-determination (Lawrence, 2004,

TABLE 15.1
continued

Session	Objective	Procedure
4	Participants will be able to state the five basic needs, will be able to state the four aspects of "Total Behavior," will understand how they are responsible for their behavior, and will begin to envision their "Quality World."	Review previous sessions. Introduce "Picture Book" exercise: Facilitator will ask participants to draw a picture or pictures of their "ideal" life, i.e., friends, a new job, etc. Group exercise: Facilitator will ask participants to share their drawings.
5	Participants will be able to state the five basic needs, will be able to state the four aspects of "Total Behavior," will understand how they are responsible for their behavior, will have a vision of their "Quality World," and will use their "Quality World" to examine their current behavior.	Review previous sessions. Group exercise Part 1: "What are you doing?" Facilitator will ask participants to share what they do on a typical day. Group exercise Part 2: Ask participants to determine if their present life is going to get them what they want (their vision of a Quality World). Process Exercise: Ask participants to think of one activity they can do to get them closer to their vision of their "Quality World."
6	Participants will be able to state the five basic needs, will be able to state the four aspects of "Total Behavior," will understand how they are responsible for their behavior, will have a vision of their "Quality World," will use their "Quality World" to examine their current behavior, and will have a plan to improve one aspect of life.	Review all previous sessions. Group exercise: Ask group members to select one aspect of their Quality World they would like to improve. Process exercise: Help the members formulate the life aspect into a measurable and observable outcome. Write down the outcome and present it to the member. Closing exercise: Ask participants what they thought of the group experience.

p. 13). In comparison with a mutual support group, the members of the reality group gained in self-regulation over the course of six weeks.

Leadership Skills

Like all counselors, reality therapists need empathy, congruence, and positive regard. They ought to enjoy the considerable amount of teaching involved in explaining choice theory and reality therapy. The nature of reality therapy also demands some specialized qualities (Wubbolding & Brickell, 1998), like a good measure of energy, because they often work with reluctant clients and in settings outside a comfortable office. Active confrontation is frequently used, so the counselor must be able to convey a caring attitude while being challenging. Counselors need a positive but not naive view of human nature because their practice requires realistic balancing of complex forces. They need hope and an ability to reframe: "For the reality therapist, a lazy person has great potential, a resistant person has deep convictions, and a manipulative person is creative" (p. 48). They also have the cultural sensitivity and competence to understand that "reality" is not the same for all clients (Wubbolding et al., 1998).

Reality therapy makes use of imaginative techniques for getting through to difficult clients, so the ability to think creatively is paramount. Paradoxical intent, metaphors, and parallel tales draw upon the counselor's creative resources. The counselor most frequently has two entities to serve—the client and the agency that wants the client to change (e.g., legal authorities, teachers, parents)—so tact and flexibility are required, as well as a firm grounding in the ethical decisions involved. Though reality therapy uses the language of everyday life, its practice is sophisticated. The William Glasser Institute (*www.wglasser.com*) awards certificates after an eighteen-month training process.

Reality therapists seek out genuine involvement with each member of the group (Glasser, 1965). The counselor needs to be confident and firm when members attempt to use the relationship for purposes that don't advance them in terms of reality therapy. For example, because clients are often under an institutional umbrella, they will want the counselor to assist them in gaining privileges within the institution, and the counselor will have to resist. Group leaders can serve as models of principled behavior while maintaining their good will toward clients.

In my opinion, a key quality for reality therapists is nonjudgmentalism. They often work with group members who have had more than their share of judgmental authorities. While the nature of reality therapy is evaluative, the evaluation comes from within each person and is considered in pragmatic terms instead of personal moral worth.

R e f l e c t i o n s

What is the difference between judgment and evaluation, as you see it? Think of instances when you have felt judged, and instances when you have felt evaluated. What was the emotional content of these instances?

Techniques in Reality Therapy Groups

A variety of techniques, especially Adlerian ones, appear in accounts of group reality therapy. I will mention a few that come up repeatedly. All are tied to the four basic needs and to the WDEP process.

Questioning

Wubbolding (2000) provides many examples of the questioning tactics reality therapists use. The leaders also model and directly teach questioning skills to the group members, so that they can assist in clarifying, brainstorming, and evaluating each other's situations. I will give you samples of questions from the WDEP cycle.

W (Wants)

What do you want for your family and the individual members of it?

How hard do you want to work?

What do you want to avoid?

D (Direction and Doing)

Where are your current choices taking you?

What were you doing the last time you felt really well?

What was your family doing last time you all enjoyed being together?

What was our group doing when everyone shut down (stopped participating) last week?

E (Evaluation)

Is what I'm doing helping me? (Or, Is what Shawna [group member] is doing helping her?)

Last time I fought with my partner, was my behavior acceptable to society?

Are my values in line with my behavior during the past week?

Is my course of action against the rules?

Am I committed enough to change to get the desired results?

P (Planning)

If you follow through with your plan, how will your life be better?

How will you be living a more need-satisfying life?

What will you have that you don't have now?

DISCUSSION IDEA

Make up at least one more question for each category of the WDEP cycle. If possible, make up questions that you see as particularly useful in the types of groups you lead or intend to lead. Discuss possible uses with your classmates.

SAMI2C3

The acronym SAMI2C3 stands for a series of questions about the characteristics of a proposed plan. The group member, the leader, and the rest of the group all work through questions about these characteristics. The questions ask whether the plan is

S = simple: clear and uncomplicated.

A = Attainable: realistically doable, possible to carry out.

M = Measurable: answers such questions as, "When?" "How many times?" "Where?" "With whom?" "How, specifically?"

I = Involved: performed sometimes with the assistance of the counselor but only if necessary.

I = Immediate: followed through soon, not put off.

C = Controlled by the planner: not a plan dependent on what others do.

C = Consistent: done repetitively.

C = Committed to: firm. (Wubbolding, 2000, p. 143)

SMALL GROUP EXERCISE

Expand on why each item in the SAMI2C3 list is important in making a good plan. Discuss how you would explain these items to groups of different ages or situations. Do you predict any problems explaining the concepts? What?

Self-Help

Members of reality therapy groups learn self-help techniques because they are expected to continue to follow the WDEP system after leaving the group and between group sessions. Charting and affirmations are two self-help techniques used.

Charting Keeping track and getting things down on paper are self-help tactics shared with many other approaches, including cognitive-behavioral and psychoeducational ones. The chart on page 419 was made by a man exploring the congruence between his values and his behavior. With help from the group, he wrote a list of ten values he espouses in the first column. Then, he recorded specific behaviors that didn't fit the values in the second column, and behaviors that do fit the values in the third column. Group members might assist in thinking of items to put in this third column—that is, alternatives to the incongruent behaviors in column two.

Affirmations Positive self-talk is another strategy taught in many therapeutic approaches. Successful people often have favorite phrases or sayings that they

Values and Behavior Chart

Describe congruent and incongruent behaviors for numbers 4 through 10.

Value. i.e., something perceived and described as important.	Specific behavior that is incongruent with the value.	Specific behavior that is congruent with the value.
1. Patience with children	1. Shouting at a child	1. Asking child, "Did it help you to do that?"
2. Communicating frankly with spouse	2. "Clamming up," the silent treatment	2. Saying what you want, etc.
3. Involving others in decision making	3. When under pressure acting like a dictator	3. Asking others for input
4. Being prompt		
5. Saving money even to the point of giving up something		
6. Being an active member of a civic or church group		
7. Using short periods of time efficiently		
8. Respecting others without putting them down		
9. Being honest with the customer		
10. Helping others		

use to boost their spirits in hard times. As a writer, when I encounter an unruly mess of ideas that seems to defy order, I always say to myself, "I've straightened out problems much harder than this one before." According to Wubbolding, affirmations are best when they are in the present tense, are positive, and are repeated.

"I am a grown, capable woman."

"I can tolerate discomfort when I have to."

"I will get the most I can out of this long meeting."

"I will be inside and toasty warm within half an hour." (Great during Iowa snowstorms!)

Humor

Reality therapy literature consistently stresses the usefulness of humor in the process. Lightening up the subject helps group members perform the self-examination necessary for the WDEP system. For example, one group leader introduced the Wants investigation by having the group imagine walking along a tropical beach, finding a bottle, and having a magic genie pop out. They then each had to contrive what three wishes they would want granted. This conversation led to laughter as members made outlandish wishes and pointed out the pitfalls of other people's wishes. On the serious side, the nature of each person's wishes revealed a great deal about what they wanted in life. The technique was a nonthreatening method for introducing this topic.

Metaphor

A metaphor is an imaginative comparison: Linda Ronstadt sings, "Love is a rose, and you'd better not pick it; it only grows when it's on the vine." Emily Dickinson wrote, "He put the Belt around my life/ I heard the Buckle snap." Delmore Schwartz described his coarse side as "The heavy bear who goes with me,/ The hungry beating brutish one/ In love with candy, anger, and sleep." Group leaders are sensitive to the metaphors people use in their speech because they lead to insights about patterns of thought and emotion. A group member who describes her marriage as a gilded cage conveys a different experience from one who describes her marriage as a heavy weight around her neck. Frequently, the leader follows up on metaphorical language by asking for extensions of the comparison: "What is that heavy weight made out of? When is it the heaviest? When was the last time you walked around without feeling that heavy weight?"

Paradox

Like Adlerians, reality group leaders sometimes use techniques with paradoxical intent, meaning that they seem to veer in an opposite direction than the expected one. For instance, in one group Clarence insisted that his situation was hopeless. The leader asked all the other group members to support this idea in as much detail as they could and to refrain from pointing out any hopeful indicators whatsoever. After a few minutes of wholehearted commiseration and doomsaying, Clarence began to argue with his group-mates and insist that the picture wasn't *that* bleak. He began enumerating positive aspects, such as having a well-paid, stable job and being in good physical shape.

Parallel Tales

Reality group counselors sometimes collect fables and stories that encapsulate messages they want their clients to take to heart. These are used when they parallel in some way the clients' stories. One group member, Tanya, seemed to be highly critical of her third-grade daughter, whose school performance was average rather than outstanding. The counselor told the group this Aesop fable and asked them to develop it in terms of Tanya's predicament.

> A boy put his hand into a pitcher full of peanuts. He grasped as many as he could possibly hold, but when he tried to pull out his hand, he was prevented from doing so by the neck of the pitcher. Unwilling to lose his peanuts, and yet unable to withdraw his hand, he burst into tears and bitterly lamented his disappointment. A bystander said to him, "Be satisfied with half the quantity, and you will readily draw out your hand."

The group was able to apply the story in several ways, with messages such as "Don't expect too much," "Be happy with the amount you can get without hurting yourself," and even in relation to the daughter, "Choose your best subject to put most of your work into, and continue to be average in the others. You are trying to do too much." The story served as an indirect confrontation.

SMALL GROUP EXERCISE

Get together to brainstorm for a fairy tale, joke, or fable that your group agrees on to convey useful messages. Practice delivering the story as though you were speaking to a counseling group.

Problems Addressed by Reality Therapy Groups

Wubbolding (2000) and Glasser (1998) assert that choice theory and reality therapy are applicable to almost all problem areas, from lower back pain to global unrest. Remember that the original applications and theory derived from settings populated by unwilling and delinquent people, such as prisons and reform schools (e.g., Wilder, 2004). The down-to-earth, pragmatic approach and everyday language of the system, as well as its step-by-step WDEP cycle, have wide appeal where most abstract and in-depth psychological concepts would flounder. The choice theory approach has been broadened to problems and institutions outside of social deviance.

Applications to Trauma

Reality therapy has proven a sound conceptual framework for healthy persons who have undergone traumatic events. An example comes from U.S. Air Force nurse Margaret McArthur (1990), who used the therapy with a group of rape victims:

> Rape has an impact on the sense of self, effecting a loss of self-esteem, creation of guilt and shame, mistrust in interpersonal relationships and distorted perceptions of self-worth. Because of this massive injury to the self, rape victims may very quickly become isolated and lonely. They may experience their pain in any of the modes previously listed: disturbances of emotions, behavior problems, disturbances of thoughts, or somatic complaints. While [these are McArthur's words] other therapeutic approaches for rape victims focus on alleviating symptoms of psychiatric illness, reality therapy treats the sense of self. The intrusive thoughts, feelings, and actions a rape victim experiences may lead her to believe she is going crazy. Other frameworks reinforce this belief by placing a value judgment on her symptoms of illness. In contrast, reality therapy changes the point at which this value judgment is made, moving the assessment up to step three [Evaluation] in the process of asking the victim to determine for herself if what she is doing is moral, legal, and is working to fulfill her needs. Reality therapy teaches the victim she is not crazy, but that she may be having difficulty in meeting her basic needs. Emphasis in reality therapy is on effective and ineffective behavior, not on the signs and symptoms of mental illness. Reality therapy offers the victim opportunities to regain self-esteem, resolve guilt and shame, rebuild trusting relationships, and renew her sense of self-worth by changing the point at which value judgments are made.
>
> Loss of the sense of competence results in loss of self-esteem for rape victims. Reality therapy helps rebuild lost self-esteem. The rape victim is given opportunities to make plans to meet her needs, plans in which she can succeed and feel powerful over her environment again. When she succeeds, her success identity is reinforced. She regains mastery over her environment. (p. 363)

McArthur delineates clearly the difference between a mental illness and a reality therapy point of view, a difference that is critical in understanding choice theory.

SMALL GROUP EXERCISE

Role-play a first session of reality therapy with survivors of a natural disaster, such as a flood or fire. One member can act as the counselor, preparing the group for the process of reality therapy, and the other members can ask questions and discuss in their roles as survivors.

Choice Theory in the Workplace

Glasser (1995) has extended the ideas of needs, quality worlds, and interpersonal enhancement to the workplace. Combined with Deming's (1986) total quality management theories, choice theory has been used to improve productivity in industrial and office settings. This improvement hinges on a change in style of management, from boss management to lead management. Lead management includes such democratic innovations as involving all workers in discussions of quality and cost of the work, having workers inspect their own work, and sharing profits from increased productivity (Glasser, 1998). Small group meetings, similar to reality therapy groups, are common features of the lead-management model.

Institutional Successes

Reality therapy remains most popular in institutional settings. In a meta-analysis of empirical research on the approach (Radtke, Sapp, & Farrell, 1997), eighteen of the studies occurred in schools and seven at residential treatment programs for at-risk, addicted, or criminal populations (one was a wilderness camp, adventure therapy as described in Chapter 14). This meta-analysis, which combines the results of several research efforts, found a .75 effect size, meaning that people in reality therapy showed a medium to large improvement over similar people who were not. Most established therapies have similar effect sizes.

One particularly apt application of reality therapy is making the best of a bad situation, as many people must within institutional bureaucracies. A friend of mine, while in the Army, was assigned to a remote outpost to oversee radio operations. Due to some kind of bureaucratic oversight, there were no radios at the post at all. After six weeks of frustration in trying to get the radios shipped so he could perform his mission, the soldier complained of his distress to the army psychologist, who gave him a copy of Glasser's *Reality Therapy* (1965) to tide him over. It did.

Adaptations to Clients' Ages

With its roots in child and adolescent treatment, reality therapy has been adapted to all age groups and many cultural backgrounds (Wubbolding, 2000). The language of four needs and WDEP is suitable for most ages, and the materials are changed according to developmental level. For example, the box on congruent and incongruent behaviors is clearly made for an adult to fill out. A child doing the same exercise might use drawings on topics like "Things I Do That Make Me Feel Bad Later" and "Things I Do That Make Me Feel Good Later." Many of reality therapy's efforts are directed at educating adults about the most productive ways to deal with children. A major enemy in choice theory is **external control,** as described in the opening selection of this chapter.

In *Reality Therapy in Action* (Glasser, 2000b), Glasser asserts that parents are the most important people in children's lives until the children are 15, and he chooses to work with parents and children together between preadolescence and age 13. For young children's problems, he often sees groups of parents, excluding the children, because he believes the parents' control habits are creating the child's problems. After age 15, children who have not followed their parents' direction can still be changed through groups of people their own age.

Glasser reveals that for years, about half of his practice was with people 15 to 20 years old, so the difficulties of these years are among his specialties.

Reality therapy professionals emphasize the need for self-evaluation skills in teenagers:

> All of us need to learn to evaluate our own behavior and adjust when what we are doing is not working. Unfortunately, challenging youth are so used to having others evaluate their behavior for them, they neglect to learn this crucial life skill. Furthermore, many challenging youth who have grown up in abusive or otherwise dysfunctional families have often received conflicting messages about what works and what doesn't. The rules change from day to day. One day, they are praised by a parent for fighting with their sibling. The next day, they are beaten for the same behavior. They are taught not to trust their own judgment. Additionally, the adult models for these youth often have a long-standing pattern of externalizing responsibility for their problems. The youth learns to avoid responsibility by blaming others. Subsequently, professionals who work with challenging youth must recognize that they may initially lack the skills to effectively self-evaluate. (Richardson, 2001, pp. 114–115)

Keep in mind that though we all have the five basic needs, at every era of life the profile of which needs are most important or most unmet may change. Children, who usually have great capacity and opportunity for fun, are frequently deficient in power. Adult men who have powerful work positions can be woefully lacking in fun. Adults who move from place to place with corporate, political, or military transfers are likely to lose their sense of belonging to a community or extended family, and the same is true of first-generation immigrants. Choice theory proponents are proud of the endless flexibility offered by analysis of needs and quality worlds, and think of their practice as the most well equipped to deal with diversity (e.g., Cunningham, 1995).

Evaluating Reality Therapy Groups

How do you know whether your reality therapy group is succeeding? Because evaluation is part of the WDEP cycle, you will get continual feedback on whether individuals' plans are working out. For group-as-a-whole evaluation, you might keep records of members contributing to WDEP discussions, because participation by all members would indicate involvement in the process. Some leaders give content quizzes on elements of choice theory such as the five basic needs and the components of total behavior to evaluate the psychoeducational part of the therapy.

Groups with shared targets for change use assessments aimed at those targets. For example, a choice-theory–based alternative high school compared students' behaviors upon entering the school with students' behaviors who had continued there for three years, in terms of attendance, grades, drug usage, and probation status (Greene & Uroff, 1991). The reality therapy group for adults with mental retardation (Lawrence, 2004) used the Arc's Self-Determination Scale (Adult Version; Wehmeyer, 1995), a self-report instrument with factors reflecting autonomy, self-regulation, psychological empowerment, and self-realization. These are directly related to the goal of the group, which was to enhance self-determination. A choice-theory based classroom group intervention with preadolescent, inner-city, learning disabled children charted daily arguments, starting with a baseline before the intervention and then graphing number of arguments with one person, arguments with two persons, and physical confrontations over the course of twenty-two days (Marandola & Imber, 1979). These are examples of evaluations tied to each group's main focus.

KEY TERMS

Basic Needs Survey an instrument designed to measure children's profiles of basic needs, outside of survival

choice theory an outgrowth of human control theory that emphasizes responsibility and free will in choosing actions and thoughts to fulfill needs

control theory a system of thought explaining how systems make internal adjustments to approximate reference points, adapted to self-regulation in people by psychological theorists

external control management of behavior by blame, recrimination, and punishment rather than natural consequences

five universal needs survival, power, belonging, fun, and freedom, essential desires that motivate humans everywhere; also called *basic needs*

natural consequences in contrast with punishment, natural consequences are real-world results of behavior, such as being tired the next morning if you stayed up too late

pragmatism a philosophy evaluating the worth of an idea or action by its usefulness in the real world

quality world each individual's mental image of valued people, ideas, items, and emotional states

total behavior the composite of actions, thoughts, feelings, and physiological responses

WDEP an analysis of Wants, Direction and Doing, Evaluation, and Plan, central to the process of reality therapy

CHAPTER REVIEW

1. In a collegiate dictionary, look up the words *choice, control,* and *reality*. Which definitions are closest to the specialized uses of these words in choice theory and reality therapy?

2. Why do you think the approach described in this chapter has claimed great success with difficult populations? Explain your answer to a person outside your class.

3. According to Carver and Scheier (1982), what are some obstacles to people's attempts to match reference states with present states?

4. List the five universal needs. Think of specific ways they are expressed in your own life. Explain the needs to someone else, and compare the ways they are meeting these needs with your own ways.

5. What do you think about Glasser's militant position against psychotropic drugs? What knowledge and experience do you bring to bear on this issue?

6. Choose one area of your own life and, on paper or on tape, go through the WDEP cycle. Apply SAMI2C3 to your plan. Reflect on your experience of doing this. Reread or listen to your tape of the process and comment on your performance. To develop your understanding of the cycle further, read or listen to a classmate's WDEP process and comment.

FOR FURTHER READING

The William Glasser Institute is an extremely active organization. On its website, *www.wglasser.com,* you will find reprints of the latest articles on choice theory, reality therapy, quality schools, and lead management. The site also provides scripted skits to help students learn choice theory, Glasser's speaking schedule if you would like to hear his presentation yourself, and details of the Institute's training program. If you think that choice theory and reality therapy are suitable for the groups you intend to lead, this site can keep you up to date.

REFERENCES

Carver, C. S., & Scheier, M. F. (1982). Control theory: A useful conceptual framework for personality-social, clinical, and health psychology. *Psychological Bulletin, 92,* 111–135.

Cunningham, L. M. (1995). Control theory, reality therapy, and cultural bias. *Journal of Reality Therapy, 15,* 15–22.

Deming, W. E. (1986). *The Deming management method.* New York: Perigee Books.

Epstein, N., & Maragos, N. (1983). Treating delinquent-prone adolescents and preadolescents. *Social Work, 28,* 66–69.

Glasser, W. (1965). *Reality therapy: A new approach to psychiatry.* New York: Harper & Row.

Glasser, W. (1981). *Stations of the mind.* New York: Harper & Row.

Glasser, W. (1992). Reality therapy. In J. K. Zeig (Ed.), *The evolution of psychotherapy: The second conference* (pp. 270–277). New York: Brunner/Mazel.

Glasser, W. (1995). *The control theory manager.* New York: HarperBusiness.

Glasser, W. (1998). *Choice theory.* New York: HarperCollins.

Glasser, W. (2000a). School violence from the perspective of William Glasser. *Professional School Counseling, 4,* 77–80.

Glasser, W. (2000b). *Reality therapy in action.* New York: HarperCollins.

Glasser, W. (2003). *Warning: Psychiatry can be hazardous to your mental health.* New York: HarperCollins.

Glasser, W. (2004). A new vision for counseling. *Family Journal, 12,* 339–341.

Greene, B., & Uroff, S. (1991). Quality education and at risk students. *Journal of reality therapy, 10,* 3–11.

Harvey, V. S., & Retter, K. (1995). The development of the Basic Needs Survey. *Journal of Reality Therapy, 15,* 76–80.

Lawrence, D. H. (2004). The effects of reality therapy group counseling on the self-determination of persons with developmental disabilities. *International Journal of Reality Therapy, 23,* 9–15.

Marandola, P., & Imber, S. C. (1979). Glasser's classroom meeting: A humanistic approach to behavior change with preadolescent inner-city learning disabled children. *Journal of Learning Disabilities, 12,* 30–34.

Maslow, A. H. (1968). *Toward a psychology of being* (2nd ed.). Princeton, NJ: Van Nostrand.

McArthur, M. J. (1990). Reality therapy with rape victims. *Archives of Psychiatric Nursing, 4,* 360–365.

Radtke, L., Sapp, M., & Farrell, W. C. (1997). Reality therapy: A meta-analysis. *Journal of Reality Therapy, 17,* 4–9.

Richardson, B. (2001). *Working with challenging youth.* Philadelphia, PA: Brunner-Routledge.

Stehno, J. J. (1995). Classroom consulting with reality therapy. *Journal of Reality Therapy, 15,* 81–86.

Wehmeyer, M. L. (1995). *The Arc's Self-Determination Scale Procedural Guidelines.* Arlington, TX: The Arc of the United States.

Wilder, S. (2004). Educating youthful offenders in a youth development center. *Journal of Addictions & Offender Counseling, 24,* 82–91.

Wubbolding, R. E. (1996). Reality therapy: Theoretic underpinnings and implementation in practice. *Directions in Mental Health Counseling, 6*(9), 1–17.

Wubbolding, R. E. (2000). *Reality therapy for the 21st century.* Philadelphia, PA: Brunner-Routledge.

Wubbolding, R. E., & Brickell, J. (1998). Qualities of the reality therapist. *International Journal of Reality Therapy, 17*(2), 47–49.

Wubbolding, R. E., Al-Rashidi, B., Brickell, J., Kakitani, M., Kim, R. I., & Lennon, B., et al. (1998). Multicultural awareness: Implications for reality therapy and choice theory. *International Journal of Reality Therapy, 17*(2), 4–6.

PART VII

Conclusion

I n this final chapter, you are encouraged once more to reflect on what you have learned and to think about this knowledge in terms of your personal growth and your preferences. I present a model of thinking about the intersection between your personality and your choices of group interventions. The distinctive ethical aspects of these choices are described for your consideration. A common ethical action is seeking supervision, and I suggest how to make the best use of your supervision hours. Finally, you will study some valuable guidelines about maintaining your personal well-being in order to operate as an effective and fulfilled group counselor.

CHAPTER 16

The Effective Group Counselor

A Selection from "In Their Own Words: An Exploratory Study of Bona Fide Group Leaders"

Commonalities in Effective Group Leadership

Ethical Decision Making in Group Counseling

Methods and Personal Style

Growing Through Supervision

The Power of Counselor Well-Being

A Selection from

"In Their Own Words: An Exploratory Study of Bona Fide Group Leaders"

By Gloria J. Galanes (2003)

[Note: This article reports on a study of twenty-three participants with reputations for excellent small-group leadership. Each leader was interviewed for one to two hours, and the responses were categorized into five major themes. The section reprinted here concerns the largest theme, "Communication Behaviors and Personal Characteristics of the Leader."]

First, leaders inspire confidence in their ability to lead by projecting reassurance and giving the "impression of command, confidence, command of all the pieces that are going to have to come together." Motivating members to support the team's vision and goals is important, but members must also have confidence that the leader will be able to get the group to its goal.

But this confidence must be tempered with humility. Effective leaders, according to these participants, must be careful not to "overly dominate or put your imprint too strongly on the work before the team even does the work." These leaders have found a way to harness their own, sometimes considerable, egos to ensure that the group does the work and gets the credit: "In business, we are all taught 'I, I, I, I' and never 'we.' Until you let go of that, you can't be a good leader'; and "There is no 'I' in TEAM." Effective leaders believe that the group's work is not about the leader but about the team developing an effective solution or plan because the team can produce "a better result than any one of those folks [including the leader] could come up with." Thus, they see their role as facilitating discussion among group members instead of driving discussion in a particular direction.

The participants believe that "as a team leader, you have to model the behaviors you want the team to practice," with several specific behaviors being particularly important. The most frequently mentioned of these was listening: "The art of listening is worth the effort." It is particularly important for leaders to listen actively before offering their own opinions and for leaders to ask good questions. It is also important for the leader to "be willing to admit if you've gone in the wrong direction," own up to mistakes, share one's own limitations, and apologize when appropriate.

Good leaders are effective communicators. They see themselves, and hope others see them, as open, approachable, and supportive. Believing that people do their best work when feeling relaxed, they strive to ensure that their own communication behavior fosters a relaxed, supportive atmosphere that encourages others to come forward. The effective leaders interviewed for this study have a high degree of self-knowledge and the ability to self-monitor. They are knowledgeable about the issues and passionate about the group's task. They have a strong work ethic and behave with great integrity and honesty. They do not expect anything of others that they are not willing to give themselves. They believe in themselves and others. (pp. 760–762)

Exploring "In Their Own Words: An Exploratory Study of Bona Fide Group Leaders"

1. Summarize the qualities needed by group leaders, according to the participants of this study.
2. What is "the ability to self-monitor"? Why is this ability important in group leaders?
3. The group leaders interviewed for this study were from education (four), private industry and business (seven), government (six), nonprofit organizations (three), and social services (three). Does it surprise you that they were not mostly counselors? Why or why not? What might be different if exclusively counselors were interviewed? What would be the same?

▪ ▪ ▪

Commonalities in Effective Group Leadership

One reason I chose the selection above for you to ponder is its highlighting of the common factors underlying good leadership. Even though the interviewees came from five distinct settings, their conclusions about leadership qualities concur remarkably, and you may have even believed that they were all counselors. The entire article established five themes running throughout the interviews:

▪ Establishing the intention for the overall project;

▪ Building the team and developing a positive group culture;

▪ Monitoring and managing the team's interaction;

▪ Managing the group's task and keeping the group focused; and

▪ Clear communication behaviors and personal integrity of the leader.

All of these themes mirror the discussions in this textbook.

In light of the huge areas of commonality among group leaders in general and group counselors in particular, it's reasonable to ask yourself whether you are being trained to be a cookie-cutter image of some ideal group guru. Where does your individuality fit in? Do you need to stifle some of your basic personality characteristics? If you're not a fast-thinking, funny, extroverted type, should you just give the whole thing up?

Of course not. People with varying personalities have become accomplished group counselors—even shy, deliberative types. Within the basic guidelines for group leadership, you will be able to choose skills and techniques that best fit your personality and worldview. In the preceding chapters, I've attempted to describe which group leadership skills are particularly adaptive for each theoretical stance. There's room for variety there. For example, if you enjoy careful planning, record-keeping, regularity, and step-by-step activities, you will find a niche in cognitive-behavioral group therapy. If you're a natural teacher, psychoeducational work is for you. In contrast, a counselor who enjoys Rogerian, person-centered counseling must thrive on spontaneity and giving up the teacher role. Your personal philosophy also affects which type of practice you embrace (Howatt, 2000). If you see the psyche as a tarn of conflict, ambiguity, and complexity, you will not give your heart to approaches imbued with sunny optimism and straightforward formulas. As you become a confident group counselor, you will gravitate toward a match between your personal qualities and your theoretical orientation:

> During graduate training, students are exposed to a broad range of knowledge and methods in research and practice, and over time they develop interests and pursue activities that fit their personal characteristics. The influences of personal characteristics and training on one another are surely reciprocal, but training experiences may have their maximum effect only for those who are prepared to be influenced by them. Students find their ways into niches in which their epistemic values and personality and cognitive strengths are further nurtured and solidified through a process of socialization. (Conway, 1988, p. 653)

Andrews (1989) related personality characteristics to the theories behind therapeutic schools of thought. He defined personality by habitual interpersonal style. For example, he identified

▪ the "executive, forceful, respected" style with cognitive approaches;

▪ the "independent, competitive" style with Gestalt approaches;

▪ the "realistic, skeptical, modest, sensitive" type to psychodynamics;

▪ and the "respectful, trustful, bland, conventional, friendly, agreeable" type to person-centered schools of thought.

▪ The "blunt, frank, critical, unconventional" style Andrews pairs with short-term confrontational approaches, where I would classify some Adlerian and most reality therapies.

These pairings may help you consider your own stance: which description of interpersonal style fits you best? Does it match Andrews's categorization of the approach you found attractive?

"Theoretical approach is a personal as well as academic phenomenon . . . encouraging students to discover their own visions of reality and to consider theory from this perspective is, I believe, an important function of counselor education" (Bernard, 1992, p. 236). To identify approaches that are good matches for your personal style, this is a good time to look back over the responses you wrote for Reflections and Chapter Review exercises. Remember the experience of doing these, and some will probably stand out as more pleasant and natural feeling to you. Think about why. Is there something you can identify about yourself that made you respond positively to the approach? The approaches you enjoyed learning about the most are probably the ones that will fit your personal style and philosophy.

Reflections

Make up a chart of the approaches in this textbook, following the template provided below. This chart will help you review for future certification tests, like the National Counselor Exam (NCE) and the Examination for Professional Practice of Psychology (EPPP). The last column, Personal Fit, encourages you to record how well this approach fits with your current personality and philosophy. It may be interesting to review what you write today in five or ten years, to see how the Personal Fit column has changed.

If time permits, exchange and discuss your chart with classmates and revise your chart to improve it, based on what you learn from others.

Approach	Distinctive Idea	Most similar to which other approach? Why?	Most different from which other approach? Why?	3–5 Key Terms	Personal Fit? Why?
Humanist					
Existential					
Psychodynamic					
Gestalt					
Psycho-educational					
Cognitive-Behavioral					
Adlerian					
Choice/Reality					

Many times, you will not be totally free to decide what approach to a group you use. Your organization or the institution that hires you may determine what they want. For example, if you are asked by a school to run a group for students with ADHD (as in the selection opening Chapter 13) with the goal of improving their school behavior, you can bet that you are expected to deliver a psychoeducational intervention, like the one described in Chapter 13. Even if you privately think that a Gestalt therapy approach would meet the goal, that is not what your employers want. Incidentally, what may strike people as an approach/goal mismatch sometimes works fine—Lantz (1989) used existential therapy to help an overweight family (a case described in Chapter 9). Though he refused to dwell on the subject of eating, the family lost weight and maintained their weight loss at one-, two- and three-year follow-ups. However, this family group must have had intense faith in Lantz's judgment to accept an approach that did not address weight loss directly.

Ethical Decision Making in Group Counseling

Ethical constraints also determine what type of approach and techniques you use. We are bound by ethical guidelines of our profession to inform clients of the treatment empirically proven to work on the problem if there is one. We can suggest other treatments that we expect to be effective in the case and say what we prefer. For weight loss, psychoeducational and behavioral methods are proven, for example. Second, ethically we can only offer treatments we are qualified to try, through being educated in them and consulting with experts. This means that even if you've read about an approach that sounds right for your group, you need to study and to arrange expert consultation before you use it on people. Third, we are not allowed to use treatments that lie outside what members of the community would find reasonable. This is a slippery guideline, but it prevents counselors from using approaches that would be considered exotic and bizarre by most of the people in the community where they work. Hypnotic regression to past lives, rebirthing experiences, group LSD trips, and nude encounter groups have their proponents, for instance, but not among most Texans. You would be at legal and ethical risk to introduce these unusual methods. If you do decide to use a method that seems unusual to the population you serve, be well prepared to explain and defend it. Remember that without your group's confidence in the treatment, you are unlikely to succeed (Frank & Frank, 1991).

Methods and Personal Style

Even within an assigned approach, your own personality and worldview lend their flavor, like the herbs in your mama's special lasagna. Almost all the counseling groups I have mentioned involve some form of confrontation, for instance, yet how you *do* confrontation will reflect many aspects of your individual self. When I was in training, I frequently had to point out to my supervisor the confrontations I had made in counseling sessions because I confront in a gentle, narrative style that my supervisor didn't recognize as confrontation. His own style of confrontation was much more direct and challenging, and that was what he saw easily in others.

Your choice of techniques within a given approach will also reflect your individuality. I hope you have learned that there are many paths to enlightenment, and in group therapy many techniques may serve as paths to one goal. I notice at meetings of group therapists that each one tends to describe techniques that obviously fit him or her as a person. People with a dramatic side enjoy role plays; people from families of teachers love creating worksheets and charts; highly emotional people make use of emotional arousal. People who love silence use the tool of silence powerfully. My own use of narrative and fondness for metaphor reflect my enchantment with literary studies. Role plays, worksheets, emotional arousal, silence, narrative, and metaphor have places in group work of many orientations, so you have choices.

As you learn group counseling, it's great to gravitate toward orientations and techniques that fit your natural inclinations. It's a way of knowing yourself and expressing your identity. However, pay attention to modes that feel alien, as well. Ask yourself why they feel alien, and what your answer to that question says about you. Give them a chance in several practice situations. If you are cozily comfortable in a teaching role, try an orientation in which the counselor abstains from teaching, like a client-centered approach. If you are skittish about silence, study its use as a technique and practice a few times in group to see what happens. If you believe you're against structured, step-by-step treatments, get involved in a study using a manualized approach and actively seek out its strengths. The broadest opportunities to experiment are likely to occur during your training years, so why stay stuck in a rut? In these years, you have the advantage of teachers to discuss your attempts to branch out with you.

Growing Through Supervision

As you lead groups, you will receive supervision from an experienced counselor. While you are in training, your school will provide you with a supervisor; when you go to work, your agency may provide one. If not, you need to seek a supervisor out for yourself, because having someone more experienced to talk with is a crucial part of making ethical decisions, evaluating your treatments, venting your deepest feelings about your work and your clients, and remaining vital in your practice (see the next section). Your supervisor is bound to the same level of confidentiality as a counselor would be, so you are quite free in this relationship.

You, and your supervisor, can make the best use of your relationship if you follow a model that ensures your attention to the complex matrix of roles, focuses, and boundaries in group counseling. Bernard and Goodyear (2004) are famous for their integrated model of clinical supervision, which they designed to be useful no matter what theoretical orientation or approach the counsel-

FIGURE 16.1   Group Supervision Model (Rubel, D., & Okech, J. E. A. [in press]. The supervision of group work model: Adapting the discrimination model for supervision of group workers. *Journal for Specialists in Group Work*.)

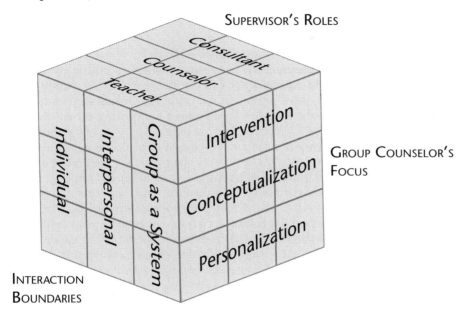

or employed. The Bernard and Goodyear Discrimination Model was created for counselors of individual clients. Rubel and Okech (in press) extended this model to pertain to supervision of group counselors. The graphic representation of this model appears in Figure 16.1. Because there are three supervisory roles, three areas of counselor focus, and three levels of interaction boundary in group counseling, the model looks like a cube (3 × 3 × 3).

The three levels of boundary in group counseling, as you have discerned throughout this textbook, are the *individual* (one person's verbal and nonverbal communication), the *interpersonal* (between two or more individuals, counselor-member or member-member or co-leader-co-leader), and the *group-as-a-whole* (the process and progress of the entire system). After any session, you can think about your group from each of these perspectives. Consider each individual's contribution and situation, the interactions between pairs and among subgroups, and the status and direction of the whole group as an organism.

You can organize these contemplations by three focuses: intervention, conceptualization, and personalization. **Intervention** concerns your application of skills and techniques. Thus, you think about the outcomes of your interventions at the individual, interpersonal, and whole-group levels. **Conceptualization** means how well you are seeing the big picture—how well you can explain what's going on, using theoretical terminology—again, at the individual, interpersonal, and whole-group level. **Personalization** pertains to you as a person—what your emotional reactions were, your estimation of your genuineness, what caught your attention, your self-disclosure, your inner conversations. This, too, operates at all boundary levels—simultaneously, you might be frustrated by one member, puzzled by a rift in a subgroup, and pleased with the overall direction of your group.

So far, your thoughts are distributed over nine pieces—one plane—of the cube. The supervisor can provide the remaining planes by taking on a **consultant role, counselor role,** and **teacher role.** In the teacher role, supervisors give you direct instruction, information, and advice. For instance, my supervisor showed me how to institute a role play in one of my groups, when I wasn't sure what technique to use or how to start it off. When you are a more experienced group leader, your supervisor serves as a consultant, a colleague to bounce ideas around with and give you fresh perspective. The relationship is more equal. While this role makes intuitive sense with advanced supervisees, it has been elusive to researchers looking at real supervision sessions (Bernard & Goodyear, 2004). Your supervisor also acts as your counselor on matters relating to your groups. This role especially comes up when you analyze your responses to and inner conversations about episodes in group sessions. For instance, most of us have found ourselves feeling intense dislike, or special affection, for one group member. Our counselor/supervisor can help us get to the source of the emotion—it may be a countertransference—and help us decide how our emotion is affecting the group and what (if anything) we should do about it. Supervisors also help us when we are feeling bored or stagnant in our group work.

The Power of Counselor Well-Being

When surveyed on the importance of character in trainees, training directors of accredited doctoral programs in clinical and counseling psychology rated highly (over 4 on a 5-point scale) the following qualities (Johnson & Campbell, 2004):

■ Integrity (honesty)
■ Prudence (good judgment)
■ Caring (respect, sensitivity)
■ Lack of personality psychopathology
■ Psychological health

These appear to be the basic requirements for appropriateness to the counseling profession. They seem self-evident; however, let me dwell upon the last quality as you draw near the end of this book and complete your course in group counseling.

Psychological health is often called well-being, and we would hope for this among all human service personnel. In counseling, the benefits of personal well-being have been empirically supported. A review of studies on therapist emotional well-being (Beutler et al., 2004) discovered a positive and significant effect of counselor well-being on client outcomes. In fact, the researchers suggest that different levels of well-being among therapists may be the "hidden moderator" creating contradictory and inconsistent findings in studies of counseling effectiveness. That is, when one form of therapy fails to pull ahead of another (or none) in an empirical study of effectiveness, it may be a result of the variable psychological health of the therapists in the study, rather than the nature of the approach.

Our profession, which requires emotional well-being to be effective, at the same time is dangerous to that well-being. Mental health services today are limited in time, money, and other resources, and professional counselors usually feel frustrated in attempts to provide top-quality care. The job stress of counselors is considerable, given that they are challenged by constantly caring for others, giving one-way empathy, and experiencing trauma through clients' reports. These are conditions that you need to take seriously throughout your career. Osborn (2004) provided Seven Salutary Suggestions for Stamina among mental health professionals, encompassing off- and on-the-job activities, ways of thinking, or dispositions that will help us ward off psychological problems that make us ineffective counselors. Osborn uses the acronym STAMINA for her list of recommendations:

Selectivity "The practice of intentional choice and focus in daily activities and long-term endeavors" (p. 322). Osborn advises making choices about matters like how much client improvement one can realistically expect. She also suggests pursuing a specialty area and focusing on specific therapeutic approaches to promote clear professional identity and develop expertise, rather than striving to be all things to all people.

Temporal Sensitivity "Time is not only something to be managed or manipulated well, . . . but also something that is viewed realistically and respectfully" (p. 322). Appreciating and focusing on the present moment is a skill to develop, rather than dwelling on the past and feeling the pressure of the future.

Accountability Osborn defines accountability not only as proof of adequate client care but also as credibility with ourselves, our clients, and the people we work with. This includes "being able to practice according to a justifiable, ethical, theoretically guided, and research-informed defense" (p. 323), something this textbook has helped you develop for yourself. Being open to feedback and new information is also part of accountability.

Measurement and Management "The counselor makes conscientious, careful, and ongoing efforts to conserve and protect those resources he or she values" (pp. 323–324). This requires an evaluation of values and then an investment of energy that reflects these values. Therefore, self-care should be high on a counselor's priority list. In a *Journal of Mental Health Counseling* article, O'Halloran and Linton (2000) list thirty self-care resources for counselors.

Inquisitiveness Curiosity about clients' worlds and the "adventure of counseling" (p. 325) must be kept alive to stave off boredom, stereotyping of clients, and impersonal responses. A lively interest in the practice comes from attending professional meetings, studying new developments, discussing issues with other counselors, and seeking ongoing supervision. Periodically writing personal vision statements, like the ones you are required to write early in school and for job searches, can help keep you excited about the field.

Negotiation "Counselors need to be responsive to and cooperate with others, while simultaneously remaining steadfast to and upholding certain values, guidelines, or standards" (p. 325). The collaborative nature of most modern counseling theories means that the therapist and clients negotiate what happens in treatment. Furthermore, interactions with peers and work superiors are effectively viewed as negotiations rather than as powerful actor/passive recipient episodes.

Acknowledgment of Agency A sense of impact and of positive influences gives a professional a feeling of agency, or instrumentality. The certainty of inner strength should extend to clients, as we perceive their everyday resources (friends, pets, talents, physical abilities, literacy, employment) as "the substance of recovery and progress" (p. 326). Many conditions and events engender hope if we prime ourselves to notice them.

In this final chapter, I have given you some modes and maps for thinking about your groups in practice. I wish you a long, vital, and exhilarating journey.

KEY TERMS

conceptualization the counselor's grasp of what is going on at the three boundary levels, expressed in professional theoretical language

consultant role supervisors' actions as colleagues to brainstorm and discuss ideas

counselor role supervisors' assistance in your personal responses to professional situations

intervention the counselor's conscious application of skills and techniques

personalization the counselor's accurate awareness of his or her own emotional and cognitive responses during a group session and in later analysis of it

teacher role supervisors' help in giving you direct instruction, information, and advice

CHAPTER REVIEW

1. Make good use of the chart you created as an exercise in this chapter. I would suggest that you look over it each day for a week or so, making changes and additions that refine your thinking. Put it in a page protector or laminate it so you can use it over and over as a study aid.

2. Review with a colleague or classmate Osborn's Seven Salutary Suggestions for Stamina. Think of your own example of how you can apply each suggestion in your own life.

3. Explain to a person outside the counseling field what supervision is and why you need it throughout your professional life.

4. Think of a system that fits your style whereby you can record your professional development over the years. This might be a blog, a journal, or a structured worksheet that you write in periodically. It could include things like accounts of ethical decision making and case studies of groups that have affected your philosophy of group counseling. Such a record will give you an accurate view of your development and serve you well in interviews and presentations of yourself as a growing professional. Besides, if you become famous, your biographer will love it.

FOR FURTHER READING

Klontz, B. T., Wolf, E. M., & Bivens, A. (2000). Effectiveness of a multimodal brief group experiential psychotherapy. *The International Journal of Action Methods: Psychodrama, Skill Training, and Role Playing, 53,* 119–135.

This article describes a brief group psychotherapy approach that blends psychodrama, art therapy, music therapy, Gestalt techniques, outdoor adventure experiences, and psycho-educational seminars. The theoretical stance was existential-humanistic. The treatment is a good example of how different techniques can be combined under a consistent theoretical umbrella. Furthermore, the researchers used pre and post tests to measure empirically the changes wrought by the program in personality, depression, symptoms, and self-actualization, giving you a good example of how you can simultaneously provide group counseling and perform outcome research.

REFERENCES

Andrews, J. D. W. (1989). Integrating visions of reality: Interpersonal diagnosis and the existential vision. *American Psychologist, 44,* 803–817.

Bernard, J. M. (1992). The challenge of psychotherapy-based supervision: Making the pieces fit. *Counselor Education and Supervision, 31,* 232–238.

Bernard, J. M, & Goodyear, R. K. (2004). *Fundamentals of clinical supervision* (3rd ed.). Boston: Allyn & Bacon.

Beutler, L. E., Malik, M., Alimohamed, S., Harwood, R. M., Talebi, H., Noble, S., & Wong, E. (2004). Therapist variables. In M. J. Lambert (Ed.), *Bergin and Garfield's Handbook of Psychotherapy and Behavior Change* (pp. 227–306, 5th ed.). New York: Wiley.

Conway, J. B. (1988). Differences among clinical psychologists: Scientists, practitioners, and scientist-practitioners. *Professional Psychology: Research and Practice, 19,* 642–655.

Frank, J. D., & Frank, J. B. (1991). *Persuasion and healing: A comparative study of psychotherapy* (3rd ed.). Baltimore: Johns Hopkins University Press.

Galanes, G. J. (2003). In their own words: An exploratory study of bona fide group leaders. *Small Group Research, 34,* 741–770.

Howatt, W. A. (2000). *The human services counseling toolbox.* Belmont, CA: Wadsworth.

Johnson, W. B., & Campbell, C. D. (2004). Character and fitness requirements for professional psychologists: Training directors' perspectives. *Professional Psychology: Research and Practice, 35,* 323–328.

Lantz, J. (1989). Family logotherapy with an overweight family. *Contemporary Family Therapy, 11,* 287–297.

O'Halloran, T. M., & Linton, J. M. (2000). Stress on the job: Self-care resources for counselors. *Journal of Mental Health Counseling, 22,* 354–364.

Osborn, C. J. (2004). Seven salutary suggestions for counselor stamina. *Journal of Counseling & Development, 82,* 319–328.

Rubel, D., & Okech, J. E. A. (in press). The supervision of group work model: adapting the discrimination model for supervision of group workers. *Journal for Specialists in Group Work.*

Name Index

Abeles, N., 359
Abramson, L. Y., 149
Adler, A., 38, 76, 129, 369–370, 372–381, 385, 388, 389, 390, 392, 393–394, 395, 396
Agras, W. S., 343
Albert Ellis Institute, 319, 325
Alcott, L. M., 315
Allport, G. W., 152, 154
American Association for Marriage and Family Therapy, 47
American Counseling Association (ACA), 47, 48, 61, 62, 65, 155, 165
American Group Therapy Association, 47
American Mental Health Counselors Association, 47
American Psychological Association (APA), 47, 155, 165, 323
American Society of Group Psychotherapy and Psychodrama, 66
Ames, D., 358
Anderson, D. C., 17
Anderson, M., 354
Anderson, N. B., 149
Anderson, T., 67
Andrews, J. D. W., 433–434
Andronico, M. P., 117
Apple, R. F., 343
Aristotle, 118
Arkowitz, H., 29
Arnett, J. J., 151, 163
Arroyo, C. G., 149
Association for Specialists in Group Work (ASGW), 8, 48–52, 60, 62, 68, 155, 165, 333, 338
Axline, V. M., 197
Azim, H. F. A., 37, 157

Bachelor, A., 178
Baltes, M., 323
Baltes, P. B., 323
Banaji, M., 162
Bandura, A., 302, 315, 342, 358
Bannister, A., 279
Barclay, D. R., 354
Barkham, M., 286
Barlow, D. H., 311
Barnes, R. C., 211, 212, 278
Barnum, K. R., 41
Barrett-Lennard, G. T., 189
Bartlett, M. Y., 147
Barton, D. A., 344
Barton, S., 40
Baruch, G., 255
Bates, J. E., 149
Bateson, G., 38
Bauman, S., 211, 212
Baumeister, R. F., 118
Baumgardner, P., 271
Beal, D., 326
Beck, A. T., 294–296, 302, 303, 320–321, 322, 343
Beck, J. S., 320
Begley, S., 150
Beisser, A., 277
Bennett, M. J., 224
Benshoff, J. M., 122
Berg, A., 225
Bergin, A. E., 356
Berglund, P. A., 77
Berman, J. S., 15
Bernard, J. M., 434, 436–437, 438
Bertalanffy, L. von., 39
Beutler, L. E., 439
Biddulph, M., 64
Bitter, J. R., 382, 385
Black, W. C., 7
Blake, W., 346

Blatner, A., 249, 277
Blazina, C., 282
Bloch, S., 118
Block, L., 301
Boisvert, J.-M., 324
Booraem, C. D., 112, 113
Borgen, W. A., 350
Borges, J. L., 8
Bowen, M., 38
Bowlby, J., 26
Brabender, V., 42
Bracke, P. E., 223
Bratton, S. C., 198
Breitbart, W., 225
Brenner, V., 354
Brickell, J., 415
Brook, D. W., 37
Brossart, D. F., 6, 141, 142
Brown, D. K., 357
Brown, N. W., 344, 345, 346, 360
Brown, R., 127, 128, 152, 160
Brownlee, K., 357
Buber, M., 137
Budman, S. H., 86, 88, 90, 93, 224, 225, 323
Bugental, J. F. T., 223
Burgess, A., 67
Burlingame, G. M., 5, 15, 17, 18, 41, 86, 324, 332
Burlingham, D., 4
Buros Institute for Mental Measurement, 359
Bushman, B. J., 118
Butler, R. N., 189, 225

Cajdric, A., 147
Callanan, P., 53
Campbell, C. D., 438
Carson, R. C., 31
Carstensen, L. L., 323
Carver, C. S., 407, 408

443

Subject Index

Encouragement, of clients, 380–381
EPPP. *See* Examination for Professional Practice of Psychology
Esprit de corps, 87. *See also* Cohesiveness
Esteem, 86, 87(fig.)
Ethics, 46–69, 435, 416
  codes of, 47, 48–52, 68
  confidentiality and, 59, 96
  decision-making and, 62–63, 435, 436
  dual relationships and, 60
  informed consent and, 50, 53–58
  leader competence and responsibility, 60–61
  legal practice and, 61–62
  multicultural sensitivity and, 60
  personality and, 68
  See also under specific group types
Ethnicity
  family and, 150–151
  therapeutic factors and, 6
  See also Culture(s)
Ethnocentrism, 159
EVS. *See* Existential Vacuum Scale
Examination for Professional Practice of Psychology (EPPP), 434
Exchange theory, 128
Exercise, law of, 299
Existential approach, to individual change, 10
Existential awareness, 199
Existential despair, 225
Existential encounter, 178
Existential factors, 134, 135–139, 207
Existential groups, 206–226, 435
  adaptations to clients' ages in, 225–226
  ethical concerns in, 64–65
  evaluating, 226
  group dynamics in, 214–215

leadership skills applied in, 215–216
problems addressed by, 222–224
stages of group work in, 214–215
techniques used in, 216–221
Existential growth, 5, 134–135
Existential guilt, 212
Existential inquiry, counselor and, 139
Existential position, 210
Existential theory, 134, 135, 137, 148
  essential concepts of, 209–214
  logotherapy and, 213–214
Existential vacuum, 212, 226
Existential Vacuum Scale (EVS), 226
Expectancy (expectations)
  cognitive-interpersonal cycles and, 30, 31
  of positive change, 76
Experiential approach, 215–216
Experimentation, in group setting, 36, 268, 270, 273, 277–279, 281, 284. *See also* Behavior experiments
Exposure and response prevention, 313
External control, 423
External control psychology, seven deadly habits of, 405–406
Extinction, of response, 298
Extraversion, 147

Facilitative conditions, 184
Fading system, 308
Faith, in group process, 5, 386
Family constellation, 375–376, 383–384, 385, 389, 396
Family photos, discussion of in group, 389
Family reenactment, 5, 114–117
  corrective emotional experiences and, 117
  counselor's role in, 116–117
Family system, 38

Family therapy, 38, 40, 283, 359, 376, 385
Fantasy, 239
Fear reduction, 311–313
Feedback, 28, 30, 33–36, 37, 89, 104, 123, 182, 262, 340, 351
  avoidance of, 121
  corrective, 34, 35, 36
  defined, 116
  examples of, 34–35
  interpretation and, 242, 243
  on patterns of relating, 116–117
  positive, 35
  to therapist, 207
Fictional finalism, 377
Fictional self, 377
Fifteen-stage process, in humanistic groups, 181–183
Figure/ground relation, 266
Fishbowl technique, modified, 256
Flow, 213
Focused listening, 216
Food abuse, 224
Forgetting, 249, 284
Free association, 235, 252, 253
Freedom
  as existential factor, 136–137, 139, 148, 224, 373
  need for, 409, 410, 413
  to choose to participate, 54–55
Free will, 206, 214
Freudian theory, 25, 27, 178, 233, 236–237, 238, 242, 246, 267, 268, 369, 370, 373, 379, 388. *See also* Psychoanalysis
Friendship(s), 11, 188, 385, 393
Frustration, low tolerance of, 325
Fun, need for, 409, 410
Fundamental attribution error, 152–153. *See also* Self-serving attributional bias

Gambling, 300
GCQ. *See* Group Climate Questionnaire
Gender
  depression and, 149, 282

Credits

15 (Figure 1.1): From G.M. MacKenzie, K.R., & Strauss, B., (2004): "Small-Group Treatment: Evidence for effectiveness and mechanisms of change," in M. J. Lambert, (ed) *Bergin and Garfield's Handbook of Psychotherapy and Behavior Change,* Fifth Edition, pg. 667. Reprinted by permission of John Wiley & Sons, Inc. **48** From ASGW. **87** (Figure 4.1): *Motivation and Personality* 2/e by Maslow, ©1970. Reprinted by permission of Pearson Education, Inc., Upper Saddle River, NJ. **142** (Table 6.1): From D.M. Kivlighan, K.D. Multon, and D.F. Brossart (1996), "Helpful Impacts in Group Counseling. Development of a Multidimensional Rating System," *Journal of Counseling Psychology, 43,* 347–355. **155** Copyright © 1996 by the American Psychological Association. Reprinted with permission. From R.B. Stuart, "Twelve Practical Suggestions for Achieving Multicultural Competence," *Professional Psychology, 35,* pp. 3–9. Copyright © 2004 by the American Psychological Association. Reprinted with permission. **176** From Carl Rogers, *Encounter Groups.* Copyright © 1970. **201** From R.R. Dies and K.R. MacKenzie, Eds., *Advances in Group Psychotherapy: Integrating Research and Practice.* **220** From M. Khatami, "Clinical application of the logochart," *International Forum for Logotherapy, 11,* pp. 67–75. **207** From Irvin D. Yalom, *The Theory and Practice of Group Psychotherapy.* Copyright © 1995. Reprinted by permission of Basic Books, a member of Perseus Books, L.L.C. **234** Excerpt from A. Wolf, "The Psychoanalysis of Groups," *American Journal of Psychotherapy, 3,* 529–557. **243** (Figure 10.1): From *Group Processes: An Introduction to Group Dynamics,* 3rd edition by Joseph Luft, 1984. Mayfield Publishing Company. Reprinted by permission of the author. **294** From A.T. Beck, A.J. Rush, B.F. Shaw, and G. Emery, *Cognitive Therapy of Depression.* Copyright © 1979. **333** Reprinted by permission of The Guilford Press. Reprinted with permission of the American School Counselor Association, www.schoolcounselor.org. **347** From *Psychoeducational Groups* by N.W. Brown. Copyright © 1998. Reprinted by permission of the publisher, Routledge, and the author. **352** Reprinted from *Psychoeducational Interventions in the Schools* by C.A. Maher and J.E. Zins, eds. Reprinted with permission from Elsevier. **353** From *Group Exercises for Enhancing Social Skills & Self-Esteem* (p. 34) by S. S. Khalsa, 1996, Sarasota, FL: Professional Resource Press. Copyright © 1996 by Professional Resource Exchange, Inc. Reprinted with permission. **370** From Rudolf Dreikurs, "Group Psychotherapy from the point of view of Adlerian Psychology," *International Journal of Group Psychotherapy, 7.* **403** Reprinted with permission of the American School Counselor Association, www.schoolcounselor.org. **414** (Table 51.1): From D.H. Lawrence, 2004, "The Effects of Reality Therapy Group Counseling on the Self-Determination of Persons with Developmental Disabilities," *International Journal of Reality Therapy, 23,* 9–15. Reprinted with permission. **419** Copyright © 1992 From *Reality Therapy for the 21st Century* by R.E. Wubbolding. Reproduced by permission of Routledge/Taylor & Francis Books, Inc., and the author. **431** From G.J. Galanes, "In their own words: An exploratory Study of Bona Fide Group Leaders," *Small Group Research, 34.* Reprinted by permission of Sage Publishing. **437** (Figure 16.1): From D. Rubel and J.E.A. Okech, "The Supervision of Group Work Model: Adapting the discrimination Model for Supervision of Group Workers," *Journal for Specialists in Group Work.* Reprinted with permission.